Using Organizational Theory to Study, Explain, and Understand Criminal Legal Organizations

Danielle S. Rudes • Jason R. Ingram
Editors

Using Organizational Theory to Study, Explain, and Understand Criminal Legal Organizations

Springer

Editors
Danielle S. Rudes
Department of Criminal Justice
and Criminology
Sam Houston State University
Huntsville, TX, USA

Jason R. Ingram
Department of Criminal Justice
and Criminology
Sam Houston State University
Huntsville, TX, USA

ISBN 978-3-031-66284-3 ISBN 978-3-031-66285-0 (eBook)
https://doi.org/10.1007/978-3-031-66285-0

This Springer imprint is published by the registered company Springer Nature Switzerland AG
The registered company address is: Gewerbestrasse 11, 6330 Cham, Switzerland

To my boys—Devin, Dylan, and Jace—with all the love in my heart
(Danielle)
To Amanda, Sam, Nora, and Amelia
(Jason)

Preface

Introduction to Using Organizational Theory to Study, Explain, and Understand Criminal Legal Organizations

What are organizations? Organizations are complex systems composed of both internal and external components and people—all of which/whom are typically working toward a common goal or purpose. This seemingly simple definition disguises the intricacy of organizations by focusing on the systems' parts, but not on the involvedness of each of these organizational parts. There are so many ways to characterize, think about, and even research organizations. Think about the decision to arrest someone for a crime. Although seemingly easy to explain, the decision to arrest a person is decidedly anything but simple. The police officer is an organizational actor serving in the role of organizational steward for a police unit. However, the police unit is part of a larger department, and the department is part of the city, county, or state (jurisdictional) police force in a given locale. Then, that police unit/department is part of a nationwide law enforcement effort with ties to global law enforcement. Additionally, and to make things even more complex, the police are just one arm of the criminal legal system with connections to courts and corrections AND nearly every part of every community is also tied (in some way) to policing. This includes schools, hospitals, social services, politicians, policymakers, government entities, recreation, sports, and so on. That's a lot! The point here is that not only are individual organizations complex, but the entire web of organizations locally, nationally, and internationally is vast and exceptionally intricate. So, something as relatively straightforward as a police officer's decision to arrest someone for criminal activity is inextricably linked to nearly every other person, organization, and system in at least some way. This may seem daunting, but rest-assured, organizational theory provides a framework for understanding these complexities.

What is organizational theory? Organizational theory, like all theories, tries to explain *why* something occurs. That is, after all, what theories do. At its core, a theory is a set of ideas or thoughts that try to explain why something is occurring.

An organizational theory, then, is an explanation for what occurs within, between, and among organizations and organizational actors. Many people credit the German sociologist, historian, and political economist, Max Weber (pronounced Vay-ber) as the grandfather (or founder) of modern organizational theory. Weber was interested in a particular type of organization: bureaucracy. For Weber, bureaucracies were rational organizational systems developed to ensure efficiency and effectiveness within organizational structures. Bureaucracies have a few fairly standard parts including record-keeping, impersonal and standardized procedures and rules, and legitimate authority. These formal organizations sprung up as cities grew and the world turned away from a mostly agrarian to a more manufacturing and production-based economy … largely in capitalist economic systems. From this origin, organizational theory grew as a way of explaining and understanding how businesses and groups organized, functioned, survived, and possibly thrived.

How can organizational theory help criminal legal organizations? Today, organizational theory is a vast and profound field that focuses on so much more than Weber may have envisioned. It is no longer just about an organization's systems and processes; it is about the *people* within that system and all the systems and people connected to an organization via other organizations and systems. This thinking comprises an Open Systems Perspective (Scott, 2013). An open system theorizes organizations as interconnected and interdependent collectivities. This means one cannot really study or try to understand an organization without seeing it within its broader context. The Open Systems perspective provides a way of understanding the organizations around us, the ones we work for and with, and the systems they belong to. Take for example, the criminal legal system. This hugely complex and multi-faceted system is a dominant component of our everyday lives. It includes the law and policies that govern us as well as all of the ways those laws and policies are enforced *AND* how we handle things when people break, bend, or stretch the laws and policies.

Organizational theory offers a formidable framework for understanding the criminal legal system and all of the organizations and sub-systems that comprise it. However, it is relatively rare for any member of the criminal legal system or any students, researchers, or scholars studying the criminal legal system to have any real understanding of organizational theory. This oversight is unfortunate. In a recent review of the top criminal justice and criminology bachelors, masters, and doctoral programs in the USA, our team found only a small handful of these programs that provide students with any coursework in organizational theory. Additionally, most police, corrections, and community corrections academies, law schools, and judicial trainings do not include organizational theory as a major (or in fact any) component of their training. There are any number of guesses as to why and how this occurs but suffice to say when the people studying and working within criminal legal organizations within the criminal legal system do not understand organizational theory it is a loss felt like a tidal wave throughout the system. These individuals do not have a framework for understanding their own organization, the system their organization is a part of, and the countless other organizations and systems that are interconnected to theirs. This challenge limits problem solving as well as advanced critical, analytic, and innovative thinking and creates a giant wall between understanding *what is* and finding ways to work toward *what is possible*.

Organizational *Theories* for Understanding and Explaining Criminal Legal Organizations

There are a myriad of organizational theories, and many of these could—if understood and used—help criminal legal actors and researchers understand the criminal legal system including law and courts, policing and security, institutional and community corrections, and juvenile justice. This book provides chapters covering six of these important theories: Neo-Institutional Theory, Bounded Rationality Theory, Systems Theory, Contingency Theory, Process Theory, and Structuration Theory. We provide a brief overview of each.

Neo-Institutional Theory A theory developed by John Meyer (1977) that moves beyond Weber's version of institutions with a focus on rational systems and into a more behavioral focused approach (new or neo-institutionalism). This theory moves beyond only thinking about efficiency and effectiveness and toward thinking about the role of legitimacy within organizations. Key scholars of note include John Meyer, Brian Rowan, Paul DiMaggio, and Walter W. Powell.

Bounded Rationality Theory A theory developed by Herbert Simon (1955) that suggests humans do not and cannot make rational decisions because they are limited by their cognitive abilities and the information they can access. Instead, Bounded Rationality Theory suggests humans make the best decisions within any given circumstance or context (called "satisficing"). Key scholars of note include Herbert Simon and James March.

Systems Theory A framework that emphasizes a holistic approach to understanding organizations. Initially, general systems theory was presented as a unified theory of science based on principles that would apply to all domains (i.e., biology, psychology, engineering, and social sciences). Systems were defined as a set of elements that are interrelated and interact with each other. All systems were described as sharing key principles, including openness, holism, equifinality, hierarchy, emergence, and feedback loops. When adapted to organizations, systems theory allows us to describe organizations based on their relationships, interactions, and process between both organizational components and the broader environment. Key concepts of organizational systems theory include inputs, outputs, and throughputs, negative entropy, boundary spanning, and event cycles. This framework emphasizes that organizations are interdependent with and must adapt to their environment using feedback and information to survive. Key scholars include Ludwig Von Bertalanffy, Daniel Katz, and Robert L. Kahn.

Contingency Theory This theory suggests that there is no one right or best way to run an organization. Instead, the way to best operate, run, or manage an organization depends (or is contingent upon) both its internal and external factors (contingencies). Contingency Theory was developed by Jay W. Lorsch and Paul R. Lawrence (1969). This thinking broadly applies to organizations of all types. Key scholars of note include Jay W. Lorsch, Paul R. Lawrence, and Fred E. Fiedler.

Process Theory Process theory is a recent approach to theory-building that focuses on identifying and examining the rules and mechanisms that drive organizational behaviors. While not a formal organizational theory, this approach is rooted in open systems thinking and is influenced by components of general systems (e.g., Von Bertalanffy, 1968) and multilevel (e.g., Kozlowski & Klein, 2000) theoretical frameworks that analyze interactions among organizational elements and actors. In doing so, process theory focuses on dynamic processes, rather than static factors, to better understand both micro-level phenomena and higher-level, emergent phenomena in organizations. Key scholars who have influenced and promoted the ideals of this approach include Craig Reynolds, James Grand, Steve Kozlowski, and Michael Braun.

Structuration Theory A sociological theory that has significant implications for the study of organizations. This perspective posits that social structures, such as organizations, and individual actions each work to shape each other. While other theories may examine these two components separately, structuration theory provides unique insight as to how organizational structures are created, maintained, and changed through the actions of organizational members. Anthony Giddens is credited with developing structuration theory.

Resource Dependency Theory This theory suggests that organizations behave in certain ways depending on what resources they have and which resources they have access to. Developed by Jeffrey Pfeffer and Gerald Salancik (1978) this theory suggests that resources are powerful and for organizations to function and thrive they must have continual access to the resources they need. As such, organizations are constantly trying to secure or maintain needed resources. In this way, power and resources are interconnected and critical. Key scholars of note include Jeffrey Pfeffer and Gerald Salancik.

By no means are these *All* the organizational theories that may be useful to understanding the criminal legal system, its organizations, and actors. There are many, many more. However, this book presents several important chapters on each of the above-mentioned theories. The chapter authors use an organizational theory to explain a particular challenge or facet of the criminal legal system (Chapters 1, 2, 3, 4, 5, and 6).

Organizational *Concepts* for Understanding and Explaining Criminal Legal Organizations

Within organizations and organizational systems there are a host of key concepts that form its building blocks. These include its culture/climate, the power and politics involved, how people make decisions and consider ethics, if/how people commit deviant acts and/or resist organizational processes/policies, and the role of authority and/or leadership within an organization or system. The chapters in Part II of this book provide readers with an overview of how these important components operate within criminal legal organizations and the broader criminal legal system. All of these ideas and concepts are part of Open Systems thinking (previously discussed) whereby organizations are not just formal, rational entities (as Weber described). Instead, they include formal *and informal* components such as the organizational actors—or people—within them. As such, to understand an organization, it is both necessary and crucial to consider how that organization operates both formally and informally. That is, it is not just about the written rules and policies … rather, it is about how those rules and policies are implemented or used in practice. The informal parts of criminal legal organizations tell us a great deal about what is happening and why it is happening. This is imperative for if we intend to change or reform any part of it, we must understand both the formal and informal systems thoroughly. For example, a law on the books does not often look much like it is written when people are using it in practice. In one study of the Prison Rape Elimination Act (PREA), Rudes and colleagues (2021) found that although PREA (a federal policy) was, in fact, implemented in most prisons and jails throughout the USA as was dictated by policy, how correctional staff used PREA in their day-to-day work varied greatly. In the correctional system of study, Rudes and colleagues found that staff felt PREA was burdensome in several salient ways including administratively, safety-wise, and culturally. As such, correctional staff did not implement PREA with fidelity (delivered as intended). So, the PREA law on the books looked one way, but in practice it looked very different. Thus, the outcomes of PREA within the US correctional system may be explainable—at least in part—by an examination of the informal organizational culture and climate within particular prisons and jails where PREA was implemented. The point here is that it is simply not enough to study the laws surrounding and the policies within an organization without studying the organization and its actors too. What is written or said is not often what is performed. We can learn a lot about the criminal legal system by asking deeper questions and using organizational theories to help us develop more explanatory answers. The chapter authors use organizational concepts or ideas to explain a particular challenge or facet of the criminal legal system (Chapters 7, 8, 9, 10, 11, 12, 13, 14, and 15).

Missing from This Book

Organizational theory, as a scholarly field, is vast and ever-growing. As such, we cannot possibly present every theory or every idea/concept in one edited volume. What we provide here is merely an introduction to organizational theory and the countless ways those theories and the related concepts/ideas provide explanatory power for understanding criminal legal organizations. There are some important areas we want to note, however, that are not covered here. To do this, we provide the topic and several key readings (not in this book) to get readers started thinking about these important areas of criminal legal organizations.

1. *Organizational Change*: This idea considers the ways organizational change occurs (or not) largely during periods of reform. For example, criminal legal organizations regularly face new laws, policies, or guidelines. Considering how each criminal legal organization and its actors adapt to, implement, and sustain the change are crucial for later understanding any outcomes related to said change.

    Rudes, D. S. (2012). Framing organizational reform: Misalignments and disputes among parole and union middle managers. *Law & Policy, 34*(1), 1–31.
    Willis, J., Mastrofski, S.D., & Weisburd, D. (2004). Making sense of COMPSTAT: A theory based analysis of organizational change in three police departments. *Law & Society Review, 41*, 147–188.

2. *Implementation Science*: Implementation Science is a both a theoretical and practical construct or framework that emerged out of the medical/health sciences. It is the study of how organizations and their actors take in/understand (called acceptability and uptake) new technologies, practices, programs, etc. Implementation science also considers other key areas of implementing something into an organization such as fidelity (adherence to the model), transportability (whether a model can be moved from one organization to another), penetration (how deeply a change goes within an organization), and feasibility (whether or not a model is appropriate for a particular organization).

    Rudes, D. S., Taxman, F. S., Portillo, S., Murphy, A., Rhodes, A., Stitzer, M., et al. (2012). Adding positive reinforcement in justice settings: Acceptability and feasibility. *Journal of Substance Abuse Treatment, 42*(3), 260–270.
    Taxman, F.S., & Belenko, S. (2011). *Implementing evidence-based practices in community corrections and addiction treatment.* Springer.

3. *Social Inequality, Feminist Theory, and Organizational Diversity*: Organizations include a diverse array of actors, and they operate within a diverse landscape of other organizations, people, and systems. As such, it is important to consider how and why an organization, a system, and its broader community thinks about, views, adheres to, and or operates within this diverse space. Using sister theories such as critical race theory, feminist theory, queer theory, or other theories that specifically consider historical discrimination, diversity, and inequality provides a powerful tool for understanding organizations and organizational actors. This

is particularly true within criminal legal organizations as our history depicts the plethora of ways the criminal legal system has and continues to discriminate against individuals and groups with less power, status, or standing.

Burdett, F., Gouliquer, L., & Poulin, C. (2018). Culture of corrections: The experiences of women correctional officers. *Feminist Criminology, 13*(3), 329–349.
Miller, S. L., Forest, K.B., & Jurik, N.C. (2003). Diversity in blue: Lesbian and gay police officers in a masculine occupation. *Men and Masculinities, 5*(4), 355–385.

4. *Bureaucracy and Street-Level Bureaucracy*: This theory originated in public administration scholarship via the work of Michael Lipsky (1969). The theory considers the work of public service workers who have direct contact with people and possess discretion to make decisions in the field when working with clients/people. For Lipsky, these street-level workers are the living embodiment of the bureaucracy and as such the informal ways they do their work is, in many ways, more effectual than the actual formal organizational processes.

   Maynard-Moody, S., & Musheno, M. (2000). State agent or citizen agent: Two narratives of discretion. *Journal of Public Administration Research and Theory, 10*(2), 329–358.
   Portillo, S., & Rudes, D. S. (2014). Construction of justice at the street level. *Annual Review of Law and Social Science, 10*, 321–334.

5. *Conflict*: There is not one but many organizational theories and concepts that consider conflict between organizations, among organizational actors, within/among systems (often associated with other theoretical frameworks like power and politics), and among organizational actors and stakeholders (often associated with power, politics, culture, change, deviance, ethics, climate, and inequality). Organizational conflict is also tied to contingencies and resources.

   Dias, C. F., & Vaughn, M. S. (2006). Bureaucracy, managerial disorganization, and administrative breakdown in criminal justice agencies. *Journal of Criminal Justice, 34*(5), 543–555.
   Morrill, C., & McKee, C. (1993). Institutional isomorphism and informal social control: Evidence from a community mediation center. *Social Problems, 40*(4), 445–463.

6. *Institutional Logics*: This organizational concept emerged (at least partially) out of neo-institutional theory with the work of Roger Friedland and Robert R. Alford (1991). The idea of an institutional logic notes that organizational actors behave and think certain ways based on their personal and organizational values, assumptions, and beliefs. Other work in this area comes from Patricia H. Thornton and William Ocasio. This work bears some similarity to another organizational concept, *sensemaking*. Largely through the work of Karl Weick (1995) which claims that personal and professional facets of workers' lived experience such as identify, retrospection, socialization, and the cues people

receive in conversations and interactions help them figure out (make sense of) organizational rules, policies, procedures, and other actors.

Chiarello, E. (2015). The war on drugs comes to the pharmacy counter: Frontline work in the shadow of discrepant institutional logics. *Law & Social Inquiry*, *40*(1), 86–122.
Rudes, D. S., Magnuson, S., Portillo, S., & Hattery, A. (2021). Sex logics: Negotiating the prison rape elimination act (PREA) against its' administrative, safety, and cultural burdens. *Punishment & Society*, *23*(2), 241–259.

The Purpose of This Book

The goal or purpose of this book is to open the world of organizational thinking to criminal legal students, scholars, and anyone else who is interested in understanding this complex system and its actors in deeper, more meaningful ways. By presenting the work of emerging scholars who are learning about organizational theory and related concepts and then using that information to explore and explain criminal legal settings and people we are hopeful it will inspire readers to do so as well. The criminal legal system is built atop formal systems and practices which are important to understand and examine, but that is just the beginning of what we need to understand about this system. The informal or "shadow structures" at play within organizational environments, locales, and spaces provide much-needed opportunities for analytical depth for understanding, and perhaps reforming, these organizations and the overall system. This is not easy work, but it is necessary. It is no longer enough to only think about the judge's decision in a case or the way a person is treated during incarceration. As thinkers, researchers, scholars, students, and fellow human beings … we must fully engage with theories that can help us gain purchase on the *why* behind the actions and activities in the black box of our criminal legal system. Organizational theory is the key to that metaphorical and paradoxical box. Let us open it, dig in, and discover what more may be possible.

Huntsville, TX, USA

Danielle S. Rudes
Jason R. Ingram

References

Bertalanffy, L. V. (1968). *General system theory: Foundations, development, applications*. G. Braziller.

Kozlowski, S. W. J., & Klein, K. J. (2000). A multilevel approach to theory and research in organizations: Contextual, temporal, and emergent processes. In K. J. Klein, & S. W. J. Kozlowski (Eds.), *Multilevel theory, research, and methods in organization: Foundations, extensions, and new directions*. Jossey-Bass.

Rudes, D. S., Magnuson, S., Portillo, S., & Hattery, A. (2021). Sex logics: Negotiating the prison rape elimination act (PREA) against its' administrative, safety, and cultural burdens. *Punishment & Society, 23*(2), 241–259.

Scott, W. R. (2013). *Institutions and organizations: Ideas, interests, and identities*. Sage Publications.

Acknowledgments

We want to acknowledge the hard work and dedication of our amazing student authors at George Mason University in Virginia and Sam Houston State University in Texas. All of the chapters produced in this book are written by doctoral students. This was no easy feat. Not only did they have to learn organizational theory (and for most of them this was the first time they were doing so), but their major assignment for the course was a book chapter that we wanted to publish. Talk about daunting! Of course, publication was optional and not part of the course grade they received, and they knew the work for the chapter would not end when the course ended. Instead, these students agreed to put in several weeks or months of additional effort revising, editing, and revising again to get their course papers ready for publication in this book. These thoughtful and dedicated souls deserve a hearty round of applause. For their time, efforts, and willingness to endure … we thank, and wholeheartedly celebrate you: Bryce, Sydney, Kennedy, Chia-Hung, Anne, Ghady, Nhi, Kayla, Clayton, Suraiya, Mary, Andrew, Lakia, Thomas, Allison, and Tyler. What bright futures you have before you and we are happy to have a ringside seat to watch you rise.

Additionally, Danielle would like to acknowledge the inspiration for this book. Dr. Calvin Morrill (University of California, Berkeley) is the professor who introduced Danielle to organizational theory while she was a doctoral student at the University of California, Irvine (Sociology). In doing so, he made the questions she had seem relevant and important and made the world of organizations literally come to life in her mind. After the quarter ended, Danielle worked as Cal's research and teaching assistant to prepare a new online graduate course for the Criminology, Law & Society department that focused on using organizational theory to explain criminal legal organizations. Through this work, Danielle started doing the work she now calls "bridging" to make organizational theories applied in other organizations and contexts work for explaining and understanding courts, corrections, policing, and juvenile justice. So, even before she knew what was happening, this book was already taking shape (albeit 16 years ago).

Additionally, Cal, with his colleague Dr. David Snow, also inspired Danielle to think about editing a volume of student's work when they published a book of qualitative papers produced by their students at the University of Arizona during their Qualitative Methods doctoral seminar.[1] So, thank you Cal for the inspiration then, and for the continued and enduring inspiration. I am forever grateful for your wisdom, guidance, and your unrelenting belief in expanding boundaries and bringing organizational theory to life within criminal legal settings.

[1]Morrill, C., Snow, D. A., & White, C. (Eds.). (2023). *Together alone: Personal relationships in public places*. Univ of California Press.

Contents

About the Editors

Danielle S. Rudes is a Professor in the Department of Criminal Justice and Criminology at Sam Houston State University. She is an organizational sociologist/criminologist who uses qualitative methods to explore key questions related to the implementation of organizational change. She first became interested in how organizations worked before graduate school while working in a large restaurant/nightclub where the culture was created, institutionalized, and socialized daily. From there, she turned her attention to correctional environments but her interest in both formal and informal organizational processes and perceptions continues today. Her substantive expertise is in institutional and community corrections. Her research considers organizational dynamics among a wide array of people, including prison/jail staff and residents, probation/parole officers and individuals under supervision, and problem-solving court teams and clients. Her work uses several organizational theories and concepts including street-level bureaucracy theory, discretionary decision-making, sensemaking, institutional logics, and implementation science. She has taught both undergraduate and graduate-level courses in corrections, reentry, and organizational theory for nearly 20 years (drudes@shsu.edu).

Jason R. Ingram is a Professor in the Department of Criminal Justice and Criminology at Sam Houston State University. He first became interested in organizational theory as a Criminal Justice PhD student at Michigan State University. Here, he developed a cognate area in Industrial and Organizational Psychology that had a significant influence on his approach to research in criminal legal organizations, especially as it relates to police culture. His primary area of research focuses on how police officers' immediate work environments shape and constrain their cultural views using multilevel theory and methods. Subsequent studies have applied this framework to understand outcomes such as culture strength, officer street-level behaviors, job satisfaction, and supervisory influences. He has also taught graduate-level courses in policing and in organizational theory that incorporate many of the theoretical frameworks and concepts in this book to help students better understand criminal legal organizations (jri004@shsu.edu).

About the Authors

Kayla Alaniz is a doctoral student in the Department of Criminal Justice and Criminology at Sam Houston State University. Her research interests include culture and climate in formal organizations and school safety. Her recent work has appeared in *Crime & Delinquency* and the *Journal of Research in Crime and Delinquency*.

Mary Catlin is a doctoral candidate at George Mason University in the Department of Criminology, Law and Society. Her work focuses on legal decision-making, particularly confessions and guilty pleas with a special interest in wrongful convictions. Mary has published in outlets such as the *Wrongful Conviction Law Review*, *Journal of Experimental Criminology*, and *Psychology, Public Policy, and Law*. Currently, she is collecting data for her dissertation, which focuses on the role of communication in plea decision-making. Her dissertation is being partially funded by the National Science Foundation through Arizona State University.

Clayton B. Drummond is a doctoral candidate in the Department of Criminology, Law and Society at George Mason University. His research focuses on social change and reform surrounding criminal legal organizations, extreme punishments, and wrongful convictions.

Lakia Faison is a doctoral student at George Mason University in the Department of Criminology, Law, and Society. She earned both a B.A. and an M.S. in Psychology from the University of Wisconsin-Milwaukee and Arizona State University, respectively. Her research interests include decision-making processes of legal officials (e.g., police, lawyers, judges), the processes of wrongful conviction and exoneration, and the stigma of wrongful conviction.

Sydney A. Fay is a doctoral candidate in the Department of Criminology, Law & Society at George Mason University. She received her M.A. in Forensic Psychology from George Washington University. She currently works full-time in an intelligence director role for a nonprofit organization that combats human trafficking and as an ad hoc research assistant at the Center for Evidence-Based Crime Policy (CEBCP). Her research interests include forensic and legal psychology, situational crime prevention, place-based criminology, cyber-assisted crime, technology-facilitated sex offending, and human trafficking.

Thomas K. Hargrove received his M.A. in Criminology, Law and Society from George Mason University. He is a retired Washington, DC, based investigative journalist and White House correspondent. Upon his retirement, Hargrove founded the nonprofit Murder Accountability Project (MAP), which uses Freedom of Information laws to obtain data about homicides not reported to the federal government. To date, MAP has gathered case-level details on more than 39,000 homicides not found in FBI files.

Ghady Hbeilini is a doctoral candidate within the Department of Criminal Justice and Criminology at Sam Houston State University. He conducts comparative and international research focusing specifically on illicit organizations and terrorism. His recent work is published in the *Journal of Applied Security Research* and *Journal of Crime and Justice.*

Tyler Houser is a doctoral student and graduate research assistant at George Mason University in the Department of Criminology, Law and Society. Prior to GMU, he was a graduate teaching fellow at Radford University in the Department of Criminal Justice where he received his master's degree. His research focuses on terrorism and extremism, gun violence and mass violence, and crime analysis. He recently published articles focused on gun violence in the *Security Journal* and *Aggression and Violent Behavior.*

Allison G. Kondrat is a doctoral student at Sam Houston State University in the Department of Criminal Justice and Criminology. Her research interests include racial and ethnic disparities in criminal justice, law and policy, and sociopolitical influencers of criminal justice issues. Her recent work has been featured in *Crime, Law, and Social Change* and *Crime & Delinquency.*

Bryce Kushmerick-McCune is a doctoral student in Criminal Justice and Criminology at Sam Houston State University. She is also a research assistant at the Center for Advancing Correctional Excellence at George Mason University. She has over 6 years of research experience working on projects looking at institutional corrections, community supervision, and opioid use disorder and treatment. As a primarily qualitative researcher, her main interests include incarcerated people's coping and adjustment to incarceration, prison staff discretion and well-being, and prison administrations. She earned her B.S. and M.A. from George Mason University in Criminology, Law & Society.

Caitlin Bauer Lasalle is a doctoral student in Criminal Justice and Criminology at Sam Houston State University. She is mainly a qualitative researcher with experience in mixed methods as well. She has over 5 years of research experience working on projects focusing on institutional corrections at both the state and local level, and the perspectives of both incarcerated individuals and staff. Her main research interests include institutional corrections, reentry, correctional programming, and differential experiences of these based on gender backgrounds. She earned her B.A. and M.S. from The University of Alabama in Psychology and Criminal Justice.

Nhi N. H. Le is a doctoral student at Sam Houston State of University, in the Department of Criminal Justice and Criminology. Her work predominantly focuses on individuals who commit sexually illicit behaviors, with additional interests in psychopathology and corrections. She has published her research in scholarly journals, including the *Journal of Criminal Justice*, and presented at various academic conferences, including the American Society of Criminology (ASC), Academy of Criminal Justice Sciences (ACJS), and the Association for the Treatment & Prevention of Sexual Abuse (ATSA).

Chia-Hung Lin is a doctoral student at Sam Houston State University (SHSU) in the Department of Criminal Justice and Criminology. Before joining SHSU, he served as a police officer in Taiwan. His research interests focus on policing, police organizations and strategies, police culture, police-public relations, and international/comparative criminal justice. His work is published in journals such as *Police Quarterly* and *Policing: An International Journal.*

Andrew Madrigal (He/Him) is a doctoral candidate in the Department of Criminology, Law and Society at George Mason University. He received his M.S. in Criminology from California State University, Long Beach. His work is dedicated to understanding and assisting wrongfully convicted people and their families. His research interests are broadly in the areas of wrongful convictions, juvenile justice, life course criminology, and qualitative research methods. His work is published in journals such as *Critical Criminology* and *the Virginia Journal of Criminal Law.*

Kennedy Suzette Ratcliff received her B.S. and M.S. in criminal justice from Lamar University and is currently a doctoral student at Sam Houston State University in the Department of Criminal Justice and Criminology. Her research interests include COVID-19 policies in criminal justice, women in criminal justice, and domestic and international terrorism.

Suraiya H. Shammi is a Ph.D. student in the Department of Criminology, Law & Society at George Mason University. She is currently developing her dissertation proposal. Her research interests include legal decision-making, focusing on guilty plea, Miranda rights, procedural justice, and police interrogation. Her recent publication a co-authored piece in *The Oxford Handbook of Psychology.*

Anne C. Wingert, M.A, is a doctoral student in the Department of Criminal Justice and Criminology at Sam Houston State University. Her research primarily focuses on life-course criminology and the outcomes of early-life victimization and offending. Additionally, her interests include victim-offender overlap, formal response to trauma, and intergenerational crime. Her most recent work is published in *Crime & Delinquency*.

Part I
Select Organizational Theories

Chapter 1
A Neo-institutional Account of Prisonization

Bryce Kushmerick-McCune

Introduction

Extant literature documents the inherent culture of correctional institutions, as well as the ways individuals adjust to life during incarceration—coined *prisonization*. This chapter examines how and why individuals become prisonized using a neo-institutional organizational framework. Neo-institutional theory, introduced by Meyer and Rowan (1977), seeks to understand why and how organizations become isomorphic (similar in form or relations) with one another and posits that a desire for legitimacy as the reasoning behind this. Neo-institutional theory traditionally operates at a macro-level, but the principles of the theory are still applicable from an individual, micro-level perspective.

This chapter first presents a literature review of both organizational culture and its theoretical applications. Next, it presents a conceptual review of neo-institutionalism and its application in many studies of organizational behavior. Prisonization presents a case study of neo-institutionalism in action, which is supplemented by a literature review of both prison culture and prisonization. The chapter ends with a discussion of policy implications and areas for future research.

B. Kushmerick-McCune (✉)
Sam Houston State University, Department of Crimial Justice and Criminology, Huntsville, TX, USA
e-mail: bck024@shsu.edu

D. S. Rudes, J. R. Ingram (eds.), *Using Organizational Theory to Study, Explain, and Understand Criminal Legal Organizations*,
https://doi.org/10.1007/978-3-031-66285-0_1

Conceptual Literature Review of Organizational Culture

Organizational culture has long captivated researchers' attention in the disciplines of sociology, management, psychology, business, and criminology. However, the complexity of organizational culture makes it a difficult concept to define precisely. A common theme among organizational literature is that organizational culture is composed of a shared set of meanings and assumptions (Bolman & Deal, 1997; Rudes & Magnuson, 2019; Schein, 1984; Terrill et al., 2003). Bolman and Deal (1997) define organizational culture as "the pattern of beliefs, values, practices, and artifacts that define for members who they are and how they are to do things" (p. 217), while Schein (1984) emphasizes the importance of cultural learning processes. In his definition, Schein argued that organizational culture is,

> The pattern of basic assumptions that a given group has invented, discovered, or developed in learning to cope with its problems of external adaptation and internal integration, and that have worked well enough to be considered valid, and therefore, to be taught to new members as the correct way to perceive, think, and feel in relation to those problems. (p. 3)

Schein (1984) expands on his definition by exploring three components which he believes are essential elements of organizational culture: (1) visible artifacts, (2) values, and (3) underlying assumptions. *Visible artifacts* are the elements that make up the environment of the organization (e.g., architecture, technology, manner of dress, language, behavior, etc). *Values* are the characteristics or behaviors of an organization that are debatable and overt. *Underlying assumptions* are unconscious thoughts that determine how members of a group perceive, think, and feel about their current situation.

Moreover, Schein (1984) argues that culture cannot exist unless there is a group that "owns" it. To constitute a *group*, there must be a collection of individuals that (1) have been together long enough to have shared significant concerns or problems, (2) have had the opportunity to solve these problems and to observe the effects of their solutions, and (3) have adopted new members (p. 6–7). Elaborating on the adoption of new members, Schein argues that the passing of solutions to new members is essential for the formation and continuation of organizational culture because it shows that the solution is considered legitimate (i.e., widely used or adopted). Further, these solutions can belong to one of two intention-minded categories—those that are designed to solve problems and those that are designed to avoid anxiety.

Adler and Adler (1988) focus their discussion of organizational culture on the development and sustainment of organizational loyalty. Organizational loyalty develops when an individual has heavily subscribed to a certain culture. Adler and Adler define organizational loyalty as "a bond formed either to an organization or to some person or group within it that can be either individually or collectively forged" (p. 401). This loyalty involves a sense of attachment and wanting to be a part of something larger than oneself, trust, voluntary alignment of oneself with a larger group, and a willingness to follow and respect leadership. Adler and Adler present five elements that they posit are essential to the development of organizational loyalty. These include *domination* (strong hierarchy or leadership), *identification* (a bond to both a group and its leader), *commitment* (occurs when leadership encourages performance or investment), *integration* (strong in-group relationships, combined with isolation from outsiders or outside influence), and *goal alignment* (if individuals believe the goal of the organization is in their best interest, they will strive for the good of the whole).

Although organizational culture is the subject of vast literature, Rudes and Magnuson (2019) argue that the study of organizational culture is still in its infancy, and that, due to its complexity, it is a poorly understood phenomenon. Quoting Pettigrew (1990, p. 413) they describe organizational culture as "a riddle wrapped in a mystery wrapped in an enigma." Referencing how existing literature cannot come to a conclusive definition of organizational culture, Rudes and Magnuson describe organizational culture as a "interactional amalgamation of beliefs, values, artifacts, behaviors, demographics, symbols, meanings, patterns, language, rituals, myths, and ceremonies" (p. 9). Although our knowledge of organizational culture requires advancement, an understanding of the nuances of organizational life and decision-making is crucial in fully understanding how organizations operate and prevail.

Organizational Culture and Theoretical Applications

Culture is inherent to organizations and extends beyond a single person (Clemmer, 1940). Neo-institutional organizational theory, which seeks to explain how organizations become isomorphic (i.e., similar) with other organizations, can be used as a tool in understanding how people assimilate and adopt the traits of an existing culture. Organizations are living systems, within which organizational actors continuously adapt to new environments, generate new knowledge and conditions, and transform existing structures (Sessa & London, 2015). Viewing organizations from an individual, micro-level perspective, rather than from a macro-level approach, allows for a far greater understanding of how organizations operate and implies that individuals and their decision making, not the overall structure, are what create and sustain organizations.

Neo-institutional theory traditionally operates from a macro-level approach, but the principles of the theory are still applicable from an individual, micro level perspective (Suddaby et al., 2013). Suddaby et al. (2013) explore the growing literature that shifted the focus of neo-institutional theory from a macro-level to a micro-level approach, most primarily research into *institutional work* (Lawrence et al., 2009; Lawrence & Suddaby, 2006). Institutional work shifts the focus of study from the outcome of institutional processes to the actual processes themselves. These processes include specific behaviors that are used to create, maintain, and change organizations (Lawrence et al., 2009, 2011; Lawrence & Suddaby, 2006), and this focus on organizational agent decision-making shifts the unit of analysis from the organization as a whole to the agents themselves. At this micro-level, the analysis is composed of practices, praxis, and practitioners (Balogun & Johnson, 2004; Jarzabkowski & Sillince, 2007; Reckwitz, 2002; Sillince et al., 2012; Spee & Jarzabkowski, 2009; Suddaby et al., 2013; Whittington, 2006). *Practices* are the routinized behaviors that organizational actors use while they are strategizing (Reckwitz, 2002), including strategic methods (Spee & Jarzabkowski, 2009) and rhetoric (Sillince et al., 2012). *Praxis* is activity guided by practices as it takes place (Suddaby et al., 2013). *Practitioners* refers to organizational agents who are implementing the activity (Balogun & Johnson, 2004). Considering neo-institutional theory from a micro-level perspective allows the theory to be applied to a variety of organizational phenomenon, including culture and assimilation.

Conceptual Literature Review of Neo-institutionalism

Neo-institutionalism was introduced by Meyer and Rowan (1977), and its primary focus is on legitimacy. Meyer and Rowan argue that "organizations are driven to incorporate the practices and procedures defined by prevailing rationalized concepts of organizational work and institutionalized in society. Organizations that do so increase their legitimacy and their survival prospects" (p. 340). In their discussion of institutionalization, Meyer and Rowan argue that institutionalization occurs when various social processes and obligations come to take on a rule-like status within the organization. Further, Meyer and Rowan discuss the concept of *rationalized myths,* which are widely accepted, but unproven, assumptions about what organizational behavior is most likely to contribute to effective functioning. Moreover, they argue that "organizations are structured by phenomena in their environments and tend to become isomorphic with them" (p. 346). In essence, people are a product of their environment.

Neo-institutional theory was expanded by DiMaggio and Powell (1983), and much of the discussion in this expansion focused on the mechanisms of isomorphic change. DiMaggio and Powell posit that there are two types of isomorphism: *competitive* isomorphism and *institutional* isomorphism. Competitive isomorphism emphasizes market competition, and institutional isomorphism proposes that organizations compete for power and legitimacy. Much of the discussion in DiMaggio and Powell's piece focuses on institutional isomorphism. Within institutional isomorphism, DiMaggio and Powell describe three mechanisms of institutional isomorphic change. *Coercive* mechanisms originate from the problem of legitimacy and involve formal controls like rules and policies. *Mimetic* mechanisms result out of a response to uncertainty. Finally, *normative* mechanisms result out of a desire to appear professional. Building on this theoretical framework, DiMaggio and Powell developed 12 hypotheses of predictors of isomorphic change. These predictors occur at both an *organizational* level and at the *field* level. Organizational level predictors seek to explain the rate at which isomorphic change occurs on a macro level. Field level predictors seek to explain the rate at which isomorphic change occurs on a micro level.

Coercive organizational level predictors include: (1) Organizations become more like other organizations when they are dependent on that organization and (2) organizations become more like other organizations when the other organizations' resource supply is highly centralized. Mimetic organizational level predictors include: (1) Organizations become more like other organizations when they are unsure of how to achieve their goal and thus model their behavior off of organizations they perceive to be successful, and (2) organizations become more like other organizations when the organization's goals are ambiguous and thus model their behavior off of organizations they perceive to be successful. Normative organizational level predictors include: (1) Organizations become more like other organizations when there is a greater emphasis on academic credentials in selecting and hiring personnel, and (2) organizations will become more like other organizations when the organizational managers participate in trade or professional associations.

Coercive field-level predictors include: (1) Organizational fields become more like other organizational fields when they rely on a single (or several similar) source for necessary resources, and (2) organizational fields become more like other organizational fields when they all frequently transact with the same state agencies. Mimetic field level predictors include: (1) Organizational fields become more like other organizational fields when there is a lack of alternative organizational models within a certain field, and (2) organizational fields become more like other organizational fields when there is a large amount of uncertainty regarding organizational field goals or new technology. Normative field level predictors include: (1) Organizational fields become more like other organizational fields when there is a large extent of professionalization within a certain field, and (2) organizational fields will become more like other organizational fields when there is a larger extent of structuration of a field.

Neo-institutional theory serves as the basis of many studies of organizational behavior. Within the field of marketing, Chaney et al. (2016) explored how neo-institutional theory can be applied towards different marketing strategies to change the culture of consumption. In the healthcare field, D'Aunno et al. (1991) applied neo-institutional theory to substance use disorder treatment providers and found that these providers adopted many conflicting practices in response to varying demands from clients and outside sources. Within the field of criminology, Rubin (2015) explored the rapid, widespread, and homogenous diffusion of prisons across America. In her analysis, she argued that across the United States, prisons became isomorphic with one another because they wanted to appear as though they could efficiently and appropriately exercise power, which would in turn make each state and their correctional system appear more legitimate.

Prisonization as a Case Study of Neo-institutionalism

The principles of neo-institutionalism can also be applied to prison culture and prisonization. Extant literature documents the pains of imprisonment and many scholars attempt to explain both the resulting prison culture, as well as an individual's adaptive response to this new, highly structured environment. With incarceration comes a loss of liberty, desirable goods, relationships, autonomy, and safety (Sykes, 1958). With the framing of neo-institutional theory on a micro-scale, as opposed to a macro-scale, neo-institutionalism offers a new perspective on how and why individuals adjust to life in incarceration, as well as how this influences the resulting prison culture.

Conceptual Literature Review of Prison Culture

In his writing of *The Prison Community*, Clemmer (1940) described prison culture as the different social interactions, both formal and informal, that permeate within an institution. Clemmer also argued that prisons have an inherent culture, one that extends beyond a single person. He argues that incarcerated people are the carriers of this culture, but that no one incarcerated person has much impact on the larger prison culture. Further, Clemmer argues that prison culture is extremely complex, as demonstrated in the below quotation. Prison culture consists of the,

> Habits, behavior systems, traditions, history, customs, folkways, codes, the laws and rules which guide inmates, and their ideas, opinions, and attitudes toward or against homes, family, education, work, recreation, government, prisons, police, judges, other inmates, wardens, ministers, doctors, guards, ball-players, clubs, guns, cells, buckets, gravy, beans, walls, lamps, rain, clouds, clothes, machinery, hammers, rocks, caps, bibles, books, radio, monies, stealing, murder, rape, sex, love, honesty, martyrdom, and so on. (p. 294–295)

Throughout the existing prison culture literature, there is debate about the origins of the present culture. Rudes and Magnuson (2019) explore the two widely held beliefs about the origins of prison culture. They argue that organizational culture is an active process that is influenced by both internal and external stimuli. Some scholars place responsibility on the pains of imprisonment as the origin of institutional culture (Goffman, 1961; Sykes, 1958; Sykes & Messinger, 1960), while others place responsibility of the influence of the external world (Irwin & Cressey, 1962).

Skarbek (2012) argues that institutions and their administrations are incapable of providing all the governance and structure that incarcerated people need to cope with their experiences. Therefore, he posits that prison culture and norms develop out of a need for informal governance. Moreover, Skarbek found that incarcerated people rely on a combination of widely accepted norms and informal organizations (e.g., prison gangs) to provide governance. He argues that

> …correctional officers may be corrupt or face monitoring, prosecution, and punishment costs that prevent them from maintaining a completely safe facility, so inmates will

> victimize each other. Inmates cannot rely on official mechanisms to support exchange in contraband markets, so they must devise self-enforcing exchange institutions to capture the benefits of trade. (p. 96)

As mentioned in the works of Clemmer (1940) and Rudes and Magnuson (2019), the culture of prisons is extremely complex and in constant flux. However, there are many aspects of prison culture that are seen across institutions. These aspects include the perpetuation of belief systems and norms, the separation of incarcerated people into different social groups, the relationships between incarcerated people and staff, contraband trading, and linguistics (Wooldredge, 2020). Early literature placed pronounced emphasis on the widely accepted norms of noncooperation and hostility towards institutional staff as the backbone of incarcerated people's culture (Adams, 1992). Further, the use of unique prison jargon can be used as a way for incarcerated people to communicate more freely with one another (Wooldredge, 2020) or as a means to express rebellion and gain emotional satisfaction (Hargan, 1935).

Conceptual Literature Review of Prizonization

The debate about the origin of prison culture is also reflected in the debate about the origin of *prisonization*, which was introduced by Clemmer (1940) and describes the adaptive response of individuals to the prison environment, as well as their eventual immersion into the existing prison culture. Lawson et al. (1996) explored the two models of prisonization. Early research on prisonization focused on the *deprivation* model, which viewed a prison as a closed system that was immune to outside influence. Later research focused on the *importation* model, which views the prison as an open system that is pervaded by outside influence. Much of the emphasis in the importation model is placed on the outside lives and personalities of people before their incarceration. Wooldredge (2020) describes this open system as one that is open to

> The influences of the prison environment (including correctional officers), particular background characteristics of offenders (including personal needs), and interactions between these micro- and macro-level effects on an individual's adaptation to incarceration. (p. 175)

According to Clemmer (1940), there are three steps of prisonization: (1) The individual is stripped of their individual identity and placed in a subordinate group; (2) the individual changes their perception of acceptable conditions and develops a new appreciation for necessities like food, shelter, and clothing; and (3) the individual develops a desire for a good job. However, not all individuals change their behavior to adapt to their new environment. Clemmer asserted that there are various reasons why an individual would or would not acculturate. Clemmer lists six reasons why individuals may not acculturate. These include stronger external relationships, a fixed personality before incarceration, whether they are involved in primary or semi-primary social groups during incarceration, their placement in a gang or cellhouse (e.g., who they are celled with), if a person accepts the norms of the prison culture, and the individuals age, criminality, nationality, race, and upbringing. He also lists seven reasons why individuals may acculturate. These include length of sentence, unstable personality before incarceration, lack of strong external relationships, a willingness or desire to integrate, a blind acceptance of the norms of prison culture, a poor placement in a work group or cellhouse, and an eagerness to engage in deviant behavior. The next section uses neo-institutional theory to understand how people become immersed in the prison culture.

Application of the Theory

As mentioned in the above literature review of DiMaggio and Powell's (1983) 12 hypotheses of isomorphic change, there are both organizational level predictors and field level predictors. Each of these hypotheses will be applied to a different aspect of prison culture and prisonization.

Hypothesis 1 involves coercive isomorphism on an organizational level and states that "the greater the dependance of an organization on another organization, the more similar it will become to that organization in structure, climate, and behavioral focus" (p. 154). In essence, organizations become more like other organizations when they are dependent on that organization. In relation to prisonization, when viewed from a micro-individual lens, incarcerated people may become more like other incarcerated people when they are dependent on them for goods or protection (e.g., illegal drugs or prison gangs for safety).

Hypothesis 2 also involves coercive isomorphism on an organizational level and states that "the greater the centralization of organization A's resource supply, the great the extent to which organization A will change isomorphically to resemble the organizations on which it depends for resources" (p. 154). In other words, organizations become more like other organizations when the other organizations resource supply is highly centralized. In relation to prisonization, when viewed from a micro-individual lens, this could serve as an elaboration to the previous hypothesis. Incarcerated people may become more like other incarcerated people, upon which they rely on for some good or service, because they interact with them so frequently. Differential association theory, proposed by Edwin Sutherland (1939) argues that, through frequent contact with others, people take on their values, attitudes, methods, and motives. Thus, in prison, when an individual is in constant contact with one individual on multiple occasions (perhaps because they are reliant on them for some good or service) they may take on their traits.

Hypothesis 3 explores mimetic isomorphism on an organizational level and states that "the more uncertain the relationship between means and ends the greater the extent to which an organization will model itself after organizations it perceives to be successful" (p. 154). Essentially, organizations become more like other organizations when they are unsure of how to achieve their goal and thus model their behavior off of organizations they perceive to be successful. In relation to prisonization, when viewed from a micro-individual lens, incoming people who have not been in incarceration before may not know how to manage their new environment. Thus, they may turn to other incarcerated people to see how they cope with the pains of imprisonment (Leban et al., 2016). These coping mechanisms would then become widely used, which would in turn lead to isomorphism between incarcerated people.

Hypothesis 4 also involves mimetic isomorphism on an organizational level and states that "the more ambiguous the goals of an organization, the greater the extent to which the organization will model itself after organizations that it perceives to be successful" (p. 155). In essence, organizations become more like other organizations when the organization's goals are ambiguous and thus model their behavior off of organizations they perceive to be successful. In relation to prisonization, when viewed from a micro-individual lens, a person who is incarcerated for the first time prison may not know how to navigate the system or what they should strive to do while incarcerated. Thus, they model their behavior off of other incarcerated people, increasing isomorphism.

Hypothesis 5 explores normative isomorphism on an organizational level and states that "the greater the reliance on academic credentials in choosing managerial and staff personnel, the greater the extent to which an organization will become like other organizations in the field" (p. 155). Essentially, organizations become more like other organizations when there is a greater emphasis on academic credentials in selecting and hiring personnel. In relation to prisonization, when viewed from a micro-individual lens, the focus may not be on academic credentials, but rather on street credibility or previous incarceration. Among units, or within prison gangs, leadership may be chosen based off of who has the most "credibility," which would lead to isomorphism between incarcerated people because they are all following the orders of the same individual.

Hypothesis 6 also explores normative isomorphism on an organizational level and states that "the greater the participation of organizational managers in trade and professional associations, the more likely the organization will be, or will become, like other organizations in its field" (p. 155). In essence, organizations will become more like other organizations when the organizational managers participate in trade or professional associations. In relation to prisonization, when viewed from a micro-individual lens, when incarcerated people become involved in commissary and/or contraband trading, they take on an aspect of prison culture and become more similar with other incarcerated people.

Hypothesis 7 explores coercive isomorphism on a field level and states that "the greater the extent to which an organizational field is dependent upon a single (or several similar) source of support for vital resources, the higher the level of isomorphism" (p. 155). In essence, organizational fields become more like other organizational fields when they all rely on similar sources for necessary resources. This hypothesis is similar to the first hypothesis—if an incarcerated person is reliant on other incarcerated people for goods and/or services, they may become isomorphic with them. At a macro-level scale in the institution, if many incarcerated people rely on each other for goods and/or services, these people may take on the traits of each other.

Hypothesis 8 also explores coercive isomorphism on a field level and states that "The greater the extent to which the organizations in a field transact with agencies of the state, the greater the extent of isomorphism in the field as a whole" (p. 155). In other words, organizational fields become more like other organizational fields when they all frequently transact with the same state agencies. In relation to prisonization, when viewed from a micro-individual lens, if incarcerated people are all reliant on the institution for some goods (e.g., meals), they may become more prisonized. Clemmer (1940) explores the idea of institutional reliance during his discussion of the three steps of prisonization.

Hypothesis 9 explores mimetic isomorphism on a field level and states that "The fewer the number of visible alternative organizational models in a field, the faster the rate of isomorphism in that field" (p. 155). Essentially, organizational fields become more like other organizational fields when there is a lack of alternative organizational models within a certain field. In relation to prisonization, when viewed from a micro-individual lens, incarceration places everyone under the same conditions. Thus, people learn how to adapt to the same environment. If all incarcerated people are adapting to the same environment, it is likely that their behavior, and thus culture, would become isomorphic.

Hypothesis 10 also explores mimetic isomorphism on a field level and states that "The greater the extent to which technologies are uncertain or goals are ambiguous within a field, the greater the rate of isomorphic change" (p. 156). In other words, organizational fields become more like other organizational fields when there is a large amount of uncertainty regarding organizational field goals or new technology. In relation to prisonization, facing uncertainty generally makes people nervous, which may in turn make them assimilate faster to their environment because of their desire for comfort or to fit in.

Hypothesis 11 explores normative isomorphism on a field level and states that "the greater the extent of professionalization in a field, the greater the amount of institutional isomorphic change" (p. 156). Essentially, organizational fields become more like other organizational fields when there is a large extent of professionalization within a certain field. In relation to prisonization and with professionalization being associated with a longer time in incarceration, Clemmer (1940) discusses how longer sentences cause many incarcerated people to "prisonize."

Hypothesis 12 explores normative isomorphism on a field level and states that "The greater the extent of structuration of a field, the greater the degree of isomorphics" (p. 156). In other words, organizational fields will become more like other organizational fields when there is a larger extent of structuration of a field. In relation to prisonization, the more routinized a prison structure, and the more incarcerated people have to interact with this prison structure, the more isomorphic they will become with one another because they are all interacting with the same structure.

Discussion

A large amount of literature has explored prison culture and the process of prisonization. However, by examining prisonization using a neo-institutional framework, we are better able to understand how and why people become immersed in the prison culture and reliant on the institution. Coercive isomorphic mechanisms originate from formal controls like rules and policies. These are illustrated in the ways in which incarcerated people rely on each other, and the ways in which people rely on formal structures within the prison, like rules regarding meals. Mimetic isomorphic mechanisms result out of uncertainty. These can be seen in the ways in which incarcerated people may adopt the traits or coping mechanisms of other people because they are unsure of how to navigate the system. Finally, normative isomorphic mechanisms result out of a desire to appear professional. These can be seen in the ways in which street credibility, time spent in incarceration, or unit structure influence prisonization. All three of these measures influence why people become part of their environment, and how and why they adopt the culture of the institution that they are entering.

Prisonization is often at odds with rehabilitation. It forces an individual to rely on an institution and often forces people to lose their sense of individual identity. However, 95% of people who are incarcerated return to their communities (Hughes & Wilson, 2004). Understanding how and why institutional policies, incarcerated people's relationships, people's uncertainty, and their desire for legitimacy or survival influence the degree to which someone prisonized can serve as the first step towards making sure that this 95% of individuals are able to successfully re-enter society (Hughes & Wilson, 2004). This framework provides many implications for both policy and future research.

Policy Implications

The policy implications that address concerns raised through a neo-institutional account of prisonization must consider individual identity, autonomy, reliance, and recidivism. Maintaining individual identity and autonomy is important, and it may make individuals less likely to re-enter the system if they do not become as reliant on it, or as comfortable in it, in the first place. Clemmer (1940) places a strong emphasis on external relationships (with family or friends) as a mechanism for preventing prisonization. Increasing visitation, supplying people with increased access to mailing materials (e.g., paper, stamps), and the general encouragement of prosocial behaviors and relationships would allow incarcerated people to maintain their external relationships, which would serve as a protective factor against prisonization. It is also important to reduce visitation barriers that the families of incarcerated people face, including financial and time-related burdens and stress from rules and regulations (Boppre et al., 2022). Additionally, Clemmer argued that long sentences can serve as a risk factor for prisonization. Implementing policies aimed at sentence reduction, or alternative sentences, could address this risk.

However, reliance on the institution is where the policy implications of prisonization become muddied. In 2009, Sharon Dolovich argued that "what the state owes its prisoners it owes not because prisoners deserve it but because of the choice the state has made to punish with incarceration" (p. 911). By virtue of the state choosing to punish through incarceration, they must supply adequate goods/services for incarcerated people. However, prisonization can only truly be addressed when policy is aimed at curbing reliance, and there is no straightforward way to navigate this quandary. Potential solutions include complete abolition of the prison system, a transformation of the existing structure, electronic monitoring, probation and parole, or new alternative sentencing structures. Future research is necessary to determine how best to navigate this conflict.

Future Research

Future research could explore how reliant incarcerated people feel on the system, how immersed in the culture they perceive themselves to be, or how much of their identity they feel is being tied up in "being a prisoner." Potential questions surrounding the idea of reliance include, "do you feel reliant on the prison system, on staff, or on other incarcerated people? What about your experience has made you feel this way?". Questions exploring the complexity of prison culture could include, "tell me about prison culture. Describe it to me. What does it mean to you? Do you feel like it exists, and if it does, do you feel like you interact with it?". Finally, questions exploring people's identity could pose the questions, "how do you define identity? How do you define your own identity? Has incarceration had any impact on your personal identity?". These questions and areas of research would provide scholars with the knowledge of how incarcerated people perceive the institution and their place in it, which provides invaluable insight into what policies may be appropriate to explore or implement.

Conclusion

Applying neo-institutional theory to the concept of prisonization allows for a unique perspective and approach to the topic. With the framing of neo-institutional theory on a micro-scale, as opposed to a macro-scale, neo-institutionalism offers a new explanation for how and why individuals adjust to life during incarceration, as well as how this influences the resulting prison culture. In particular, the exploration of coercive, mimetic, and normative influences that encourage individuals to prisonize expands upon Clemmer's (1940) discussion of risk and protective factors by providing a more in-depth explanation of the influences behind each factor.

Finally, by applying neo-institutional theory on a micro-level scale, the scope of neo-institutional theory is greatly increased. Applying neo-institutional theory on a micro-level scale allows for the theory to be applied to a variety of organizational phenomenon that might have otherwise been ignored, including culture and assimilation. This moves both the organizational theory and criminology fields forward and makes room for deeper theoretical analysis on a variety of topics. Within the field of penology, an understanding of how and why people react to incarceration provides scholars and practitioners with a wide array of policy implications and future research directions. These policy implications and future research directions are especially useful when considering how many people return to their communities from incarceration.

References

Adams, K. (1992). Adjusting to prison life. *Crime and Justice, 16*, 275–359. http://www.jstor.org/stable/1147565

Adler, P. A., & Adler, P. (1988). Intense loyalty in organizations: A case study of college athletics. *Administrative Science Quarterly*, 401–417. https://doi.org/10.2307/2392716

Balogun, J., & Johnson, G. (2004). Organizational restructuring and middle manager sensemaking. *Academy of Management Journal, 47*(4), 523–549. https://doi.org/10.5465/20159600

Bolman, L. G., & Deal, T. E. (1997). *Reframing organizations: Artistry, choice, and leadership* (2nd ed.). Jossey-Bass.

Boppre, B., Dehart, D., & Shapiro, C. J. (2022). "The prison system doesn't make it comfortable to visit": Prison visitation from the perspectives of people incarcerated and family members. *Criminal Justice and Behavior, 49*(10), 1474–1494. https://doi.org/10.1177/00938548221094823

Chaney, D., Ben Slimane, K., & Humphreys, A. (2016). Megamarketing expanded by neo-institutional theory. *Journal of Strategic Marketing, 24*(6), 470–483. https://doi.org/10.1080/0965254X.2015.1052539

Clemmer, D. (1940). *The prison community*. Holt, Rinehart & Winston.

D'Aunno, T., Sutton, R. I., & Price, R. H. (1991). Isomorphism and external support in conflicting institutional environments: A study of drug abuse treatment units. *Academy of Management Journal, 34*(3), 636–661. https://doi.org/10.5465/256409

DiMaggio, P., & Powell, W. (1983). The iron case revisited: Institutional isomorphism and collective rationality in organizational fields. *American Sociological Review, 48*, 147–160. https://doi.org/10.1515/9780691229270-005

Dolovich, S. (2009). Cruelty, prison conditions, and the eighth amendment. *NYU Law Review, 84*, 881–979. https://heinonline.org/HOL/P?h=hein.journals/nylr84&i=889

Goffman, E. (1961). On the characteristics of total institutions: The inmate world. In D. R. Cressey (Ed.), *The prison: Studies in institutional organization and change* (pp. 312–338). Holt, Rineheart and Winston, Inc..

Hargan, J. (1935). The psychology of prison language. *The Journal of Abnormal and Social Psychology, 30*(3), 359–365. https://psycnet.apa.org/doi/10.1037/h0057784

Hughes, T. & Wilson, D. J. (2004). *Reentry trends in the United States*. Retrieved from https://bjs.ojp.gov/content/pub/pdf/reentry.pdf

Irwin, J., & Cressey, D. R. (1962). Thieves, convicts and the inmate culture. *Social Problems, 10*(2), 142–155. https://doi.org/10.2307/799047

Jarzabkowski, P. A., & Sillince, J. (2007). A rhetoric-in-context approach to shaping commitment to multiple strategic goals. *Organization Studies, 28*(10), 1639–1665. https://doi.org/10.1177/0170840607075266

Lawrence, T. B., & Suddaby, R. (2006). Institutions and institutional work. In S. R. Clegg, C. Hardy, T. B. Lawrence, & W. R. Nord (Eds.), *Handbook of organization studies* (pp. 215–254). Sage.
Lawrence, T. B., Suddaby, R., & Leca, B. (2009). Introduction: Theorizing and studying institutional work. In T. B. Lawrence, R. Suddaby, & B. Leca (Eds.), *Institutional work: Actors and agency in institutional studies of organizations* (pp. 1–27). Cambridge University Press.
Lawrence, T. B., Suddaby, R., & Leca, B. (2011). Institutional work: Refocusing institutional studies of organization. *Journal of Management Inquiry, 20*(1), 52–58. https://doi.org/10.1177/1056492610387222
Lawson, D. P., Segrin, C., & Ward, T. D. (1996). The relationship between prisonization and social skills among prison inmates. *The Prison Journal, 76*(3), 293–309. https://doi.org/10.1177/0032855596076003004
Leban, L., Cardwell, S. M., Copes, H., & Brezina, T. (2016). Adapting to prison life: A qualitative examination of the coping process among incarcerated offenders. *Justice Quarterly, 33*(6), 943–969. https://doi.org/10.1080/07418825.2015.1012096
Meyer, J. W., & Rowan, B. (1977). Institutionalized organizations: Formal structure as myth and ceremony. *American Journal of Sociology, 83*(2), 340–363. https://www.jstor.org/stable/2778293
Pettigrew, A. M. (1990). Conclusion: Organizational climate and culture: Two constructs in search of a role. In B. Schneider (Ed.), *Organizational climate and culture* (pp. 413–434). Jossey-Bass.
Reckwitz, A. (2002). Toward a theory of social practices: A development in culturalist theorizing. *European Journal of Social Theory, 5*(2), 243–263. https://doi.org/10.1177/13684310222225432
Rubin, A. T. (2015). A neo-institutional account of prison diffusion. *Law & Society Review, 49*(2), 365–400. https://doi.org/10.1111/lasr.12136
Rudes, D. S., & Magnuson, S. (2019). Scapegoating culture: Misunderstanding organizational culture as the problem in carceral institutions and beyond. *Sociology Compass, 13*(2), 1–12. https://doi.org/10.1111/soc4.12657
Schein, E. H. (1984). Coming to a new awareness of organizational culture. *Sloan Management Review, 25*(2), 3–16. https://www.proquest.com/scholarly-journals/coming-new-awareness-organizational-culture/docview/1302988646/se-2
Sessa, V. I., & London, M. (2015). *Continuous learning in organizations: Individual, group, and organizational perspectives*. Psychology Press.
Sillince, J. A. A., Jarzabkowski, P. A., & Shaw, D. (2012). Shaping strategic action through the rhetorical construction and exploitation of ambiguity. *Organization Science, 23*(3), 743–757. https://doi.org/10.1287/orsc.1110.0670
Skarbek, D. (2012). Prison gangs, norms, and organizations. *Journal of Economic Behavior & Organization, 82*(1), 96–109. https://doi.org/10.1016/j.jebo.2012.01.002
Spee, A. P., & Jarzabkowski, P. A. (2009). Strategy tools as boundary objects. *Strategic Organization, 7*(2), 223–232. https://doi.org/10.1177/1476127009102674
Suddaby, R., Seidl, D., & Lê, J. K. (2013). Strategy-as-practice meets neo-institutional theory. *Strategic Organization, 11*(3), 329–344. https://doi.org/10.1177/1476127013497618
Sutherland, E. H. (1939). *Principles of criminology*. JB Lippincott Company.
Sykes, G. (1958). *The society of captives*. Princeton University Press.
Sykes, G., & Messinger, S. (1960). The inmate social system. In R. A. Cloward, D. R. Cressey, G. H. Grosser, R. McCleery, L. E. Ohlin, G. M. Sykes, & S. L. Messinger (Eds.), *Theoretical studies in social organization of the prison* (pp. 5–19). Social Science Research Council.
Terrill, W., Paoline, E. A., III, & Manning, P. K. (2003). Police culture and coercion. *Criminology, 41*(4), 1003–1034. https://doi.org/10.1111/j.1745-9125.2003.tb01012.x
Whittington, R. (2006). Completing the practice turn in strategy research. *Organization Studies, 27*(5), 613–634. https://doi.org/10.1177/0170840606064101
Wooldredge, J. (2020). Prison culture, management, and in-prison violence. *Annual Review of Criminology, 3*, 165–188. https://doi.org/10.1146/annurev-criminol-011419-041359

Chapter 2
"Out of Bounds": The Influence of Personal and Institutionalized Bounded Rationality on Judicial Decision Making

Sydney A. Fay

Introduction

Herbert A. Simon would likely have disputed Aristotle's famous claim that the law is free from passion, or at least, he would have pointed out that legal decision-making is free from rationality. Simon did not argue that the law, or legal actors, were somehow irrational, but that human rational decision making was a fallacy. Simon (1955) said that the "classical" concepts of rationality assumed that the decision maker can attach pay-offs to each alternative, predict what will happen without any unanticipated outcomes, and select the best outcome with certainty. However, decision makers cannot literally make calculations to come to non-mathematical decisions. Hagle (1990) agreed that the theoretical rational decision maker would have access to and examine all available information and alternatives, selecting the one that produced exacted anticipated outcomes (from the cost-benefit analysis) and would consider all possibilities and consequences associated with each possibility before deciding. According to Hagle (1990), an ideal rational decision maker using such an exhaustive and comprehensive model of rational decision-making faces common barriers: control, unintended results, missing or unavailable data, and goals. Decision makers cannot usually control all elements of the problem at hand; cannot predict unforeseen results that may occur for the people the decision affects; cannot have at her disposal all complete data necessary to make an accurate cost-benefit analysis of possible solutions to the given problem; and the decision maker's goals may not be known or adequately identified. To cope with the constraints of the rational decision-making model, Simon explored the concept of bounded rationality.

S. A. Fay (✉)
George Mason University, Department of Criminology, Law & Society, Fairfax, VA, USA
e-mail: sboone6@gmu.edu

D. S. Rudes, J. R. Ingram (eds.), *Using Organizational Theory to Study, Explain, and Understand Criminal Legal Organizations*,
https://doi.org/10.1007/978-3-031-66285-0_2

Simon's behavioral choice model, including bounded rationality, is a critique of the rational decision-making model, as it illuminates the limits of rational adaptation (Jones, 2002). Simon (1979) explained that bounded rationality is a consequence of not knowing all of the possible alternatives to a problem, having uncertainty about exogenous events, and being unable to calculate consequences of the decision. Simon first conceptualized bounded rationality in 1957, explaining that the principle of bounded rationality is:

> [t]he capacity of the human mind for formulating and solving complex problems is very small compared with the size of the problems whose solution is required for objectively rational behavior in the real world — or even for a reasonable approximation to such objective rationality. (Simon, 1957, p. 198, see also p. 202)

Later Simon (1997b) extrapolated on bounded rationality, insisting that this type of behavioral rationality is consistent with how humans actually make decisions as they search for alternatives using incomplete and inaccurate knowledge of the consequences of those actions, and then choose a satisfactory enough action (Simon, 1997b, p. 17). Simon (1957) elaborated that one way to simplify a choice problem was to replace the goal of maximizing (i.e., seeking the "best" outcome after exhaustively considering all possibilities and their consequences, with complete information) with *satisficing,* which includes selecting a "good enough" choice. By 1979, Simon defined the two concepts underlying mechanisms of choice under conditions of bounded rationality as *searching* and *satisficing* (p. 502).

While Simon (1957) suggested that his behavioral choice model of decision making, bounded rationality, applied to all decision makers, bounded rationality may easily be applied to legal decision makers in particular. By design, legal decision makers (especially judges and prosecutors) operate as boundedly rational individuals. They cannot be omniscient beings but are held to such a standard since their decisions may formally affect the rest of peoples' lives (and may even end them under the death penalty). Engel and Gueth (2018) contended that judicial decision making consists of four steps, all of which may be understood under the theory of bounded rationality. According to Engel and Gueth (2018), judicial decision making consists of the four steps of scenario construction, removing implausible scenarios, acceptable outcomes, and the ultimate decision-making, as follows:

- *Scenario construction:* Under the theory of bounded rationality, the decision maker will only consider scenarios that s/he "dares" not neglect. This very process is institutionalized in the courts when parties plead their cases by telling a story, supported by evidence. The defendant has only two scenarios: The defendant can either tell another story or try to weaken prosecution's case so that they cannot prove that the defendant is guilty beyond a reasonable doubt.
- *Removing implausible scenarios:* After a set of scenarios to consider are available to consider, the trier of fact must qualify relevant scenarios based on plausibility. This element of boundedly rational decision making is also institutionalized: The standard of proof creates a relevance criterion. When the standard of proof is beyond reasonable doubt and the scenario would support the claim, the trier of fact must dismiss that claim if any reasonable doubt remains.

- *Acceptable outcomes:* The trier of fact wants to choose a scenario that is "good enough" by weighing the gain-loss balance. All the trier of fact is concerned about is error, not the gain-loss balance between parties (assuming the trier of fact is unbiased).
- *Decision-making:* All the trier of fact requires is confidence in discriminating between the two alternative interpretations of the evidence. Then a decision can be made and rendered.

Since judicial decision making occurs in the context of such high stakes, understanding legal decision making under the model of bounded rationality would help justice organizations understand the internal constraints (i.e., cognitive limitations) and external constraints (i.e., environmental constraints) that judicial decision makers face. Beyond the individual decision-maker, recognizing the extent to which the concept of bounded rationality is institutionalized in the US court system is imperative for understanding how our justice organizations either limit or assist legal decision makers.

The US court system was purportedly designed to help triers of fact make better decisions (Engel & Gueth, 2018). At the simplest level, a court case consists of two sides (e.g., defendant, prosecutor) pleading their case to a judge who must determine whether a certain standard of proof is met before deciding on an outcome, such as guilty or innocent, or determining a mode and length of sentencing. In this way, the court system is set up to limit the number of outcomes a judge can even select. Further, most judges have complex and ever-increasing caseloads, which are not compatible with a judge making an optimal ruling in every case—bounded rationality is almost necessary and encouraged. The judge also only knows the evidence as it is presented to him or her and often relies on precedence and memory to make decisions. Thus, the US court system is further restricting the already personally bounded rationality of a judicial decision maker by institutionalizing bounded rationality and baking it into the criminal legal system.

Ultimately, understanding how an individual's bounded rationality interacts with that institutionalized bounded rationality and how this interaction impacts final decision outcomes is critical to understanding how persons and organizations influence each other to produce verdicts and sentences. Therefore, the central questions addressed in this chapter are:

- What are the *cognitive* mechanisms responsible for bounded rationality within the judiciary?
- What other *environmental* constraints (or external "bounds") are placed on judicial decision makers who already use their own bounded rationality to make decisions?
- To what extent is bounded rationality institutionalized?
- How does the judicial decision maker's bounded rationality interact with that institutionalized bounded rationality to produce final outcomes?

Literature Review

Vallbé (2015) assumed that while judges act rationally (meaning they pursue their goals using rational means), they are limited by their cognition and their institutional environments. Understanding both the cognitive and the environmental factors that limit or "bound" decision-makers' rationality must be understood from a layman's and a judicial agent's context. The extent to which cognitive limitations are married to the decision-making environment and the extent to which bounded rationality is institutionalized at an organizational level is also discussed.

The Cognitive Mechanisms Responsible for Bounded Rationality

Cognitive mechanisms are responsible, in part, for a decision maker's bounded rationality. Humans have a limited ability to process information and judges are no exception (Glöckner, 2008; Hagle, 1990; Tsaoussi & Zervogianni, 2010). While judges and other judicial actors (e.g., prosecutors, attorneys) do make decisions in different contexts and often with larger stakes, their cognition as experts does not vary considerably from a layperson's cognitive mechanisms for making decisions (Hagle, 1990; Vallbé, 2015). Humans use a variety of cognitive mechanisms to make decisions, a full discussion of which is beyond the scope of this chapter. However, to understand how rational choice is bounded, we will focus on cognitive shortcuts related to processing information to arrive at a decision, with an emphasis on selective searching, heuristics, and take-the-best-strategy as a satisficing approach.

Selective Searches

Simon (1990) called decision-making heuristics "selective searches." He likened human bounded rationality to the abilities of a computer: A computer can solve many complex tasks but not every single possible task. A standard computer cannot, for example, cook a six-course meal, because it was not designed to do that. That is outside of its programming, outside of its scope, in much the same way that humans cannot have unbounded limits of understanding and perception. Like a computer with programming constraints, a human decision maker in the real world faces cognitive limitations. Kalantari (2010) posited that, specifically, decision makers in the real world are constrained by aspiration level (i.e., how an individual explores alternatives to a problem, related to past experiences). They often complete their searches using a stop rule (i.e., deciding when a search is over and a decision can be made). Simon (1979) proposed that satisficing is such a stop mechanism (Barros, 2010). But, how do we even begin to search?

Heuristics

When people are uncertain about a decision's outcome, they often begin searching for answers within the bounds of what they already know or have experienced. Tversky and Kahneman (1974), revered for their work on conceptualizing heuristics, start one of their seminal papers using judicial decision makers as an example of actors who may use heuristics to make important decisions: "Many decisions are based on beliefs concerning the likelihood of uncertain events such as the outcome of an election, the guilt of a defendant, or the future value of the dollar" (p. 1124). Heuristics, then, are well-documented cognitive mechanisms people use to make decisions using limited sets of information in the context of their decision-making scenarios (e.g., Tversky & Kahneman, 1974). Particularly, heuristics are used to simplify and manage selective searches (Hagle, 1990). Hagle (1990) pointed that for organizations, heuristics can take the form of Standard Operating Procedure manuals and explicit rules. For people, heuristics may take the shape of more informal rules, like a rule of thumb. For example, a common decision heuristic involves students tending to sit in the same chairs each class, even if the seats are unassigned. Hagle (1990) argued that after making an initial set of decisions during the first class (e.g., choosing a window seat close to the front, next to a friend), by the next class, people tend to choose the same seat using the heuristic solidified in the first class.

Judges also rely on heuristics to make sentencing and other critical decisions (Marder & Pina-Sánchez, 2020). Perez (2016) explained that judges use cognitive shortcuts in part due to institutional pressures to turn over high caseloads, which limits judges' ability to deeply understand the expert testimony and its subject matter. Perez (2016) found that when Israeli judges had to contend with conflicting expert evidence in a sample of tort cases, they were more likely to appoint their own expert, especially when the case was labeled highly controversial. Another potential issue was that in cases with a court-appointed expert, the court sided with that expert's opinion in more than 90% of cases. Perez (2016) argued that judicial actors hired their own experts in cases where there had been conflicting expert opinions and thus indirectly employed a second-order heuristic to resolve an evidentiary dispute: The judges did not make a first-order decision (i.e., seek to understand the scientific evidence that multiple experts disagreed on), but a second-order decision, wherein they hired their own expert and deferred to their judgement in most cases. This is not an optimal solution, but one again that is "good enough."

Take-the-Best Satisficing Strategy

Sometimes decision makers are faced with new situations that limit their ability to rely on heuristics. Another application of bounded rationality is a cognitive mechanism often called take-the-best (or drop-the-worst) strategy. The take-the-best-strategy is arguably a satisficing strategy. Humans cannot review or even fathom all alternatives to any given problem. One strategy for selecting the best choice is to focus on cues. Bergert and Nosofsky (2007) conducted several experiments that showed that strategy choice depends on characteristics of the relevant task and stimuli. They found that if a decision task lends different strategies with different levels of accuracy, people chose the most accurate strategy. However, if strategies produce the same level performance, people chose the simplest strategy. Furthermore, increases in time pressure, "information-acquisition costs," and presentation formats lead to increased use of take-the-best strategies. This validates Kalantari's (2010) notion that once a person reaches an aspirational level (i.e., using the most accurate strategy, or if there are multiple accurate strategies, then the simplest strategy is used), they will stop searching and make a decision. In other words, people take the first "best" cue (e.g., is it the most accurate? Is it the simplest?) and stop searching to come to their decision using this take-the-best strategy.

Selective searches, heuristics, and satisficing strategies such as the take-the-best strategy are all employed in situations where the decision maker has limited information, searches selectively, relies on past experiences, and if all fails, takes-the-best approach. These are some of the fundamental ways in which human rationality is bound by cognitive limitations and how people adapt to arriving at the best choice without exhausting cognitive capacities in the process. Our searches are limited by effort, but also by our environment. Even if we had the cognitive capacity to determine all alternative solutions to a problem, we do not often have the luxury of infinite time to review them. External constraints do not often allow for such an extended search (Hagle, 1990). This is especially true for judicial decision makers, who have additional environmental constraints placed upon them by the very institutions in which they serve.

The Environmental Constraints for Judicial Decision Makers

There are other environmental constraints (or external "bounds") confronting judicial decision makers who already use their own individual bounded rationality to make decisions. Physical environment, workgroup members, competing roles, uncertainty, and time pressure to work with and complete large and complex caseloads are all contributors to the additional pressures judicial decision makers face every day (Cauthen & Peters, 2003; Engel & Gueth, 2018; Gibson, 1980, 1983; Gilboa & Schmeidler, 1995; Hagle, 1990; Hall & Brace, 1996; Jones, 2002; Li, 2020; Metcalfe, 2016; Nardulli et al., 1984; O'Brien, 2009; Oh et al., 2016; Sunstein & Ullmann-Margalit, 1999; Sunstein, 2000; Tsaoussi & Zervogianni, 2010).

Physical Environment

Gibson (1980) discovered that the physical environment in which judges operate may affect their sentencing decisions. Gibson (1980) examined the linkages between criminal trial courts in Iowa and the sociopolitical attributes of their environments, focusing on variations in sentencing policies. Gibson (1980) surmised that the environment in which a judge renders a sentence affects the severity of that sentence. Gibson (1980) concluded that judges who had more contact with constituencies have been defeated in election and who assumed "delegate" role orientation were much more influenced by environmental factors when making a sentencing decision.

More recently, Cauthen and Peters (2003) found that Louisiana Supreme Court justices supported the state (i.e., voting against criminal defendants) and voted conservatively in cases from their home districts compared to similar cases coming from outside their home districts. Cauthen and Peters (2003) believed that judges were intentionally supporting their districts' interests in part to please their constituents to secure their district election votes. Hall and Brace (1996) similarly determined that, across eight states, state supreme court justices' decisions were impacted by the environment in which the case was heard. Hall and Brace (1996) saw that judges made death sentence decisions differently depending on the ideological environment of the state in which the case was heard, even when controlling for crimes of extreme similarity (for example, when the defendant killed identical types of victims in the same manner, they were given different sentences depending on the state where the decision was made).

Workgroup Members

Gibson (1983) later argued that judges' decisions are a combination of what they prefer to do, what they should do (e.g., role theory), and what they are constrained from doing (e.g., their group or institution's constraints). However, it is important to remember that judges do not act alone. Take for instance, a typical working group consisting of a judge, prosecutor, and defense attorney when deciding plea deals. Nardulli et al. (1984) examined the contextual factors (such as the type of criminal case, prosecutor office policies restricting discretion, and workgroup configuration[1]) and individual factors (attitude toward punishment, Machiavellianism, and operating styles) at play when a set of groups of judges, prosecutors, and defense attorneys worked face-to-face to make sentencing decisions in felony guilty pleas in nine counties in the United States. They found that contextual and individual factors interacted to produce final decisions and could not be considered independently from each other. Notably, they found that while some sentencing decisions adhered to tradition or precedent, others were complex and the product of personal views, working styles, and personality traits of the triad making the decision.

More recent courtroom workgroup research found that courtroom triads influence case outcomes and even the mode of case disposition. When studying how courtroom workgroup (i.e., the judge, prosecutor, and defense attorney) interactions affected guilty plea convictions, Metcalfe (2016) found that workgroups more

[1] Workgroup characteristics were defined as the specific configuration of judge, prosecutor, defense counsel dealing with the case.

familiar with each other were more likely to take a case to trial rather than have the defendant take a plea bargain. Familiarity between the prosecutor and judge increased the chance that a case would end in a plea deal, while a defense attorney familiar with the other actors of the workgroup was actually more likely to erode that cooperative process between the prosecutor and judge. These findings demonstrate again that the interactions among courtroom actors influence case processing, and that the judge does not act alone in his or her decision-making process.

Competing Roles

While legal actors face challenges between-persons in their workgroups (such as in a triad of a judge, prosecutor, and defense attorney), prosecutors in particular can face competing roles within-person. O'Brien (2009) stated that prosecutors have two competing roles: They must prosecute defendants vigorously while also balancing the rights of the defendants they prosecute. O'Brien (2009) argued that if prosecutors were indeed rational actors, then any judicial errors they made were due to rigged institutional incentives, or more likely, their cognitive limitations were exacerbated when they were held accountable for their ability to persuade others of a suspect's guilt. Prosecutors also have their reputations to worry about:

> Accuracy must also be weighed against efficiency: proceeding quickly and decisively against a suspect may preclude pursuing alternate avenues of investigation. And once a prosecutor decides to proceed against a suspect, changing course in response to every new piece of information could be perceived by superiors (and perhaps ultimately voters) as weak and indecisive. (O'Brien, 2009, p. 1013)

Uncertainty

No matter the judicial actor's member role or interactions in their workgroup, all legal decision makers usually face inherent uncertainty. Li (2020) contended that the balancing of legality and the rationality of the ruling is what generates uncertainty in legal decisions. For example, if facts or precedented cases are in conflict or ambiguous, the judge cannot be wholly certain of the outcome before careful deliberation. To deal with this, Engel and Gueth (2018) developed a decision-making model in the face of uncertainty about past behavior (with the assumption this will help with future decision making) so that judges may feel more confident in their decisions moving forward. Their approach was modeled after Simon's (1979) notion of satisficing, insofar as that the judicial decision maker minimizes the chance that their decision is made in error. While there is a level of uncertainty present in all decision making, judicial decision makers arguably face more uncertainty (e.g., defendants are not always truthful) with higher stakes (e.g., the removal of the defendant's freedom or life).

Time Pressure and Increasing Caseloads

Another pressure facing judicial decision makers in particular is time pressure under growing caseloads (Hagle, 1990). Oh et al. (2016) conducted three experiments of decision making under different units of time pressure, extending:

> the previous work on bounded rationality by documenting, for the first time, that under much higher time pressure that enforces split-second decision making, subjects instead adopted a "drop-the-worst" heuristic, whereby the least valuable cues are simply ignored (or discounted) altogether. This difference in satisficing strategy likely represents an adaptive shift in information integration to accommodate the less certain nature of cue information and much higher time pressure in the present task. (p. 1953)

Oh et al. (2016) found that to use the take-the-best approach, the subject must be confident in her knowledge of exact rankings of cue validities. Experts with this knowledge use the take-the-best approach, making judicial actors no different than decision makers in other professions. Therefore, humans cope with uncertainty and time pressure by adopting a take-the-best or drop-the-worst cue decision-making strategy to minimize cognitive time and effort while considering the most diagnostic cue information to maintain "good enough" accuracy to make a decision.

While the average judicial decision maker's environmental constraints include the physical environment in which they render decisions, their workgroup members, often competing roles, uncertain situations, and time pressure with increasing caseloads, these are constraints that can affect the individual decision maker. But, what about the bounded rationality that is baked into our court system? Bounded rationality, for better or worse, is institutionalized in the US criminal justice system, the extent to which we discuss next.

Institutionalized Bounded Rationality

Recall from the introduction that judicial decision making consists of four steps: scenario construction, removing implausible scenarios, acceptable outcomes, and decision-making (Engel & Gueth, 2018). Engel and Gueth (2018) argued that bounded rationality is institutionalized in each of these four steps, respectively: A limited number of sides (e.g., defendant, prosecution) plead their case with a limited number of outcomes (e.g., guilty, not guilty); triers of fact use the standard of proof to create a relevance criterion to help them come to a decision (e.g., the standard is met or is not met); the decision maker weighs a "good enough" outcome to ensure she is not incorrect in her ruling; then the judicial actor renders a decision after considering the believability of each alternative interpretation of the evidence. While judicial decision making is complex, Engel and Gueth (2018) made a strong case for how the choices judges and other legal actors make is actually constricted and therefore bounded.

Engel and Gueth (2018) applied their model of decision making on court procedure, stating that court procedure's institutional design was constructed to assist triers of fact to make better decisions. This may be true if bounded rationality is helpful at the organizational level. But institutionalized bounded rationality can restrict already rationally bound decision makers. First, we must assess the extent to which bounded rationality institutionalized. We argue that bounded rationality is institutionalized at multiple levels.

Institutional Incentives and Increasing Caseloads Are Not Compatible with Maximization

Tsaoussi and Zervogianni (2010) contended that institutional incentives are not compatible with maximization, meaning that judicial actors are not rewarded for maximizing the bounds of their rationality. They are rewarded for satisficing; taking the most optimal strategy without considering all possibilities available to them. Judges are satisficers due to an inefficient and overloaded criminal justice system that disincentivizes maximization. Triers of fact, in this way, are forced to function within the boundaries of their institution. Tsaoussi and Zervogianni (2010) continued that in particular judges are satisficers who adjudicate under the bounded rationality model's constraints. Thus, they cannot perform at an optimal level, only the best they can under their circumstances. Tsaoussi and Zervogianni (2010) continued that judges must also be satisficers because of the constrains of large caseloads and complex cases. Hagle (1990) affirmed that Americans are litigious and court caseloads are ever increasing.

Prosecutors Only Know What Investigators Relay to Them

O'Brien (2009) stipulated another institutional constraint: Prosecutors are limited by what information investigators present to them. In this way, the bounds of rationality are formed beyond individual cognitive limitations. In fact, O'Brien (2009) found that prosecutors are especially susceptible to confirmation bias. Recall that "once a prosecutor decides to proceed against a suspect, changing course in response to every new piece of information could be perceived…as weak" (O'Brien, 2009, p. 1013). So, not only are prosecutors limited by the information they obtain about an investigation, they are bounded by specific cognitive limitations that may be promoting their career progress over expanding their selective searches for alternative information, even if that is not their intention.

Judicial Decision Makers Rely on Precedence and Memory

Hagle (1990) insisted that as a society, we assume that legal actors study individual cases to make their unique decisions. However, each individual case decision is almost always in some way based on preceding cases. The principle of using precedent to determine points in a new litigation is called stare decisis. Essentially, stare decisis binds the courts to follow previous decisions when making new decisions in similar cases. While this is a legally binding principle in and of itself, case-based decision making using past cases is also a cognitive heuristic device, according to Tsaoussi and Zervogianni (2010). Since it is so difficult to deal with the outcome of uncertainty among legal alternatives, judges reduce their cognitive burden by relying on their reasoning in past cases (Sunstein, 2000). Gilboa and Schmeidler (1995) confirmed that case-based decision making like this is common in the courtroom.

Oh et al. (2016) claimed that the most basic heuristic for decision making is memory. Relying on memory supports Tsaoussi and Zervogianni's (2010) contention that judges rely on an adherence to precedent. Bounded rationality helps explain judicial conformity and their commitment to existing patterns of choice. Satisficing practices become a source of "path dependence" where sequences of past actions inform the current decision outcome (Tsaoussi & Zervogianni, 2010). Jones (2002) agreed that people rely on previous solutions to guide their selective searches. Jones even asserted that the way in which organizations encode experiences into rules and routines that specify action to take under certain circumstances serves as a kind of organizational memory. Jones (2002) sought to demonstrate how bounded rationality could serve as a foundation for connecting individual decision maker behavior with a collective choice, or policy. In this way, a judge's bounded rationality used to make a decision feeds back into the institutionalized bounded rationality when that case informs future policy. Arguably, this effect is exponentially tightening the rational bounds of the decision maker and the organization like water circling the drain.

While relying on precedence may be seen as a cognitive limitation in the form a heuristic, Sunstein and Ullmann-Margalit (1999) may have called this an adaptive "small steps" decision-making strategy. Sunstein and Ullmann-Margalit (1999) said that "small steps," unlike chance, are a form of choosing, like moving in with a romantic partner before deciding on a more permanent marriage status. When judges use small steps, Sunstein and Ullmann-Margalit (1999) said, it is because they know their rules create precedents; in doing so, they narrow the scope of future applications of their rulings. Specifically, "[j]udges face similar problems, and incremental decisions are a good way of responding to the particular problem of bounded rationality created by ignorance of possible adverse effects" (Sunstein & Ullmann-Margalit, 1999, p. 27). Sunstein (2000) also iterated that decision makers decrease their burden by reasoning from past cases for case-based decisions.

Clearly, bounded rationality is institutionalized in the US court procedures themselves. Institutional incentives are incompatible with legal decision makers using maximizing strategies, having access to limited investigative information, and relying on memory heuristics and precedence all are intrinsic forms of bounded rationality that the judicial decision makers cannot escape. What is left to determine is whether the judicial decision makers' bounded rationality, the constraints of their environments, and the institutionalized bounded rationality interact to serve or hinder the judicial decision-making process. Does bounded rationality help decision makers or keep them from making fair decisions? What can be done moving forward? It is these questions to which we turn in our discussion now.

Discussion

Importantly, a judicial decision maker's bounded rationality may interact with institutionalized bounded rationality to produce final outcomes. We outline three major applications in the criminal legal system that focus on how a judicial actor's own bounded rationality may interact with institutionalized bounded rationality. There are major implications for all three interaction models, which consist of decision fatigue, human influence, and sentencing decisions. Limitations and recommendations for current research are also stressed.

Interacting Applications

Decision Fatigue

As Tsaoussi and Zervogianni (2010) attest, judges have the same cognitive limitations as everyone else, yet the stakes are perhaps much higher when they make errors. When judges become overburdened with the number and complexity of cases ever increasing, they may use second-order decision strategies (i.e., heuristics) to reduce cognitive burden. However, such heuristics may result in mistakes (Sunstein & Ullmann-Margalit, 1999). While judges are also bound by time limitations imposed upon them by their institutions, which want to turn over a large number of complex cases quickly, they are also bounded by their own mental overload and must then rely on heuristics and cognitive shortcuts to make decisions. With such a burden comes the possibility that judges are lowering their aspirational level during their selective searches and coming to a stop sooner, meaning that they may not be even looking at all of the "good enough" outcomes before settling on the first thing that "sounds fine" in a take-the-best (or drop-the-worst) cue satisficing strategy.

Danziger et al. (2011) studied this kind of decision fatigue in the Israeli parole courts system. Decision fatigue is the notion that our judgements get worse throughout the day as our mental workload begins to strain and fail (Jones, 2013). Jones (2013) reasoned that to compensate for reduced access to mental resources as the day goes on, people become increasingly conservative and risk-averse when making decisions, especially if they made many decisions that day (as judges do). Danziger et al. (2011) supported this position, finding in their landmark study that the chance of a prisoner securing parole declined from about two-thirds in the morning to almost zero as the day went on, with the exception of food breaks—rulings after a judge's food break resulted in the prisoners' chance of parole spiking again to about 65%.

However, Danziger et al.'s (2011) study did not account for how decision fatigue may build over years of intense decision-making. It stands to reason that prolonged decision-heavy days, over years and even decades for experienced judges, may compound that fatigue. A systematic reliance on heuristics may inadvertently lead a judicial decision maker to further restrict the bounds in which s/he operates. In this way, precedence plays a large role in trying to ameliorate decision fatigue. Precedence is a court-sanctioned boundedly rational tool that judges use to make decisions. When judges are bound by their past cases as a day drags on, decision fatigue and precedence may work together to produce highly restricted outcomes when the optimal solution actually exists outside of those boundaries. In other words, the best decision may become "out of bounds." Tsaoussi and Zervogianni (2010) went as far as to say that judges inflict harm through negligence when they satisfice this way, arguing that judges come to only satisfactory decisions instead of optimal decisions, though these decisions often affect the rest of someone's life.

Human Influence

We must remember that judges do not act alone. They often exist in workgroups and elected judges serve their constituents. Judges may well halt their selective searching once their workgroups come to a satisfactory decision and may well rely on the organizational binds of precedent, which they themselves may have often helped create. Preserving the contentedness of their constituents (i.e., securing future votes) and the informal relationships with their colleagues that preserve their plea decision pipeline offer great incentives for judges to stay the course. Judicial actors who are uncertain of plea or trial outcomes are also presumably more likely to rely on their recollections of past cases, formally using precedent or more informally using memory heuristics. "The way it has always been" is a safe and boundedly rational way for judicial actors to make difficult and subjective decisions in the course of their everchanging task environment.

For instance, Dhami (2003) found that judges relied on simple heuristics in a group context when making bail decisions. Dhami (2003) reasoned that judges relied on prior decisions made by, in part, the police and prosecutor. Dhami (2003) thought that when these judges made decisions as a group, their shared responsibility of coming to a decision allowed them to need few cues before deciding. This line of reasoning exemplifies the take-the-best cue satisficing strategy, which possibly compounds as more people share decision-making responsibly. Does the diffusion of responsibility for coming to a decision result in the group using fewer cues, and can this lead to poorer or at least rasher outcomes? Does the workgroup assist in alleviating a judge's uncertainty about a particular outcome? More research is necessary to answer these questions.

Jones (2002) argued that policies are really authoritative collective choices and that in this way, bounded rationality links procedures of human choice with organizational processes. Simon (1997a) said this was a good thing that organizations help individuals approach near objective rationality. However, we argue that these suggestions need further, and more contemporary, support.

Sentencing Decisions

Whereas decision fatigue and human influence are two common components of most organizations, sentencing decisions fall squarely in the courts of judicial decision makers. While the criminal legal system mandates certain minimum sentences or provides sentencing guidelines for judges to use as rational decision-making tools, judges are still bound by their own biases. Research has demonstrated that the judicial decision maker's personal bounded rationality interacts with the contextual organization's bounded rationality to produce final outcomes in certain circumstances. One such crucial application lies in sentencing decision making.

Ekpunobi (1999) applied bounded rationality to sentencing decision-making behavior in Michigan. Ekpunobi (1999) found that even when Michigan Sentencing Guidelines served as a rational decision-making tool for sentencing judges, judges still were influenced by extralegal factors such as defendant gender and race when deciding on incarceration. Extralegal factors, such as gender and race, are a form of bounded rationality. A purely rational decision maker would rely solely on all available legal information, not accounting for personal biases or using simple heuristics to come to a decision. However, we know that is not the case in the real world. Factoring extralegal factors into judicial decision making is a way of inserting the judicial actor's own bounded rationality. In other words, if judges are anything like the general population, their worldview is restricted by their life experiences and background—they are bounded by their worldview. In this way, judges are using their own personal bounded rationality when they are selectively searching for alternative sentencing options (e.g., community corrections, incarceration). If they are able to rely on their institution's bounded rationality model that are sentencing guidelines, they are even further restricted in their (limitedly bounded) discretion. This interaction of personal and institutionalized bounded rationality may very well lead to sentencing disparities and unfair rulings. Judges may selectively search for a ruling only to be bound by minimum sentencing guidelines as their stop rule.

Clearly, more research must be conducted to determine the utility of sentencing guidelines, especially since judicial decision makers can still operate under their personal bounded rationality decision-making models, not necessarily incorporating the guidelines in a meaningful way. If bounded rationality may be even partially responsible for sentencing disparities, research on how to expand personal bounded rationality's limits must be translated into policy. Sentencing disparities not only undermine our criminal justice system and unnecessarily financially burden our society if the rates of incarceration are heightened because of it, at the microlevel, people are being unjustly incarcerated. As Josef Stalin allegedly claimed, "the death of one man is a tragedy; the death of millions is a statistic." It is time we stop treating mass incarceration as a numbers problem, and look at how each person came to be incarcerated in the first place. If bounded rationality is a contributor to disparate sentencing, it requires further scientific investigation. One such avenue could include attitudinal research with judicial decision makers. It may be beneficial to supplement attitudinal surveys with ethnographic interviews to better understand how judicial decision makers decide, and how bounded rationality affects those decisions.

Conclusion

There are, of course, dissenters who claim that bounded rationality is no longer a viable theory, while others postulate that certain constraints, such as time pressure, can actually aid decision makers. For instance, Glöckner (2008) claimed that the bounds of rationality have been "outstretched." Glöckner (2008) believed that evolution has in fact dramatically shifted the bounds of rationality, in that people are actually better at quickly integrating a lot of information to make a decision than previously realized.

Certain constraints, other researchers noted, may actually help a decision maker. For example, people engage in more selective information searches and use memory-based heuristics when they can if they are under time pressure, which can actually lead to even better choices than if they had a long deliberation time (Oh et al., 2016). Therefore, some of the environmental constraints that legal actors face, such as time pressure, may be beneficial in making an optimal decision.

While the limits of bounded rationality are open to debate, it is clear that there are at least some cognitive limitations and environmental constraints that synergize to create the reality in which legal decision makers operate. The theory of bounded rationality and how it can operate in legal contexts deserves a revival and much research is left to be done. For example, we do not know whether more experienced judges are more or less susceptible to personal and/or institutionalized bounded rationality. On one hand, the satisficing strategies may be well engrained, on the other hand, they have more "intuition." Glöckner (2008) explained that decision making mandates a dual-processing approach, which combines deliberate and intuitive systems. Glöckner (2008) defined "intuition" as meaning automatic, unconscious processing of information. If intuition is really just drawing on past experiences, which is what Simon (1987) argued, then judges with more experience must have a heightened sense, and perhaps usage of, intuition-based decision-making processes. Is such bounded rationality beneficial or stifling? This is another of many applications of bounded rationality in a legal setting that may benefit judicial actors in making more just, or even simply more self-aware, decisions. In reality, the applications of bounded rationality for judicial decision makers are, ironically, limitless.

References

Barros, G. (2010). Herbert A. Simon and the concept of rationality: Boundaries and procedures. *Revista de Economia Política, 30*(3), 455–472. https://doi.org/10.1590/S0101-31572010000300006

Bergert, F. B., & Nosofsky, R. M. (2007). A response-time approach to comparing generalized rational and take-the-best models of decision making. *Journal of Experimental Psychology: Learning, Memory, and Cognition, 33*(1), 107–129. https://doi-org.mutex.gmu.edu/10.1037/0278-7393.33.1.107

Cauthen, J. N. G., & Peters, C. S. (2003). Courting constituents: District elections and judicial behavior on the Louisiana Supreme Court. *The Justice System Journal, 24*(3), 265–281. http://www.jstor.org/stable/27977160

Danziger, S., Levav, J., & Avnaim-Pesso, L. (2011). Extraneous factors in judicial decisions. *Proceedings of the National Academy of Sciences – PNAS, 108*(17), 6889–6892. https://doi.org/10.1073/pnas.1018033108

Dhami, M. K. (2003). Psychological models of professional decision making. *Psychological Science, 14*(2), 175–180. https://doi.org/10.1111/1467-9280.01438

Ekpunobi, A. E. (1999). *Judicial decision-making under Michigan sentencing guidelines*. ProQuest Dissertations Publishing. http://mutex.gmu.edu/login?url=https://www.proquest.com/dissertations-theses/judicial-decision-making-under-michigan/docview/304544997/se-2?accountid=14541

Engel, C., & Gueth, W. (2018). Modeling a satisficing judge. *Rationality and Society, 30*(2), 220–246. https://doi.org/10.1177/1043463118767406

Gibson, J. L. (1980). Environmental constraints on the behavior of judges: A representational model of judicial decision making. *Law & Society Review, 14*(2), 343–370. https://doi.org/10.2307/3053317

Gibson, J. L. (1983). From simplicity to complexity: The development of theory in the study of judicial behavior. *Political Behavior, 5*(1), 7–49. http://www.jstor.org/stable/586347

Gilboa, I., & Schmeidler, D. (1995). Case-based decision theory. *Quarterly Journal of Economics, 110*(3), 605. https://doi-org.mutex.gmu.edu/10.2307/2946694

Glöckner, A. (2008). How evolution outwits bounded rationality. In C. Engel (Ed.), *Better than conscious?: Decision making, the human mind, and implications for institutions* (pp. 259–284). MIT Press. https://doi.org/10.7551/mitpress/9780262195805.003.0012

Hagle, T. M. (1990). So many cases, so little time: Judges as decision makers. In D. Madsen, A. H. Miller, & J. A. Stimson (Eds.), *American politics in the heartland*. Kendall/Hunt. https://www.researchgate.net/publication/44208624_So_Many_Cases_So_Little_Time_Judges_as_Decision-makers

Hall, M. G., & Brace, P. (1996). Justices' responses to case facts: An interactive model. *American Politics Quarterly, 24*(2), 237–261. https://doi.org/10.1177/1532673X9602400206

Jones, B. D. (2002). Bounded rationality and public policy: Herbert A. Simon and the decision foundation of collective choice. *Policy Sciences, 35*(3), 269–284. http://mutex.gmu.edu/login?url=https://www-proquest-com.mutex.gmu.edu/scholarly-journals/bounded-rationality-public-policy-herbert-simon/docview/221248645/se-2?accountid=14541

Jones, C. E. (2013). The troubling new science of legal persuasion: Heuristics and biases in judicial decision-making. *Advocates' Quarterly, 41*(1), 49–122.

Kalantari, B. (2010). Herbert A. Simon on making decisions: Enduring insights and bounded rationality. *Journal of Management History, 16*(4), 509–520. https://doi.org/10.1108/17511341011073988

Li, Y. (2020). Analysis on uncertainties in judicial decision based on cognitive psychology. *Revista Argentina De Clínica Psicológica, 29*(1), 1016. https://doi.org/10.24205/03276716.2020.142

Marder, I. D., & Pina-Sánchez, J. (2020). Nudge the judge? Theorizing the interaction between heuristics, sentencing guidelines and sentence clustering. *Criminology & Criminal Justice, 20*(4), 399–415. https://doi.org/10.1177/1748895818818869

Metcalfe, C. (2016). The role of courtroom workgroups in felony case dispositions: An analysis of workgroup familiarity and similarity. *Law & Society Review, 50*(3), 637–673. https://doi.org/10.1111/lasr.12217

Nardulli, P., Flemming, R., & Eisenstein, J. (1984). Unraveling the complexities of decision making in face-to-face groups: A contextual analysis of plea-bargained sentences. *The American Political Science Review, 78*(4), 912–928. http://www.jstor.org/stable/1955798

O'Brien, B. (2009). A recipe for bias: An empirical look at the interplay between institutional incentives and bounded rationality in prosecutorial decision making. *Missouri Law Review, 74*(4), 999–1050. https://web-a-ebscohost-com.mutex.gmu.edu/ehost/pdfviewer/pdfviewer?vid=2&sid=3afd4bb8-a62b-4f47-bfad-8567fa8c9bfe%40sdc-v-sessmgr01

Oh, H., Beck, J. M., Zhu, P., Sommer, M. A., Ferrari, S., & Egner, T. (2016). Satisficing in split-second decision making is characterized by strategic cue discounting. *Journal of Experimental Psychology: Learning, Memory, and Cognition, 42*(12), 1937–1956. https://doi.org.mutex.gmu.edu/10.1037/xlm0000284

Perez, O. (2016). Judicial strategies for reviewing confliction expert evidence: Biases, heuristics, and higher-order evidence. *American Journal of Comparative Law, 64*(1), 75–120.

Simon, H. A. (1955). A behavioral model of rational choice. *Quarterly Journal of Economics, 69*(1), 99–118. https://doi-org.mutex.gmu.edu/10.2307/1884852

Simon, H. A. (1957). *Models of man, social and rational: Mathematical essays on rational human behavior in a social setting*. John Wiley and Sons.

Simon, H. A. (1979). Rational decision making in business organizations. *American Economic Review, 69*(4), 493–513. https://doi-org.mutex.gmu.edu/http://www.aeaweb.org/aer/

Simon, H. A. (1987). Making management decisions: The role of intuition and emotion. *The Academy of Management Executive, 1*(1), 57–64.

Simon, H. A. (1990). Invariants of human behavior. *Annual Review of Psychology, 41*(1), 1–19. https://doi.org/10.1146/annurev.ps.41.020190.000245

Simon, H. [1945] (1997a). The psychology of administrative decisions. In *Administrative behavior: A study of decision making processes in administrative organizations* (pp. 92–117). Free Press.

Simon, H. A. (1997b). *An empirically based microeconomics*. Cambridge University Press.

Sunstein, C. R. (Ed.). (2000). *Behavioral law and economics*. Cambridge University Press.

Sunstein, C. R., & Ullmann-Margalit, E. (1999). Second-order decisions. *Ethics, 110*(1), 5–31. https://doi.org/10.1086/233202

Tsaoussi, A., & Zervogianni, E. (2010). Judges as satisficers: A law and economics perspective on judicial liability. *European Journal of Law and Economics, 29*(3), 333–357. https://doi.org/10.1007/s10657-009-9123-9

Tversky, A., & Kahneman, D. (1974). Judgment under uncertainty: Heuristics and biases. *Science (American Association for the Advancement of Science), 185*(4157), 1124–1131. https://doi.org/10.1126/science.185.4157.1124

Vallbé, J.-J. (2015). *Frameworks for modeling cognition and decisions in institutional environments: A data-driven approach* (1st ed.). Springer Netherlands. https://doi.org/10.1007/978-94-017-9427-5

Chapter 3
A Systems Approach to Criminal Justice Policymaking

Kennedy Suzette Ratcliff

Introduction

The criminal legal system is comprised of multiple subsystems. There are many ways to describe what a system is, but briefly, one description is when multiple interconnected components work together for the common good of the overall system functioning. Taken from a statement made by Aristotle, Ludwig Von Bertalanffy says regarding a system: "The whole is more than the sum of its parts" (Von Bertalanffy, 1972, p. 407). This description stems from general systems theory pioneered by Ludwig Von Bertalanffy (1972). While von Bertalanffy himself was a biologist, his theory is relevant and applicable to a number of disciplines, including but not limited to engineering, computer science, chemistry, and the broader field of social science.

Von Bertalanffy's general systems theory is applicable to explaining and understanding our criminal legal system. This framework can help us view the criminal legal system holistically in order to help us understand how each component of the system impacts its intended goals. Understanding how the system works can allow us to evaluate, study, and test the system to not only see what works, but to also see what does not work and how to improve its faults. This applies to all organizational systems, but specifically concerning the criminal legal system, it is especially important to understand it from a policymaking perspective.

Policymaking is an influential component of our criminal legal system. Policymaking can be considered the backbone of the criminal legal system as effective policies keep the system running, correctly use resources, do not waste money,

K. S. Ratcliff (✉)
Sam Houston State University, Department of Crimial Justice and Criminology, Huntsville, TX, USA
e-mail: ksr047@shsu.edu

D. S. Rudes, J. R. Ingram (eds.), *Using Organizational Theory to Study, Explain, and Understand Criminal Legal Organizations*,
https://doi.org/10.1007/978-3-031-66285-0_3

and achieve justice, but ineffective policies can have harmful effects, unfairly punish the wrong people, waste resources, and promote distrust in the American people. Because the different components of the criminal legal system are connected, ineffective policies can have broad, negative consequences for the system.

Criminal justice policymakers, as well as criminal justice scholars, do not always look at criminal justice policymaking with a general systems theory perspective. This can be detrimental and can cause issues to rise within criminal justice policymaking; both in the short-term and in the long-term. General systems theory offers an all-encompassing perspective while scholars and policymakers tend to look at their particular policies with only one specific part of the criminal legal system in mind. The criminal legal system is comprised of multiple systems, including policing, courts, and corrections. Furthermore, within these systems there are smaller subsystems. When scholars and legislators create policies, they generally only gear these policies towards one section of the criminal justice system without taking into account how such policies will affect other sections of the criminal justice system. For example, a classic example of this interdependence is when aggressive enforcement tactics by law enforcement are used as a "get tough on crime" approach leading to more arrests of individuals. Such approaches do not take into consideration what all those extra arrests will do to the court system and the prison system. Courts are constantly backlogged, and prisons have dealt with overcrowding issues for decades, so adding more bodies (unnecessarily) to those sections of the criminal legal system will bring additional consequences to this subsystem component (Albrecht et al., 2022; Alkon, 2022; Ekland-Olson et al., 1983; Nagel, 1977; Pitts et al., 2014).

Aside from not considering the criminal justice system as a whole, there are other issues concerning general systems theory and criminal justice policymaking, such as an overemphasis on punitiveness, media portrayals, and ineffective collaboration among system components, including legislators, researchers, and practitioners. The roadmap for the rest of this chapter includes a review of the literature relating to previous examples of policymaking, a more detailed section on general systems theory, a section on how to apply general systems theory into criminal justice policymaking, a section on implications for researchers and practitioners within the criminal justice field, and a conclusion.

Issues with Criminal Justice Policymaking

Historically, there have been multiple examples within criminal justice policymaking that, although enacted decades ago, are still currently affecting the criminal legal system. The types of policies that have negatively affected the criminal legal system the most are the popular, prominent, and historic get tough on crime policies. Punishment has always been a major factor in the American criminal legal system, but general ideologies and practices within the system have also come in waves (Levinson et al., 2019). During the Warren court era (1950s and 1960s), criminal justice policies were more liberal and progressive in nature, but soon afterward, there was a hard pendulum swing from the more progressive side to the more punitive side; it was not a slow and steady change, it was an extreme, reactive, and strong change to counteract the Warren era ideals. Some decisions and ideas that were a part of the Warren/progressive era include the *Miranda v. Arizona* decision, *Gideon v. Wainwright* decision, push for rehabilitation for those convicted of a crime, and a general expansion of citizens' due process rights (Dressler, 2020). On the other side of the spectrum, starting in the 1970s, the general ideas regarding the criminal legal system and how it should be run include a major push for crime control no matter the cost (even if the citizens' rights are stepped on a little bit), incarceration and punitiveness over rehabilitation, and just getting tough on crime in general.

Although the shift to more punitive approaches intended to decrease crime and increase public safety, the tough ways that legislators went about it were significantly more consequential than beneficial based on empirical examinations. Instead of looking at the crime issue broadly (as in with the *whole* criminal justice system in mind), policymakers focused on narrow parts of the crime issue. Not only did they not look at the system broadly, but they did not look at the long-term impacts that these tough policies may cause, not just for the system but for the people affected by the system. Increases in punishments are only short-term fixes, not constructive long-term fixes. The three specific tough on crime policies/laws enacted that I will cover in detail include the War on Drugs, the Violent Crime Control and Law Enforcement Act of 1994, and the three-strikes laws. I will discuss their backgrounds and the issues that have arisen from their improper implementations.

The War on Drugs

Though American leaders have always tried to combat the use and distribution of drugs, the War on Drugs was not officially declared until the early 1970s when President Nixon proclaimed that drug use was "America's public enemy number one" (Fouch, 2023, p. 6). Just like the name of the era, instead of critically looking at the root problem of drug use (such as through a medical lens as opposed to a criminal lens), and instead of making it a mission to help individuals affected by drugs, American politicians quickly waged "war" on drugs. Funding for combatting drugs was increased significantly, and mandatory prison sentences for drug crimes were enacted. There was such fervor in combatting drugs in the United States that Nixon established the Drug Enforcement Administration (DEA), a federal agency, in 1973 to tackle illegal drug use as well as the smuggling of drugs (Executive Order No. 11,727, 1973). While Nixon did officially declare the War on Drugs, his primary focus concerning the punishment aspect was based more on drug distributors more so than drug users (not that drug users were *completely* immune from punishment), but he did also make an effort to expand treatment for those affected by drug use.

Combatting the issue of drugs is justified, but the *way* that politicians went about combatting it is the problem, particularly after Nixon left office. The 1980s and President Ronald Reagan's presidency cracked down even harder regarding drug crimes. Unlike Nixon, Reagan had no room for rehabilitation, his sole method of combatting drug crimes was punishment and deterrence, which significantly increased during his presidency while treatment and rehabilitation significantly decreased (Ramirez, 2022). In the 1980s, there was also a "crack epidemic" that was spurred by significant media attention, which then led to the enactment of the Anti-Drug Abuse Act of 1986, signed by Reagan (Ahmed, 2017). A major part of this bill included expanding the use of mandatory minimum sentences for various drug offenses (Ahmed, 2017). Notably, there were quite large disparities within this legislation. For example, an extreme and controversial enactment was difference in criminalization between crack cocaine and powder cocaine; possessing merely 5 g of crack cocaine warranted a 5-year minimum sentence while possessing a whopping 500 g of powder cocaine garnered the same sentence (Ahmed, 2017). This legislation was especially questionable since it appeared to target certain demographics. Black individuals were understood to be the main demographic that used crack cocaine, while white individuals were the main demographic of powder cocaine. Another negative aspect of the War on Drugs is the issue of it having hidden racial agendas.

Decades after the official declaration of the War on Drugs, America is dealing with consequences even today. As of March 2024, the Federal Bureau of Prisons (BOP) finds that almost half (44.4%) of inmates in federal prisons are incarcerated for drug offenses (Federal Bureau of Prisons, 2024). Overcrowding has been a significant prison problem for decades, and this problem has been exacerbated by housing individuals charged for merely a drug offense. Simple drug use is a non-violent and victimless crime (Vitiello, 2021). In the latter half of the twentieth century, politicians did not think about the aftermath of what the War on Drugs would bring. The "war" is still going on over half a century later and we are still obviously losing. Simply locking people up and throwing away the key is not an adequate way of combatting drug crimes, or crimes in general. The primary problem concerning the War on Drugs is that politicians thought that giving out harsh punishments would solve the drug problem, but clearly that line of thinking was seriously flawed. People still do drugs, and people are still getting locked up for it.

Violent Crime Control and Law Enforcement Act of 1994

Drug crimes were not the only crimes heavily targeted in the latter half of the twentieth century, crime in general was severely scrutinized and more intensely penalized. The Violent Crime Control and Law Enforcement Act of 1994, drafted by then Senator Joe Biden and signed into law by President Bill Clinton, is arguably America's largest crime bill ever enacted. The bill aimed to employ 100,000 more police officers and gave prisons $9.7 billion in funding. Other aspects of the bill included a federal ban on assault weapons (this ban eventually expired), a Violence Against Women Act (which is one of the more beneficial and less extreme enactments), adding multiple new offenses subject to the death penalty, making it much more difficult for inmates to receive a higher education, enforcing even tougher guidelines and regulations against sex offenders, creating "boot camps" for juveniles (which empirically do not work long-term), adding 50 new federal offenses, and adding truth-in-sentencing laws (which essentially awarded states for making inmates complete 85% of their sentence before giving them the opportunity to be on parole) (Muchnick, 1995; H.R. 3355, 1994).

As stated earlier, wanting to protect the general public is a necessary legislative function, however, the Crime Bill of 1994 also had negative consequences for the criminal legal system as a whole. Mass incarceration is something that came about after the enactment of this bill. Today, the United States is still dealing with overcrowding issues. If laws require those convicted of drug crimes to go to prison for even longer lengths such as per the 1994 Crime Bill, incarceration rates increase, but release rates are substantially lower. Increases in arrests and sentencing take a toll on the courts as well. The increase in arrests and court cases encouraged the use of plea bargaining much more frequently simply to go through cases quicker. Multiple parts of the criminal justice system were negatively impacted by the 1994 Crime Bill.

Three Strikes Laws

Though the general idea of three-strikes laws has been around even before the enactment of the 1994 Crime Bill, three-strikes laws did not significantly come about until that bill was enacted. While the 1994 Crime Bill is a federal piece of legislation, three-strikes laws vary across states, but the way they all operate is generally the same; if an individual has two previous serious convictions and is convicted of a third serious crime, that individual is given a mandatory life sentence usually without the option of parole (or *at least* 25 years imprisonment) (Ahmed, 2017). It is important to note that not all states incorporate some sort of three-strikes law, but many of them do. They all also vary in what they consider to be "serious" offenses. Unfortunately, despite these policies' intentions, many offenders who do not even commit violent crimes or crimes that involve other individuals are subject to these harsh sentences (Fiber-Ostrow & Tucker, 2013). Whether these individuals commit violent or non-violent crimes, the states' answer to decreasing crime is simply to lock them up and throw away the key, so these individuals are never even given the chance to be rehabilitated. Not only that but considering the amount of people currently incarcerated in the United States, these deterrence-based policies obviously did not work.

Issues Concerning Criminal Justice Policymaking

The above example legislative policies have had long-lasting consequences that led to negative consequences for the criminal legal system (Lee, 2020). The criminal legal system is comprised of many parts, and legislation, especially acts that emphasize tough on crime policies, has not considered the long-term effects of the changes on subsystem components. Concerning crime and punishment as a whole, the United States is the country that incarcerates the most people with roughly two million individuals incarcerated at any given time; there are also roughly five million people under community supervision at any given time (Bagaric et al., 2023; Jacobi & Maguire, 2023). Before the tough on crime era, rehabilitation and treatment seemed to dominate criminal justice policymaking. The general public started to believe that policymakers were too "soft" on crime, so soon after, the pendulum swung from one extremity (too soft on crime) to the other extremity (too tough on crime). To better the criminal justice system, as in the *whole* system and not just certain parts, policymakers need to be objective and not lean towards extremities.

Another issue that policymakers had in the previous three examples is not including research in their criminal justice policymaking. Policymakers capitalized off of negative media attention surrounding crime and the (understandable) fear that the citizens had of crime. "Gut feelings" and "common sense" are not good enough when implementing policies, empirical research can and does provide adequate pathways for policymaking (Wagner, 2009). It is understandable (and necessary) that policymakers take into account of the general public's feelings and opinions, they did indeed vote them in, but on the other hand, politicians need to do what is best for everybody (Lucas & Tasic, 2015). Empirical research certainly does not provide *all* the answers, but policymakers should consider researchers' findings on crime related topics. Unfortunately, policymakers either refuse to listen to researchers, or they use the research findings in a skewed manner to further their own agendas (Mears, 2017).

Description of General Systems Theory

After examining previous issues regarding criminal justice policymaking, I would like to provide some more information on what general systems theory is. We have already established that a system consists of multiple subsystems working independently yet together for the common purpose of the overall system, so what else is there? Systems can either be closed or open; an open system is influenced by its environment while closed systems are not (Katz & Kahn, 1966). Most systems (organizations), including the criminal legal system, are considered open systems. Concerning the criminal justice system specifically, a type of environment that may affect or influence the system may be the current political environment of the nation or jurisdiction. Systems also have inputs, throughputs (also known as processes), and outputs. Inputs are what goes into the system (such as resources or employee labor), throughputs are what are processed after being inputted, and outputs are the products made or the services finally provided from the system. In the criminal legal context, those accused of crimes could be considered inputs, their cases throughputs, and finally their convictions, punishments, releases, or dropped cases could be considered outputs (Van Gigch, 1978; Bernard et al., 2005). Finally, feedback is an important part of the general systems theory. Feedback can be positive or negative, and it can help improve the overall functioning of the system. Criminal justice policymaking relies on feedback, or at least it *should*; policymakers do have the authority to dismiss feedback (positive or negative) as they please.

Application of Systems Theory to Policymaking

This section discusses how applying a general systems theory approach can help us better understand how policies aimed at one particular part of the criminal legal system can affect (positively, negatively, or even neutrally) other parts of the criminal justice system. Policymakers implement (and researchers advocate for) policies directed at specific parts of the system, such as law enforcement, courts, or corrections, without considering how they will impact other parts of the system. Emphasizing certain aspects of the general systems theory within criminal justice policymaking can prove useful in helping improve criminal justice policymaking in the long-term.

Establishing Goals

One of the more basic and arguably one of the more important parts of implementing the general systems theory into criminal justice policymaking is establishing a goal or goals. Though all the subsystems within the criminal legal system may have their own secondary goals, what is the *overall* goal of the American criminal justice system? Is its purpose to achieve "justice" for all victims, spend/save taxpayer and government money, to process cases in and out of the system indefinitely, or a mixture of many of these goals (Bernard et al., 2005)? Has our overall goal changed since the inception of the system? The criminal legal system and its purpose has indeed been evolving (rehabilitation versus punishment), but though the methods implemented have changed, has the overall *goal* stayed the same? Without clearly defined goals, it is difficult to implement policymaking effectively across criminal justice subsystems (Skoler, 1977; Duffee, 1990). As a nation, providing and establishing an official goal(s) of the criminal legal system will not only allow us to look at policymaking from a general systems theory perspective, but it will also simply make the system better and more cohesive. Establishing a goal at the top level will help the lower levels (the subsystems) achieve their secondary and interconnected goals while achieving the criminal justice system's *overall* goal at the same time.

Establishing Inputs, Throughputs, and Outputs

In order to improve criminal justice policymaking from a general systems theory perspective, we need to thoroughly describe what *exactly* our inputs, throughputs, and outputs are as well as their purposes. Currently, in terms of criminal justice policymaking, we have not established what our inputs, throughputs, and outputs are. As mentioned above, our inputs *could* be the individuals who come into contact with the system, throughputs be their case in the system, and outputs be their convictions, releases, or just generally their end of their time in the system. Like establishing overall goals at the national level, establishing inputs, throughputs, and outputs at the national level would allow the subsystems within the criminal justice system to have their own secondary and interconnected inputs, throughputs, and outputs. For example, at probation offices specifically, their inputs could be individuals entering their system, throughputs *processing* their case (deciding what level of probation they need to be on), and outputs treating the individuals, meeting with them, and upon successful completion, allowing the offender to leave probation. These examples are all hypothetical and theoretical; it is up to policymakers and criminal justice administrators to officially determine what our criminal justice system's inputs, throughputs, and outputs should be. Then, the lower-level jurisdictions/subsystems would be able to make their secondary inputs, throughputs, and outputs from there.

An Open System and the Environment

Understanding what *type* of system the criminal legal system is can help us implement policies based on the general systems theory. As per the general systems theory, organizations are either closed or open, and the criminal justice system is considered an open system. Being an open system means the criminal justice system is subject to its environment; that would include the political environment of the nation or local jurisdiction. The criminal justice system is *especially* subject to the political environment, and polarization in the United States also has particularly increased in recent years (Hart et al., 2020). However, taking advantage of this or at least understanding this can help in improving criminal justice policy from the general systems theory perspective. Since the entire system can be affected by one part of the system, it would be wise to understand political trends (or environmental trends in general, such as the economy) concerning the overall system as well as the subsystems. For example, if the police have been subject to relentless political scrutiny, the aftermath of potential changes in police policies will affect the rest of the system, such as prisons and the courts. Preparing for such changes will better the criminal justice system overall. Also, if a subsystem is struggling financially, such as the prison system, that too would affect the rest of the overall criminal justice system. Being aware of the environment at the national level and the individual subsystem levels, as well as actually working together to combat these environmental setbacks, would vastly improve the criminal justice system as well as policymaking.

Understanding Interdependence

While it may seem quite straightforward and obvious, fully understanding interdependence will help greatly in improving criminal justice policymaking. As per general systems theory, interdependence is how all subsystems within an organization interconnect with each other and how they affect each other when changes are made, including both positively and negatively. Within the criminal legal system specifically, this includes how subsystems such as the courts, police, and prisons all interconnect and interact with each other, and it also includes what exactly happens to offenders once they are put into the system. There are so many potential routes for individuals once they enter the system—initial arrest/interaction with the police, bail, initial trial, community service, probation, GPS monitoring, complete dismissing of a case, appellate court, jail time, prison time, probation, parole, registering on the sex offender registry if convicted of a sex crime, treatment, rehabilitation, the potential routes for individuals are limitless; and once those incarcerated are released, that still does not necessarily mean that they are completely out of the system. Fully understanding how all of the subsystems interact and potentially affect one another allows policymakers to have more educated ideas on what types of policies to implement. If a policy implemented in subsystem X has the potential to negatively impact subsystem Y, then either that policy should potentially be amended, or a policy should be implemented for subsystem Y to combat the negative effects of the policy implemented for subsystem X. The entire system is one interconnected web.

Feedback Loops

Finally, feedback loops are important in constantly improving policies regarding the criminal legal system and keeping it successful. Feedback can be positive or negative, but that does not necessarily mean "good" or "bad"; positive feedback is more like a reinforced/award-based type of feedback while negative feedback is primarily a correcting type of feedback. Let's say that we as a nation learn that rehabilitation is the better option than pure punishment, although many individuals would still disagree. The state could give positive incentives to prisons with high rates of successful treatments, such as more money or resources (this is just a theoretical example, these types of incentives would have to realistically be implemented cautiously so that prisons do not merely say that every inmate was "successful" in treatment just to get monetary compensation). Policies involving states being awarded for being successful in providing adequate treatment would be considered positive feedback. Having constant feedback loops and other forms related to evaluation helps in improving criminal justice policymaking.

Taking multiple aspects from the general systems theory such as establishing goals, understanding and establishing inputs, throughputs, and outputs, taking advantage of the open criminal justice system and its environment, fully understanding interdependence, promoting feedback loops, and incorporating them into criminal justice policymaking will significantly improve criminal justice policymaking and the system as a whole. It is imperative that policymakers look at the criminal legal system both broadly and intricately. That will help improve the system in the long-run and not only make it successful, but it will help to *keep* it successful.

Practical Implications

This section discusses the practical implications for both researchers and practitioners. What should they do in order to incorporate general systems theory into their perspective fields and to improve criminal justice policymaking?

Researchers

Concerning criminal justice researchers specifically, it is common and quite normal for them to specialize and research just a few very specific topics within the field of criminal justice. Their research interests may evolve a little bit throughout their academic career, but for the most part, they will continue to specialize in just a few topics. While I am not advocating for them to specialize in *all* criminal justice topics and subtopics, I am suggesting that research areas should focus more broadly on the interconnected criminal justice system. At the end of their research papers, researchers almost always have their own "Implications" section towards the end, and they mostly write it solely from the perspective of their specialized topic. When they give policy suggestions, they do not give policy suggestions that would relate to the *whole* system, only their specific part. I would suggest that researchers have a better overall understanding of the whole criminal justice system and base their policy implications not solely just on their specialized topic, but how their suggested policy implications could affect the *whole* system. If a researcher specializes in corrections and knows hardly anything about the court system, it would be best for them to at least become more familiar with the court system and especially how it connects to the prison system.

Another implication regarding researchers is related to how they disseminate or publish their research. In the world of researching, researchers normally publish their work in peer-reviewed journals, and these journals usually require paid subscriptions in order to read the journal. This limits access to these works for practitioners and even the general public to be more informed regarding the criminal legal system. Researchers themselves cannot really help this, many of them work at universities, and universities emphasize producing peer-reviewed published research as a core criteria for tenure, a goal of practically all scholars that work at a university (Mears, 2017). Even if researchers *did* provide easier and less financially draining ways for practitioners and the public to read their findings, they do not write in ways that non-academics can understand; and on top of that, no practitioner or member of the public can easily comprehend technical specialized language in lengthy journal articles (Latessa, 2004).

While researchers possess great knowledge of the criminal legal system, practitioners and the general public are constantly *affected* by the system both indirectly (taxpayer dollars) and directly (being a victim of a crime as well as actually working for the system), so they should be better informed about how the *whole* system works. Them being better informed also pushes for them to advocate for better policies (Lucas & Tasic, 2015). Ultimately, the general culture of researching should be changed just slightly. There should be easier opportunities for practitioners and the general public to be educated on the criminal legal system. For practitioners especially, they should be given documents with less scholarly jargon. Producing more executive summaries of scholarly research with easier to understand language to give to practitioners would be a great start. Even if some practitioners were more familiar with the scholarly language, they simply do not have the time to read such lengthy documents, so shorter executive summaries would be great to give practitioners and even make available to the general public.

Collaboration

Another implication is to facilitate researcher-practitioner collaborative partnerships, as learning from both perspectives are highly important. Practitioners see what happens within the system on a day-to-day basis, and researchers are able to have an outside perspective, a perspective that practitioners may not be able to see while working from within the system. This collaboration between researchers and practitioners is called translational criminology, and it is slowly receiving more attention in the field of criminal justice. Here, researchers and practitioners can work together to not only better understand each other, but to better the criminal legal system as a whole and to improve criminal justice policymaking. Having both researchers and practitioners on the same page allows them to both propose better ideas and push for legislators to implement more beneficial criminal justice policies.

Conclusion

The American criminal legal system has existed for many years, and it is still adapting and evolving, though some could say that there have also been times where it has de-evolved. When discussing the criminal legal system, it is usually done as a general matter, but according to the general systems theory, systems are made up of multiple interconnected parts that work together to achieve the overall goals of the whole system, so all individual parts should be acknowledged, especially when it comes to policymaking. Criminal justice policymaking affects all parts of the system and concerning the current and recent state of the criminal justice system, the policies implemented have done more harm than good for the system.

Starting in the 1970s, the American criminal justice system increasingly implemented more tough on crime policies, such as the War on Drugs, the Violent Crime Control and Law Enforcement Act of 1994, and three-strikes laws that varied across jurisdictions. These policies were intended to curb the crime problem, but as of 2024, the effectiveness of these policies is questionable. Taking a look at the criminal legal system through the lens of general systems theory helps us to understand the system both broadly and intimately. Establishing goals, understanding *exactly* how the system works, understanding the interdependence of all of the systems related to the system, and promoting constant feedback loops can help guide better criminal justice policymaking, which would then help the criminal justice system be more successful long-term. That is where researchers and practitioners come in. Researchers can look at the system from the outside while practitioners look at it from the inside; collaborating together helps both sides better understand the system. Having both researchers and practitioners see eye to eye allows them both to work together more cohesively and to advocate to policymakers for better criminal justice policies that would benefit everyone.

Understanding the general systems theory, *applying* this theory to our criminal legal system and its policymaking, and collaborating can help improve the system long-term. Unlike the tough on crime policies implemented before, these ideas I mentioned would help long-term instead of short-term. Doing so could assist in developing more permanent solutions of the underlying challenges currently facing the criminal legal system.

References

Ahmed, S. (2017). Is history repeating itself: Sentencing young American Muslims in the War on Terror. *Yale Law Journal, 126*(5), 1520–1576.

Albrecht, K., Hawilo, M., Geraghy, T. F., & Rountree, M. M. (2022). Justice delayed: The complex system of delays in criminal court. *Loyola University Chicago Law Journal, 53*(4), 747–792.

Alkon, C. (2022). Criminal court system failures during Covid-19: An empirical study. *Ohio State Journal on Dispute Resolution, 37*(4), 453–532.

Bagaric, M., Svilar, J., & Bagaric, B. (2023). Continuing principled sentencing reform and winding back mass incarceration against the backdrop of America's surge in violent crime. *Nevada Law Journal, 23*(2), 411–462.
Bernard, T. J., Paoline, E. A., III, & Parea, P.-P. (2005). General systems theory and criminal justice. *Journal of Criminal Justice, 33*(3), 203–211.
Dressler, J. (2020). Reflections on the Warren Court's criminal justice legacy, fifty years later: What the wings of a butterfly and a Yiddish proverb teach me. *University of the Pacific Law Review, 51*(4), 727–740.
Duffee, D. E. (1990). *Explaining criminal justice* (2nd ed.). Prospect Heights, IL7 Waveland.
Ekland-Olson, S., Barrick, D. M., & Cohen, L. E. (1983). Prison overcrowding and disciplinary problems: An analysis of the Texas prison system. *Journal of Applied Behavioral Science, 19*(2), 163–176.
Exec. Order No. 11,727, 3 C.F.R. 38 Fed. Reg. 18,357 (1973). https://www.federalregister.gov/executive-order/11727
Federal Bureau of Prisons. (2024). *Federal Bureau of Prisons*. BOP Statistics: Inmate Offenses. https://www.bop.gov/about/statistics/statistics_inmate_offenses.jsp. Retrieved on March 29, 2024.
Fiber-Ostrow, P., & Tucker, J. A. (2013). Third Strikers under three strikes and you're out: Politics and prosecutions. *California Journal of Politics and Policy, 5*(2), 168–205.
Fouch, P. (2023). Decriminalization: A way out of the unwinnable War on Drugs. *Appalachian Journal of Law, 22*(2), 1–16.
H.R. 3355 – 103rd Congress (1993–1994): Violent Crime Control and Law Enforcement Act of 1994. (1994, September 13). https://www.congress.gov/bill/103rd-congress/house-bill/3355
Hart, P. S., Chinn, S., & Soroka, S. (2020). Politicization and polarization in COVID-19 news coverage. *Science Communication, 42*(5), 679–697.
Jacobi, T., & Maguire, A. (2023). Searches without suspicion: Avoiding a four million person underclass. *Brigham Young University Law Review, 48*(6), 1769–1830.
Katz, D., & Kahn, R. L. (1966). *The social psychology of organizations*. Wiley.
Latessa, E. J. (2004). The challenge of change: Correctional programs and evidence-based practices. *Criminology & Public Policy, 3*(3), 547–560.
Lee, K. (2020). Pandemic, protests, and prison reform? Why 2020 is catalyst to rethink drug policy. *St. Thomas Law Review, 33*(1), 1–26.
Levinson, J. D., Smith, R. J., & Hioki, K. (2019). Race and retribution: An empirical study of implicit bias and punishment in America. *UC Davis Law Review, 53*(2), 839–892.
Lucas, G. M., & Tasic, S. (2015). Behavioral public choice and the law. *West Virginia Law Review, 118*(1), 199–266.
Mears, D. P. (2017). *Out-of-control criminal justice: The Systems Improvement Solution for more safety, Justice, accountability, and efficiency*. Cambridge University Press.
Muchnick, J. Y. (1995). The assault weapons ban- saving lives. *University of Dayton Law Review, 20*(2), 641–652.
Nagel, W. G. (1977). On behalf of a moratorium on prison construction. *Crime & Delinquency, 23*(2), 154–171.
Pitts, J. M. A., Griffin, O. H., III, & Johnson, W. W. (2014). Contemporary prison overcrowding: Short-term fixes to a perpetual problem. *Contemporary Justice Review, 17*(1), 124–139.
Ramirez, S. A. (2022). The racist roots of the War on Drugs 7 the myth of equal protection for people of color. *University of Arkansas at Little Rock Law Review, 44*(4), 453–490.
Skoler, D. L. (1977). *Organizing the non-system: Governmental structuring of criminal justice service*. MA7 Lexington Books.
Van Gigch, J. P. (1978). *Applied general systems theory* (2nd ed.). Harper and Row Publishers.
Vitiello, M. (2021). The war on drugs: Moral panic and excessive sentences. *Cleveland State Law Review, 69*(2), 441–484.
Von Bertalanffy, L. (1972). The history and status of general systems theory. *Academy of Management Journal, 15*(4), 407–426.
Wagner, L. A. (2009). Sex offender residency restrictions: How common sense places children at risk. *Drexel Law Review, 1*(1), 175–210.

Chapter 4
Application of Contingency Theory to the "Workforce Crisis" in Policing

Chia-Hung Lin

Introduction

Policing, traditionally seen as a stable career field, is currently facing a workforce crisis. Factors like diminishing public perception and legitimacy of law enforcement, particularly after incidents like the George Floyd case and the COVID-19 pandemic, have exacerbated this issue. A survey by the Police Executive Research Forum (PERF) showed a 63% decline in new officer applications over 5 years, with resignations and retirements spiking post-2019 (PERF, 2019). College students' growing reluctance to pursue policing careers, influenced by negative public opinions, and a sharp increase in voluntary resignations following the George Floyd protests further complicate recruitment and retention. This crisis reflects a broader shift in attitudes towards law enforcement, underscoring the need for reforms to address financial and perceptual challenges in the police workforce.

Contingency theory provides a suitable theoretical framework for understanding the problem of the police workforce crisis. The core of contingency theory is that organizational success depends on adapting structures and strategies to specific internal and external circumstances, such as size, technology, environment, and objectives. Its key principles include recognizing there is no one-size-fits-all solution, differentiating between mechanistic and organic systems, balancing differentiation and integration, considering both internal and external factors, and employing the Structural Adaptation to Regain Fit (SARFIT) framework. This approach underscores the importance of flexibility and adaptability in solving organizational

C.-H. Lin (✉)
Sam Houston State University, Department of Crimial Justice and Criminology, Huntsville, TX, USA
e-mail: cxl102@shsu.edu

D. S. Rudes, J. R. Ingram (eds.), *Using Organizational Theory to Study, Explain, and Understand Criminal Legal Organizations*,
https://doi.org/10.1007/978-3-031-66285-0_4

problems emphasizing the need for leaders to align their strategies with their unique operational realities.

This chapter begins by exploring the current "workforce crisis" in policing, examining potential factors that contribute to this issue. Following this, it explores the framework and key tenets of contingency theory. The chapter then presents some studies that apply contingency theory within the realm of criminal legal contexts, summarizing the principles from these studies that might be relevant to the application in police organizations. Finally, this chapter offers strategic recommendations aimed at addressing the workforce crisis in policing using a contingency framework.

The Workforce Crisis in Policing

Traditionally, many people regard policing as a stable profession, offering job security, civil service benefits, and a middle-class salary (McLean et al., 2023). However, according to Boylan's (2022) peer-reviewed paper, from 1972 to 2017, over 521 US municipalities, ranging in population from 1000 to 200,000, disbanded their police forces primarily due to budget constraints. Furthermore, between 2021 and 2022, at least 12 smaller towns eliminated their police departments. In 2022, a nationwide recruitment crisis in policing was attributed largely to shifting public views of police as less legitimate entities. This recruitment challenge received wide coverage; on September 6, 2023, the Associated Press noted that incidents like the Floyd case and the COVID-19 pandemic were contributing factors (Dazio et al., 2021), and local news echoed similar sentiments about staffing shortages in various regions.

A national survey conducted by the Police Executive Research Forum (PERF) revealed that over the past 5 years, 63% of the participating agencies witnessed a decline in new police officer applications, a notable finding given that this survey was conducted before George Floyd's incident (Police Executive Research Forum, 2019). Furthermore, central to this issue is the mass departure from the police profession. In comparison to 2019, the year preceding both the pandemic and Floyd's incident, officer resignations surged by 47%, and retirements increased by 19%. These statistics are based on a survey involving nearly 200 police agencies, as reported by the PERF, a Washington, D.C.-based research organization (Dazio et al., 2021). Chuck Wexler, the executive director of PERF, remarked on the alarming trend, stating that the number of police officer applicants is decreasing while retirements and resignations are increasing tremendously. This has resulted in a nationwide police officer shortage (Ahmed & Salter, 2023).

Recent studies indicate that college students are increasingly hesitant to consider a career in policing largely due to negative public opinions and perceptions toward the profession (Morrow et al., 2019; Todak, 2017). This sentiment is further supported by many law enforcement agencies that are voicing challenges in recruiting and filling their vacant positions (Duncan, 2021; Rasmussen, 2022). Aggravating the complexity of the issue, Mourtgos et al. (2022) highlighted a sharp increase in voluntary resignations from police departments in the aftermath of the George Floyd protests during the summer of 2020. This trend underscores the changing dynamics and challenges faced by law enforcement in recent times.

To sum up, two primary factors contribute to the crisis in the police workforce. First, there is a declining interest that fewer people want to be police officers, and second, many existing officers are choosing to retire or leave the profession. The decreased inclination to join the police force can be traced back to issues such as insufficient salary, financial constraints, and more significantly, the shifting public perception or trust towards law enforcement officers. On the other hand, the challenges with retaining current officers are deeply intertwined with their levels of job satisfaction and the prevailing problems associated with turnover. Both challenges highlight the pressing need for comprehensive reforms and strategies to address the concerns of potential recruits as well as current officers. Consequently, the following is relevant literature on addressing the interplay of public perception, and job satisfaction or turnover causing the workplace crisis in policing.

Public Perception

The series of high-profile incidents, starting with the death of Michael Brown in Ferguson in 2014 and including the highly publicized case of George Floyd in Minneapolis in 2020, have placed police practices at the center of debate and national discourse in the United States. These events, among others, have significantly heightened media focus on police actions, casting a shadow over the profession due to negative public scrutiny (Morrow et al., 2019; Adams et al., 2023). Some argue, primarily through anecdotal evidence, that growing dissatisfaction with American police forces has led to a phenomenon known as de-policing. This term refers to a situation where officers may reduce proactive policing activities, driven by the fear of becoming targets of accusations related to racial profiling or the use of excessive force; a trend believed to contribute to rising crime rates (MacDonald, 2017). Furthermore, this prevailing negative perception of the police affects current policing strategies but influences the willingness of individuals to pursue careers in police enforcement. As such, the impact of public opinion on the motivation to join police departments emerges as an area of significant importance and concern.

Morrow et al. (2019) delved into the ramifications of the Ferguson Effect and the public scrutiny it brought upon police forces, focusing specifically on its influence on college students' motivation to become police officers. The research utilized data gathered from 654 students enrolled at two large US universities, each boasting a student population exceeding 20,000. The findings revealed a significant correlation: Students who believed that negative media coverage had adversely affected both officer motivation and the perceived danger of the profession were considerably more likely to strongly agree that such scrutiny has unfavorably altered their professional motivations in police enforcement (Morrow et al., 2019). Furthermore, these students displayed higher log odds of strongly agreeing that the current climate of scrutiny heightened their hesitance to apply for positions in police departments, compared to a reference group (Morrow et al., 2019). This research underscores the extent to which the negative public perception of the police department is detrimentally impacting the motivation of college students to pursue careers in the police force.

Therefore, a range of problematic police practices have triggered extensive public discourse and examination. The heightened media scrutiny resulting from these events has shone a negative light on the police profession. This situation has led to a trend known as de-policing, which is impacting both the recruitment of new officers and the retention of current personnel within the police force. The cumulative effect of these developments underscores the need for a nuanced understanding of the relationship between public perception and police force efficacy, and the necessity for strategies that address both the internal dynamics of police departments and their interaction with the communities they serve.

Job Satisfaction and Turnover Related Reasons

Numerous factors influence an employee's decision to remain in or depart from their current position. These factors might range from their commitment to the organization and the quality of their work life to the levels of stress they experience and so on. Turnover, in particular, is a complex issue often intertwined with many of these factors. Job satisfaction plays a pivotal role in this context. When employees feel satisfied and valued in their roles, they are more likely to stay loyal to the organization, be more productive, contribute positively to the workplace environment, and want to stay in the organization (Sageer et al., 2012). Lack of job satisfaction can lead to increased turnover rates, which not only disrupts the organization's workflow but also incurs significant costs in terms of recruitment and training for replacements (Ramlawati et al., 2021). In the following discussion, we will particularly explore the intricacies of job satisfaction and its direct impact on turnover.

Job satisfaction, universally recognized as a key predictor of an employee's intent to stay and their overall performance at the workplace, holds significance across all organizations, whether private or public (Judge et al., 2001; Scanlan & Still, 2013). For policing agencies worldwide, this aspect is especially crucial. Researchers have shown the interest in understanding police job satisfaction for the last three decades, leading to numerous studies drawing samples not just from the United States but from various countries around the world (Abdulla et al., 2011; Adebayo, 2005; Ahmad & Islam, 2019; Donner et al., 2015; Ingram & Lee, 2015). The research underscores the multi-faceted impact of job satisfaction. Beyond its influence on job performance and retention, job satisfaction has profound effects on officers' well-being. A lack of satisfaction in policing roles may lead to several issues. Scholars draw connections between dissatisfaction with police roles and escalating mental health concerns, such as stress and burnout (Lambert et al., 2018; Wang et al., 2014). Moreover, a direct correlation has been observed between low job satisfaction and increased turnover rates, which can have a ripple effect on the performance and financial aspects of police departments (David & Venatus, 2019).

Moreover, Adams et al. (2023) conducted an analysis using historical monthly data to assess the changes in turnover within 14 major US police agencies before and after the George Floyd protests. The results of this study revealed a marked rise in both resignations and retirements among police officers in the 2-year period following the protests. The turnover crisis was extensive, with approximately 80% of the surveyed agencies reporting an increase in either resignations, retirements, or both (Adams et al., 2023). Notably, this trend was more pronounced in larger metropolitan police departments as compared to smaller local agencies (Adams et al., 2023). The implications of this increased turnover rate are profound, posing significant challenges to effective crime control, the operational capabilities of police forces, and the maintenance of high recruitment standards.

Thus, the above findings underscore the critical need for police agencies to prioritize and continuously monitor job satisfaction levels, taking proactive measures to enhance the retention of their officers.

Understanding Contingency Theory

Origins and Development

Contingency theory was first proposed by Tom Burns and G.M. Stalker in their 1961 book, *The Management of Innovation.* Burns and Stalker (1961) argued that there are two main systems of organizational design: mechanistic and organic. Mechanistic organizations are characterized by a high degree of formalization, specialization, and centralization. Organic organizations are characterized by a low degree of formalization, specialization, and centralization. Moreover, Burns and Stalker (1961) concluded that the best type of organizational design for a particular organization depends on its environment. Mechanistic organizations are more effective in stable environments, while organic organizations are more effective in unstable environments.

The theory has been further developed by other scholars, such as Fred Fiedler, Henry Mintzberg, Paul Lawrence, Jay Lorsch, and Lex Donaldson. Lawrence and Lorsch (1967) studied different industries and concluded that the degree of uncertainty in an organization's environment determined the internal characteristics of that organization. Firms in stable environments benefited from a mechanistic structure, while those in more uncertain environments required a more organic setup. Because organizational structures are various, Mintzberg (1979) identified five main types of organizational structures: simple structure, machine bureaucracy, professional bureaucracy, divisionalized form, and adhocracy. Mintzberg's framework of five organizational structures provides valuable insights into organizational design. It aids managers in selecting the most suitable structure for their entity and pinpointing areas that might require enhancement.

Moreover, Fiedler (1967) provides a contingency model, emphasizing the interplay between leadership style and situational favorability. Fiedler introduced the Least Preferred Co-worker metric to determine whether a leader is more relational or task-oriented based on their assessment of a challenging colleague. The model defines situational favorability through three dimensions: the leader-member relationship, the structure of the task, and the leader's position power, with situations being most favorable when all three are high.

In conclusion, contingency theory suggests that there is no one best way to solve organizational problems. Contingency theory operates on the premise that organizational success is not predicated on a singular, universally applicable model. Instead, the best way to solve the organization problems depends on the specific circumstances of the organization. These circumstances might encompass the organization's size, the technological tools it utilizes, the external environment in which it operates, and the objectives it seeks to achieve. In fact, what works best for one organization might not be suitable for another due to differences in their specific circumstances. This theory underscores the importance of flexibility and adaptability in organizational design, highlighting the need for leaders to be attuned to their specific context and make decisions that align with their unique operational realities.

Key Principles

Today's contingency theory, having been developed and expanded by numerous scholars, features a variety of perspectives and entry points. However, it is possible to identify some fundamental principles common to this theory. These include the concept that there is no one best solution, the distinction between mechanistic and organic systems, the balance of differentiation and integration, the influence of both internal and external factors, and the overarching framework of Structural Adaptation to Regain Fit (SARFIT). Theory. Each of these key principles is further explored in the sections that follow.

No One Best Solution

The theory posits that there is no single best way to organize a corporation, lead a company, or make decisions. In the early twentieth century, the field of organizational theory was largely shaped by classical theorists, whose perspectives were molded by the industrial revolution and the emergence of factory systems. These theorists concentrated on developing universal organizational principles aimed at maximizing productivity. The most notable example of this approach was Taylor's (1911) scientific management method, representing the "one best way" ideology. However, by the 1960s, this rigid perspective was challenged, leading to the development of the contingency approach in organizational studies (Kessler et al., 2017). This approach, also known as structural contingency theory, proposes that there is no one best solution to structure an organization. What proves effective in one organizational context may not be suitable in another, underlining the importance of tailoring organizational structures to the specific nature of the tasks at hand and the environmental context (Lawrence & Lorsch, 1967).

Mechanistic and Organic Systems

In their 1961 work, Burns and Stalker introduced two sets of organizational characteristics known as the elements of mechanistic structures and organic structures. They suggested viewing these characteristics as polarities or ideal types. According to their analysis, mechanistic systems are more suitable for stable conditions, whereas organic systems thrive in dynamic environments.

Burns and Stalker (1961) further detailed these elements and offered additional observations. Firstly, they observed that organic systems, unlike mechanistic ones, do not have a traditional hierarchy. Instead, they have varying levels of authority and stratification, likely based on individual capability rather than seniority. Secondly, they noted a difference in employee commitment between the two systems. In organic systems, employee commitment is more extensive, resembling the dedication of professional scientists to their work, making it difficult to separate informal from formal organizational structures.

Thirdly, they pointed out that in organic systems, shared beliefs and values often take the place of the formal control structures found in mechanistic systems. Fourth, Burns and Stalker emphasized that neither system is universally superior; the choice depends on the organization's external environment. This implies that an organization might shift between organic and mechanistic systems depending on its internal and external environmental fit.

Differentiation and Integration

Lawrence and Lorsch (1967) explained the interplay of differentiation and integration within organizations, particularly in relation to external environmental factors. Differentiation refers to how an organization is divided into distinct subunits, each with specialized roles and functions (Lawrence & Lorsch, 1967). This specialization allows organizations to handle complex tasks and adapt to specific challenges. However, differentiation often leads to internal conflicts due to varying objectives and approaches among different units. Thus, integration is the process of ensuring that these differentiated units work together harmoniously. As organizations become more differentiated, achieving effective integration becomes increasingly challenging (Lawrence & Lorsch, 1967). This requires strong interpersonal skills and collaborative efforts to align the diverse segments toward common organizational goals. Moreover, the influence of the external environment (such as external pressures and demands) impacted different segments of the organization (Lawrence & Lorsch, 1967).

They concluded that the more an organization is differentiated, the greater the need for effective integration. Balancing these aspects is crucial for organizational efficiency and effectiveness. This balance is particularly important in dynamic environments where the rate of change is high, and the organization must respond quickly and cohesively to external pressures (Lawrence & Lorsch, 1967). This balance of differentiation and integration is a dynamic process requiring continuous assessment and adjustment in response to both internal developments and external environmental changes.

Internal and External Factors

Fiedler's, 1967 work emphasizes the complexity of many internal and external factors influencing the optimal structure of an organization. He identifies a range of internal aspects, such as the organization's size, the technology employed, compensation strategies, leadership styles, and the ability to pivot strategy when needed. External factors are equally significant, encompassing the organization's location, political climate, and public opinion.

Building on this, Burns and Stalker (1961), Donaldson (1995, 2001), and Lawrence and Lorsch (1967) further assert that the key to organizational success lies in aligning the organizational structure and practices with these internal and external contingencies. This perspective views organizations as open systems, which necessitates a careful balancing act between managing internal needs and responding to external environmental changes. Thus, the effective management of an organization requires a nuanced understanding of its context. The dynamics within an organization—such as its culture, employee skills, and resources—must harmoniously interact with external factors like market trends, public opinion, and regulatory changes.

Structural Adaptation to Regain Fit (SARFIT)

Structural contingency theory, traditionally viewed as an equilibrium theory, suggests organizations achieve a state of fit and then remain static. However, SARFIT, as described by Donaldson (2001), is a disequilibrium theory where organizations temporarily achieve fit, leading to surplus resources and expansion. This expansion alters variables like size or diversification, causing a misfit with the existing structure. Consequently, organizations oscillate between fit and misfit, with each fit leading to expansion and misfit (Donaldson, 2006). This dynamic cycle results in performance fluctuations and incremental growth, transitioning organizations from small and local to larger and diversified entities (Donaldson, 2006).

Configuration theory, a modern variation of contingency theory, posits limited configurations or fits between structural and other organizational variables (Miller,

1986). In contrast, Cartesianism (Donaldson, 2001) argues for a continuous line of fits, with each contingency level matched by a structural level. This continuous fit line, aligning with the SARFIT model, facilitates incremental changes in contingency and structure, explaining frequent, smaller-scale organizational changes, as opposed to the less frequent major changes suggested by configurationalism (Donaldson, 2006).

Despite criticism, structural contingency theory and the concept of quasi-fit (Donaldson, 2001) suggest that organizations do not always achieve full fit but rather a partial fit that still enhances performance. This quasi-fit, though not optimal, generates enough improvement to propel the organization into growth, leading to a cycle of incremental changes and substantial growth over time. Donaldson (2001) also argues that the notion of quasi-fit allows managers to reduce misfits and engage in the SARFIT cycle, even if they do not fully understand the fit states prescribed by the theory.

In conclusion, the evolution of organizational theory from the early twentieth century to the present day highlights a shift from the classical "one best way" approach to a more dynamic contingency perspective (no one best solution). This shift, as noted by theorists like Lawrence and Lorsch (1967), and Donaldson (2001, 2006), reflects an understanding that organizational effectiveness depends on adapting structures to specific internal and external factors. Mechanistic and organic systems, as proposed by Burns and Stalker (1961), offer different approaches suited to various environmental contexts. The balance of differentiation and integration within organizations is crucial in responding to these environmental factors. SARFIT, a disequilibrium theory, suggests that organizations constantly oscillate between states of fit and misfit, leading to incremental growth and adaptation. This ongoing process underscores the importance of structural flexibility and the ability to achieve quasi-fit, allowing organizations to continuously evolve and respond effectively to changing internal and external demands.

Applying Contingency Theory to Criminal Legal Contexts

Given that every organization possesses unique characteristics and follows its own management model, it is worth deliberating if contingency theory is an appropriate framework to apply to criminal legal agencies. Although the theory was initially employed in studying corporations and companies, it was soon applied to examining public bureaucracies, such as Greenwood and Hinings' research in 1976. Police organizations were certainly among the research targets with their fairly bureaucratic structures; for example, Zhao et al. (2010) examine the utility of contingency theory in its application to police organizational structures during the 1990s. The key question here is not just the applicability of this theory, but also identifying specific areas within criminal legal organizations where its' principles might be most effectively utilized.

As previously noted, contingency theory encompasses various principles, and it is debatable whether all of them are suitable for implementation in criminal justice agencies. Therefore, this discussion will focus on summarizing literature that has adeptly incorporated contingency theory into criminal legal research. By delving deeply into these studies, this discussion aims to extract valuable findings and insights that lay a solid groundwork for applying these principles as effective, practical strategies in future policing organizations. This approach is tailored to align with the distinctive characteristics of criminal legal agency management and operations. The key principles discussed below offer a framework to comprehend and tackle the intricate challenges encountered by police forces.

Mechanistic and Organic Systems

Contingency theory highlights the critical role of organizational flexibility. Traditionally, police organizations operate within a bureaucratic and hierarchical framework, similar to a mechanistic system, which is known for its efficiency in stable and predictable environments, as noted by Kuykendall and Roberg (1982). Similarly, Zhao et al. (2010) conclude that the organizational structure in a police department is highly stable and apparently highly resistant to change. This mechanistic approach ensured a consistent and balanced approach to salary and compensation. However, the post-COVID-19 era has presented significant challenges to this model. The increasing gap between inflation rates and salary increments has posed financial strain and dissatisfaction among police personnel. Moreover, the public perception of the police force, which was traditionally neutral or even positive, has taken a hit. Various incidents involving law enforcement, often negatively portrayed by the media, have contributed to a growing sense of mistrust and criticism from the public (Morrow et al., 2019; Todak, 2017). These factors combined have revealed the limitations of the traditional, mechanistic organizational structure in adapting to rapidly changing and unpredictable situations.

Moreover, Küçükuysal and Beyhan (2011) observed a significant shift in police operations over the past few decades, transitioning from a force-focused approach to one that is more service-oriented. Community policing has emerged as a highly favored method among law enforcement agencies globally, with many countries adopting this strategy in recent years. However, they identified a key issue in implementing community policing programs: the failure to consider the unique characteristics of different environments and communities. This oversight often leads to unsuccessful outcomes when programs successful in one setting are replicated elsewhere without modifications. Programs copied without adapting to the distinct needs and conditions of the target environment, community characteristics, and police organizational structures often fail to deliver the desired outcomes. This issue is particularly pronounced in environments characterized by uncertainty, rapid market changes, and technological advancements, which have different demands compared to more stable settings.

Küçükuysal and Beyhan (2011) underscore that the success of community policing relies on adapting organizational structures to fit environmental demands, a core tenet of contingency theory. This theory has evolved to suggest that mechanistic systems are more suitable for stable conditions, whereas organic systems thrive in dynamic environments. Organizational design decisions should be based on environmental conditions, implying that organizations must align their internal features with external demands for optimal adaptation. However, in community policing, the significance of organizational structure is frequently overlooked or underestimated. For an effective community policing program, certain structural changes within police departments are necessary, such as decentralized decision-making and flattened hierarchies. This approach aligns the organizational structure with the dynamic needs and conditions of the community, enabling more effective community policing.

Responding to these challenges necessitates a paradigm shift in the organizational structure of police departments. Moving towards a more organic system, as conceptualized by Burns and Stalker (1961), implies embracing a model that thrives in dynamic and uncertain environments. Such a system is characterized by its adaptability and responsiveness to various external and internal factors. This would involve fundamental changes in several aspects of police organization operations, including how compensation is structured, how resources are allocated, and how the needs of the public are addressed. A key aspect of this transformation is the shift towards decentralized decision-making processes and the flattening of hierarchical structures (Küçükuysal & Beyhan, 2011). This approach fosters a more responsive and agile organization, capable of adapting to the evolving landscape of law enforcement.

Internal and External Factors

The studies related to "Police Compensation" by Giblin and Galli (2017) and "County Prosecutor Salaries" by Choi and Giblin (2023) provide a focused analysis of salary structures within law enforcement agencies, utilizing the lens of contingency theory. This theoretical framework is instrumental in examining how various factors within and outside an organization impact its salary levels.

Giblin and Galli (2017) conducted a study to examine if unfavorable contingencies like high living costs and rigorous application standards correlate with the compensation levels—supplemental incentives and reimbursements—of officers in large metropolitan police departments. They propose that structural contingency theory is a valuable framework for understanding the variations in recruitment strategies of police departments, particularly in terms of financial compensation for officers (Balkin & Gomez-Mejia, 1987; Rynes & Barber, 1990). The study posits that differences in police officer compensation across agencies may be linked to both internal and external organizational contingencies. As recruitment becomes more challenging, reducing the attractiveness of the organization and its setting, police departments, like other organizations, are compelled to find ways to overcome the shortage of job candidates. This necessitates adaptation or regaining fit when faced with unfavorable contingencies.

The dependent variable of the study is compensation, encompassing salary, incentives, and reimbursements. The research examines six independent variables: screening techniques, educational requirements, employment rates, competition, crime rates, and median home values. These variables are chosen as contingencies that potentially influence the attractiveness of working for an organization, with higher scores indicating less appealing features or greater recruitment challenges. Additionally, the study considers control variables such as agency size, fiscal capacity, and collective bargaining agreements. Their findings largely align with the principles of contingency theory, particularly regarding salaries. Police departments are observed to offer higher salaries as a means to counterbalance more rigorous hiring criteria, elevated living costs, and other unfavorable contingencies.

Similarly, Choi and Giblin (2023) applied the contingency theory to examine the county prosecutor salaries. The study discovered that numerous prosecutor offices face difficulties in recruiting and retaining competent prosecuting attorneys. A 2005 survey revealed that about 24% of these offices encountered challenges in hiring new attorneys, while 35% faced retention issues, a problem more pronounced in larger jurisdictions (Perry, 2006). Furthermore, the same survey highlighted that low salaries were the main obstacle for offices struggling to recruit and keep qualified attorneys (Perry, 2006). Therefore, the study aimed to identify both organizational factors (like fiscal capacity) and environmental factors (such as median rent) that influence the compensation in prosecutor offices, integrating these variables into the framework of contingency theory.

The research adopted a contingency perspective, suggesting that an organization's success depends on aligning its structure and practices with both internal and external factors or contingencies (Burns & Stalker, 1961; Lawrence & Lorsch, 1967). The internal organizational variables examined included fiscal capacity, office size, felony caseload, and perceived threats. The external environmental variables consisted of aspects like the form of county government, community conservatism, the county-level unemployment rate, rurality, and median rent. The dependent variable of interest in the study was the minimum salary for entry-level prosecutors. The central question of the research was to identify what factors contribute to the variations in prosecutors' salaries across the United States. The predictive factors were assessed within the lens of contingency theory, viewed as challenges that prosecutors' offices must adapt to for effective recruitment. A key finding of the study was the consistent and significant correlation between (a proxy for cost of living) and the minimum entry-level salary across the 2 years. This aligns with contingency theory, where a higher cost of living requires higher salaries. Additionally, the study found that factors like organizational size, perceived threats, fiscal capacity, and unemployment rate also influenced salaries.

Contingency theory, as applied in both studies, underscores the concept that no single organizational structure or practice is universally effective; instead, the efficacy is contingent upon the internal and external factors at play. These studies examine the intricacies of how internal organizational aspects like fiscal capacity, office size, and crime rates influence the setting of salary levels in law enforcement agencies. The works of Burns and Stalker (1961), Donaldson (1995, 2001), and Lawrence and Lorsch (1967) have significantly contributed to this field by asserting that the success of an organization is largely dependent on how well it aligns its structure and practices with both internal and external contingencies. They advocate for the perception of organizations as open systems, implying a need for a dynamic balance. This balance involves managing the internal operational needs while simultaneously adapting to the changing external environment. In the context of law enforcement agencies, this means navigating through the complexities of internal operational requirements while being responsive to external socioeconomic conditions.

Furthermore, the internal factors examined in these articles, such as fiscal strength, size of the organization, and the quantity of the crime caseload, are crucial in determining how law enforcement agencies structure their compensation. On the other hand, external factors like median rent and home values in the surrounding area play a significant role in shaping salary scales. These external elements reflect broader economic conditions, such as market trends and inflation rates, which directly influence the cost of living and, consequently, the salary expectations of employees. This intricate interplay between internal organizational dynamics and the external environmental context highlights the need for a nuanced understanding and adaptability in organizational management. This adaptability is key to ensuring the success and sustainability of law enforcement agencies in a rapidly evolving socio-economic landscape.

Differentiation and Integration

Hu and Lovrich's (2019) research, examining the correlation between organizational complexity and social media (Facebook, Twitter, and YouTube) usage in police departments, is deeply rooted in the concepts of differentiation and integration as outlined in contingency theory. Similarly, Roberts et al. (2012) noted that police agencies with more complex organizational structures are likelier to perceive the advantages of new innovations and possess the capacity to utilize them based on previous successful implementations of innovations. In this context, organizational complexity is a reflection of the levels of differentiation and integration within an organization, which in turn influences its performance.

Lawrence and Lorsch (1967) provided a detailed explanation of how differentiation and integration function within organizations. Differentiation is characterized by the division of an organization into distinct subunits, each specializing in specific roles and functions. This specialized structuring allows organizations to efficiently manage complex tasks and respond adeptly to unique challenges. However, a high degree of differentiation can lead to internal conflicts, as each unit may develop its own objectives and methods, potentially leading to misalignments within the organization. To counteract this, integration becomes essential. Integration involves the process of ensuring these diverse units operate in a cohesive and coordinated manner. As organizations grow more differentiated, the challenge of achieving effective integration intensifies. It demands robust interpersonal communication and concerted efforts to unify the different segments of the organization toward shared goals.

Usually, the higher the level of differentiation within an organization, the more crucial it becomes to have effective integration mechanisms. Striking this balance is vital for maintaining both efficiency and effectiveness, especially in dynamic environments where rapid changes are common, and the organization needs to react swiftly and in a united manner to external stimuli (Lawrence & Lorsch, 1967). In line with this, Hu and Lovrich (2019) found that a higher degree of organizational complexity, which includes both high levels of differentiation and the need for integration, is associated with an increased adoption of social media in police agencies. This suggests that as police departments become more complex, with various specialized units and functions, they are more likely to utilize social media platforms to facilitate communication, coordination, and integration across their diverse components. The use of social media, in this case, can be seen as a tool to bridge the gaps brought about by differentiation, fostering a more integrated and cohesive organizational operation.

In summary, these principles of contingency theory provide a robust framework for understanding and addressing the diverse and complex workforce crises in policing. By applying these principles, police forces can enhance their effectiveness, adaptability, and responsiveness to the ever-changing landscape of law enforcement.

Strategies for Addressing the Policing Workforce Crisis

The existing literature suggests that the current crisis in the police workforce primarily arises from two significant challenges: a lack of interest among potential recruits in joining the police force and a high turnover rate among existing personnel. This crisis could largely be attributed to two key factors: the uncompetitive nature of police salaries and the prevailing negative public perception of the police force. Moreover, numerous studies indicate that existing employees' satisfaction with their salary can significantly enhance their job satisfaction and organizational commitment (Matz et al., 2014; Muhammad et al., 2011). Then, it can lead to reduced employee turnover and a greater willingness to retain in the police departments (Lee et al., 2020; Schuck & Rabe-Hemp, 2018; Wilson et al., 2010). The following sections will outline strategic measures, grounded in the principles of contingency theory, to effectively address and mitigate this workforce crisis.

Compensation Structures

When questioned about individuals' reasons for working, many individuals commonly mention money as a primary motivator (Jurgensen, 1978). Balkin and Gomez-Mejia (1987) emphasize that "compensation is considered an important part of the strategic thrust of human resource management" (p. 170). Similarly, Locke et al. (1980) even asserted that in terms of its instrumental value, no incentive or motivational technique rivals money. Moreover, Diener and Seligman (2004) revealed that individuals' income levels positively correlate with their reported well-being.

Thus, these arguments are equally applicable to police organizational policies. Similar to how corporations utilize competitive compensation packages to distinguish themselves in the marketplace, police departments can employ financial incentives as a strategy to enhance their appeal. For recruitment endeavors to be successful, it is crucial that departments can draw from and select candidates from a substantial applicant pool. To boost their attractiveness to potential recruits, they might provide both monetary and non-monetary incentives to promote employment (Rynes & Barber, 1990). In the realm of policing, different agencies have adopted diverse incentive strategies. Some offer tangible perks like signing bonuses, additional bonuses for holding a college degree, and grants for uniforms (Taylor et al., 2005). Alternatively, some departments prioritize offering competitive salaries, a factor that has been consistently highlighted as a significant motivator in surveys exploring the reasons individuals choose a career in policing (e.g., Ridgeway et al., 2008; White et al., 2010).

Furthermore, as posited by scholars, individuals spend on themselves in various manners, not merely for immediate gratification but in anticipation of future financial and non-financial gains (Blaug, 1976; Becker, 1962). Giblin and Galli (2017) argue that potential candidates might be hesitant to invest time and resources into acquiring skills and knowledge, such as obtaining a college degree, if similar employment opportunities can be accessed elsewhere without such extensive commitment. Conversely, they might decline job offers if the proposed salary seems inadequate and does not align with their previous investments. Offering a higher salary may enable organizations to enhance their performance, especially when paired with criteria that seek higher-quality of applicants (Giblin & Galli, 2017). In essence, competitive compensation attracts candidates who view it as a justifiable return on their educational and training investments.

Thus, the compensation structures within police organizations should evolve towards more flexible pay scales that account for varying external environmental factors, such as fluctuating inflation rates or the regional unemployment situation. This need for adaptability in pay scales becomes especially critical during periods of significant external change, like the economic upheaval witnessed during the COVID-19 pandemic when inflation rates saw rapid and considerable increases. In response to such economic fluctuations, it is essential for police remuneration to be adjusted accordingly. This will not only ensure alignment with the broader economic environment but also enhance the competitiveness of police salaries compared to those offered by private sector companies.

Moreover, in a more dynamic, organic framework, salary should be increasingly linked to individual performance and merit, moving away from the traditional emphasis on seniority. This change in pay structure aims to cultivate a more dynamic and performance-oriented culture within police organizations. Such an approach aligns more closely with the current expectations of accountability and effectiveness in modern law enforcement. A performance-linked pay system encourages officers to strive for excellence and efficiency, aligning personal success with organizational goals. Furthermore, this transformation enhances the responsiveness of police organizations, enabling them to adapt more effectively to the complex and evolving challenges of modern policing.

By adopting this organic model, police departments can significantly enhance their adaptability to both internal developments and external social changes. This increased flexibility in responding to changes ensures that police officers are not only fairly compensated in line with the current economic climate but also motivated to perform at their best. In turn, this can lead to increased effectiveness in law enforcement operations and a positive impact on public relations. The adoption of a more responsive and merit-based pay structure is an important step towards modernizing police forces and fostering a more motivated, accountable, and publicly respected police workforce.

To sum up, the evolving compensation structures serve a dual purpose. Firstly, it acts as a magnet, drawing in potential candidates. Secondly, it signifies the organization's recognition and appreciation of its officers' efforts and expertise. This dual approach not only fills vacancies but also instills a sense of pride and worth among employees, ensuring they recognize and satisfy their integral role and value within the institution. Moreover, a competitive compensation structure can also improve police officers' job satisfaction and reduce turnover rates.

Managing Internal Crises

If adjusting the police's entrenched bureaucratic structure proves challenging, then the creation of an internal contingency department within the organization becomes essential. Creating a contingency department within an organization is a strategic approach to effectively manage and mitigate internal crises. This specialized department would focus not on external crime-related issues, but rather on addressing internal administrative challenges within the organization. It should include the leadership of various departments, working in tandem with quantitative data analysts to effectively manage and resolve these internal matters. The establishment of such a department signifies a proactive stance towards organizational resilience, ensuring the organization is well-equipped to handle unforeseen situations that might otherwise disrupt its smooth functioning.

For example, in tackling a workforce crisis within a police organization, a contingency department can be instrumental by conducting comprehensive assessments to identify root causes, such as uncompetitive salaries or negative public perception. This department would develop and implement targeted strategies, like restructuring compensation packages and improving community relations, in collaboration with various organizational departments. Continuous monitoring and adjustment of these strategies ensure their effectiveness, while the department also focuses on long-term planning to prevent future crises. By facilitating dynamic responses to both internal and external challenges, the contingency department plays a crucial role in enhancing the organization's resilience and adaptability.

Finally, the contingency department would play a pivotal role during actual crisis situations. It would coordinate the organization's response efforts, ensuring effective communication and swift action. This coordination is critical for minimizing the impact of the dissatisfaction of personnel and to increase their commitment and willingness to stay in the organization. Through these activities, the contingency department would significantly contribute to the organization's overall resilience, enabling it to navigate through internal crises with minimal disruption and emerge stronger from each challenge.

Maintaining Positive Relationships

A strategy to maintain positive police-community relations or to leverage social media to promote a favorable image of the police organization can be an effective response to a workforce crisis. Contingency theory emphasizes the importance of an organization's adaptability to its external environment. In this context, the external environment includes public perception and community relationships, which are crucial for the police force.

Firstly, understanding the specific community needs and perceptions is essential. This involves assessing how different communities view the police, which can vary significantly based on demographic, geographic, and social factors. Based on this assessment, tailored strategies can be developed to improve relations. This might involve community outreach programs, participation in local events, or initiatives that address specific community concerns.

Secondly, using social media as a tool to promote a positive image is aligned with contemporary communication trends. Social media platforms can be used to highlight positive stories, community engagement activities, and transparency efforts of the police force. This approach also allows for real-time communication and feedback, providing an avenue for building trust and dispelling misconceptions.

In both cases, the strategies should not be static but adaptive to changing circumstances and feedback. For instance, if certain community initiatives are not yielding the expected improvement in relations, the approach should be re-evaluated and adjusted accordingly. Similarly, the content and strategy on social media should evolve based on the engagement and response from the public.

By improving public perception and community relations through these methods, a police organization can create a more positive working environment. This, in turn, can make the profession more attractive to potential recruits and help retain current officers, thus addressing aspects of the workforce crisis. The key, as highlighted by contingency theory, is the flexible and responsive adaptation of strategies to the specific and evolving needs of the external environment.

Conclusion

Contingency theory, a classical theory of organizational theory, has seen widespread and successful application across various sectors of the private industry. Currently, the police workforce is facing with a significant workforce crisis, primarily attributed to the lack of competitive salaries and negative public perceptions, leading to low recruitment interest and high turnover rates among officers. In response to this, the present chapter aims to apply the principles of contingency theory to address this crisis, offering practical and actionable recommendations. Based on a review of existing literature, several strategies are proposed: evolving compensation structures to make them more competitive, establishing a dedicated contingency department to manage internal organizational crises, and enhancing police-community relations or utilizing social media effectively to foster a positive image of the police force.

Moreover, echoing the foundational premise of contingency theory, which posits that there is no one-size-fits-all solution, the chapter suggests a practical approach to the police workforce crisis. While contingency theory offers valuable insights, integrating it with the computational models of process theory could yield a more in-depth and holistic evaluation of the salary structure. Furthermore, incorporating the legitimacy of institutional theory could help in moderating police behaviors, reducing instances of excessive enforcement or inaction. These additional theoretical perspectives could enhance the robustness and comprehensiveness of the strategies devised to tackle the workforce crisis in policing. By combining these diverse theoretical frameworks, the approach to resolving the crisis can be more nuanced, addressing not just the symptoms but the underlying structural and perceptual issues within the police organization.

References

Abdulla, J., Djebarni, R., & Mellahi, K. (2011). Determinants of job satisfaction in the UAE: A case study of the Dubai police. *Personnel Review, 40*(1), 126–146.

Adams, I. T., Mourtgos, S. M., & Nix, J. (2023). Turnover in large US policing agencies following the George Floyd protests. *Journal of Criminal Justice, 88*, 102105.

Adebayo, D. O. (2005). Perceived workplace fairness, transformational leadership and motivation in the Nigeria police: Implications for change. *International Journal of Police Science & Management, 7*(2), 110–122.
Ahmad, R., & Islam, T. (2019). Does work and family imbalance impact the satisfaction of police force employees? A "net or a web" model. *Policing: An International Journal, 42*(4), 585–597.
Ahmed, T., & Salter, J. (2023). Some small towns in America are disbanding police forces, citing hiring woes. *ABC News*. https://abcnews.go.com/Business/wireStory/americas-small-towns-disbanding-police-forces-citing-hiring-102924860
Balkin, D. B., & Gomez-Mejia, L. R. (1987). Toward a contingency theory of compensation strategy. *Strategic Management Journal, 8*(2), 169–182.
Becker, G. S. (1962). Investment in human capital: A theoretical analysis. *Journal of Political Economy, 70*(5), 9–49. http://www.jstor.org/stable/1829103
Blaug, M. (1976). The empirical status of human capital theory: A slightly jaundiced survey. *Journal of Economic Literature, 14*(3), 827–855.
Boylan, R. T. (2022). Should cities disband their police departments? *Journal of Urban Economics, 130*, 103460.
Burns, T., & Stalker, G. M. (1961). Mechanistic and organic systems. *Classics of Organizational Theory, 10*, 209–214.
Choi, M., & Giblin, M. (2023). The environmental and organizational determinants of county prosecutor salaries. *Journal of Crime and Justice, 46*(3), 383–396.
David, A., & Venatus, V. K. (2019). Job satisfaction and turnover intentions of police officers in rural communities in Dekina Local Government Area of Kogi State, Nigeria. *Bangladesh e-Journal of Sociology, 16*(1), 65–81.
Dazio, S., Bleiberg, J., & Brumback, K. (2021, June 11). Law enforcement struggles to recruit since killing of Floyd. *AP News*. https://apnews.com/article/government-and-politics-george-floyd-racial-injustice-only-on-ap-coronavirus-pandemic-d434cc8023875ddb996abb7df0a7bc44
Diener, E., & Seligman, M. E. P. (2004). Beyond money: Toward an economy of well-being. *Psychological Science in the Public Interest, 5*(1), 1–31. https://doi.org/10.1111/j.0963-7214.2004.00501001.x
Donaldson, L. (1995) American anti-management theories of organization: A critique of paradigm proliferation, New York, NY: Cambridge University Press.
Donaldson, L. (2001). *The contingency theory of organizations*. Sage.
Donaldson, L. (2006). The contingency theory of organizational design: Challenges and opportunities. In *Organization Design: The evolving state-of-the-art* (pp. 19–40). Springer.
Donner, C., Maskaly, J., Fridell, L., & Jennings, W. G. (2015). Policing and procedural justice: A state-of-the-art review. *Policing: An International Journal of Police Strategies & Management, 38*(1), 153–172.
Duncan, K. (2021, December 31). Who wants to join the force in 2022? Eagle county law enforcement agencies struggle to staff up. *Vail Daily*. https://www.vaildaily.com/news/who-wants-to-join-the-force-in-2022-eagle-county-law-enforcement-agencies-struggle-to-staff-up/
Fiedler, F. E. (1967). *A theory of leadership effectiveness*. McGraw-Hill.
Giblin, M. J., & Galli, P. M. (2017). Compensation as a police candidate attraction tool: An organizational-level analysis. *Police Quarterly, 20*(4), 397–419.
Greenwood, R., & Hinings, C. R. (1976). Contingency theory and public bureaucracies. *Policy & Politics, 5*(2), 159–180.
Hu, X., & Lovrich, N. P. (2019). Social media and the police: A study of organizational characteristics associated with the use of social media. *Policing: An International Journal, 42*(4), 654–670.
Ingram, J. R., & Lee, S. U. (2015). The effect of first-line supervision on patrol officer job satisfaction. *Police Quarterly, 18*(2), 193–219.
Judge, T. A., Thoresen, C. J., Bono, J. E., & Patton, G. K. (2001). The job satisfaction–job performance relationship: A qualitative and quantitative review. *Psychological Bulletin, 127*(3), 376.

Jurgensen, C. E. (1978). Job preferences (What makes a job good or bad?). *Journal of Applied Psychology, 63*(3), 267.
Kessler, S. R., Nixon, A. E., & Nord, W. R. (2017). Examining organic and mechanistic structures: Do we know as much as we thought? *International Journal of Management Reviews, 19*(4), 531–555.
Küçükuysal, B., & Beyhan, E. (2011). Contingency theory approach for effective community policing. *Süleyman Demirel Üniversitesi Fen-Edebiyat Fakültesi Sosyal Bilimler Dergisi, 2011*(23), 259–268.
Kuykendall, J., & Roberg, R. R. (1982). Mapping police organizational change: From a mechanistic toward an organic model. *Criminology, 20*(2), 241–256.
Lambert, E. G., Qureshi, H., Frank, J., Klahm, C., & Smith, B. (2018). Job stress, job involvement, job satisfaction, and organizational commitment and their associations with job burnout among Indian police officers: A research note. *Journal of Police and Criminal Psychology, 33*, 85–99.
Lawrence, P. R., & Lorsch, J. W. (1967). Differentiation and integration in complex organizations. *Administrative Science Quarterly, 12*(1), 1–47.
Lee, H. W., Robertson, P. J., & Kim, K. (2020). Determinants of job satisfaction among US federal employees: An investigation of racial and gender differences. *Public Personnel Management, 49*(3), 336–366.
Locke, E. A., Feren, D. B., McCaleb, V. M., Shaw, K. N., & Denny, A. T. (1980). The relative effectiveness of four methods of motivating employee performance. *Changes in Working Life, 363*(1), 388.
MacDonald, H. (2017). *The war on cops: How the new attack on law and order makes everyone less safe*. Encounter Books.
Matz, A. K., Woo, Y., & Kim, B. (2014). A meta-analysis of the correlates of turnover intent in criminal justice organizations: Does agency type matter? *Journal of Criminal Justice, 42*(3), 233–243.
McLean, K., Cherry, T., & Alpert, G. P. (2023). Recruiting for change: Shifting focus to address a workforce crisis. *Police Practice and Research, 24*(4), 446–460.
Miller, D. (1986). Configurations of strategy and structure: Towards a synthesis. *Strategic Management Journal, 7*(3), 233–249.
Mintzberg, H. (1979). *The structuring of organizations: A synthesis of the research*. Prentice-Hall.
Morrow, W. J., Vickovic, S. G., Dario, L. M., & Shjarback, J. A. (2019). Examining a Ferguson effect on college students' motivation to become police officers. *Journal of Criminal Justice Education, 30*(4), 585–605.
Mourtgos, S. M., Adams, I. T., & Nix, J. (2022). Elevated police turnover following the summer of George Floyd protests: A synthetic control study. *Criminology & Public Policy, 21*(1), 9–33.
Muhammad, S. C., Hazoor, M. S., Rafi, N., & Masood, N. K. (2011). Exploring the relationship between salary satisfaction and job satisfaction: A comparison of public and private sector organizations. *The Journal of Commerce, 3*(4), 2218–8118.
Perry, S. W. (2006). *Prosecutors in state courts, 2005*. US Department of Justice, Office of Justice Programs, Bureau of Justice Statistics.
Police Executive Research Forum. (2019). *The workforce crisis, and what police agencies are doing about it.* https://www.policeforum.org/assets/WorkforceCrisis.pdf
Ramlawati, R., Trisnawati, E., Yasin, N., & Kurniawaty, K. (2021). External alternatives, job stress on job satisfaction and employee turnover intention. *Management Science Letters, 11*(2), 511–518.
Rasmussen, E. (2022, January 10). *Recruiting realities: Policing staffing crisis not the same in every city, data shows*. KSTP.com. https://kstp.com/kstp-news/top-news/recruiting-realities-police-staffing-crisis-not-the-same-in-every-city-data-shows/
Ridgeway, G., Lim, N., Gifford, B., Koper, C., Matthies, C., Hajiamiri, S., & Huynh, A. (2008). *Strategies for improving officer recruitment in the San Diego Police Department, Santa Monica, CA*. RAND.

Roberts, A., Roberts, J. M., Jr., & Liedka, R. V. (2012). Elements of terrorism preparedness in local police agencies, 2003–2007: Impact of vulnerability, organizational characteristics, and contagion in the post-9/11 era. *Crime & Delinquency, 58*(5), 720–747.

Rynes, S. L., & Barber, A. E. (1990). Applicant attraction strategies: An organizational perspective. *Academy of Management Review, 15*(2), 286–310.

Sageer, A., Rafat, S., & Agarwal, P. (2012). Identification of variables affecting employee satisfaction and their impact on the organization. *IOSR Journal of Business and Management, 5*(1), 32–39.

Scanlan, J. N., & Still, M. (2013). Job satisfaction, burnout and turnover intention in occupational therapists working in mental health. *Australian Occupational Therapy Journal, 60*(5), 310–318.

Schuck, A. M., & Rabe-Hemp, C. E. (2018). Investing in people: Salary and turnover in policing. *Policing: An International Journal, 41*(1), 113–128.

Taylor, F. W. (1911). *The principles of scientific management*. NuVision Publications, LLC.

Taylor, B., Kubu, B., Fridell, L., Rees, C., Jordan, T., & Cheney, J. (2005, December). *Cop crunch: Identifying strategies for dealing with the recruiting and hiring crisis in law enforcement*. Police Executive Research Forum.

Todak, N. (2017). The decision to become a police officer in a legitimacy crisis. *Women & Criminal Justice, 27*(4), 250–270.

Wang, Y., Zheng, L., Hu, T., & Zheng, Q. (2014). Stress, burnout, and job satisfaction: Case of police force in China. *Public Personnel Management, 43*(3), 325–339.

White, M. D., Cooper, J. A., Saunders, J., & Raganella, A. J. (2010). Motivations for becoming a police officer: Re-assessing officer attitudes and job satisfaction after six years on the street. *Journal of Criminal Justice, 38*(4), 520–530.

Wilson, J. M., Dalton, E., Scheer, C., & Grammich, C. A. (2010). *Police recruitment and retention for the new millennium* (p. 10). RAND Corporation.

Zhao, J., Ren, L., & Lovrich, N. (2010). Police organizational structures during the 1990s: An application of contingency theory. *Police Quarterly, 13*(2), 209–232.

Chapter 5
An Organizational Process Approach for Identifying Side Effects of Juvenile Justice System Reforms

Anne C. Wingert

Introduction

Throughout the past few decades, society's preferences for addressing youth crime drove numerous shifts in the philosophies of the Juvenile Justice System (JJS). The JJS's initial view of youth as vulnerable and dependent yielded state protections from the punitive nature of adult criminal courts and the prioritization of nonpunitive and rehabilitative responses to crime. However, the rise in youth crime in the decades following altered society's perception, and a "get tough" era commenced, prioritizing offense type, retribution, and criminal responsibility. The passing of the 1974 Juvenile Justice and Delinquency Prevention Act (JJDPA) kickstarted reform efforts to prioritize more humane and empirically backed practices (i.e., rehabilitation, prevention, and diversion) in numerous states across the country. The goal of improving the JJS and reducing youth contact through reform led to the implementation of different policies, laws, and practices (e.g., zero-tolerance and diversion policies). The implemented changes in reform efforts, however, produced unforeseen side effects. A few detected JJS side effects include the school-to-prison pipeline, the concept of net-widening, and difficulties addressing gun violence. The term *side effect* conceptualizes adverse, undesired, and unforeseen events that stem from the implementation of some form of organizational intervention (Watts et al., 2022). Historically, side effects in the JJS are detected *after* the implementation of a change in policy, practice, or approach. Thus, challenges remain in understanding how the JJS can better anticipate, monitor, and assess potential side effects before they become an issue.

A. C. Wingert (✉)
Sam Houston State University, Department of Crimial Justice and Criminology, Huntsville, TX, USA
e-mail: acw074@shsu.edu

D. S. Rudes, J. R. Ingram (eds.), *Using Organizational Theory to Study, Explain, and Understand Criminal Legal Organizations*,
https://doi.org/10.1007/978-3-031-66285-0_5

This chapter proposes one promising solution through the lens of organizational theory. Specifically, a process theory approach can advance the current understanding and detection of unanticipated side effects for juveniles who encounter the justice system to better identify, minimize, and eliminate the persistent side effects. Additionally, this process approach can help identify the potential for JJS side effects before they occur to prevent future reform outcomes from harming youth. This chapter first details the history of the juvenile justice system, discussing its various shifts from its establishment to the present day. Then, the author presents three notable side effect examples in JJS research to underline the pattern of reactive approaches to reform and the need for alternative methods to address side effects. Following this, the author defines process theory and applies it to the identification of side effects in the JJS. Lastly, the author details the recommendations for implementing this process theory approach and offers avenues for future empirical assessment.

The Juvenile Justice System

Prior to the establishment of the juvenile justice system (JJS) in the early nineteenth century, children age seven and older could be tried in criminal court and potentially sentenced to prison or death in the United States (National Research Council, 2001). Ironically, those younger than seven were exempt from such punishment, as society assumed they were too young to form criminal intent. Reformers proposed the development of special courts and incarceration facilities for juveniles with the goal of facilitating optimal child development and diverting young offenders from the harmful punishments of criminal courts and, instead, encouraging rehabilitation based on their needs. Without the establishment of a distinct system for juveniles, youth would likely still be vulnerable to public court proceedings, charged with criminal offenses, found guilty, and serving prison sentences. Nevertheless, the JJS has encountered numerous shifts in philosophies throughout history, which have not always translated positively in practice (e.g., yielding organizational side effects).

The Progressive Era kickstarted the development of a juvenile justice system (i.e., JJS; Bishop & Feld, 2012; Feld, 1999; Platt, 1977; Tanenhaus, 2004). At the time (i.e., 1899), reformers perceived youth as immature, dependent, vulnerable, and highly influenced by external factors (Bishop & Feld, 2012). Subsequently, reformists founded a separate justice system to safeguard youth from the stigmatizing punitiveness of criminal courts and the corruption imposed by adult correctional facilities (i.e., jails and prisons). These perceptions bolstered the philosophical underpinnings of the juvenile court, which upheld a doctrine of parens patriae (i.e., the idea that the state was an arbiter of child-rearing).

For the next 60 years, the juvenile court was thought of as a nonpunitive and therapeutic institution whose founders implemented private proceedings, reworded stigmatizing terminology (e.g., charges, convictions) utilized in criminal contexts, eliminated formal court actors (e.g., lawyers and juries), and offered judges administrative flexibility to decide the stipulations of youth supervision (Bishop & Feld, 2012; Ryerson, 1978; Tanenhaus, 2004). This new system introduced a civil-therapeutic model of justice, seeking to identify the source of one's problem behaviors and offer direction and supervision to aid in their development into responsible and law-abiding citizens (Bishop & Feld, 2012; Zimring, 1998). Rather than have concern regarding the defense of youth from false adjudications of delinquency, reformers placed their trust in juvenile court interventions to execute benign treatment from which they believed youth would always benefit (Bishop & Feld, 2012). Consequently, the scope of the state's authority had no bounds, and the juvenile court's jurisdiction expanded to encompass those accused of crimes, status offenders, dependent children, and those "at risk" for delinquency.

From its commencement, the JJS was a delicate development, as its continuation relied on public and political backing (Tanenhaus, 2004). However, the behavior of violent and chronic offenders threatened this support, as the public often perceived them as "adult-like" and pushed for extensive sentences beyond the capacity of the JJS (Bishop & Feld, 2012). Similarly, recidivists challenged the juvenile court, as their failure to respond to interventions suggested that youth may be more obstinate than once assumed. The most serious and persistent cases were often transferred to criminal court. Although this waiver of jurisdiction contested the court's founding principles, it was politically practical to appease public fear and preserve the court's intended rehabilitative function for the remaining majority.

A Punitive Shift to "Get Tough"

Ultimately, the prioritization of rehabilitative ideals placed the JJS on cultural, legal, and criminological fault lines. Binary distinctions between the juvenile and criminal justice system became accepted: either "child or adult," "irresponsible or responsible," "treatment or punishment," "devoid of rules and informal, or formal and adversarial" (Bishop & Feld, 2012, p. 902). However, from the 1960s onward, shocking realities regarding abuses of authority in the adjudicatory stage and the truth of "rehabilitation" in the juvenile correctional system sparked a shift to the latter of each distinction. Observable over the past century, the JJS no longer reflects its foundational ideals and origins. Rather than prioritizing juvenile's needs, the focus is on their offense. Emphasis on punishment and accountability completely overshadows the social welfare model, and the traditional perceptions of delinquents as youth who need space to reform directly contrast with the current view that convicted juveniles are responsible for their crimes (Zimring, 1998).

A "get tough" approach to juvenile justice gained stride in the 1980s, as "macro-structural, economic, and racial demographic changes and an increase in gun violence" provided an ideal environment for the adoption of harsh policies (Bishop & Feld, 2012, p. 904). The rise in youth gun violence was particularly impactful in political motivations to transform juvenile justice policy (Feld, 1999). Juveniles convicted of criminal activity were virtually portrayed as menacing, cruel, and morally impoverished "super-predators" who were predicted to reach 270,000 by 2010 (Dilulio, 1995). Politicians and political scientists drove public fears of this "demographic crime bomb" (Fox, 1996), focusing on violent gun crime to advocate for "get tough" policies. Consequently, many US legislatures amended their juvenile codes to prioritize punishment, accountability, and public safety, enacting sentencing guidelines and mandatory minimums (Bishop, 2006) that applied principles of proportionality to rationalize sentencing decisions, demonstrate legislative toughness, and increase the severity of sanctions (Bishop & Feld, 2012). By the end of the twentieth century, the court's historical inclusiveness (i.e., encompassing those convicted of delinquency, status offenses, and pre-delinquents) relinquished to "front end" diversion policies and exclusionary "back end" transfer policies (Bishop & Feld, 2012). Consequently, the observable disjunction between the implementation of juvenile justice practices and written juvenile law and policy prompted systemic reforms.

A Shift to Humane Practices

The JJS's excessive reliance on harmful and punitive measures in response to youth offenses resulted in the need for more humane and empirically backed practices (Bishop & Feld, 2012). Although some states continued to expand punitive measures across issues related to juvenile justice, other jurisdictions adopted new policies and practices to move away from punitive reforms with a newfound focus on rehabilitation, prevention, and diversion. Several developments appear to have driven the shift to more humane practices, including the significant drop in youth violence, evidence of wide-ranging public support for prevention and treatment programs (Cullen et al., 2000; Moon et al., 2000), advances in social science research on effective treatment methodologies (Greenwood & Turner, 2011; MacKenzie & Freeland, 2011), and the development of juvenile advocacy groups (Bishop & Feld, 2012).

Worth noting, the Juvenile Justice and Delinquency Prevention Act (JJDPA) was enacted in 1974, yielding numerous provisions whose influence remains pertinent today. The JJDPA aimed to make certain that states upheld shared standards for the treatment of youth in the justice system across the country (Coalition for Juvenile Justice, 2018). This Act established two protections: a ban on youth incarceration for status offenses (i.e., noncriminal adult conduct) and a mandate that juveniles have sight and sound separation from incarcerated adults. Through subsequent reauthorization, the Act expanded to protect against housing youth in adult facilities while anticipating trial and required that states address disproportionate minority contact.

Nevertheless, Congress passed the Juvenile Justice Reform Act (JJRA) in 2018 to update the former, placing additional focus on de-incarceration efforts and the reduction of juvenile contact with the criminal justice system. Under this new Act, youth violating a valid court order can be detained for up to 7 days if found necessary. However, the detainment order must (1) identify the violated court order; (2) state the basis for deciding that there is reasonable cause to believe that an individual convicted of a status offense has violated such an order; (3) include fact findings showing that there is no appropriate less restrictive alternative available to placement in a secure facility, with consideration of the juveniles best interest; and (4) specify the amount of time the individual shall remain in a secure facility, including a release plan. Although policies and practices vary by state, juvenile justice reforms have been implemented to address issues regarding youth incarceration.

State officials have persistently sought to reduce youth contact with the criminal legal system and endorsed modifications to lengthy prison terms for young defendants (Porter, 2017). Within the past decade, at least 19 states (e.g., Colorado, Utah, and South Dakota) have prohibited life sentences without parole for juveniles. For example, through *Senate Bill 140*, South Dakota barred juvenile life without parole as a sentencing option, eliminating all life sentences for defendants younger than 18 at the time of their crime. Similarly, Louisiana and South Carolina increased the age of criminal responsibility for juvenile defendants through *Senate Bill 324* and *Senate Bill 916*, respectively. Although alternative mechanisms can result in the transfer of juveniles to adult court, 43 states have fixed the upper limit of juvenile court jurisdiction to 17 years old. Lastly, through *House Bill 95*, states like Vermont limit prosecutorial discretion in charging juvenile defendants as adults. However, multiple states still authorize prosecutorial discretion to adjudicate youth in criminal court, and age requirements range depending on charge type. While the proliferation of these developments provides hope for continued advances toward more humane juvenile justice practices, their establishment has created unanticipated *side effects* that this chapter seeks to acknowledge.

Ultimately, the JJS has encountered multiple shifts in philosophies, ranging from (1) the system's initial emphasis on nonpunitive and rehabilitative responses; (2) the "get-tough" period emphasizing retribution and harsh sanctions to youth violence (e.g., zero-tolerance policies); and (3) the most recent emphasis on the importance of humane, empirically backed, and youth-specific practices (e.g., rehabilitation, prevention, and diversion programs; Bishop & Feld, 2012; National Research Council, 2001). While the success of each philosophy has varied, each shift in reform intended to improve the JJS, whether through limiting youth contact with the formal justice system, implementing harsh policies in public settings to deter future offenses, or establishing alternative programs for those convicted of repeat offenses. Nevertheless, each shift in philosophy has led to unanticipated side effects that have impacted youth and their likelihood of encountering and being harmed by the justice system.

Side Effects of Shifts in JJS Reforem

Scholars underline the complexity of organizational systems, like the JJS, as they are multilevel and constructed of interacting processes (Braun et al., 2022; Kozlowski & Klein, 2000). For instance, the JJS comprises multiple stages, including referral, intake/diversion, transfer, detention, adjudication, disposition, corrections, and aftercare. *Organizational interventions* are implemented at every stage of the JJS, encompassing all deliberate changes in policies, programs, procedures, or systems anticipated to alter employee mindsets or behaviors (Watts et al., 2022). Generally, organizational interventions are employed to yield a positive influence on specific processes (Braun et al., 2022), such as the implementation of rehabilitative treatment programs in juvenile justice. However, side effects may occur through such interventions, altering processes and outcomes not intentionally targeted (Watts et al., 2021). Side effects comprise unforeseen changes in some secondary criteria, ranging from "hard" behavioral, performative, or organizational outcomes to "soft" attitudinal, cognitive, and health outcomes (Watts et al., 2022). These events differ from those in which an intervention fails to initiate an intended change in a primary criterion of interest (i.e., a failed organizational intervention). Some may consider failed interventions as unintended consequences (e.g., a training program's failure to advance safety communication), but they distinctly differ from side effects. Whether explicitly labeled as such, scholars document a multitude of side effects through the different shifts in JJS policy, reflecting the priorities at the time. To demonstrate the practical significance of developing a greater understanding of side effects within the JJS, the following sections discuss noteworthy examples that resulted from a range of organizational interventions (e.g., the school-to-prison pipeline, net-widening, and difficulties addressing gun violence).

School-to-Prison Pipeline

A preceding example of side effects stemming from the JJS's prioritization of retributive responses to rising youth violence is the development of the "School-to-Prison Pipeline." Countering the surge in juvenile violence at the end of the twentieth century, states and schools adopted zero-tolerance policies and hired School Resource Officers (Pinard, 2003; Redding & Shalf, 2001). Zero-tolerance policies and practices that criminalize student misbehavior and respond with punitive consequences strengthen this pipeline, resulting in the removal and arrest of thousands of youths and their transfer to the JJS (Bishop & Feld, 2012; Ruiz, 2016).

Scholars thoroughly document this pipeline in the state of Texas. In response to fears regarding school violence in the 1990s, the Texas Federation of Teachers and the State Board of Education ordered school discipline policies (Fowler et al., 2019). Subsequently, the Texas legislature passed an education bill in 1995 that included zero-tolerance measures, and school districts increased their own measures so that exclusion was allowed for low- and high-level behavior in schools. Consequently, lawmakers implemented punitive school actions across the state that (1) removed students from their classrooms (e.g., through suspensions, expulsions, and alternative placements) and (2) criminalized misconduct resulting in school-based ticketing and arrests that drive students (i.e., disproportionately those of color and special education) out of the state's schools, diminishing their chances of academic success and increasing their risk of subsequent JJS involvement (Fowler, n.d.). Regarding suspensions and expulsions in Texas public schools, one national study found that more than half of the students (60.0%) in grades 7 through 12 received some form of exclusionary discipline referral (i.e., suspension or expulsion) from 2000 to 2009 (Fowler, n.d.). Relatedly, most (97.0%) Texas school officials had discretion to employ these disciplinary actions rather than suspensions or expulsions mandated by state law. Consequently, receiving a discretionary disciplinary action tripled the probability of JJS contact in the following school year.

Regarding school-based arrests and ticketing, most arrests are for misdemeanor offenses (e.g., theft and simple assault). However, students of color and students with disabilities continue to be overrepresented in exclusionary discipline, resulting in their disproportionate contact with the JJS (Fowler et al., 2019). In this "get-tough" era, the JJS upheld the philosophy that to address crime, policies must be harsh on crime (Bishop, 2006; Bishop & Feld, 2012). While Texas provides one example in which the JJS's retributive goals yielded unforeseen side effects, legislatures across all 50 states enacted similar school policies to address delinquency and violence, leading to the development of the school-to-prison pipeline.

Net-Widening

Another example of side effects unintentionally produced from shifts in juvenile justice policy is "net-widening." This phenomenon comprises the implementation of prevention and early intervention programs for youth (i.e., often referred to as diversion programs), which have unexpectedly drawn more youth into contact with juvenile justice agencies to their detriment (Prichard, 2010). These diversion programs and policies received widespread attention during the JJS's shift to more humane practices (i.e., in the early 1990s), with the new goal of reducing youth exposure to traditional (i.e., legal) system processing. Unexpectedly, rather than decrease the number of juveniles formally processed through the JJS, prevention and early intervention policies yield the opposite effect, subjecting more juveniles to formal system intervention (Macallair & Males, 2004; Macallair & Roche, 2001). Addressing these net-widening side effects is important; left unaddressed, the limited resources are diverted away from youth in most need of interventions to those who may require no intervention at all. Throughout the past few decades, empirical work shows that approximately 70.0% of youth arrested one time never encounter the JJS again. This suggests that the state can reach a 70.0% success rate with first-time juveniles convicted of criminal activity by taking no action. By reducing net-widening, empirical work underlines that systems can better endorse public safety and improve their effectiveness (Macallair & Males, 2004). Notably, programs designed for those in personal crises should be voluntary and unassociated with the JJS. Furthermore, the favored models for effective justice-system intervention are those reaching high-risk youth who have been involved with the system three or more times. Some argue that the quantity of total contact points with the JJS is the only reliable method of predicting the risk of subsequent system involvement.

Scholars document the concept of net-widening in San Francisco, California (Macallair & Males, 2004). During the late 1990s, the city launched a significant undertaking to enforce juvenile justice reform to reduce San Francisco's traditional reliance on custodial detention and reallocate resources to community-based youth programs. This reform work was important to expunge the prior stigmatization that followed a delinquent identity, prevent the acceleration of further JJS involvement, and reduce overcrowding of juveniles in detention facilities. Approximately $20 million of state and federal funding went to the establishment of new prevention and diversion programs targeting individuals convicted of first-time and nonserious crimes (e.g., home-based supervision and day treatment programs). Reflecting the San Francisco Juvenile Justice Comprehensive Action Plan of 1944, the reform efforts established a decentralized intake system to refer youth to community-based services and reduce unnecessary detention. Contrary to the anticipated results, the reform efforts yielded increases in the processing of juveniles convicted of criminal activity who were previously excluded from the JJS, with the most substantial impact on minority females, reflecting "net widening" side effects. This example is particularly disturbing given the overarching consensus on the need for systematic reform and the unintended side effects disproportionately harming minority youth.

Difficulties Addressing Gun Violence

The final example of side effects stemming from the JJS's shift to more humane practices concerns cases of gun violence in the United States. Across jurisdictions, various juvenile justice laws were implemented with the objective of reducing juvenile contact with the criminal legal system (Prichard, 2010). Most notably, the JJRA passed in 2018 with the intention of reducing youth contact with the criminal justice system. For instance, some jurisdictions increased the age of juvenile defendants and altered the length of sentences for juveniles. In some jurisdictions, however, the implementation of JJRA laws yields unforeseen difficulties in addressing gun violence. Consequently, in some jurisdictions juveniles are recruited to be shooters in violent gun crimes because it is known that if caught, they will be adjudicated in the JJS for lengthier periods.

Cambridge, Maryland, is one city encountering side effects such as these (Spy & WHCP Community Radio, 2023). State legislatures passed the Juvenile Justice Reform Act of 2022 with the goal of protecting the rights of children. Specifically, the Act prohibited the detainment of youth under 13 years old after committing most crimes (i.e., including assault) to deter youth from formal processing, protect their due process rights, protect against deceiving interrogation methods, limit solitary confinement and restraints, and prevent issues regarding long separation from their families. Unprecedently, this Act yielded a rise in auto theft and weapon possession by juveniles. The Chief of Police in Cambridge noted that the law has resulted in gangs' recruitment of children, as juveniles now viewed themselves as free to commit serious crimes without consequences. Until the state lawmakers address these side effects through a reform bill, these unexpected crime patterns will likely persist.

The aforementioned examples (e.g., the school-to-prison pipeline, net-widening, and difficulties addressing gun violence) comprise just a few scenarios of side effects associated with shifts in JJS philosophies and reforms. These examples underline the pattern of reactive approaches to JJS reform, as states tend to identify side effects after they occur rather than before policy implementation. Applying process theory to the understanding of JJS interventions offers a promising solution to the detection of side effects prior to formal implementation.

Process Theory

Process theory provides a framework for understanding organizational side effects (Braun et al., 2022). Process theories place focus on organizational actors and their actions, with the goal of articulating *why* and *how* they perform actions (i.e., affectively, cognitively, behaviorally, and socially) across contexts toward goal completion (i.e., processes; Braun et al., 2022; Macy & Willer, 2002; Strauss & Grand, 2022). Contrary to alternative organizational frameworks that seek to explain covariance relationships, process theory focuses on specifying "the underlying process mechanisms or rules driving system phenomena" (Kozlowski, 2022, p. 6). This theory assesses how system phenomena develop, evolve, or shift over time, often across multiple entity levels (i.e., micro, meso, macro). Process theory is particularly useful in detecting the process mechanisms responsible for the visible series of actions (Kozlowski, 2022); the objective underlying process theory is to clarify why each employee (i.e., actor) in a focal system executes a "particular action at a particular time in a particular way" (Braun et al., 2022, p. 5). While not the focus of this chapter, it is helpful to note that computational modeling encompasses an emergent method supporting process theory (i.e., see Braun et al., 2022; Kozlowski, 2022).

A process approach has many benefits for conceptualizing and implementing organizational interventions and the negative outcomes that stem from such interventions (Braun et al., 2022). Process theory's alignment with the observable actions performed by actors provides an avenue to the processes targeted by interventions (Braun et al., 2022; Macy & Willer, 2002; Strauss & Grand, 2022). Ultimately, using process approaches to examine the effectiveness of JJS reforms will aid in detecting, mitigating, and/or eliminating side effects.

Process Theory's Application to JJS Reforms

The presented JJS side effects were unanticipated because the reforms lacked exactness and specificity regarding *how, why, when,* and *which* processes needed modification at critical times. Each organizational intervention aimed to broadly reduce juvenile contact with the justice system, whether through prevention and early intervention (i.e., diversion) programs, punitive consequences (e.g., zero-tolerance policies), or changes in sentence length for violent offenses. However, these interventions failed to target specified actions at specified time points and, thus, could not to anticipate the side effects resulting from the altering of such tangential processes. Consequently, the implemented JJS interventions yielded increases in youth crime, disproportionate punitiveness targeting minorities and disabled individuals, and the misallocation of resources toward diversion programs that unsuccessfully reintegrated youth after their justice-system encounters (Bishop & Feld, 2012; Macallair & Males, 2004; Macallair & Roche, 2001).

The association linking process theory and action holds direct benefits for JJS reform efforts and their outcomes. As Braun et al. (2022) successfully articulate, process theories can seamlessly translate into interventions that target explicit actions in explicit contexts during related performance incidents. By applying a process theory framework to the development of JJS interventions and focusing on actions, policymakers can more easily assess the number and severity of potential side effects to safeguard youth from further harm and reduce their likelihood of future involvement with the criminal legal system (Watts et al., 2021). By taking a process approach, researchers and policymakers alike can become more informed of the types of processes potentially influenced by their interventions (Braun et al., 2022). Nevertheless, for theory and research to be maximally useful in understanding the consequences related to JJS reforms, more attention and effort must be placed on understanding the processes before, during, and after the intervention takes place. Most importantly, using process theory to understand the side effects of past JJS interventions may help prevent harmful outcomes for youth moving forward.

Recommendations for Identifying JJS Side Effects

The side effects of interventions (e.g., JJS reforms) are often ignored or overlooked due to organizational complexity and the typical methods of conducting empirical assessments, hindered by limitations, such as resource constraints, lack of accountability, and simplification bias (Watts et al., 2022). Therefore, it is important to discuss the existing strategies for advancing empirical attention toward understanding JJS intervention-associated side effects (e.g., posing different questions, designing reporting systems, incentivizing research, determining effect-size guidelines, disseminating known side effects, and educating future scholars). While these strategies cannot solve every consequence stemming from shifts in the JJS philosophies and reform interventions mentioned previously, the widespread understanding and adoption of such strategies can aid policymaker and scholar conceptualizations of how to analyze, disseminate, and monitor unanticipated side effects. First, scholars and policymakers may advance their examination and assessment of the JJS's side effects by posing different research questions that are utilized to strategize reform interventions (Watts et al., 2022). The possibility of side effects must be considered at the planning stages of interventions; otherwise, individuals can only respond post-implementation (Watts et al., 2022). For instance, rather than ask: "Do zero-tolerance policies reduce youth violence in schools?" one could begin anticipating side effects of the intervention, stating, "If we implement zero-tolerance policies to address youth violence, how might it also affect their subsequent involvement in the JJS?" By adjusting the research questions, practitioners and academics can better forecast the potential consequences stemming from different intervention strategies and identify if any are worth pursuing.

Following the identification of side effects concerning JJS intervention, some evaluative infrastructure is needed to capture the negative events. One example of this may be a state database that periodically records, stores, and monitors the outcomes of early intervention policies to ensure youth are receiving the services they need to reintegrate. Developing one universal database to track the implementation of JJS interventions, the unanticipated outcomes of the interventions, and the decisions regarding *how* the organization implemented each intervention likely comes with great challenges (Watts et al., 2022). Nevertheless, the compilation of such information is pivotal for identifying whether side effects result from specific interventions or from the individual characteristics of the context in which implementation occurred.

Another strategy for encouraging research on the effectiveness of JJS interventions is to form relationships with juvenile justice agencies and express persistent interest in safeguarding juveniles from potential side effects. Strategies for aggregating information about such side effects include qualitative and quantitative post-intervention methods, process evaluations, and conducting follow-up surveys to assess any adverse incidents. Lastly, all known side effects of organizational interventions should be advertised and widely disseminated through publicly accessible channels (Watts et al., 2022). The advertisement of known side effects is particularly important for JJS reforms, as the impact of such interventions may place youth at increased risk of subsequent system involvement, hinder their educational success, and cause harm to their physical and mental states (Bishop & Feld, 2012; Macallair & Roche, 2001; Macallair & Males, 2004; Ruiz, 2016). Ultimately, learning to anticipate, assess, and report JJS reform side effects and identify the circumstances in which they are most likely to occur should be the focus for future policymakers and scholars.

Conclusion

Empirical research examining intervention-associated side effects related to juvenile justice is sparse. Even less work examines a process theory application to the detection of related organizational side effects. While this chapter highlighted three salient examples pertaining to shifts in JJS philosophy, additional side effects remain to be discovered and empirically assessed. Future research is needed to establish the severity and frequency of JJS side effects associated with policy reform, as well as the conditions under which these side effects are most likely to surface. Optimistically, further development of when and why side effects are associated with JJS reform efforts will yield more sophisticated mechanisms of intervention to detect, eliminate, compensate for, and reduce potential side effects while increasing the likelihood of positive outcomes (Watts et al., 2022). A process theory approach to better anticipate, monitor, and understand potential side effects of JJS reforms *before* they become an issue is essential to avoid negative outcomes in the future. However, until widespread understanding and application of this theory to the detection of JJS side effects, they will likely persist and go undetected, harming youth's ability to rehabilitate and, therefore, increasing their likelihood of future system involvement.

References

Bishop, D. M. (2006). Public opinion and juvenile justice policy: Myths and misconceptions. *Criminology & Public Policy, 5*, 653–664.

Bishop, D. M., & Feld, B. C. (2012). Trends in juvenile justice policy and practice. In *The Oxford handbook of juvenile crime and juvenile justice*. Oxford University Press.

Braun, M. T., Kuljanin, G., Grand, J. A., Kozlowski, S. W., & Chao, G. T. (2022). The power of process theories to better understand and detect consequences of organizational interventions. *Industrial and Organizational Psychology, 15*(1), 99–104.

Coalition for Juvenile Justice. (2018, December 13). *Summary of the Juvenile Justice Reform Act of 2018*. https://www.juvjustice.org/sites/default/files/resource-files/Summary%20of%20the%20Juvenile%20Justice%20Reform%20Act%20of%202018.pdf

Cullen, F. T., Fisher, B. S., & Applegate, B. K. (2000). Public opinion about punishment and corrections. *Crime and Justice, 27*, 1–79.

Dilulio, J. (1995). The coming of the super-predators. *The Weekly Standard, 1*(11), 23.

Feld, B. C. (1999). *Bad kids: Race and the transformation of the juvenile court*. Oxford University Press.

Fowler, D. (n.d.). *The Texas School-to-Prison Pipeline*. https://www.texasappleseed.org/sites/default/files/152-STPP-FactSheet.pdf

Fowler, D., Sloan, M., & Stone, E. (2019). Making the case for a school-and-neighborhood desegregation approach to deconstructing the school-to-prison pipeline. *UALR L. Rev., 42*, 723.

Fox, J. A. (1996). *Trends in juvenile violence: A report to the United States Attorney General on current and future rates of juvenile offending*. US Department of Justice, Bureau of Justice Statistics.

Greenwood, P. W., & Turner, S. (2011). Probation and other noninstitutional treatment: The evidence is in. In *The Oxford handbook of juvenile crime and juvenile justice*. Oxford University Press.

Kozlowski, S. W. J. (2022). The data revolution and the interplay between theory and data. In K. R. Murphy (Ed.), *Data, methods, and theory in the organizational sciences: A new synthesis*. Routledge.

Kozlowski, S. W. J., & Klein, K. J. (2000). A multilevel approach to theory and research in organizations: Contextual, temporal, and emergent processes. In K. J. Klein & S. W. J. Kozlowski (Eds.), *Multilevel theory, research, and methods in organizations: Foundations, extensions, and new directions* (pp. 3–90). Jossey-Bass.

Macallair, D., & Males, M. (2004). A failure of good intentions: An analysis of juvenile justice reform in San Francisco during the 1990s. *Review of Policy Research, 21*(1), 63–78.

Macallair, D., & Roche, T. (2001). *Widening the net in juvenile justice and the dangers of prevention and early intervention*. http://www.cjcj.org/files/widening.pdf

MacKenzie, D. L., & Freeland, R. (2011). Examining the effectiveness of juvenile residential programs. In *The Oxford handbook of juvenile crime and juvenile justice*. Oxford University Press.

Macy, M. W., & Willer, R. (2002). From factors to actors: Computational sociology and agent-based modeling. *Annual Review of Sociology, 28*(1), 143–166.

Moon, M. M., Sundt, J. L., Cullen, F. T., & Wright, J. P. (2000). Is child saving dead? Public support for juvenile rehabilitation. *Crime & Delinquency, 46*(1), 38–60.

National Research Council. (2001). *Juvenile crime, juvenile justice*. National Academies Press.

Pinard, M. (2003). From the classroom to the courtroom: Reassessing Fourth Amendment standards in public school searches involving law enforcement authorities. *Ariz. L. Rev., 45*, 1067.

Platt, A. M. (1977). *The child savers: The invention of delinquency*. University of Chicago Press.

Porter, N. D. (2017). *State advances in criminal justice reform, 2016*. The Sentencing Project. https://www.sentencingproject.org/app/uploads/2022/08/State-Advances-in-Criminal-Justice-Reform-2016-1.pdf

Prichard, J. (2010). Net-widening and the diversion of young people from court: A longitudinal analysis with implications for restorative justice. *Australian & New Zealand Journal of Criminology, 43*(1), 112–129.

Redding, R. E., & Shalf, S. M. (2001). The legal context of school violence: The effectiveness of federal, state, and local law enforcement efforts to reduce gun violence in schools. *Law & Policy, 23*(3), 297–343.

Ruiz, R. R. (2016). School-to-prison pipeline: An evaluation of zero tolerance policies and their alternatives. *Houston Law Review, 54*, 803.

Ryerson, E. (1978). *The best-laid plans: America's juvenile court experiment* (p. 137). Hill and Wang.

Spy, & WHCP Community Radio. (2023, October 13). *The unintended consequences of juvenile justice reform: A chat with Cambridge Chief Justin Todd.* https://chestertownspy.org/2023/10/13/the-unintended-consequences-of-juvenile-justice-reform-a-chat-with-cambridge-chief-justin-todd/

Strauss, J. A., & Grand, J. A. (2022). Applying systems science to advance research on team phenomena. In J. Dulebohn, B. Murray, & D. Stone (Eds.), *Managing team centricity in modern organizations*. IAP.

Tanenhaus, D. S. (2004). *Juvenile justice in the making*. Oxford University Press.

Watts, L. L., Gray, B. E., & Medeiros, K. E. (2021). Side effects associated with organizational interventions: A perspective. *Industrial and Organizational Psychology: Perspectives on Science and Practice. 15(1)*, 76–94.

Watts, L. L., Gray, B. E., & Medeiros, K. E. (2022). Side effects associated with organizational interventions: A perspective. *Industrial and Organizational Psychology, 15*(1), 76–94.

Zimring, F. E. (1998). Toward a jurisprudence of youth violence. *Crime and Justice, 24*, 477–501.

Chapter 6
An Application of Structuration Theory to Criminal Organizations

Ghady Hbeilini

Introduction

Criminal organizations, and subsequently organized crime, are an issue for most governments and law enforcement agencies in many countries (Naylor, 1995; Okoli & Nwangwu, 2023; Shelley, 1995; Van Duyne, 1995). The threat of criminal organizations largely stems from their multifaceted nature that is associated with the concern of the crime-terror nexus, the interaction between crime and terrorism, thus increasing the threat that organized criminal groups pose overall (Okoli & Nwangwu, 2023; Phillips & Schiele, 2023). However, the study and understanding of criminal organizations is unique as these organizations function through the use of multiple disciplines (Finckenauer, 2005; Kemp, 2001; Robbins, 1990; Southerland & Potter, 1993). For example, their structure, function, and business are similar to legitimate organizations and their economic processes (Finckenauer, 2005; Kemp, 2001; Robbins, 1990; Southerland & Potter, 1993). However, there is an inherent difference between legitimate and illicit organizations by the simple nature of their operations. While legitimate organizations operate within the realm of legitimacy and follow the rule of law, illicit organizations operate outside the rule of law and have their own code of conduct described as criminal behavior (Smith, 1980; Southerland & Potter, 1993; Thompson, 2003; Von Lampe, 2006, 2015). Therefore, this issue requires a multidirectional approach to understand and combat criminal organizations. In other words, to understand the differences between illicit and legitimate organizations, it is necessary to first understand that they are in fact similar in many ways. Establishing their similarities in terms of structure, function, and other

G. Hbeilini (✉)
Sam Houston State University, Department of Crimial Justice and Criminology, Huntsville, TX, USA
e-mail: gxh040@shsu.edu

D. S. Rudes, J. R. Ingram (eds.), *Using Organizational Theory to Study, Explain, and Understand Criminal Legal Organizations*,
https://doi.org/10.1007/978-3-031-66285-0_6

factors, would then seem to be a beneficial approach as it provides a clear and previously established analysis of organizations, giving way to the expansion upon their differences.

As such, scholars regularly utilize various frameworks to analyze organized criminal groups; these frameworks include but are not limited to, psychology (Robles-Mendoza, 2023), business and economics (Cavgias et al., 2023; Mocetti & Rizzica, 2023), security studies (Okoli & Nwangwu, 2023; Phillips & Schiele, 2023), and criminology (Poppi & Ardila, 2023; Zabyelina, 2023). Other scholars also explored the possibilities of studying criminal organizations and have since advocated for the use of interdisciplinary approaches using organizations theory (Southerland & Potter, 1993; Von Lampe, 2006).

Southerland and Potter (1993) were among the first to apply an organizational perspective to study and understand organized crime. While their study focused more on the structural components of criminal organizations, they base their approach on Smith's (1980) initial concept of a spectrum based theory of enterprise that mentions and encourages the need to evaluate organized crime from an interdisciplinary lens given its unique nature involving a complex entanglement of crime, business and economy, psychology, organizations, and politics, among other facets. Incorporating organizational theory as a framework to understand the complexity of organized crime, however, poses specific advantages such as identifying key individuals or structures within the organization that are crucial for its operations, or the manner through which they exert control over people and places (Balsamo, 2006; Battisti et al., 2022a, b; Block, 2017; Von Lampe, 2006).

This chapter specifically discusses the application of organization sciences and theory to understand criminal organizations. It also highlights the importance of examining this issue from a multidisciplinary perspective that integrates both the organizational and criminological literature. The key to combating criminal organizations and organized crime is to first understand them in terms of their structure and function, and subsequently identify ways to address them (Smith, 1980; Southerland & Potter, 1993; Thompson, 2003; Von Lampe, 2006, 2015). To aid in such an endeavor, this chapter seeks to expand the knowledge of the operational and structural components of organizations in terms of applicable organizational theory. Specifically, this chapter seeks to apply Giddens' (1984) structuration theory which considers that the concepts of structure and agency are two sides of the same coin and must both be considered to understand the competing perspectives of macro-micro views, thus enabling a subsequent understanding of organizational behavior (Turner, 1986; Yates, 1997).

Therefore, examining the similarities between legitimate organizations and illicit organizations may prove beneficial given the advantages gained by understanding structure, function, agency, and other sub-factors. Criminal organizations have been a challenge to national and international law enforcement entities since their inception. While there has been great effort in understanding their structure and function, very scarce research has attempted to utilize a theoretical framework that encompasses both these aspects, while taking into consideration criminal organizations as organizational entities as opposed to simply criminal entities.

This chapter seeks to fill this gap in the literature by analyzing criminal organizations from an organizational perspective using Giddens' structuration theory and institutional forms. By applying this framework to the Sicilian Mafia, this chapter aims to provide the utility of a multidisciplinary approach, particularly utilizing an organizational science approach, to understand and combat criminal organizations. The implications of the findings following the case study are discussed and emphasized by addressing the central question of this endeavor (Southerland & Potter, 1993). For example, legitimate organizations improve their development and achieve their goals by addressing any shortcomings that their structure or function presented. Similarly, criminal organizations optimize their performance and development by altering their structure, function, and agency, and other sub-factors based on prior experiences, goal attainment, and, in this case, organization persistence (Balsamo, 2006; Battisti et al., 2022a, b; Kleinbaum et al., 2013; Southerland & Potter, 1993). It is this subsequent understanding that will make way for the elaboration on the differences which will, in turn, lead to policy recommendations and responses to organized crime, thus facilitating tackling such a pervasive problem. As such, the main questions addressed in this book chapter are:

1. How are illicit organizations defined from an organizational lens?

   How can Giddens' structuration theory be applied to understand the structure and functioning of criminal organizations?

   (a) How do organized crime groups compare to legal organizations in this context?
   (b) How do criminal organizations behave according to their organizational characteristics?

2. What are the main points that can be drawn from such an approach to aid in addressing organized crime?

To address these questions, it is necessary to first present the definition of organized crime, followed by its differentiation as criminal organizations. It is also necessary to present the theoretical framework, structuration theory (Giddens, 1984), to make way for a case study that seeks to analyze the Sicilian Mafia (also known as Cosa Nostra) through an organizational lens. Finally, this chapter concludes with a discussion presenting the advantages and implications of these findings.

Literature Review

According to the United Nations Convention against Transnational Organized Crime (2000), an organized criminal group is defined using the following four criteria: (1) a structured group of three or more persons; (2) the group exists for a period of time; (3) the group acts in unison with the goal of committing at least one serious crime; and (4) with the goal of attaining (either directly or indirectly) a material, usually financial, benefit (Kemp, 2001). While this definition accounts for some factors of organized crime, there are other facets that have been developed since there is no single definition that is universally used (Finckenauer, 2005; Hagan, 2006). Historically, for example, organized crime is used synonymously and solely to describe the Italian Mafia when in fact it is a term that encompasses many Transnational or Drug Trafficking Organizations, or even smaller groups that fit the descriptions mentioned above (Finckenauer, 2005; Kemp, 2001).

Finckenauer (2005) provides ample information on the different contributors to the definition of organized crime. First, he presents certain elements that must be present to not only define organized crime, but also to differentiate it from other types of criminal activity that have been associated with it. Therefore, his framework included the elements of ideology (or lack thereof) to separate organized crime from terrorism despite their occasional crossovers, structured and organized hierarchy, continuity, violence and use of force, restricted membership, illegal enterprises, infiltration of legitimate businesses, and corruption (Finckenauer, 2005). While each of these concepts has its specific definition, the complexity in defining organized crime lies in the entities that seek to combat it. For example, since organized crime affects laws, investigations, research, and so much more, each of these entities defines it in a manner that fits its respective needs. Flanigan (2012) presents evidence that delineates the idea of labeling cartels as terrorists. The advantages for law enforcement of applying the definition of terrorists and terrorism to the Mexican cartels is then to increase the severity of sanctions and punishments in their fight against organized crime (Flanigan, 2012). As such, regarding the definition of organized crime, the two most important notions to keep in mind is the role that definitions play in the fight against criminal organizations, and the importance of understanding the contextual factors that have contributed to that specific definition, thus allowing for a more informative approach to understand and address organized crime.

Organized Crime as Criminal Organizations

The definition of organized crime, as has been mentioned, is contingent on many aspects, must meet a number of conditions, and varies based on these criteria (Finckenauer, 2005). For the purposes of this chapter, however, the definition of organized crime and subsequently criminal organizations is based on the aspects and conditions that fall in line with an organizational perspective. Southerland and Potter (1993) examine organized crime and criminal organizations by disregarding the controversies existing in the literature. Instead, they identify criminal enterprises that fit into their criteria of production/distribution of goods and services to make profit through the illicit market, a consumer population providing a constant demand for these goods, and some illegal nature to the core aspect of the enterprise.

However, Southerland and Potter (1993) apply an organizational lens to criminal organizations and organized crime solely from a structural perspective, taking into account (1) centralization (i.e., an aspect of the organization that is characterized by the degree of vertical and horizontal allocation of authority and decision-making power; vertical centralization is when these responsibilities and decision-making powers are reserved for leaders and higher levels of management within the organization), (2) complexity (i.e., the extent of the division of labor within an organization; meaning how numerous subparts of an organization differentiate among themselves), and (3) formalization (i.e., an aspect that is characterized by the explicitness of operating rules and procedures in the organization that dictate how members should behave) as core characteristics of organizational structure. This is based on Robbins' (1990) understanding of organizational structure that requires formal control and mechanisms that are guiding an organization and how it allocates work (Child, 1973; Dalton et al., 1980; Lewis, 2006). Additionally, their conclusions were drawn prior to the establishment of a more universal definition of organized crime, thus possibly excluding the contextual factors of definition that play a role in defining and addressing criminal organizations (Finckenauer, 2005; Kemp, 2001; Southerland & Potter, 1993).

Structural Aspects

Aside from the criminal aspect, criminal organizations do not differ much when compared to legal organizations. In fact, they share many characteristics, so much so that, when compared to legitimate organizations, similar structural characteristics exist (Southerland & Potter, 1993). In their argument, Southerland & Potter explain how criminal organizations resemble legitimate ones in terms of centralization, complexity, formalization, and hierarchy. Centralization reflects the extent of vertical (i.e., clear definition of leadership and top down filtration of management influence) and horizontal (i.e., a flat structure that has few levels of management) delegation of responsibilities in the organization, as well as the level of authority needed for decision-making regarding the actions taken and issues dealt with in the organization. Criminal organizations centralize their most major and impactful decisions, as well as their information at the top, in more of a vertical organization. This is to ensure proper hierarchical functioning, implement favorable security practices, and prevent any leaks that could lead to member or, more importantly, leadership arrest (Andrews et al., 2009; Hage & Aiken, 1970; Mansfield, 1973; Moch & Morse, 1977; Southerland & Potter, 1993). These aspects still exist in criminal organizations as there is a clear centralization of structure between leadership and members, playing a role in current organized crime (Carpenter, 2009; Chatagnier et al., 2012).

Another aspect of organizational structure examined in criminal organizations that mirrors legitimate ones is complexity. While complexity looks at the extent of division of labor among members of an organizations, it also describes organizations as either horizontal or vertical by either having functional task units at the same level or multiple levels of managerial tasks (Dooley, 2002; Hage & Aiken, 1970; Southerland & Potter, 1993). At the time, Southerland & Potter described criminal organizations as having simple structures given the absence of the need of sophisticated skills or education to carry out tasks, and the absence of specializations and departmentalization, both of which play a role in creating an organization's sub-units. However, criminal enterprises and organizations are constantly and significantly expanding their operations. While they may not yet have many specific specializations, criminal organizations such as cartels and terrorist groups repeatedly exhibit sophisticated skills in the deployment of their attacks and tactics (Bunker & Sullivan, 2021; Hoenig, 2014), as well as the creation of specialized sub-units with specific tasks geared towards completing a particular aim of the organization (Carpenter, 2009).

Finally, discussing the operating rules and procedures of an organization, the final structural characteristic is that of formalization. According to Southerland & Potter, organized criminal groups are able to show a certain degree of formalization such as the level of purity that is expected of their drug supplies or in terms of the manner through which their operations are being conducted (Perrow, 1967; Pugh et al., 1969; Southerland & Potter, 1993). Another aspect to formalization is that of programs aimed at training newly recruited individuals for acceptance into the organization or promotion (Perrow, 1967). Currently, there are many programs that criminal organizations use to train their recruits (Wainwright, 2016). Terrorist organizations may recruit from other looser social network organizations to bolster their ranks, with particular attention being drawn on their process of decision-making. For example, Chatagnier et al. (2012) highlight the important factors that go into terrorist leadership decisions and discuss a form of unspoken "code" that plays a role in these discretionary practices (Chatagnier et al., 2012; Milward & Raab, 2006).

Criminal Organizations: Entrepreneurial Nature and Functioning

Given that a major component of analyzing organized crime through an organizational perspective relies on the structural aspect, it would be insightful to also define and understand criminal organizations from their entrepreneurial and functional nature as well as their similarities where this is concerned. Organized crime, and subsequently, criminal organizations have been well known for having a business aspect to their day-to-day functions (Milward & Raab, 2006; Smith, 1980; Von Lampe, 2015; Wainwright, 2016). Though it may not have been as visible or explorable in past years, Klaus von Lampe (2015) was able to delineate the organized approach some types of criminal organizations take to conduct their operations. Von Lampe focused on cocaine trafficking as one of his main examples in studying organized crime, bringing to light how criminal Drug Trafficking Organizations (DTOs), for example, begin first by harvesting coca leaves, produce cocaine, transport certain intermediary products, proceed to smuggle cocaine to the desired location, and concludes with wholesale and retail distribution (Thompson, 2003; Von Lampe, 2015).

Interestingly enough, when compared to the regular functioning of some legitimate organizations, such as pharmaceutical companies, their supply chains sound similar to that of DTOs. Pharmaceutical supply chains involve the attainment of base materials to then produce the desired medication, transport the end product to specific locations for wholesale distribution to be sold to patients as prescribed (Jaberidoost et al., 2013; Shah, 2004). The difference between pharmaceutical companies and DTOs lies in the illegal nature of the material being produced and sold, and in the illegal nature of operation. Therefore, perhaps the difference between organizations and criminal organizations is simply the presence of the aspect of "criminal activity" as both seek to maximize profit-making opportunities off of the manufacturing and distribution of certain goods (Block, 2017; Perrow, 1986; Schelling, 1971; Thompson, 2003; Vold et al., 1998).

Although it is now clear how legitimate and illegitimate enterprises are similar (Block, 2017; Schelling, 1971; Von Lampe, 2015), this similarity cannot be described in a simple fashion given the differences in the nature of the activity. As such, Smith (1980) not only established what he referred to as the enterprise spectrum that highlights the commonalities between criminal and legal organizations in terms of their business, but was also able to differentiate between them through a unified perspective that includes both legal and illegal businesses. Smith's assumption begins with identifying enterprise as a spectrum that includes both business and certain types of crime, behavioral theory can be applied to organizations generally, and business specifically, and that conspiracy and ethnicity play a role in organized crime, but are subordinate to a theory of enterprise (Smith, 1980). Therefore, the argument made based on Paragons, Pariahs, and Pirates, a spectrum-based theory of enterprise takes into account the commonality of enterprises instead of the differences suggested in prior theories (i.e., the alien conspiracy notions of organized crime that initially separated crime and business (Smith, 1980)).

The discussion provided by Southerland and Potter (1993) established the centralization and formalization of criminal organizations, but not their complexity. Additionally, they focused largely on structural and contingency factors without delving into the entrepreneurial nature of criminal organizations as presented for example by Smith (1980), and paying little to no attention to aspects such as organizational functioning or climate and culture. Although the arguments and evidence presented by Southerland and Porter provided substantial insight into criminal organizations, they do not establish the effect structure has on function or that of function on structure. Similarly, Smith (1980) provides a perspective on the functioning of criminal organizations without focusing much on the importance of structure. Despite the insight provided, and based on arguments made in both studies (Smith, 1980; Southerland & Potter, 1993) as well as other prior literature (Balsamo, 2006; Battisti et al., 2022a, b; Kleinbaum et al., 2013), it seems that structure and function should be integrated together as both sides of the same coin with a sort of bidirectional influence, thus improving the understanding of criminal organizations from both perspectives. Therefore, the next section briefly examines Giddens' (1984) structuration theory that addresses these shortcomings in prior applications of organizations theory to criminal enterprises. This will then make way for the case study of the Sicilian Mafia and how structuration theory can help fill the gaps mentioned in prior literature and provide novel insight into the understanding of and addressing criminal organizations.

Theoretical Framework

Giddens (1984) introduced structuration theory to present the main divisions that have existed historically between function and structure on one side, which Giddens identified as having shared naturalistic and objectivist perspectives. On the other side, hermeneutics and interpretative sociology; he identified and emphasized the radical difference between the social and natural sciences placing subjectivity at the center of human experience. As these divisions exist, Giddens suggests, structuration theory seeks to move past them by stating that the basic level of social sciences is social practices that are ordered in space and time. Therefore, the theory sees human activities as recursive and reflexive while advocating for a stratification model that considers the body, mediations, and the coherence of the act itself (Giddens, 1984; Turner, 1986; Yates, 1997). For these reasons, structuration theory is important to consider as a theoretical application to understand criminal organizations as it provides the framework to investigate such organizations in a multifaceted perspective, thus expanding on prior work (Southerland & Potter, 1993).

To give further clarity and elaboration on structuration and its elements, it is imperative to first discuss the stratification model of the agent which distinguishes between intentions, motives, and unintended consequences where human behavior is concerned (Giddens, 1984). As such, practical consciousness is introduced and identifies agency as an individual's capability to perform an action rather than the intention behind it. While unintended consequences are integral and examined in various perspectives, they are important to enable tracing events that were initiated by a single circumstance, examining patterns as a result of intentional conduct, and exploring the mechanisms of institutionalized practices' reproduction through unintended consequences (Giddens, 1984; Yates, 1997). Furthermore, drawing on the association between agency and power, Giddens explores the connection between these two elements stating that an agent with agency is involved in the ability to intervene in the environment and in the world to influence specific processes. As such, power is influence, and agency has been identified as the gateway to achieving that sort of power that allows for transformation within the broader organization (Giddens, 1984).

This interaction between an organization providing agents with power and agents using that power to influence change in the organization is then identified by Giddens as the duality of structure. Structures are then perceived as both the medium and the outcome of the conduct that forms social systems as people shape structure, it is the structure that determines what people do and how they act, contributing to system reproduction based on rules and resources (Giddens, 1984; Turner, 1986). Agents are then responsible for reproducing the conditions making action possible by reproducing structural properties. At the same time, unintended consequences and conditions of such actions serve as part of the flow by acting as feedback to further the understanding of the duality of structure. The entirety of the process, however, is done as a form of system integration as it is independent of space and time which differentiates this approach from social integration involving face-to-face interaction (Giddens, 1984; Turner, 1986).

Finally, to focus on the most relevant aspect of structuration theory for the purposes of this chapter, the different forms of institutions (signification, domination, and legitimation) are introduced (Giddens, 1984). These forms arose by dividing rules into different modes of (1) signification which addresses the inferred through the use of structures where agents utilize past experiences to draw out meaning; (2) domination which is also referred to as either authoritative resources which permits agents to exert control over persons, or allocative resources which permits agents to exert control on objects; and (3) legitimation is included to take into account influence from external contexts, conditions, and results of behavior that are all based on norms (Giddens, 1984). This aspect of structuration is also integral in its meaning as the different modes are derived from interdisciplinary work as Giddens highlights in his theorization.

Case Study

With the delineation of Giddens' theory of structuration (Giddens, 1984), it is now time to apply that theory to illicit organizations as other researchers also explored the applications of specific theories in such regard (Finckenauer, 2005; Milward & Raab, 2006; Southerland & Potter, 1993). As scholars are working consistently to try and understand dark networks and organized crime, the only viable option is to do so using theoretical applications onto a non-experimental case study given the dangerousness of the situation.

With that being the case, this chapter seeks to understand a specific criminal organization, the Sicilian Mafia (or la Cosa Nostra), to evaluate its structure and function, and how it differs from regular, legitimate organizations where structuration theory is concerned. To do so, a brief background into the Sicilian Mafia is first provided, followed by an analysis of its function and structure, and finally the different forms of institutions.

Background and History

The Sicilian Mafia has been labeled as one of the most infamous institutions that has operated in the Western World after its initial appearance in Sicily, Italy in the 1870s. Shortly after that, it quickly infiltrated both the economic and political sectors of Italy and the United States, posing a threat to both countries (Catanzaro &

Rosenthal, 1992). While its operations included instances of murder, bombings, and other violent attacks, of particular relevance for this chapter is its origin story. According to Dimico et al. (2017), the Sicilian Mafia was able to propel itself into success through the citrus and lemon market. While sounding ridiculous in the twenty-first century, when the period of time is taken into context, the mental image is put into perspective. In the 1800s, Scurvy had already plagued and taken the lives of millions (Magiorkinis et al., 2011). Upon the discovery of the effective use of citrus fruits in curing scurvy (Lind, 1757), the demand for such fruits rose exceptionally.

As Sicily in and of itself was the perfect ground for citrus fruits prosperity, Lind's discovery resulted in the increase in demand and a subsequent large influx of revenues to towns such as Sicily's. Given the specific conditions required for the production of citrus, few local producers profited off of this caveat. Additionally, the Italian government at the time did not have the resources or the power to effectively enforce issues such as property rights, forcing producers to hire mafias for protection as well as mediators between retailers and exporters. Therefore, and with the unique combination of a substantial increase in profits, a weak rule of law, low levels of interpersonal and governmental trust, as well as a high level of poverty, the Sicilian Mafia saw the lemon producers of Sicily as an irreplaceable target for profit (Dimico et al., 2017).

Based on solely the background of the Sicilian Mafia's rise, it is possible to draw out some themes that mimic those discussed in the theoretical framework section.

Signification, domination, and a concept of legitimation can be seen through the operating procedures that the mafia has exhibited in the brief overview of its history. While this requires significant elaboration to draw out concrete conclusions and implications, it is important to first establish the Sicilian Mafia as a criminal organization that fits into Giddens' structuration theory. This will be achieved in the next section to make way for an application pertaining to institutional forms.

Structure, Function, and Agency

The Sicilian Mafia is a large criminal organization that had significant business dealings and illicit trades in many instances and concerning many goods (Catanzaro & Rosenthal, 1992). There exists a number of evaluations that have examined the structure of such an entity, however, with its widespread influence and multi-geographic spread, the best approach to understand each of the mafia's structure, function, and agency is to draw findings from multiple disciplines that have applied multiple methods. To begin, the structure of the Sicilian Mafia is examined by Battisti et al. (2022a) through an exploration using social network analysis and econometric analysis. They found the Sicilian Mafia to be a small world network that was described as disassortative (i.e., higher node degrees are connected to lower node degrees and vice versa, with a decreased probability of connection between two higher nodes). Compared to regular organizations, such brief descriptions do not highlight many differences given that disassortative mimics a hierarchical structure. However, the detailed exploration reveals key differences that show how the Sicilian Mafia has adjusted its structure to accommodate its functioning due to its criminal nature (Battisti et al., 2022a, b).

Contrary to typical organizations following a hierarchy where managers and other "bosses" are central in their corresponding network, this is not always the case for mafia bosses. Instead, there exists a cell-dominated hierarchy where it is not a key member that is central, but it is that key members are connected to a relative with a central position (Baccara & Bar-Isaac, 2008; Battisti et al., 2022a, b). This alteration in hierarchical structure is a strategy to increase efficiency by increasing coordination and ensuring a speedy relay of information across Mandamentos (a district of three geographically contiguous Mafia cosche in Sicily) (Battisti et al., 2022a). Additionally, the adjusted structure, function, and agency of the Sicilian Mafia is not only to ensure efficiency, but to also ensure security (Battisti et al., 2022a, b). The adaptation of the mafia into a small world network is the main aspect that is linked to its illegal nature. While small world networks of a legal nature have a higher clustering coefficient (i.e., a high level of familiarity with the surrounding network) and a lower diameter (i.e., a short distance between members of different networks), networks such as the Sicilian Mafia are the opposite. This is largely due to the previously mentioned cell-dominated hierarchy in which key agents are protected from the remaining network by sharing a link with another agent who plays the significant role of information hub, allowing for the dispersal of information (Baccara & Bar-Isaac, 2008; Battisti et al., 2022a).

Another tactic to increase the efficiency and security of this criminal organization is the probability of link formation, the probability of two separate individuals of different networks to form a link. Battisti et al. (2022a) found that the probability of link formation between two agents is higher when these agents share a larger number of similar tasks, and belong to the same Mandamento. These findings are in line with previous research which has established a multidivisional form as the structural description for the Sicilian Mafia (Kleinbaum et al., 2013). The multidivisional form operates on at least three different levels and resembles the structure of a family tree for example. This form is characterized by having the top position (e.g., General Office) branching out into multiple subdivisions (e.g., Product Division), each of which is further divided into specific sections or roles (e.g., Marketing, Production, Engineering, and Finances) (see Hoskisson et al., 1993). In a criminal organization, for example, this can be equated to having the leader as the topmost position, who is in contact with various subdivisions and Mandamentos, each of which has multiple members or individuals reporting to them on various roles. This form of organizational structure makes sense when compared to legitimate ones as it allows the Mafia to disperse its revenue and operations across various divisions and markets, thus increasing its efficiency and preventing its downfall should one division perish (Hoskisson et al., 1993; Kleinbaum et al., 2013).

Signification, Domination, and Illegitimation

So far, the structure, function, and agency of the Sicilian Mafia has been identified as being in line with Giddens' structuration theory (Giddens, 1984; Turner, 1986; Yates, 1997). In other words, the structure and function of the Sicilian Mafia can be described as bidirectional in that the structure acted as both the medium and the outcome of the function and agency (Giddens, 1984; Turner, 1986). In order to expand further the understanding of this criminal organization in regard to structuration, the next step is an application of the different forms of institutions and how the Sicilian Mafia fits into these.

Signification

First, to begin with signification, which uses structures where agents utilize past experiences to draw out meaning (Giddens, 1984), the Sicilian Mafia like most Mafias around the mid to late 1900s had to re-examine its structure and function due to experiences and events that have unfolded. For example, after the "second mafia war" in the early 1980s, there were thousands of homicides and assassinations of judges, prosecutors, and politicians, that also resulted in the reconfiguration of the Casa Nostra from a pluralistic organization based on democratic rule to a dictatorship built on terror (Balsamo, 2006; Catanzaro & Rosenthal, 1992). This reconfiguration was based on the mentioned war, and its subsequent decisions and behaviors are based on a long historical evolution of what worked and what did not work, allowing for decision-making based on prior experiences.

Another example presented by Blok (2008) also examines the transformations of the Sicilian Mafia that shifted from a democratic norm to more of a dictatorship (Balsamo, 2006; Catanzaro & Rosenthal, 1992) due to the Italian state's new initiative of passing new legislation in an effort to combat the growing illicit trades the Mafia was involved in while holding key positions in state power. The shift in the state's stance regarding the mafia from cooperation to legislation caused the Sicilian Mafia to retaliate (Blok, 2008). The combination of legalization, prior Mafioso's acting as state witnesses, and the decline in political protections of the mafia caused the decline in their activities. However, it did not cause its end. Based on the primary dissolving of the Mafia in the 1950s (Balsamo, 2006; Catanzaro & Rosenthal, 1992) and the shift in organizational structure, it was deduced that the mafia now holds a segmented structure rather than the previously believed centralized structure, leading to its longevity (Blok, 2008).

Domination

Second, in terms of authoritative and allocative resources, both of which fall under domination, the Sicilian Mafia seems to exert control over either persons or objects respectively (Giddens, 1984). The example provided for signification fits perfectly under this form as well. As the decline of Mafiosos as public figures and political representatives became the new reality, and the subsequent mandate of the mafia and its members to live clandestine lives as outlaws, the tactics of this criminal organization changed. This change, however, involved the use of threat, bribery, and coercion to take control of key influential personnel in the state to regain some form of the influence that had been lost (Balsamo, 2006; Blok, 2008; Catanzaro & Rosenthal, 1992). While these efforts seem to control only persons, the criminal nature of the Sicilian Mafia gave rise to both authoritative and allocative resources simultaneously.

In instances where politicians, judges, prosecutors, and even transport personnel were bribed, coerced, or threatened and served the mafia as a consequence, it also gave rise to the control of objects (Balsamo, 2006). The mafia had not simply chosen these individuals for revenge or spite. Although that sometimes was the case, their choice in who to target was more strategic. Whether to control courts, prisons, the state, or transshipment companies to move their goods and provide services, the Sicilian Mafia carefully and strategically exerted control over persons to exert subsequent control over objects in an effort to enable the attainment of its goals (Balsamo, 2006; Blok, 2008; Catanzaro & Rosenthal, 1992; McWeeney, 1987).

Illegitimation

Finally, legitimation in regards to the Sicilian Mafia takes a more unique perspective based on its criminal nature. While Giddens (1984) examines organizations and one of their institutional forms as legitimate, i.e. abiding by the theory of normative regulations based on the rules and norms provided by legal institutions, it would only make sense that criminal organizations undergo more so of an illegitimation. The very nature of criminal organizations relies on the illicit methods they utilize to achieve their goals and further their agenda. These methods can be seen throughout the previous application of structuration theory provided. The tactics and methods the Sicilian Mafia used, whether to influence, control, and achieve goals have relied on illegitimate means (Blok, 2008). Therefore, while normative regulation relies on the law, as well as moral systems, systems regulating social relations… among others (Krecht, 1986), the Sicilian Mafia deviates from this.

The Sicilian Mafia, and the broader criminal organizations roster, relies then on anormativity. As the mafia does not abide by the regular norms and rules of day-to-day life of which community members and society deem appropriate, the behavior and subsequent operations of Sicilian Mafia is anormative (Archer, 2016; Blok, 2008; Catanzaro & Rosenthal, 1992). This deviation from the classic forms stated in structuration theory is key in differentiating legitimate organizations from illegitimate ones. Many scholars have already established that the major differences between legitimate and illicit organizations is the simple use of the term "illicit" and its synonyms to describe these entities (Smith, 1980; Southerland & Potter, 1993; Thompson, 2003; Von Lampe, 2006, 2015). As such, here lies the crucial information needed to understand the Sicilian Mafia and other criminal organizations.

While in the case of legitimate organizations, understanding them requires regular thought within the realm of legitimacy, understanding criminal organizations would now require a shift in perspective. Archer (2016) identified anormative social behavior as a coping mechanism for social morphogenesis, which examines changes in society. It is then the societal facets of structure, culture, and agency that play a role in social powers and dictate morphogenetic characteristics. This not only further reinforces the importance of examining structure, and agency, but also provides a perspective into how to examine the actions of criminal organizations to better combat them by understanding decision making and methods based on illegitimation (Archer, 2016; Blok, 2008).

Discussion

So far, the delineation of the purpose of this book chapter, the presentation of criminal organizations as organization entities, the theoretical framework of structuration theory, and the application of that theory to the Sicilian Mafia were discussed to draw out the general fit of this theory to criminal organizations and allow for a clearer analysis. Now, the analysis and discussion that highlights the importance and significance of all that has been put forth will allow for a much clearer visualization of the advantages of these methods.

First, in terms of the applicability of structuration theory, it is clear that criminal organizations, at the very least the Sicilian Mafia, necessitates an interaction between structure and functioning and agency. As was evidenced in the prior section, the structure of the Sicilian Mafia allows for the performance of its functioning which in turn, dictates its structure (Battisti et al., 2022a, b; Giddens, 1984; Turner, 1986). To explain this more in a conceptualized perspective, it is the interaction between individual agents based on the number of tasks and the degree of importance that they hold that dictates the structure of the Sicilian Mafia. Consequently, the structure of the mafia is what allows for the execution of the tasks that each individual agent holds.

Structure and Function

While the presentation of evidence using historical examples and methods of social network analysis highlighted the structure of the Sicilian Mafia, the transformation from a single unified organization that follows the functional structure to the more segmented multidivisional structure bears significance on the response efforts to these criminal organizations (Baccara & Bar-Isaac, 2008; Battisti et al., 2022a, b; Hoskisson et al., 1993; Kleinbaum et al., 2013). This provides evidence to law enforcement at the difficulty of addressing the operations of criminal organizations like the Sicilian Mafia as it is apparent that these efforts need to be adapted to a multidivisional structure as opposed to focusing on one division at a time. This approach will ensure a more decisive blow to such organizations as opposed to cutting off one division so that two more can take its place.

Moreover, identifying significant agents within the organization could prove immeasurably advantageous in hindering the operations of the Sicilian Mafia. As this organization consists of an agent that is hidden from other members and the outside world to facilitate the establishment of an information hub, identifying and apprehending this and similar agents within the organization can help in the fight against criminal enterprises. An agent identified as an information hub is much more difficult to replace given the role that agent plays in the overall organization, as well as the information that agent holds (Battisti et al., 2022a, b).

Signification, Domination, and Illegitimation

In terms of forms of institutions, there are several insights that can be derived from the application presented. First, in terms of signification, it allows for the understanding of decision-making processes, at least in part, of criminal organizations such as the Sicilian Mafia (Blok, 2008) as it is clear that la Cosa Nostra takes into consideration past experiences to inform its current structure and decision. Therefore, creating a form of understanding on the part of law enforcement where this is concerned could help the responses criminal organizations have to some intervention strategies, allowing for quicker adaptations to shifts in organizational behavior (Balsamo, 2006).

Looking at domination, it is clear that criminal organizations have more of an advantage where the control of persons and objects is concerned as they do not need to target persons and objects separately. The control of persons provides them with the access needed to control certain objects thus achieving both allocative and authoritative resources (Balsamo, 2006; Blok, 2008; McWeeney, 1987). This understanding of the way through which criminal organizations achieve control of key individuals and subsequent key objects, including institutions, permits responses to criminal organizations by identifying more appropriate and strategic targets that could disrupt their operations.

Finally, the illegitimation approach taken by criminal organizations is the most deviating aspect when compared to mainstream structuration. However, it could be the most informative. Given that this illegitimation is linked back to an anormativity response to societal morphogenesis (Archer, 2016; Blok, 2008; Krecht, 1986), it is clear that the agency of individuals within criminal organizations such as the Sicilian Mafia could be based, at least partly, on these types of morphogenetic characteristics. Therefore, examining these concepts from a more specific perspective, such as criminology or security studies, disciplines which evaluate such societal characteristics and their effects on individuals or groups, would allow for evidence-based practices that could yield better results.

Even though the application and the subsequent implications discussed have targeted practical concerns, following the delineation of the evidence presented as well as the analysis, there seems to also be a theoretical suggestion that can be made. In Giddens' theory of structuration (1984), signification, domination, and legitimation seem to be discussed in more of a disconnected fashion. Going through the evidence in the case study, however, it seems that there is some form of transference between the three. While signification relies on past experiences to make sense of certain issues, it also serves to inform better practices of domination and illegitimation. This can be seen in the decision of the Sicilian Mafia to take control of key personnel and subsequent objects due to experiences learned from the past and in an effort to regain power. While domination allows for the facilitation of illegitimate techniques and helps inform the process involved in signification given the methods through which the Mafia achieved its control over these individuals and objects, as well as the role they serve in potentially relaying information to the Mafia. Similarly, illegitimation is involved in the achievement of domination as the methods required to achieve both allocative and authoritative resources while also providing information to the process involved in signification and subsequent decision making by examining what works and what does not. For a clearer visualization of the deduced model, see Fig. 6.1.

Limitations

Considering the findings and the implications that have resulted from the analysis of the case study, this approach is not without its limitations. Although structuration theory was a good fit to assess such an organization, other theoretical frameworks might be more appropriate for this or other criminal organizations. This is not to say

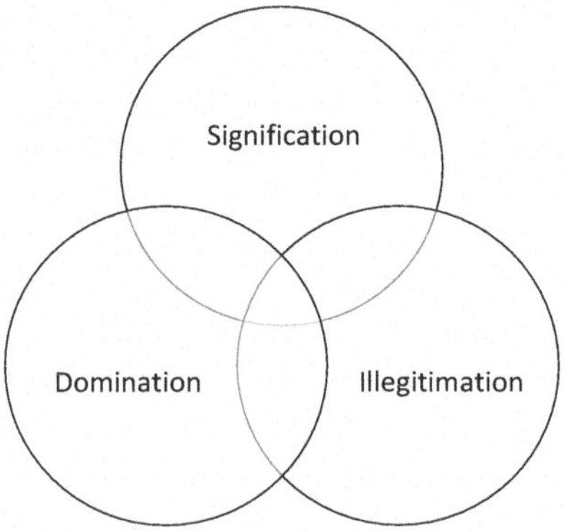

Fig. 6.1 A suggested model for the interactions between institutional forms

that structuration theory does not provide enough insight to explain the ideas presented, to the contrary, this framework provided valuable results and conclusions. However, it did highlight the need to examine criminal organizations from varying disciplines and perspectives which could, in turn, yield better or different results. Another limitation here is the constriction of time concerning the Sicilian Mafia and the information available about this organization. As real-time information is difficult to procure, these findings are based on information that has ranged in year of conducting the study and in the timeline respective to the Sicilian Mafia. Therefore, the findings of this project must be interpreted in light of this limitation, and must be expanded upon to provide more up-to-date suggestions.

While the suggestion of the need to examine such concepts and applications in further detail is not a limitation, it is important to mention that the implications mentioned above in the discussion section provide specific areas that require further research and investigation to unveil the true effects and effectiveness of such approaches in combating organized crime. Given that the specifics of each investigation is beyond the scope of this chapter, future research should examine these issues in greater detail to better inform research and stakeholders where this is concerned.

Conclusion

Criminal organizations have been a challenge to national and international law enforcement entities since their inception. While there has been great effort in understanding their structure and function, little research has attempted to utilize a theoretical framework that encompasses both these aspects, while taking into consideration criminal organizations as organizational entities as opposed to simply criminal entities. This chapter sought to fill this gap in the literature by analyzing criminal organizations from an organizational perspective using Giddens' structuration theory and institutional forms. By applying this framework to the Sicilian Mafia, this chapter aimed to provide the utility of a multidisciplinary approach, particularly utilizing an organizational science approach, to understand and combat criminal organizations.

This is by no means the only or best solution to combat the Sicilian Mafia and organized crime. There are other disciplines, methods, and theoretical frameworks from multiple disciplines that provide insight into options for combating criminal organizations. While the presented theoretical framework of structuration theory and the case study of the Sicilian Mafia enabled the emphasis on multiple aspects to understand and combat the Sicilian Mafia, the most important aspect that this investigation has highlighted is the necessity to examine organized crime from an interdisciplinary perspective.

The application of structuration provides implicit evidence that fields such as criminology, economics, and security studies… among others, are integral to the analysis of criminal organizations, even in applying an organizational science perspective (Archer, 2016; Balsamo, 2006; Battisti et al., 2022a, b; Blok, 2008; Giddens, 1984; Southerland & Potter, 1993). However, without the use of an organizational perspective initially, such a deduction of interdisciplinary importance is impossible. Therefore, structuration theory and other such frameworks that aim at understanding the structure and function of criminal organizations is perhaps an irreplaceable starting point as it informed the necessary types of interventions needed at various levels of the organization.

While much research remains to be done in this field to better understand and better inform decision and policy makers, this is a great starting point as future research can now target specificities unveiled through this application. For example, utilizing organizational sciences and social network analysis to determine possible unintended consequences of certain law enforcement interventions, thus improving results. Another example highlights the importance of considering criminogenic factors that contribute to the illegitimation methods of organizations based on societal morphogenesis. As the field of organizational sciences expands upon various types of organizations, taking into account criminal ones to understand and counteract them is just as important as examining legitimate ones to understand and improve them. There are strong benefits of examining criminal organizations from this approach to allow for the understanding of the functional and operational aspects of criminal organizations and to identify structural shortcomings, allowing for law enforcement and future research to better address organized crime.

References

Andrews, R., Boyne, G. A., Law, J., & Walker, R. M. (2009). Centralization, organizational strategy, and public service performance. *Journal of Public Administration Research and Theory, 19*(1), 57–80. https://doi.org/10.1093/jopart/mum039

Archer, M. S. (2016). Anormative social regulation: The attempt to cope with social morphogenesis. In *Morphogenesis and the crisis of normativity* (pp. 141–168). Springer.

Baccara, M., & Bar-Isaac, H. (2008). How to organize crime. *The Review of Economic Studies, 75*(4), 1039–1067. https://doi.org/10.1111/j.1467-937X.2008.00508.x

Balsamo, A. (2006). Organized crime today: The evolution of the Sicilian mafia. *Journal of Money Laundering Control, 9*(4), 373–378.

Battisti, M., Lavezzi, A. M., & Musotto, R. (2022a). Organizing crime: An empirical analysis of the Sicilian mafia. *arXiv preprint arXiv:2205.02310*. https://doi.org/10.48550/arXiv.2205.02310

Battisti, M., Lavezzi, A. M., & Musotto, R. (2022b). Taking care of everyone's business: Interpreting Sicilian mafia embedment through spatial network analysis. *Global Crime, 23*(2), 171–192. https://doi.org/10.1080/17440572.2022.2073440

Block, A. (2017). *East side-west side: Organizing crime in New York, 1930–50*. Routledge.

Blok, A. (2008). Reflections on the sicilian mafia: Peripheries and their impact on centres. In *Organized crime: Culture, markets and policies* (pp. 7–13). Springer.

Bunker, R. J., & Sullivan, J. P. (2021). Mexican cartel tactical note# 35: Weaponized drone/UAV/UAS seized in valtierrilla, Guanajuato with remote detonation IED ('papa bomba') payload. In *Criminal drone evolution: Cartel weaponization of aerial IEDS* (p. 9). Xilbris.

Carpenter, T. (2009). *Troubled neighbor* (p. 4). Cato Institute.

Catanzaro, R., & Rosenthal, R. (1992). *Men of respect: A social history of the Sicilian mafia*. Free Press.
Cavgias, A., Bruce, R., & Meloni, L. (2023). Policy enforcement in the presence of organized crime: Evidence from Rio de Janeiro. *Journal of Development Economics, 162*, 103071. https://doi.org/10.1016/j.jdeveco.2023.103071
Chatagnier, J. T., Mintz, A., & Samban, Y. (2012). The decision calculus of terrorist leaders. *Perspectives on Terrorism, 6*(4/5), 125–144. https://www.jstor.org/stable/26296880
Child, J. (1973). Predicting and understanding organization structure. *Administrative Science Quarterly*, 168–185. https://doi.org/10.2307/2392061
Dalton, D. R., Todor, W. D., Spendolini, M. J., Fielding, G. J., & Porter, L. W. (1980). Organization structure and performance: A critical review. *Academy of Management Review, 5*(1), 49–64.
Dimico, A., Isopi, A., & Olsson, O. (2017). Origins of the Sicilian mafia: The market for lemons. *The Journal of Economic History, 77*(4), 1083–1115. https://doi.org/10.1017/s002205071700078x
Dooley, K. (2002). Organizational complexity. In *International encyclopedia of business and management* (Vol. 6, pp. 5013–5022). Thompson Learning.
Finckenauer, J. O. (2005). Problems of definition: What is organized crime? *Trends in Organized Crime, 8*(3), 63–83. https://doi.org/10.1007/s12117-005-1038-4
Flanigan, S. T. (2012). Terrorists next door? A comparison of Mexican drug cartels and middle eastern terrorist organizations. *Terrorism and Political Violence, 24*(2), 279–294. https://doi.org/10.1080/09546553.2011.648351
Giddens, A. (1984). *The constitution of society*. The University of California Press.
Hagan, F. E. (2006). "Organized crime" and "organized crime": Indeterminate problems of definition. *Trends in Organized Crime, 9*(4), 127–137.
Hage, J., & Aiken, M. T. (1970). *Social change in complex organizations*. Random House.
Hoenig, M. (2014). Hezbollah and the use of drones as a weapon of terrorism. *Public Interest Report, 67*(2), 5.
Hoskisson, R. E., Hill, C. W., & Kim, H. (1993). The multidivisional structure: Organizational fossil or source of value? *Journal of Management, 19*(2), 269–298. https://doi.org/10.1016/0149-2063(93)90055-R
Jaberidoost, M., Nikfar, S., Abdollahiasl, A., & Dinarvand, R. (2013). Pharmaceutical supply chain risks: A systematic review. *DARU Journal of Pharmaceutical Sciences, 21*, 1–7.
Kemp, G. (2001). The United Nations convention against transnational organized crime: A milestone in international criminal law. *South African Journal of Criminal Justice, 14*, 152.
Kleinbaum, A. M., Stuart, T. E., & Tushman, M. L. (2013). Discretion within constraint: Homophily and structure in a formal organization. *Organization Science, 24*(5), 1316–1336. https://doi.org/10.1287/orsc.1120.0804
Krecht, J. (1986). The Normative Regulation. ARSP: Archiv Für Rechts- Und Sozialphilosophie / Archives for Philosophy of Law and Social Philosophy, 72(4), 514–522. http://www.jstor.org/stable/23679783
Lewis, D. (2006). *The management of non-governmental development organizations*. Routledge.
Lind, J. (1757). *A treatise on the scurvy*. A. Millar.
Magiorkinis, E., Beloukas, A., & Diamantis, A. (2011). Scurvy: Past, present and future. *European Journal of Internal Medicine, 22*(2), 147–152. https://doi.org/10.1016/j.ejim.2010.10.006
Mansfield, R. (1973). Bureaucracy and centralization: An examination of organizational structure. *Administrative Science Quarterly*, 477–488. https://doi.org/10.2307/2392200
McWeeney, S. M. (1987). The Sicilian Mafia and its impact on the United States. *FBI Law Enforcement Bulletin, 56*, 1.
Milward, H. B., & Raab, J. (2006). Dark networks as organizational problems: Elements of a theory. *International Public Management Journal, 9*(3), 333. https://doi.org/10.1080/10967490600899747
Mocetti, S., & Rizzica, L. (2023). Organized crime in Italy: An economic analysis. *Italian Economic Journal*, 1–22.

Moch, M. K., & Morse, E. V. (1977). Size, centralization and organizational adoption of innovations. *American Sociological Review*, 716–725. https://doi.org/10.2307/2094861

Naylor, R. T. (1995). From cold war to crime war: The search for a new "national security" threat. *Transnational Organized Crime, 1*(4), 37–56.

Okoli, A. C., & Nwangwu, C. (2023). Organized crime–terror nexus: Interrogating the linkage between banditry and terrorism in northern Nigeria. *Journal of Asian and African Studies, 58*(5), 766–778. https://doi.org/10.1177/00219096211069650

Perrow, C. (1967). A framework for the comparative analysis of organizations. *American Sociological Review, 32*(2), 194–208. https://doi.org/10.2307/2091811

Perrow, C. (1986). *Complex organizations: A critical essay*. McGraw-Hill.

Phillips, B. J., & Schiele, A. (2023). Dogs and cats living together? Explaining the crime-terror nexus. *Terrorism and Political Violence*, 1–17. https://doi.org/10.1080/09546553.2023.2189968

Poppi, F. I. M., & Ardila, A. (2023). In nomine diaboli: The ideologies of organized crime. *European Journal of Criminology, 20*(2), 401–421. https://doi.org/10.1177/14773708211006642

Pugh, D. S., Hickson, D. J., Hinings, C. R., & Turner, C. (1969). The context of organization structures. *Administrative Science Quarterly, 14*(1), 91–114. https://doi.org/10.2307/2391366

Robbins, S. P. (1990). *Organization theory: Structures, designs, and applications* (3rd ed.). Pearson Education India.

Robles-Mendoza, A. (2023). Legal psychology from social psychology. Historical introduction of forensic psychology. *Forensic Research & Criminology International Journal, 11*(1), 5–7.

Schelling, T. C. (1971). What is the business of organized crime? *The American Scholar, 40*(4), 643–652. Retrieved October 15, 2023, from http://www.jstor.org/stable/41209902

Shah, N. (2004). Pharmaceutical supply chains: Key issues and strategies for optimization. *Computers & Chemical Engineering, 28*(6–7), 929–941. https://doi.org/10.1016/j.compchemeng.2003.09.022

Shelley, L. I. (1995). Transnational organized crime: An imminent threat to the nation-state? *Journal of International Affairs, 48*(2), 463–489. https://www.jstor.org/stable/24357599

Smith, D. C. (1980). Paragons, pariahs, and pirates: A spectrum-based theory of enterprise. *Crime & Delinquency, 26*(3), 358–386. https://doi.org/10.1177/001112878002600306

Southerland, M. D., & Potter, G. W. (1993). Applying organization theory to organized crime. *Journal of Contemporary Criminal Justice, 9*(3), 251–267. https://doi.org/10.1177/104398629300900306

Thompson, J. D. (2003). *Organizations in action: Social science bases of administrative theory*. Transaction Publishers.

Turner, J. H. (1986). The theory of structuration the constitution of society: Outline of the theory of structuration. Anthony Giddens. *The American Journal of Sociology, 91*(4), 969–977. https://doi.org/10.1086/228358

Van Duyne, P. C. (1995). The phantom and threat of organized crime. *Crime, Law and Social Change, 24*, 341–377.

Vold, G. B., Bernard, T. J., & Snipes, J. B. (1998). *Theoretical criminology*. Oxford University Press.

Von Lampe, K. (2006). The interdisciplinary dimensions of the study of organized crime. *Trends in Organized Crime, 9*(3), 77–95.

Von Lampe, K. (2015). *Organized crime: Analyzing illegal activities, criminal structures, and extra-legal governance*. Sage Publications.

Wainwright, T. (2016). *Narconomics: How to run a drug cartel*. Public Affairs.

Yates, J. (1997). Using Giddens' structuration theory to inform business history. *Business and Economic History, 26*(1), 159–183. https://www.jstor.org/stable/23703305

Zabyelina, Y. (2023). Revisiting the concept of organized crime through the disciplinary lens of economic criminology. *Journal of Economic Criminology, 1*, 100017. https://doi.org/10.1016/j.jeconc.2023.100017

Part II
Select Organizational Concepts & Ideas

Chapter 7
Sexual Harassment in Police Organizations: Applying the Lens of Organizational Culture and Climate

Nhi N. H. Le

Introduction

Between 2018 and 2021, the U.S. Equal Employment Opportunity Commission (EEOC, 2022) received 27,291 charges alleging workplace sexual harassment, and 78.2% of those charges were filed by women. Although there are efforts to paint sexual harassment as a crime, instead of a boogeyman that all working professionals must look out for, it still remains largely underreported, especially in areas with obvious sex/gender imbalances (Taylor et al., 2020). Sexual harassment is a prevailing challenge to the workplace given that harassers hold power over those who survive such incidences, and that power intersects with demographic characteristics (i.e., age, race/ethnicity, sex/gender), need for employment, and organizational hierarchy (Ford & Ivancic, 2020). Research on the consequences of sexual harassment in the workforce predominantly focuses on individual-level impacts, ignoring how sexual harassment impacts organizations (Willness et al., 2007). Focusing on the impacts to organizations is warranted because such incidences can test an organization's stability. Specifically, sexual harassment is a negative phenomenon that forces organizations to examine or reexamine their policies and procedures. Given its prevalence and the negative consequences felt by survivors and organizations, it is important to understand what factors make an organization fertile ground for sexual harassment, which can further help guide potential prevention strategies.

To date, the research on sexual harassment in criminal legal organizations is diverse, but these studies rarely explain its emergence in the workforce from an organizational lens, and rarely within public, human service organizations like

N. N. H. Le (✉)
Sam Houston State University, Department of Crimial Justice and Criminology, Huntsville, TX, USA
e-mail: nnl010@shsu.edu

D. S. Rudes, J. R. Ingram (eds.), *Using Organizational Theory to Study, Explain, and Understand Criminal Legal Organizations*,
https://doi.org/10.1007/978-3-031-66285-0_7

policing. The following question remains unanswered: *How do we understand the existence of sexual harassment in organizations meant to represent virtue and justice?* Its presence in police organizations is especially problematic as these officers represent guardians of the community. Claiming that sexual harassment in police organizations is the result of "bad apples" is problematic because this perspective does not explain why sexual harassment persists after these harassers are reprimanded or fired (Taylor et al., 2020). Instead of attributing sexual harassment as a defunct characteristic in officers, further exploration as to how it infiltrates criminal legal organizations is necessary.

The purpose of this chapter is to explore how sexual harassment in criminal legal organizations can be understood through the lens of organizational theories, specifically focusing on the culture and climate of police organizations. Culture and climate research focuses on the attitudes of the workers and their perceptions of policies and procedure (see Ostroff et al., 2013; Schneider et al., 2013). This research is especially relevant for understanding sexual harassment given that organizational policies and actors' attitudes determine whether it matures within this system. Exploring sexual harassment in police organizations is especially relevant when studying female police officers (FPO) as sexual harassment is riddled with sex/gender and power imbalances, and these individuals already struggle to adapt to the hypermasculine culture of police organizations (Davis et al., 2023; Kaiser et al., 2022). The first part of this chapter introduces definitions of sexual harassment and organizational culture and climate. The next part interprets sexual harassment in police organizations through the culture and climate lens and proposes practical implications based on extant research.

Conceptualizing Sexual Harassment

The EEOC defines sexual harassment as unwelcome sexual advances, unwelcome requests for sexual favors, and physical and verbal harassment on the basis of an individual's sex (Sexual Harassment, n.d.). Activities that constitute as sexual harassment are those that make a workplace or environment hostile, such as sexually explicit comments, comments about an individual's gender, and unwanted contact and may result in adverse decisions regarding the survivor's employment (Quick & McFadyen, 2017; Sexual Harassment, n.d.). Behaviors such as inappropriate jokes and comments, pressure for sexual favors, and sexual assault classify as sexual harassment because the behaviors are unwanted, one-sided, and offensive towards survivors (Chaiyavej & Morash, 2009; Pina et al., 2009). The EEOC states that survivors and harassers can be of any gender identity or status (e.g., supervisors, co-workers) (Sexual Harassment, n.d.). Given the broadness of this definition, scholars have debated the best ways to conceptualize sexual harassment in research, accounting for the psychological consequences (see Berdahl, 2007; Fitzgerald et al., 1997b; Willness et al., 2007). Specifically, there is disagreement on how to accurately capture mild forms of sexual harassment (e.g., sexual propositions, sexist remarks) in research (McCabe & Hardman, 2005). Some researchers rely on the Sexual Experience Questionnaire (SEQ) and separate sexual harassment into two dimensions, gender harassment (e.g., misogynistic comments, sexist behaviors) and unwanted sexual attention (e.g., sexual imposition, seductive behaviors), to represent the phenomena in the workplace (Quick & McFadyen, 2017; Willness et al., 2007).

Given that there is no universal standard for sexual harassment, there is also no standard typology for harassers or survivors (Pina et al., 2009). The stereotypical description of a sexual harassment incident depicts a man as a perpetrator and a woman as a survivor; this depiction has expanded to account for other marginalized groups as survivors. For example, the EEOC recently updated the legal definition of sexual harassment to account for LGBTQ+ survivors, which is important given that these individuals are more likely to simultaneously experience harassment because of their gender and sexual orientation (Quick & McFadyen, 2017). All members of an organization will experience negative consequences when sexual harassment occurs (Quick & McFadyen, 2017). Thus, sexual harassment is not exclusive to heteronormative identities and the literature must increase its diversity by exploring such incidents.

Women represent an overwhelming majority, approximately 72%, of survivors of sexual harassment, but such numbers do not account for unreported incidences (Quick & McFadyen, 2017). Traditional sex roles, with men as dominant and women as submissive, fuel the stereotypes of perpetrators and survivors. For example, the McCabe and Hardman (2005) study observed that blue- and white-collar employees were more likely to perceive an event as sexual harassment when the perpetrator was a man and the survivor was a woman, but not for the reversal. Even if women hold positions of power or discretion in decision-making, women are socialized to be subordinate (Cleveland & Kurst, 1993). Past works suggest women are more likely to be blamed for the harassment, and this level of blame further depends on the severity of the event, if the event was reported, and whether the woman considered it to be sexual harassment (Kiebler & Stewart, 2022). Research on sexual harassment explores the effects of gender stereotypes, especially regarding women who do not fall under traditional femininity. Kaiser et al. (2022) used a prototype model to examine perceptions of sexual harassment, with the prototypical woman being heterosexual, White, and conventionally attractive. Results indicated that women who contrasted with the prototypical woman were less likely to be perceived as a survivor, limiting their access to victims' resources and increasing their experiences with negative organizational consequences (Kaiser et al., 2022). Additionally, Yu (2022) found that women of color were more likely to report sex-based discrimination, compared to their White counterparts, suggesting that the duel subordination from race and gender roles negatively impacts women of color in organizations.

Conceptualizing Organizational Culture and Climate

Importantly, although organizational culture and climate are concepts used to discuss how individuals interact with the environment of an organization, they are not interchangeable terms. Organizational climate refers to the perception of policies, practices, and procedures shared by members and derived from the interconnected experiences associated with membership while culture refers to assumptions, values, and beliefs that are shared by members and characterize a specific setting (Ostroff et al., 2013; Schneider et al., 2013, 2017). In simpler terms, climate can explain what organizational behavior occurs while culture can explain why it occurs (Ostroff et al., 2013). Ostroff et al. (2013) argued that organizational climate and culture may overlap but are equally necessary as independent concepts to interpret an organization's social structure and study organizational behavior. More specifically, organizational climate and culture are "social and symbolic processes" that can influence "individual and group behaviors," contributing to organizational functioning and outcomes (Ostroff et al., 2013, p. 643).

Climate research, overall, is important for understanding an organization's functioning and outcomes because climate represents the internal consistency of units within an organization: More specifically, weak climate may serve as an indicator that an organization has poor or inconsistent policies and procedures (Schneider et al., 2013). In contrast, organizations with strong climate are marked with higher levels of interaction, communication, and interdependence, implying that increased cohesion demonstrates stronger internal consistency (Schneider et al., 2013). Some scholars conduct research on focused climates, referring to specific dimensions of climate (e.g., service, safety), while others research on process climates, referring to how climates target organizational processes (e.g., procedural justice, diversity) (Schneider et al., 2013, 2017). Schneider et al. (2013) argued that the shift from researching overall climate to more specific avenues improved the validity and contextual understanding of climate in organizational research. Additionally, in-depth examinations within climate research provides practitioners with specific strategies and behaviors to better serve their organization and increase performance (Schneider et al., 2013). Research on how organizational climate is associated with perceptions of an organization's goals and values is mixed, with results ranging from a positive to a limited impact on performance (Zhang & Liu, 2010). Research on climate chronologically predates research on culture, and more recent literature focuses on the latter (Ostroff et al., 2013; Schneider et al., 2013). Schneider et al. (2013) argued this shift was explained by culture being able to capture and measure "the richness of organizational environment" in ways beyond climate (p. 363).

Although researchers have not standardized the definition of organizational culture, the existing commonalities suggest organizational culture is a social construct capturing a shared phenomenon, which is influenced by historical and spatial factors (Ostroff et al., 2013). There are various interpretations regarding the existence of culture in an organization: Culture can be seen as part of the system, referring to the attributes, or as the system, referring to the development of meaning and shared assumptions (Schneider et al., 2013). Culture is typically cemented through everyday interactions between members and later passed down to new inductees, those who become introduced to the culture through socialization and communication of shared ideologies (Ford & Ivancic, 2020; Ostroff et al., 2013; Schein, 2010). Additionally, most organizations are multicultural and consist of subcultures, defined as "distinctive clusters of ideologies, cultural forms, and other practices" that is shared amongst smaller groups of individuals within an organization (Trice & Beyer, 1993, p. 174). Schein (2010) further argued that culture is composed of three fundamental layers: (1) *observable artifacts*, items (e.g., symbols, language) that represent the organization's underlying values and ideologies; (2) *espoused values*, values endorsed by management or the overall organization; and (3) *basic assumptions*, values that transform into unobservable core assumptions. Previous works have not fully identified whether culture influences effectiveness. Specifically, the relationship between culture and effectiveness wavers in terms of statistical significance and effects, and researchers often find other confounding factors moderating the relationship (Ostroff et al., 2013). Such results are related to difficulties conceptualizing levels of culture, unit of analyses, and best dimensions, and previous works have only tested the direct relationship between culture and performance (Schneider et al., 2013). Recent works have examined whether culture moderates relationships among other organizational constructs (e.g., cooperation, leadership-member exchanges), assessing the various levels of culture within specific contexts (Schneider et al., 2013). To further assess the influence and effectiveness of an organization's culture and climate, it is important to examine the roles of leaders.

The Role of Leadership

Leaders rely on climate and culture to understand an organization's unique processes and outcomes, and they, themselves, contribute to climate and culture as antecedents to its development (Schneider et al., 2013, 2017). They are typically indifferent towards the conceptual differences between climate and culture, more concerned about whether culture or climate affects performance and efficiency (Schneider et al., 2013). Regarding climate, leaders are responsible for creating climate, and their specific leadership style will affect members' behaviors and attitudes (Ostroff et al., 2013; Schneider et al., 2013). Leaders concerned with improving group performance must maintain strong climate, given that organizational climate exerts influence on a unit's performance, collective identity, and loyalty to the organization (Zhang & Liu, 2010). Regarding culture, leaders use culture-embedding mechanisms to articulate and reinforce specific values, ideologies, and assumptions (Ostroff et al., 2013; Schein, 2010; Schneider et al., 2013). Given that they are responsible for creating norms, leaders also serve as role models for acceptable behaviors (Perry et al., 2021).

Just as leaders play an important role in the development of climate and culture, leaders are fundamental for responding to adverse events. The durability of an organization's leader is especially tested in moments of crises. Bowers et al. (2017) analyzed leader responses to various historical crises, applying the Crisis Response Leadership Matrix (CRLM) to identify what type of leader is most efficient during a crisis event. There were four types of leadership styles: (1) the *directive style*, characterized by decisiveness, well-defined expectations, and clear communication; (2) the *transformational style*, characterized by self-assurance, adaptability, and logic; (3) the *transactional style*, characterized by following procedures to the letter, and (4) the *cognitive style*, characterized by strong perception and imagination (Bowers et al., 2017). Additionally, organizational culture was conceptualized by three distinct styles: (1) *hierarchy*, characterized by a rigid tiered structure with definitive values and processes; (2) *clan/adhocracy*, characterized by both rigidity and empowerment of the workforce, and (3) *elitist*, characterized by power only given to few and dictatorial in nature (Bowers et al., 2017). Bowers et al. (2017) found the transformational leadership style was the most appropriate for handling events of crises, while transactional style was the least appropriate. Furthermore, Bowers et al. (2017) argued that preparation for crises was predetermined by both leadership style and cultural dynamics, and in-depth understanding of culture will better prepare an organization for responding to adverse events. Sexual harassment is a form of crisis that disrupts an organization's internal harmony, affecting performance and outcomes; leaders are responsible for responding to the concerns of both individual workers and the organization. However, there are very few empirical studies focused on whether leadership mediates the association between sexual harassment and organizational climate and culture (Perry et al., 2021).

Understanding Sexual Harassment Prevalence from an Organizational Perspective

Understanding how sexual harassment "fits" within an organization is important because sexual harassment affects all types of organizations and is tied to various characteristics of employment, such as job status and the atmosphere of the workplace (Hertzog et al., 2008; Pina et al., 2009). For example, in addition to negative individual-level consequences, sexual harassment affects the organization through poor employee performance (such as a response to the traumatic experience) and high turnover (Cleveland & Kurst, 1993; Willness et al., 2007; Yu, 2022). Modern interpretations of sexual harassment define the act as an expression of dominance and status maintenance, with perpetrators attempting to restore their power by undermining the peers they view as subordinate (Berdahl, 2007; Perry et al., 2021). Unlike other theories, the organizational perspective acknowledges power inequalities through a gender-neutral approach (Pina et al., 2009). Cleveland and Kurst (1993) argued that power can be categorized in three contexts: (1) *societal*, referring to the expectations and acceptance of power within a hierarchy; (2) *organizational*, referring to disparities between occupational status; and (3) *interpersonal*, referring to individual behavior towards others. Organizational interpretations of power focus on the role of harassers. Harassers in the workforce can be the survivor's supervisor, coworker, or subordinate (Cleveland & Kurst, 1993; Dougherty & Smythe, 2004). These statuses can impact a survivor's vulnerability in an organization: supervisors represent the most formal level of authority, coworkers represent informal and social power, and subordinates represent the least amount of formal power (Cleveland & Kurst, 1993). Organizational conditions and responses to instances of sexual harassment will either weaken or strengthen sexual harassment within the workplace: Such reactions inform workers as to whether an organization tolerates or punishes sexual harassment (Cleveland & Kurst, 1993). Organization responses can affect the perceptions of both harassers and survivors, specifically whether these parties are supported or devalued, and such attitudes can be further exacerbated by how leaders respond (i.e., failure to acknowledge complaints, only implementing minimal prevention efforts) (Cleveland & Kurst, 1993; Timmerman & Bajema, 2000). If an organization allows sexual harassment to continue unpunished, then the likelihood of future harassment increases (Cleveland & Kurst, 1993).

Examining sexual harassment through the lens of organizational climate and culture can be very informative: Members refer to an organization's culture and climate to determine whether sexual harassment is normalized (Dougherty & Smythe, 2004; Fitzgerald et al., 1997a). Higher levels of sexual harassment are associated with higher levels of tolerance and male dominance in an organization (Fitzgerald et al., 1997a). McCabe and Hardman (2005) examined Australian employees' attitudes towards perceptions of sexual harassment while accounting for individual and organizational factors. When examining organizational factors, results revealed gender differences regarding tolerance in white-collar organizations, but not blue-collar ones: Men in white-collar organizations exhibited higher levels of tolerance for sexual harassment, compared to women, but levels of tolerance in blue-collar organizations were the same regardless of gender (McCabe & Hardman, 2005). Additionally, tolerance was inversely related to perceptions of sexual harassment, meaning individuals who labeled more behaviors as sexual harassment were less likely to be tolerant of them (McCabe & Hardman, 2005). Other early studies suggest that altering the organization's climate to oppose sexual harassment would better address and reduce sexual harassment, but such suggestions do very little to address other forms of sex-based mistreatment or the perpetuation of unequal status of workers (Perry et al., 2021).

Sexual Harassment in Police Organizations

In police organizations, sexual misconduct can range from arguably harmless behaviors, such as flirting or consensual sex while on duty, to serious violent offenses, such as sexual assault or coercion (Maher, 2003; Rabe-Hemp & Braithwaite, 2012). Approximately 35% of police officers engage in some form of sexual misconduct (Maher, 2003), but the true prevalence of inappropriate sexual behaviors by police officers is masked by lack of reporting and restricted access to data (Rabe-Hemp & Braithwaite, 2012). In the United States, 50–75% of women in law enforcement reported surviving some form of sexual harassment, but only 15–25% of women submitted formal complaints (Kobayashi, 2018). Despite being the guardians for justice, police are severely lacking when punishing sexual harassment within the organization (Carter Collins, 2004; Rabe-Hemp & Braithwaite, 2012). Examining whether culture and climate contribute to sexual harassment in police organizations is important for addressing an institution-wide dilemma, instead of focusing on individual actors.

Culture and Climate of Police Organizations

The culture and climate of police organizations do not match a one-size-fits-all approach because culture and climate varies over time, space, context (Silvestri, 2017; Westmarland, 2012). In other words, side-by-side comparisons can still produce different results because no two departments are completely alike. One approach at understanding this unique organization is to interpret the culture of police from an occupational perspective. Police organizations create an occupational culture, with individuals sharing the experiences and risks attached with their job (Trice & Beyer, 1993; Westmarland, 2012). Workers are taught their organization's expectations, values, and norms when they are new, and consistent socialization results in internalization of the ideals associated with the profession (Trice & Beyer, 1993). One's occupation holds lasting influence over an organization because individuals derive their identities and social status from their profession, and the shared goals and norms of an organization are reinforced by the culture (Trice & Beyer, 1993; Westmarland, 2012). In the context of police, officers share a goal of exercising authority and, when necessary, demonstrating force to combat crime; the subcultures of the organization allow officers to reinforce these goals (Westmarland, 2012). Additionally, an unofficially established value shared among officers is loyalty: Allegiance amongst officers perpetuates a "blue code/wall of silence" that penalizes any officer who betrays that loyalty, especially when speaking out against misconduct (Davis et al., 2023; Lee & Yu, 2020; Sweeting et al., 2022). This blue wall of silence is the colloquial phrase used to describe the reluctance of police officers to report misconduct or corruption, out of fear of ostracization or reprisals (Sweeting et al., 2022). Sweeting et al. (2022) assessed whether the blue wall of silence interfered with reporting of sexual harassment: Although men were more likely to report sexual misconduct than women, results suggested the effect of the blue wall was less substantial in reference to such instances. The authors hypothesized that the criminal nature of sexual harassment outweighed the loyalty of the blue wall.

Lee and Yu (2020) argued that gendered organizations may implement "glass walls," referring to how gendered organizations segregate or restrict women to certain roles, which perpetuates gender imbalances. Given that police organizations meet the criteria of a gendered organization (Lee & Yu, 2020), an understanding of how masculinity influences police culture is warranted. Reiner (2000) argued that police organizations follow traditional notions of masculinity and "machismo" as rulers of the street fighting crime. In police culture, emphasis is placed on masculine traits (i.e., aggression, competition), meaning feminine traits (i.e., sensitivity, empathy) contradict the dominant norms (Davis et al., 2023). An example of how police culture exemplifies these masculine ideals is the concentration on officer's physicality: Qualifications for police officers require candidates to meet certain physical standards which isolates non-males on the basis of biology (Silvestri, 2017).

Understanding Sexual Harassment Through Culture and Climate

Female police officers (FPO) entering the police force must acclimate to the masculine-dominated atmosphere of the police organization (Chaiyavej & Morash, 2009; Davis et al., 2023; Taylor et al., 2020). Unfortunately, numbers reveal that uniformed services see the highest levels of sexual harassment (Davis et al., 2023). One approach to understanding sexual harassment in police organizations is to assess how policing perpetuates a culture of heterosexual masculinity. Police organizations represent one of the most gendered organizations: Law enforcement agencies are male-dominated and value masculine traits (Lee & Yu, 2020). FPO inherently threaten this dominance with their biological femininity and are expected to act more masculine if they wish to fit in with their peers (Lee & Yu, 2020). The fact that women who enter male-dominated organizations have a higher likelihood of facing harassment may be partially explained by identity crises; specifically, men who believe women are threatening their masculine identity may overcompensate through harassment (Carter Collins, 2004; Chaiyavej & Morash, 2009; Perry et al., 2021). Sexual harassment of women becomes a part of a "masculinity contest culture," in which traditional masculinity is juxtaposed with status and harassment towards minorities translates into demonstrations of power (Perry et al., 2021). In other words, a culture of competition is created and sexual harassment is a consequence of this culture. A code of silence stemming from organizational loyalty prevents FPO from reporting incidences of harassment out of fear of reprisal and further isolation (Chaiyavej & Morash, 2009; Davis et al., 2023; Lee & Yu, 2020). Members learn whether such harassment is tolerated through their everyday interactions and whether harassers are held accountable for their actions, further cementing the importance of policy and procedures (Ford & Ivancic, 2020). This close-knit nature, specifically the fear of their reputations tarnished or of reciprocating bullying, heavily contributes to FPO avoiding reporting (Davis et al., 2023).

Another approach is to assess organizational climate, specifically the policies implemented. Even though organizational climate is considered an antecedent of sexual harassment in the workplace (e.g., Willness et al., 2007), few studies have examined whether specific policies or procedures perpetuate tolerance for sexual harassment. In general, organizational climate is a significant predictor for sexual harassment, and how organizations deal with sexual harassment has significant associations with psychological, physical, and occupational outcomes (Willness et al., 2007). Ford and Ivancic (2020) studied whether tolerance of sexual harassment is related to sexual harassment fatigue, referring to feelings of "helplessness, anger, or an emotionless state" as a result of repeat occurrences within an organization (p. 5). Results suggest that an organization's tolerance of sexual harassment is associated with workers' feelings of resilience, with individuals experiencing lower levels of tolerance if they perceive their workplace as tolerant of such actions (Ford & Ivancic, 2020). Policies are intended to clarify how the organizations are expected to react and discipline, and formal restrictions are intended to tell workers that harassment is being taken seriously as well as assure survivors that they are not being ignored (Chaiyavej & Morash, 2009). Previous works suggest that women are more likely to report incidences if their organization had long-standing policies, education, procedures, and punishments for sexual harassment (Chaiyavej & Morash, 2009). Furthermore, women's confidence to report sexual harassment to their organization is contingent on how clearly policies prohibit this harassment (Chaiyavej & Morash, 2009).

Practical Implications

The most obvious solution to sexual harassment in the workplace includes changing the culture and climate that tolerates such deviance. This is not easy to accomplish as it requires tasking organizations with completely restructuring themselves (Lee & Yu, 2020; Yu, 2022). The most often proposed solution to workplace sexual harassment is to offer organizations more training and workshops, keeping workers informed about the realities of sexual harassment (Chaiyavej & Morash, 2009; Pina et al., 2009). Notably, there is no current universal standard for effective programs. If/when developed, these programs then require standardized, validated program evaluations to properly determine the effectiveness of trainings in combating sexual harassment (Pina et al., 2009). However, previous work suggests that training and mentoring increase worker empowerment, which benefits individuals as well as the organization as a whole (Chaiyavej & Morash, 2009; Yu, 2022). Given that organizational climate is associated with policies and procedures, strengthening policies to better punish sexual harassment is warranted. Chaiyavej and Morash (2009) argue that involving women in decision-making would further empower them and reinforce their trust in the organization.

Additionally, it is important to consider the role of leaders in police organizations specifically. Leadership influences how organizational cultures and climate develop and maintain, sometimes leaders even contribute to the potential formation and destruction of culture/climate (Wolfe & Piquero, 2011). Leaders in police organizations (i.e., administrators, section chiefs) are the paradigm of a good officer, setting the standards for rule compliance, risk management, and health and wellness

(Simmons-Beauchamp & Sharpe, 2022). If these leaders are ineffective, demonstrate values that contradict the organization, or fail to maintain a healthy culture and climate, then their legitimacy is questioned (Simmons-Beauchamp & Sharpe, 2022; Timmerman & Bajema, 2000; Wolfe & Piquero, 2011). FPO awareness of an organization's hierarchy may act as a barrier to reporting sexual harassment, with survivors concerned they will be perceived as rude, disrespectful, or dishonest if they speak up (Carter Collins, 2004; Davis et al., 2023). Survivors who reported the instances to their superiors felt discouragement when leaders were reluctant to pursue their claims or remove the perpetrators from the organization (Sands et al., 2023). Additionally, the lack of women in leadership roles may contribute to FPO inability to properly acclimate within police organizations: Specifically, FPO without such mentors can affect turnover, promotions, and empowerment (Sands et al., 2023).

Conclusion

Given that sexual harassment is a prevalent issue in the workplace, understanding this phenomenon through an organizational culture and climate lens provides further information on the role organizations play in either the tolerance or acceptance in an institution. Studying police organizations provides further context on how organizations driven by masculine ideals are especially susceptible to this type of harassment (see Davis et al., 2023; Quick & McFadyen, 2017). Understanding how organizations play a role in sexual harassment may provide further information regarding its impacts. For example, survivors of sexual harassment often report that the incident significantly impacted their work, with women feeling that scrutinized or that the incident hindered their future career prospects (Davis et al., 2023). Organizations cannot effectively function when their workers are experiencing trauma, especially if their workplace plays a role in the trauma. It is the organization's responsibility to implement clear policies regarding discipline of sexual harassment, to ensure survivors concerns are addressed and harassers are held accountable.

References

Berdahl, J. L. (2007). Harassment based on sex: Protecting social status in the context of gender hierarchy. *The Academy of Management Review, 32*(2), 641–658.

Bowers, M. R., Hall, J. R., & Srinivasan, M. M. (2017). Organizational culture and leadership style: The missing combination for selecting the right leader for effective crisis management. *Business Horizons, 60*(4), 551–563. https://doi.org/10.1016/j.bushor.2017.04.001

Carter Collins, S. (2004). Sexual harassment and police discipline: Who's policing the police? *Policing: An international Journal, 27*(4), 512–538. https://doi.org/10.1108/13639510410566253

Chaiyavej, S., & Morash, M. (2009). Reasons for policewomen's assertive and passive reactions to sexual harassment. *Police Quarterly, 12*(1), 63–85. https://doi.org/10.1177/1098611108327309

Cleveland, J. N., & Kurst, M. E. (1993). Sexual harassment and perceptions of power: An under articulated relationship. *Journal of Vocational Behavior, 42*(1), 49–67. https://doi.org/10.1006/jvbe.1993.1004

Davis, H., Lawrence, S., Wilson, E., Sweeting, F., & Poate-Joyner, A. (2023). 'No one likes a grass' Female police officers' experience of workplace sexual harassment: A qualitative study. *International Journal of Police Science & Management, 25*(2), 183–195. https://doi.org/10.1177/14613557231157185

Dougherty, D. S., & Smythe, M. J. (2004). Sensemaking, organizational culture, and sexual harassment. *Journal of Applied Communication Research, 32*(4), 293–317. https://doi.org/10.1080/0090988042000275998

Equal Employment Opportunity Commission. (2022). *Sexual harassment in our nation's workplaces*. https://www.eeoc.gov/data/sexual-harassment-our-nations-workplaces

Fitzgerald, L. F., Drasgow, F., Hulin, C. L., Gelfand, M. J., & Magley, V. J. (1997a). Antecedents and consequences of sexual harassment in organizations: A test of an integrated model. *Journal of Applied Psychology, 82*(4), 578–589.

Fitzgerald, L. F., Swan, S., & Magley, V. J. (1997b). But was it really sexual harassment?: Legal, behavioral, and psychological definitions of the workplace victimization of women. In W. O'Donohue (Ed.), *Sexual harassment: Theory, research, and treatment* (pp. 5–28). Allyn & Bacon.

Ford, J. L., & Ivancic, S. R. (2020). Surviving organizational tolerance of sexual harassment: An exploration of resilience, vulnerability, and harassment fatigue. *Journal of Applied Communication Research, 48*(2), 186–206. https://doi.org/10.1080/00909882.2020.1739317

Hertzog, J. L., Wright, D., & Beat, D. (2008). There's a policy for that: A comparison of the organizational culture of workplaces reporting incidents of sexual harassment. *Behavior and Social Issues, 17*, 169–181.

Kaiser, C. R., Bandt-Law, B., Cheek, N. N., & Schachtman, R. (2022). Gender prototypes shape perceptions of and responses to sexual harassment. *Current Directions in Psychological Science, 31*(3), 254–261. https://doi.org/10.1177/09637214221078592

Kiebler, J. M., & Stewart, A. J. (2022). Gender stereotypes, class, and race in attributions of blame for women's gender-linked mistreatment. *Analyses of Social Issues and Public Policy, 22*(1), 351–377. https://doi.org/10.1111/asap.12299

Kobayashi, Y. (2018). Exploring sexual harassment in the police force in Japan: A comparative study between Japan and the United States. *Journal of Asia-Pacific Studies (Waseda University)*. Retrieved March 7, 2024 from https://core.ac.uk/download/pdf/159504225.pdf

Lee, D., & Yu, H. H. (2020). Breaking the code of silence: Who are the women reporting sex-based discrimination in federal regulatory agencies? *Policing: An International Journal, 43*(4), 575–589. https://doi.org/10.1108/PIJPSM-01-2020-0008

Maher, T. M. (2003). Police sexual violence: Officers' perceptions of its extent and causality. *Criminal Justice Review, 28*, 355–381.

McCabe, M. P., & Hardman, L. (2005). Attitudes and perceptions of workers to sexual harassment. *The Journal of Social Psychology, 145*, 719–740. https://doi.org/10.3200/SOCP.145.6.719-740

Ostroff, C., Kinicki, A. J., & Muhammad, R. S. (2013). Organizational culture and climate. In N. W. Schmitt & S. Highhouse (Eds.), *Handbook of psychology* (2nd ed., pp. 646–676). Wiley.

Perry, E. L., Block, C. J., & Noumair, D. A. (2021). Leading in: Inclusive leadership, inclusive climates and sexual harassment. *Equality, Diversity and Inclusion, 40*(4), 430–447. https://doi.org/10.1108/EDI-04-2019-0120

Pina, A., Gannon, T. A., & Saunders, B. (2009). An overview of the literature on sexual harassment: Perpetrator, theory, and treatment issues. *Aggression and Violent Behavior, 14*(2), 126–138. https://doi.org/10.1016/j.avb.2009.01.002

Quick, J. C., & McFadyen, M. A. (2017). Sexual harassment: Have we made any progress? *Journal of Occupational Health Psychology, 22*(3), 286–298. https://doi.org/10.1037/ocp0000054

Rabe-Hemp, C. E., & Braithwaite, J. (2012). An exploration of recidivism and the officer shuffle in police sexual violence. *Police Quarterly, 16*(2), 127–147. https://doi.org/10.1177/1098611112464964
Reiner, R. (2000). *The politics of the police* (3rd ed.). Dartmouth.
Sands, A., Westerman, L., Prochnau, J., & Blankenau, H. (2023). Police sexual violence: A study of policewomen as victims. *Police Quarterly, 26*(1), 3–23. https://doi.org/10.1177/10986111211058032
Schein, E. H. (2010). *Organizational culture and leadership*. Jossey-Bass.
Schneider, B., Ehrhart, M. G., & Macey, W. H. (2013). Organizational climate and culture. *Annual Review of Psychology, 64*, 361–388. https://doi.org/10.1146/annurev-psych-113011-143809
Schneider, B., González-Romá, V., Ostroff, C., & West, M. A. (2017). Organizational climate and culture: Reflections on the history of the constructs in the Journal of Applied Psychology. *Journal of Applied Psychology, 102*(3), 468–482. https://doi.org/10.1037/apl0000090
Sexual Harassment. (n.d.). *U.S. Equal Opportunity Commission*. Retrieved October, 17, 2023, from https://www.eeoc.gov/sexual-harassment
Silvestri, M. (2017). Police culture and gender: Revisiting the 'cult of masculinity'. *Policing, 11*(3), 289–300.
Simmons-Beauchamp, B., & Sharpe, H. (2022). The moral injury of ineffective police leadership: A perspective. *Frontiers in Psychology, 13*, 766237. https://doi.org/10.3389/fpsyg.2022.766237
Sweeting, F., Cole, T., & Hills, P. (2022). Is the blue wall of silence a fallacy in cases of police sexual misconduct? *International Journal of Police Science & Management, 24*(3), 285–297. https://doi.org/10.1177/14613557221085504
Taylor, B. G., Maitra, P., Mumford, E., & Liu, W. (2020). Sexual harassment of law enforcement officers: Findings from a nationally representative survey. *Journal of Interpersonal Violence*, 1–25. https://doi.org/10.1177/0886260520978180
Timmerman, G., & Bajema, C. (2000). The impact of organizational culture on perceptions and experiences of sexual harassment. *Journal of Vocational Behavior, 57*, 188–205. https://doi.org/10.1006/jvbe.1999.1741
Trice, H. M., & Beyer, J. M. (1993). *The cultures of work organization*. Pretince Hall.
Westmarland, L. (2012). Police cultures. In T. Newburn (Ed.), *Handbook of policing* (2nd ed., pp. 253–280). Willan Publishing.
Willness, C. R., Steel, P., & Lee, K. (2007). A meta-analysis of the antecedents and consequences of workplace sexual harassment. *Personnel Psychology, 60*(1), 127–162.
Wolfe, S. E., & Piquero, A. (2011). Organizational justice and police misconduct. *Criminal Justice and Behavior, 38*(4), 332–353. https://doi.org/10.1177/0093854810397739
Yu, H. H. (2022). Intersectionality and non-reporting behavior: Perceptions from women of color in federal law enforcement. *Review of Public Personnel Administration, 42*(3), 574–592.
Zhang, J., & Liu, Y. (2010). Organizational climate and its effects on organizational variables: An empirical study. *International Journal of Psychological Studies, 2*(2), 189–201.

Chapter 8
Toward an Organizational Climate of Delinquency Prevention: The Missing Link for Understanding School Delinquency

Kayla Alaniz

Introduction

Although schools are generally safe places, in-school delinquency, crime, and violence remain a concern for students and staff (Fissel et al., 2019). Acts of delinquency in schools, ranging from substance use to rarer events such as school shootings, can pose threats to academic achievement, physical and mental health, and the overall well-being of school occupants (Aldridge et al., 2018). With this, school leaders are charged with creating safe and supportive settings to foster effective teaching and learning by minimizing the harmful effects of delinquency.

In response to the growing concern for safety, school leaders and legislators have mandated or implemented policies, procedures, and practices aimed at preventing and reducing the harmful effects of delinquency in schools (Fissel et al., 2019; Schreck & Miller, 2003; Tillyer et al., 2011). These initiatives range from punitive discipline practices (e.g., zero-tolerance policies; Fissel et al., 2019; Teske, 2011; Welch & Payne, 2018), security implementations (e.g., metal detectors and school resource officers [SROs]; Canady et al., 2012; Fisher & Hennessy, 2016; Na & Gottfredson, 2013), and programming (e.g., after school programs and student-teacher morale; Gottfredson, 2001; Tillyer et al., 2011). These strategies and interventions are aimed at preventing school delinquency; however, the effectiveness of these efforts is mixed in the literature and is often associated with adverse outcomes (Tillyer et al., 2011).

Although these efforts are considered environment-focused interventions, they are not products developed for a specific school environment. In other words, these

K. Alaniz (✉)
Sam Houston State University, Department of Criminal Justice and Criminology, Huntsville, TX, USA
e-mail: kxa045@shsu.edu

D. S. Rudes, J. R. Ingram (eds.), *Using Organizational Theory to Study, Explain, and Understand Criminal Legal Organizations*,
https://doi.org/10.1007/978-3-031-66285-0_8

efforts intended to address school delinquency are general strategies that do not consider how stakeholders perceive these initiatives. The perceptions of those subjected to the prevention strategies and contexts of the school environment can be meaningful in understanding delinquency engagement and further inform efforts to reduce these acts.

Organizational climate is a relevant framework that captures individuals' perceptions of a social environment and how they influence related outcomes. Furthermore, organizational climate poses that the interconnected experiences of policies, procedures, and practices of individuals and their perceptions of what is expected, valued, and promoted in an organization can become shared through meaningful interactions and influence organizational outcomes (James & Jones, 1974; Jones & James, 1979; Schneider et al., 2017). If a climate is shared, then it reflects a higher, school-level phenomenon (i.e., Kozlowski & Klein, 2000). Research in school settings shows that student perceptions of school are associated with various outcomes, such as academic performance and school satisfaction (Battistich et al., 1995; Stewart, 2008; Thapa et al., 2013; Verkuyten & Thijs, 2002); however, a climate dimension that centers on students' views of delinquency prevention initiatives has not been established. Developing a climate of delinquency prevention, especially in the areas of discipline, security, and programming, would assist our understanding of how students perceive their school environment in order to enhance targeted interventions and initiatives (Fan et al., 2011), such as school delinquency.

This chapter proposes three main points to enhance the current understanding of school delinquency and prevention. First, it is imperative to measure students' perceptions of delinquency interventions. How students view these initiatives as beneficial or detrimental (i.e., climate) can be the missing link in explaining subsequent engagement in school delinquency. Second, student perceptions can become shared and reflect a school-level phenomenon through a multilevel process of emergence. Third, if student perceptions of their school's interventions are shared, this climate of school delinquency prevention should be investigated to determine if it is related to delinquency engagement. To accomplish this argument, this chapter uses a multilevel organizational framework.

The chapter is organized as follows. First, I cover scholarship centered on the prevalence, explanations, and prevention programs of school delinquency. Next, I provide an overview of the organizational climate framework for understanding how perceptions of procedures, policies, and practices shape a collective phenomenon through an emergent process. Within this discussion, differences between the organizational climate framework offered here and the concept of school climate within the educational literature is offered. Then, I describe how organizational climate can serve as a mechanism between the school environment and school delinquency and any work that has examined this relationship. Lastly, I advocate for further research in this area and offer recommendations for future research to examine this relationship.

School Delinquency

Conceptualizing School Delinquency

Research aimed at understanding and examining students' problematic behavior or misconduct in schools employ numerous titles and definitions to capture their behaviors of interest. For example, school crime reflects a range of behaviors, from fighting to school shootings (Gottfredson et al., 2020). In contrast, school misconduct may include minor misbehavior such as tardiness and non-attendance (Hart & Mueller, 2012). With an interest in capturing all types of delinquent behavior in school settings, I use the term school delinquency in this chapter. I prefer school delinquency as it distinguishes delinquency occurring on or around school campuses and encompasses behavior from student misconduct to school crime (Hart & Mueller, 2012; Jenkins, 1997; Welsh et al., 1999). Additionally, a comprehensive term capturing all problematic behavior is important because regardless of the level of severity, all forms of juvenile delinquency in schools can hinder students' feelings of safety and security, which are vital for learning environments (DeVoe et al., 2004; Hart & Mueller, 2012).

Prevalence of School Delinquency

The National Center for Education Statistics (NCES) collects and reports information on school crime, safety, and violence in K-12 schools in the United States. Although they are considerably rare, school shootings and violent deaths on campuses can have detrimental effects on the school and neighboring community. The most recent data shows that the 2020 to 2021 academic year yielded 93 casualties within public schools, the highest count since the start of the millennium when data collection began (Irwin et al., 2022). Additionally, the 2020 to 2021 academic year was the first year where elementary schools ($N = 59$) outnumbered high schools ($N = 57$) in school shooting occurrences (Irwin et al., 2022).

Other more common occurrences of school delinquency are fights, substance use, and weapon possession or use. Involvement in physical fights anywhere on a school campus (as either aggressor or victim) among high school students decreased from 11% in 2009 to 8% in 2019 (Irwin et al., 2022). Adolescent alcohol use overall also declined from 2009 to 2019, decreasing from 42% to 29% (Irwin et al., 2022). In 2019, 22% of high school students reported use of marijuana on school campuses at least once in the past 30 days. Additionally, 22% of high school students reported being offered, given, or sold an illegal substance on school property in the past year (Irwin et al., 2022). These trends were considerably stable compared to 2009. Regarding weapons (e.g., guns, knives, or clubs), weapon possession on school campuses decreased from 6% to 3% between 2009 and 2019 (Irwin et al., 2022). Overall, while some of these indicators of delinquency and disorder are on the decline, the negative effects of these behaviors can be detrimental to the students and overall school population.

Prevention Initiatives

To address the concerns over safety on school campuses, school leaders and legislators have mandated or implemented policies, procedures, and practices aimed at reducing or preventing the prevalence of delinquency in schools, including zero tolerance policies, security implementations, and behavior modification and counseling (Fissel et al., 2019; Schreck & Miller, 2003; Tillyer et al., 2011; Welsh & Harding, 2015).

Zero Tolerance Policies Zero tolerance policies became widespread throughout the United States as an operable approach for maintaining safe classrooms by removing students who commit school infractions, such as fighting, smoking, and class disruption (Teske, 2011; Welch & Payne, 2018). Zero tolerance policies mandate that after one considerably deviant offense, students are removed from the classroom or school via in-school suspension, out-of-school suspension, or expulsion. The zero-tolerance framework is rooted in deterrence theory and asserts that severe punishment will deter future engagement in delinquency and rule violation (Fissel et al., 2019; Quackenbush, 2011). However, zero-tolerance policies are associated with numerous negative outcomes. Specifically, there is a lack of empirical support on whether zero-tolerance policies significantly impact the prevention of violence or enhance safety (American Psychological Association Zero Tolerance Task Force, 2008). In fact, zero-tolerance policies have been scrutinized for the number of unintended consequences associated with them (Welch & Payne, 2018). Research has suggested these policies have increased the likelihood of misconduct in schools rather than decreased (Fabelo et al., 2011). Additionally, students punished by zero-tolerance policies have an increased likelihood of experiencing poor academic performances, dropping out, future engagement in delinquent acts, and entering the juvenile or criminal justice system (Fabelo et al., 2011; Gardella, 2015; Lasnover, 2015; Nickerson & Cornell, 2019; Skiba & Rausch, 2006; Wald & Losen, 2003; Welch & Payne, 2018).

Security Initiatives The concerns about safety in school settings led to the increased presence of security initiatives, such as school resource officers (SROs), across schools in the United States. Briefly, SROs are sworn police officers assigned to patrol certain schools or school districts to maintain safe and stable conditions (Canady et al., 2012; Fisher & Hennessy, 2016). SRO implementation is considered a "hard control strategy" as they are assigned to target problematic juveniles and punish them accordingly (Brown, 2005). Research has suggested that the presence of SROs increases punitive discipline usage, such as suspension and expulsion (Fisher & Hennessy, 2016). Studies suggest the presence of SROs heightens the risk that students will face exclusionary or punitive discipline, such as arrests, for non-serious violations once solely handled by the school administration (Almanza et al., 2023; Bleakley & Bleakley, 2018; Chan et al., 2019; Na & Gottfredson, 2013). Additionally, Gottfredson et al. (2020) found that in a sample of 33 American public schools, the increased presence of SROs not only increased the usage of exclusionary discipline but also increased the number of drug and weapon-related incidents.

After-school Programs An intervention less punitive than the former in addressing school delinquency is after-school programs (ASP). ASPs were created to make up for unsupervised periods of time between school conclusion and parents returning home from work. By proxy, they have also been suggested to target common delinquency risk factors to mitigate problematic behavior (Taheri & Welsh, 2016). ASPs are viewed as instruments of delinquency reduction because they provide education, social and psychological development, informal social control, and formal supervision (Durlak et al., 2010; Eccles & Templeton, 2002; Gottfredson et al., 2007; Taheri & Welsh, 2016) during the after-school hours, which are considered a prime opportunity for delinquent behavior (Fox & Newman, 1997; Snyder & Sickmund, 2006; Vandell et al., 2005). With this, it is possible that ASPs can reduce criminal or deviant opportunities and be a source reflective of acceptable behavior (Cross et al., 2009, 2010; Gottfredson et al., 2007).

Studies have shown a positive relationship between ASPs and academic success and social skills (see Durlak et al., 2010; Zief et al., 2006); however, their effectiveness in reducing delinquent behavior is mixed. Jones and Offord (1989) found significant reductions in antisocial behavior outside and within school related to a non-skill development program in Ontario. Contrastingly, other examinations of this relationship suggested ASPs increased involvement in delinquency (Durlak et al., 2010). A recent meta-analysis by Taheri and Welsh (2016) examined research in this area and found that ASPs have a small and non-statistically significant effect on juvenile delinquency. Although beneficial in other forms to students, ASPs have not been sufficiently proven to effectively reduce delinquency in schools.

Organizational Climate and School Delinquency

The initiatives described previously have been evaluated in their effectiveness as policies, practices, and procedures in reducing delinquency; however, they could also serve as a basis for a climate of school delinquency prevention. Organizational climate is a popular and empirically supported theoretical framework for explaining organizational outcomes. Organizational climate represents the shared perceptions of and attachment to experiences of situations, such as procedures, policies, practices, and routines of individuals within the same environment (James & Jones, 1974; Ostroff et al., 2013; Schneider et al., 2011, 2013, 2017). According to James et al. (1978), if individuals in the same context form attitudes based on their assignment of unique meanings to situations and engage in behavior based upon these meanings, then the meanings themselves are meaningful in predicting attitudes and behavior. In other words, perceptions of the organizational atmosphere, objectives, social context, and conditions have meaningful consequences for an organization's effectiveness and outcomes.

Historically, organizational climate faced a series of conceptualization and measurement issues (Schneider et al., 2017). The early eras of climate research utilized survey data from individuals in an organization and aggregated the results to reflect a higher level of analysis. This strategy raised concerns regarding the reliability of employing individual perceptions of situations to represent an organizational measure (Schneider et al., 2017). James and Jones (1974) clarified these concerns by distinguishing the difference between psychological (individual level) and organizational climate (unit level). Their work explained that individual perceptions can only reflect a higher unit if shared (James & Jones, 1974; Jones & James, 1979; Schneider et al., 2017). This distinction by James and Jones (1974) implies that climate can operate at lower and higher levels of analysis. Examining the unit level can reveal between-organization effects, while the individual level is limited to assessing within-organization effects (Griffith, 1997).

Climate as an Emergent Phenomenon

The concept of emergence is important to the organizational climate framework. Organizations are multilevel structures of individuals working in groups, teams, units, departments, and branches toward a specific goal in a specific industry (Fischer, 2015). Considering this, it is essential for organizational theory to explain behavior across these levels. Individual assessments of features of an organization can be meaningful in understanding relevant outcomes if there is a consensus among those in the environment (James, 1982; Ostroff et al., 2013).

A consensus across individual perceptions infers a sharedness among those in the same environment at the organizational level. This is also known as a bottom-up process or emergence in organizational theory. Emergence describes how lower-level entities (i.e., individuals, workgroups, units) combine and interact to create a collective phenomenon over time (Kozlowski et al., 2013; Kozlowski & Klein, 2000). Emergence develops through the combination of two factors: elemental content and interaction (Kozlowski & Klein, 2000). The perceptions, norms, and behaviors individuals formulate serve as the elemental content of emergence. This information is the context of how the organization influences its members' cognitions and behavior. The process of interaction is how these individual characteristics can become shared. Individuals within the same environment communicate and share their ideas, information, feelings, and moods, which can yield homogeneous perceptions. If there is evidence of homogeneity at the individual level, these perceptions could be aggregated to represent a higher-level phenomenon, or climate, to represent the organization (James & Jones, 1974; Kozlowski & Klein, 2000).

Organizational climate possesses emergent qualities as it summarizes the cumulative perceptions of procedures, policies, practices, and routines of individuals in an organization to create a collective phenomenon (Kozlowski & Klein, 2000). With this in mind and the fact that school systems are formal multilevel organizations with hierarchies of power, communication patterns, rules, roles, and coordination schemes to function like traditional organizational systems (Thomas, 1976), it is appropriate to apply this framework to school settings.

Regarding school delinquency, student perceptions of delinquency interventions can emerge through a multilevel process. As students interact with each other in school settings, their attitudes toward delinquency interventions can become shared and representative of a school-level construct through emergent processes. If perceptions of these features of delinquency interventions are homogeneous among students or teachers, they can reflect a collective school climate and be theoretically meaningful in understanding subsequent engagement in delinquency behavior. Before detailing how organizational climate can be applied to school delinquency prevention, however, it is necessary to differentiate how this framework differs from the concept of school climate in the educational literature.

Organizational Climate Versus School Climate

Climate has extensively been discussed within school settings. A generally accepted definition offered by the National School Climate Council (2007) asserts that "school climate is based on patterns of people's experiences of school life and reflects norms, goals, values, interpersonal relationships, teaching and learning practices, and organizational structures" (p. 4). Notably, school climate represents every function and experience within a school environment and expands upon the academic learning context (Wang & Degol, 2016). In addition to the academic element, school climate commonly incorporates community, safety, and institutional environment categorizations to provide a comprehensive insight into the school climate condition (see Thapa et al., 2013 and Wang & Degol, 2016 for thorough reviews).

Researchers and educators have increasingly examined predictors and outcomes associated with school climate to foster and promote supportive school environments (Thapa et al., 2013). With this, school climate research commonly examines how positive or negative connotations influence student outcomes (Koth et al., 2008; Wang & Degol, 2016). There is a general consensus that school climate is associated with student academic achievement (Cornell et al., 2016; Kwong & Davis, 2015; Wang & Holcombe, 2010), problematic behavior (e.g., aggression, misconduct, delinquency) (Meyer-Adams & Conner, 2008; Wang & Dishion, 2012), and psychological outcomes (Klein et al., 2012; Way et al., 2007). In sum, there is a solid foundation in research that suggests a positive school climate enhances student experiences in schools and reduces risk behaviors. Despite its contribution to the field, the concept of school climate does have some current conceptual limitations.

First, most of the related studies are theoretically and methodologically lacking in examining how school climate operates as a link between the school environment and school delinquency. School climate research has traditionally relied on individual perceptions or statistical aggregation of individual perceptions without considering the possibility of diversity in views among school occupants (Bradshaw et al., 2021; Griffith, 1997). It is possible that although students, staff, and faculty interact in the same environment that their perceptions of the school's policies, practices, and procedures may differ. Suppose dissimilarities exist among the school population (whether it is students or faculty). In that case, the meanings attached to the school environment cannot reflect an overall school climate and are better represented at the individual level.

In this sense, traditional school climate literature has not incorporated the concept of emergence, which is the theoretical mechanism for treating climate as a school-level measure, into the framework. Few of the previously mentioned studies aggregated the student perceptions to the school level to determine if they reflected a collective phenomenon. Rather, researchers will simply implicate that school climate operates at the individual and school level rather than substantively examining the between-school effects (Griffith, 1997). An example of this being adequately done is a study by Griffith (1997). Griffith (1997) assessed student perceptions of their school and social environment and its influence on academic performance. The paper used hierarchical linear modeling analyses to examine the between-school differences in school climate (e.g., social order and social action) and found that dimensions of school climate were the strongest predictors of academic achievement. Other contemporary works have applied multilevel statistical modeling to produce school-level measures (e.g., Fan et al., 2011; Tillyer et al., 2011); however, they lack the theoretical discussion of why individual perceptions can potentially be reflective of a school-level climate or have not examined a relative climate dimension for understanding school delinquency.

Second, climate—in all types of organizations—has been conceptualized differently and taken on different forms (Ostroff & Schulte, 2014). A majority of climate research has analyzed climate monolithically, trying to capture the inner workings of the organization in one measure. Another body of research has examined focused climates within organizations (Schneider et al., 2017). This body of work suggests that a singular and uniform approach to climate would be too multifaceted to be useful in understanding specific outcomes (Ostroff et al., 2013; Schneider, 1975). To mend this, Schneider (1975) proposed a strategic climate approach that centered on conceptualizing climate dimensions relative to their specific goals. In other words, when specific procedures and practices are relevant to specific outcomes and goals, focused climates are more meaningful for examination (Schneider, 1975).

Common examples of strategic climates include climates for safety, justice, service, ethics, diversity, and excellence (Schneider et al., 2013, 2017). The purpose of these strategic climate dimensions is to examine how procedures, policies, and practices relevant to their respective area influence relevant outcomes. Regarding delinquency, a focused dimension of climate can be explanatory of the effectiveness of delinquency prevention strategies and student engagement in delinquency. The procedures, policies, and practices related to school delinquency can shape the perceptions of students and can be directly related to delinquent behavior or lack thereof. With this, there is reason to measure a strategic climate of school delinquency prevention in future research examining school delinquency. The following sections describe the appropriate framework to accomplish this.

Toward a Climate of School Delinquency Prevention

Schools implement several policies, practices, and programs in an effort to reduce and deter school delinquency. While these implementations are extensively evaluated to determine effectiveness, a missing link in the explanation of school delinquency engagement is students' perceptions and interpretations of these initiatives. As described earlier, multiple focused climates can exist within an organization that relate to specific outcome measures. This application of organizational climate can be particularly meaningful in the examination of school delinquency. Specifically, examining a climate of school delinquency prevention that captures students' perceptions of prevention initiatives (i.e., zero-tolerance policies, SROs, and ASPs) can be explanatory of subsequent delinquency engagement.

Unfortunately, research narrowly considers how students perceive initiatives to address delinquency. For example, when looking at zero-tolerance policies, McNeal and Dunbar Jr (2010) found that students at urban high schools in the Midwest viewed the enforcement of zero-tolerance policies as ineffective, applied inconsistently and that they did not enhance overall school safety. Among a sample of teachers and students who had formerly been expelled for misconduct outside of violence and aggression, Borrego and Maxwell (2021) revealed a disconnect between the two groups. Overall, teachers applying the zero-tolerance policies accordingly believed they were good for students and enhanced campus safety; however, former students revealed the experience of exclusionary discipline left lingering effects, including feelings of alienation, negative views of educators, and experiences of stigmatization (Borrego & Maxwell, 2021).

Additionally, empirical research on SROs is mixed on how positively students rate SROs and the effectiveness of their presence (Theriot & Orme, 2016). It is possible this is a product of the use of different operationalizations and methodologies in reporting this relationship. Interestingly, like zero-tolerance policies, literature examining students' and educators' perceptions of SROs has suggested a disconnect between the two. Kupchik and Bracy (2009) found that school personnel and parents held more favorable perceptions of SROs than students. Additionally, there are a number of studies that reveal generally positive perceptions of SRO presence, but there is a lack of consensus on their perceived effectiveness in making schools safer (Booren & Handy, 2009; Bracy, 2011) or reducing crime (Kupchik & Bracy, 2009).

Collectively, these examples in the zero-tolerance policy and SRO literatures can serve as a basis for developing a climate of school delinquency prevention measure. To determine if school delinquency prevention climate is associated with delinquent behavior, researchers should measure students' perceptions of their school's delinquency intervention measures to understand how detrimental or beneficial they view them. Theoretically, students who perceive these initiatives as detrimental or beneficial can be influential over their future engagement in delinquency. From here, researchers can assess if these perceptions become shared and reflect a school-level phenomenon.

School Delinquency Prevention Climate and Delinquent Behavior

Examining schools' climate of school delinquency prevention can explain why traditional delinquency implementations may be ill-fitting. Schools implement procedures, policies, and practices intended to reduce delinquency and create safer environments. Applying an organizational climate framework to school delinquency, it is asserted that how students perceive delinquency interventions and form attitudes based upon them represent important interpretations of the school environment that influences subsequent behavior (James et al., 1978), such as delinquency. Again, as students interact with each other in school settings, their attitudes toward delinquency interventions can become shared and represent a school-level construct through emergent processes. Students' shared meanings can then reflect a collective phenomenon relevant at the school level.

In this regard, it is possible that the effectiveness of delinquency interventions are mixed in literature because they are general and uniform in nature. Thus, it is important to understand the differences between schools to create interventions suitable to the specific school setting. To properly examine a climate of delinquency prevention as a mechanism of school delinquency, future research should (1) measure students' perceptions of delinquency interventions, (2) determine whether these individual-level perceptions have emergent properties that reflect a school-level phenomenon, and (3) investigate how the school-level climate is a device for individual-level school delinquency. Step 2 is the most important part of this process. Most school climate literature is void of the theoretical rigor organizational scientists apply in their climate examinations. With this, researchers should only aggregate student perceptions when they reflect a consensus (Kozlowski et al., 2013; Kozlowski & Klein, 2000). If a shared view of delinquency is present, researchers can employ multilevel modeling methods to account for the use of nested data (Hox, 1998).

The relationship between school climate and problematic student behavior has generally been examined in the literature. This body of work generally supports the significant association between negative school climate and problem behaviors, such as rule-breaking and telling lies (Reaves et al., 2018; Way et al., 2007). A recent meta-analysis by Reaves et al. (2018) examining the relationship between school climate and problematic student behavior concluded that, over time, there was a small statistically significant association between the two. Notably, the studies included in Reaves et al.'s (2018) study varied in their school climate dimension construction with conceptualizations including school connectedness, school satisfaction, school commitment, school attachment, fairness, and more. None of these projects, however, directly examine student perceptions of school delinquency intervention policies and programs and how these perceptions influence delinquent behavior.

Practical Implications

Understanding how school climate operates as a mechanism between school delinquency and targeted interventions can inform practical implications for school leaders and government officials. As argued throughout the chapter, how students perceive the target delinquency interventions can influence subsequent engagement in delinquent behavior; thus, student perceptions should be used to inform future delinquency interventions. As prior research has suggested, punitive efforts such as zero-tolerance policies and SRO presence are generally poorly rated among students and associated with negative unintended consequences (Booren & Handy, 2009; Borrego & Maxwell, 2021; Kupchik & Bracy, 2009; McNeal & Dunbar Jr, 2010). Additionally, although there is a lack of research considering student perceptions of ASPs—a form of non-punitive programming not directly targeted at delinquency reduction—they are seemingly ineffective in mitigating problematic behavior (Taheri & Welsh, 2016). It is evident that the current and widespread interventions targeted at school delinquency are questionable in their effectiveness, regardless of the severity of punitiveness. As such, the mixed conclusions on the effectiveness of these interventions are a direct result of the lack of understanding of students' perceptions of school climate. School officials should prioritize understanding student perceptions of current or future school delinquency interventions to inform future strategies. Additionally, considering the robust amount of literature showing the influence of school climate on behavioral and educational outcomes (see Thapa et al., 2013; Wang & Degol, 2016), school leaders should seek to improve the overall quality of their school environments (Bradshaw et al., 2021).

Conclusion

The widespread concern for school safety has led to an increased focus on understanding delinquency in school settings. While statistics have suggested some delinquent acts are on the decline, trends show that the most lethal forms of delinquency have led to more lives lost than any year prior (Irwin et al., 2022). Although well-intended, the traditional and considerably punitive interventions implemented by school leaders and legislators have not garnered sufficient evidence supporting their effectiveness (American Psychological Association Zero Tolerance Task Force, 2008; Fabelo et al., 2011; Theriot & Orme, 2016). There may be a missing piece of information that can explain engagement in school delinquency. Specifically, how students perceive their school's prevention initiatives can serve as a mechanism for future behavior. With this, there are grounds for exploring other theoretical frameworks and arguments to explain delinquency in hopes of adequately informing policy and practice that can be more effective in reducing delinquency behavior in school settings.

Organizational scientists have long applied an organizational climate framework to understand different organizational outcomes. This book chapter applied this framework to explain the disconnect between school delinquency and targeted school interventions. As asserted by the organizational climate framework, how students perceive delinquency interventions and form attitudes based upon these unique meanings influences subsequent delinquent behavior (James et al., 1978). If perceptions of these interventions in school settings are homogeneous among students, they can reflect a collective school climate and be meaningful in understanding outcomes such as delinquency. With this, it is imperative for future research examining school delinquency to take into consideration student perceptions of these policies in order to curate interventions that are specific to the climate of the school. Doing so can potentially be more effective in reducing delinquent behavior in schools than the traditional forms of intervention.

References

Aldridge, J. M., McChesney, K., & Afari, E. (2018). Relationships between school climate, bullying and delinquent behaviours. *Learning Environments Research, 21*, 153–172.

Almanza, M., Mason, M., & Melde, C. (2023). Perceptions of school resource officers: Protectors or prosecutors? *Criminal Justice Review, 48*(3), 318–338.

American Psychological Association Zero Tolerance Task Force. (2008). Are zero tolerance policies effective in the schools?: An evidentiary review and recommendations. *The American Psychologist, 63*(9). https://doi.org/10.1037/0003-066X.63.9.852

Battistich, V., Solomon, D., Kim, D. I., Watson, M., & Schaps, E. (1995). Schools as communities, poverty levels of student populations, and students' attitudes, motives, and performance: A multilevel analysis. *American Educational Research Journal, 32*(3), 627–658.

Bleakley, P., & Bleakley, C. (2018). School resource officers, 'zero tolerance' and the enforcement of compliance in the American education system. *Interchange, 49*, 247–261.

Booren, L. M., & Handy, D. J. (2009). Students' perceptions of the importance of school safety strategies: An introduction to the IPSS survey. *Journal of School Violence, 8*(3), 233–250.

Borrego, R., & Maxwell, G. M. (2021). The lingering effects of zero-tolerance: Perceptions of educators and former students. *Research in Higher Education Journal, 40*, 1–6.

Bracy, N. L. (2011). Student perceptions of high-security school environments. *Youth & Society, 43*(1), 365–395.

Bradshaw, C. P., Cohen, J., Espelage, D. L., & Nation, M. (2021). Addressing school safety through comprehensive school climate approaches. *School Psychology Review, 50*(2–3), 221–236.

Brown, B. (2005). Controlling crime and delinquency in the schools: An exploratory study of student perceptions of school security measures. *Journal of School Violence, 4*(4), 105–125.

Canady, M., James, B., & Nease, J. (2012). *To protect and educate: The school resource officer and the prevention of violence in schools*. National Association of School Resource Officers.
Chan, P. E., Counts, J., Katsiyannis, A., & Ryan, J. (2019). Litigation and school resource officers. *Journal of Child and Family Studies, 28*, 3296–3306.
Cornell, D., Shukla, K., & Konold, T. R. (2016). Authoritative school climate and student academic engagement, grades, and aspirations in middle and high schools. *Aera Open, 2*(2), 2332858416633184.
Cross, A. B., Gottfredson, D. C., Wilson, D. M., Rorie, M., & Connell, N. (2009). The impact of after-school programs on the routine activities of middle-school students: Results from a randomized, controlled trial. *Criminology & Public Policy, 8*(2), 391–412.
Cross, A. B., Gottfredson, D. C., Wilson, D. M., Rorie, M., & Connell, N. (2010). Implementation quality and positive experiences in after-school programs. *American Journal of Community Psychology, 45*, 370–380.
DeVoe, J. F., Peter, K., Kaufman, P., Miller, A., Noonan, M., Snyder, T. D., & Baum, K. (2004). Indicators of school crime and safety, 2004. In *NCES 2005-002*. National Center for Education Statistics.
Durlak, J. A., Weissberg, R. P., & Pachan, M. (2010). A meta-analysis of after-school programs that seek to promote personal and social skills in children and adolescents. *American Journal of Community Psychology, 45*, 294–309.
Eccles, J. S., & Templeton, J. (2002). Extracurricular and other after-school activities for youth. *Review of Research in Education, 26*(1), 113–180.
Fabelo, T., Thompson, M. D., Plotkin, M., Carmichael, D., Marchbanks, M. P., & Booth, E. A. (2011). *Breaking schools' rules: A statewide study of how school discipline relates to students' success and juvenile justice involvement*. Council of State Governments Justice Center.
Fan, W., Williams, C. M., & Corkin, D. M. (2011). A multilevel analysis of student perceptions of school climate: The effect of social and academic risk factors. *Psychology in the Schools, 48*(6), 632–647.
Fischer, R. (2015). Multilevel approaches in organizational settings: Opportunities, challenges, and implications for cross-cultural research. In *Multilevel analysis of individuals and cultures* (pp. 175–198). Taylor and Francis.
Fisher, B. W., & Hennessy, E. A. (2016). School resource officers and exclusionary discipline in US high schools: A systematic review and meta-analysis. *Adolescent Research Review, 1*, 217–233.
Fissel, E. R., Wilcox, P., & Tillyer, M. S. (2019). School discipline policies, perceptions of justice, and in-school delinquency. *Crime & Delinquency, 65*(10), 1343–1370.
Fox, J. A., & Newman, S. A. (1997). *After-school crime or after-school programs: Tuning in to the prime time for violent juvenile crime and implications for national policy. A Report to the United States Attorney General*. Fight Crime: Invest in Kids.
Gardella, J. H. (2015). *Restorative practices: For school administrators considering implementation*. Vanderbilt University.
Gottfredson, D. C. (2001). *Schools and delinquency*. Cambridge University Press.
Gottfredson, D. C., Cross, A., & Soulé, D. A. (2007). Distinguishing characteristics of effective and ineffective after-school programs to prevent delinquency and victimization. *Criminology & Public Policy, 6*(2), 289–318.
Gottfredson, D. C., Crosse, S., Tang, Z., Bauer, E. L., Harmon, M. A., Hagen, C. A., & Greene, A. D. (2020). Effects of school resource officers on school crime and responses to school crime. *Criminology & Public Policy, 19*(3), 905–940.
Griffith, J. (1997). School climate as "social order" and "social action": A multilevel analysis of public elementary school student perceptions. *Social Psychology of Education, 2*(3–4), 339–369.
Hart, C. O., & Mueller, C. E. (2012). School delinquency and social bond factors: Exploring gendered differences among a national sample of 10th graders. *Psychology in the Schools, 50*(2), 116–133.

Hox, J. (1998). Multilevel modeling: When and why. In *Classification, data analysis, and data highways: Proceedings of the 21st Annual Conference of the Gesellschaft für Klassifikation eV, University of Potsdam, March 12–14, 1997* (pp. 147–154). Springer Berlin Heidelberg.
Irwin, V., Wang, K., Cui, J., & Thompson, A. (2022). *Report on indicators of school crime and safety: 2021 (NCES 2022-092/NCJ 304625)*. National Center for Education Statistics, U.S. Department of Education, and Bureau of Justice Statistics, Office of Justice Programs, U.S. Department of Justice. Retrieved [date] from https://nces.ed.gov/pubsearch/pubsinfo.asp?pubid=2022092
James, L. R. (1982). Aggregation bias in estimates of perceptual agreement. *Journal of Applied Psychology, 67*(2), 219.
James, L. R., & Jones, A. P. (1974). Organizational climate: A review of theory and research. *Psychological Bulletin, 81*(12), 1096.
James, L. R., Hater, J. J., Gent, M. J., & Bruni, J. R. (1978). Psychological climate: Implications from cognitive social learning theory and interactional psychology. *Personnel Psychology, 31*(4), 783–813.
Jenkins, P. H. (1997). School delinquency and the school social bond. *Journal of Research in Crime and Delinquency, 34*(3), 337–367.
Jones, A. P., & James, L. R. (1979). Psychological climate: Dimensions and relationships of individual and aggregated work environment perceptions. *Organizational Behavior and Human Performance, 23*(2), 201–250.
Jones, M. B., & Offord, D. R. (1989). Reduction of antisocial behavior in poor children by nonschool skill-development. *Journal of Child Psychology and Psychiatry, 30*(5), 737–750.
Klein, J., Cornell, D., & Konold, T. (2012). Relationships between bullying, school climate, and student risk behaviors. *School Psychology Quarterly, 27*(3), 154.
Koth, C. W., Bradshaw, C. P., & Leaf, P. J. (2008). A multilevel study of predictors of student perceptions of school climate: The effect of classroom-level factors. *Journal of Educational Psychology, 100*(1), 96.
Kozlowski, S. W., & Klein, K. J. (2000). A multilevel approach to theory and research in organizations: Contextual, temporal, and emergent processes. In K. J. Klein & S. W. J. Kozlowski (Eds.), *Multilevel theory, research, and methods in organizations: Foundations, extensions, and new directions*. Jossey-Bass.
Kozlowski, S. W., Chao, G. T., Grand, J. A., Braun, M. T., & Kuljanin, G. (2013). Advancing multilevel research design: Capturing the dynamics of emergence. *Organizational Research Methods, 16*(4), 581–615.
Kupchik, A., & Bracy, N. L. (2009). *To protect, serve, and mentor?. Schools under surveillance: Cultures of control in public education* (p. 21).
Kwong, D., & Davis, J. R. (2015). School climate for academic success: A multilevel analysis of school climate and student outcomes. *Journal of Research in Education, 25*(2), 68–81.
Lasnover, S. (2015). The early of effects of the removal of willful defiance from the discipline policy at urban high schools (Doctoral dissertation). UCLA.
McNeal, L., & Dunbar, C., Jr. (2010). In the eyes of the beholder: Urban student perceptions of zero tolerance policy. *Urban Education, 45*(3), 293–311.
Meyer-Adams, N., & Conner, B. T. (2008). School violence: Bullying behaviors and the psychosocial school environment in middle schools. *Children & Schools, 30*(4), 211–221.
Na, C., & Gottfredson, D. C. (2013). Police officers in schools: Effects on school crime and the processing of offending behaviors. *Justice Quarterly, 30*(4), 619–650.
National School Climate Council. (2007). *The School Climate Challenge: Narrowing the gap between school climate research and school climate policy, practice guidelines and teacher education policy*. Retrieved from http://www.schoolclimate.org/climate/advocacy.php
Nickerson, A., & Cornell, D. (2019). School crisis prevention, response, and recovery. In M. J. Mayer & S. R. Jimerson (Eds.), *School safety and violence prevention: Science, practice, policy* (pp. 223–246). American Psychological Association. https://doi.org/10.1037/0000106-010

Ostroff, C., & Schulte, M. (2014). *A configural approach to the study of organizational culture and climate*. Oxford University Press.
Ostroff, C., Kinicki, A. J., & Tamkins, M. M. (2013). Organizational culture and climate. In W. C. Borman, D. R. Ilgen, & R. J. Klimoski (Eds.), *Handbook of psychology* (I/O psychology) (Vol. 12, pp. 565–594). Wiley.
Quackenbush, S. L. (2011). Deterrence theory: Where do we stand? *Review of International Studies, 37*(2), 741–762.
Reaves, S., McMahon, S. D., Duffy, S. N., & Ruiz, L. (2018). The test of time: A meta-analytic review of the relation between school climate and problem behavior. *Aggression and Violent Behavior, 39*, 100–108.
Schneider, B. (1975). Organizational climates: An essay. *Personnel Psychology, 28*, 447–479.
Schneider, B., Ehrhart, M. G., & Macey, W. H. (2011). Organizational climate research: Achievements and the road ahead. In N. M. Ashkanasy, C. P. M. Wilderom, & M. F. Peterson (Eds.), *The handbook of organizational culture and climate* (2nd ed., pp. 29–49). Thousand Oaks, CA: Sage.
Schneider, B., Ehrhart, M. G., & Macey, W. H. (2013). Organizational climate and culture. *Annual Review of Psychology, 64*, 361–388.
Schneider, B., González-Romá, V., Ostroff, C., & West, M. A. (2017). Organizational climate and culture: Reflections on the history of the constructs in the Journal of Applied Psychology. *Journal of Applied Psychology, 102*(3), 468.
Schreck, C. J., & Miller, J. M. (2003). Sources of fear of crime at school: What is the relative contribution of disorder, individual characteristics, and school security? *Journal of School Violence, 2*(4), 57–79.
Skiba, R., & Rausch, M. K. (2006). School disciplinary systems: Alternatives to suspension and expulsion. In G. G. Bear & K. M. Minke (Eds.), *Children's needs III: Development, prevention, and intervention* (pp. 87–102). National Association of School Psychologists.
Snyder, H. N., & Sickmund, M. (2006). *Juvenile offenders and victims: 2006 national report*. Office of Juvenile Justice and Delinquency Prevention.
Stewart, E. B. (2008). School structural characteristics, student effort, peer associations, and parental involvement: The influence of school-and individual-level factors on academic achievement. *Education and Urban Society, 40*(2), 179–204.
Taheri, S. A., & Welsh, B. C. (2016). After-school programs for delinquency prevention: A systematic review and meta-analysis. *Youth Violence and Juvenile Justice, 14*(3), 272–290.
Teske, S. C. (2011). A study of zero tolerance policies in schools: A multi-integrated systems approach to improve outcomes for adolescents. *Journal of Child and Adolescent Psychiatric Nursing, 24*(2), 88–97.
Thapa, A., Cohen, J., Guffey, S., & Higgins-D'Alessandro, A. (2013). A review of school climate research. *Review of Educational Research, 83*(3), 357–385.
Theriot, M. T., & Orme, J. G. (2016). School resource officers and students' feelings of safety at school. *Youth Violence and Juvenile Justice, 14*(2), 130–146.
Thomas, A. R. (1976). The organizational climate of schools. *International Review of Education, 22*, 441–463.
Tillyer, M. S., Fisher, B. S., & Wilcox, P. (2011). The effects of school crime prevention on students' violent victimization, risk perception, and fear of crime: A multilevel opportunity perspective. *Justice Quarterly, 28*(2), 249–277.
Vandell, D. L., Reisner, E. R., Brown, B. B., Dadisman, K., Pierce, K. M., Lee, D., & Pechman, E. M. (2005). *The study of promising after-school programs: Examination of intermediate outcomes in year 2*. Policy Studies Associates.
Verkuyten, M., & Thijs, J. (2002). School satisfaction of elementary school children: The role of performance, peer relations, ethnicity and gender. *Social Indicators Research, 59*, 203–228.
Wald, J., & Losen, D. J. (2003). Defining and redirecting a school-to-prison pipeline. *New Directions for Youth Development, 2003*(99), 9–15.

Wang, M. T., & Degol, J. L. (2016). School climate: A review of the construct, measurement, and impact on student outcomes. *Educational Psychology Review, 28*(2), 315–352.
Wang, M. T., & Dishion, T. J. (2012). The trajectories of adolescents' perceptions of school climate, deviant peer affiliation, and behavioral problems during the middle school years. *Journal of Research on Adolescence, 22*(1), 40–53.
Wang, M. T., & Holcombe, R. (2010). Adolescents' perceptions of school environment, engagement, and academic achievement in middle school. *American Educational Research Journal, 47*(3), 633–662.
Way, N., Reddy, R., & Rhodes, J. (2007). Students' perceptions of school climate during the middle school years: Associations with trajectories of psychological and behavioral adjustment. *American Journal of Community Psychology, 40*, 194–213.
Welch, K., & Payne, A. A. (2018). Zero tolerance school policies. In *The Palgrave international handbook of school discipline, surveillance, and social control* (pp. 215–234). Palgrave Macmillan.
Welsh, W. N., & Harding, C. (2015). School effects on delinquency and school-based prevention. In *The handbook of juvenile delinquency and juvenile justice* (pp. 181–198). Wiley Blackwell.
Welsh, W. N., Greene, J. R., & Jenkins, P. H. (1999). School disorder: The influence of individual, institutional, and community factors. *Criminology, 37*(1), 73–116.
Zief, S. G., Lauver, S., & Maynard, R. A. (2006). Impacts of after-school programs on student outcomes. *Campbell Systematic Reviews, 2*(1), 1–51.

Chapter 9
Administrative Burdens in Correctional Programming

Caitlin Bauer Lasalle

Introduction

Although the increase in incarcerations has started to slow in recent years, over 1.2 million people are currently incarcerated in US prisons (Carson, 2023). Most incarcerated individuals will eventually be released. In this regard, the programs and experiences individuals encounter while incarcerated are intended to help them succeed post-release and reduce recidivism. Even with the programs currently in place though, 70% of those released reoffend within 5 years (U.S. Prison Population, 2019). Incarcerated individuals experience daily obstacles in obtaining the programs and services they need to be successful (Carson, 2022). These obstacles that residents (and all citizens) face are referred to as administrative burdens in the literature. Administrative burdens can be seen in many different processes; obtaining Medicaid, disability forms, taxes, financial aid, enrolling in foreclosure prevention programs, and so much more (Herd & Moynihan, 2020; Bell et al., 2022; Pierce & Moulton, 2023; Yates et al., 2021).

Participation in programs while incarcerated helps to increase the safety of the facility and lower the recidivism of residents (Davis et al., 2013; Perez & Leon, 2020; Vur & Nguyen, 2023) but administrative burdens make it more difficult to participate in and complete them. Addressing the administrative burdens that exist in programming facilities can increase participation and, in turn, reduce recidivism of the residents.

While different burdens or barriers have been examined in the literature regarding incarcerated individuals (residents), the literature has not focused on the

C. B. Lasalle (✉)
Sam Houston State University, Department of Crimial Justice and Criminology, Huntsville, TX, USA
e-mail: cmb212@shsu.edu

D. S. Rudes, J. R. Ingram (eds.), *Using Organizational Theory to Study, Explain, and Understand Criminal Legal Organizations*,
https://doi.org/10.1007/978-3-031-66285-0_9

administrative burdens that residents face within prison programs. Previous studies that have looked at correctional programming focus on evaluating the effectiveness of those programs in terms of both recidivism and how well the goals of programs are achieved (Vur & Nguyen, 2023; Duwe, 2015; Clark & Duwe, 2015; Schubert et al., 2016; Huynh et al., 2015). When burdens are mentioned, it is in the context of how they prevent program goals from being achieved, again not in the form of administrative burdens.

In this chapter, I will begin with an overview of the administrative burden literature. I will discuss in more detail the three mechanisms that make up administrative burdens and the issue of human capital as it relates to burdens, as well as how this framework fits withing the organizational theory of resource dependency. Next, I will give an overview of the literature on programming in correctional facilities. This section will contain information about the different programs that are available to correctional residents, how much they engage with those programs, the types of programming, and the benefits of residents engaging with programs. Third, I will discuss how administrative burdens and human capital are present in correctional programming. This will include the specific burdens residents may face in engaging with programming, how these burdens make residents lives more difficult, and where the gaps in the literature are regarding this topic. Finally, I will discuss how we can use administrative burden information to improve correctional programming. This will include information on the burdens we can see in the literature as well as how to use administrative burden literature to improve research on correctional programming and what those studies may look like. Ideas for practices to be used in prisons to overcome administrative burdens will also be presented.

Literature Review

Administrative Burdens

Administrative burdens are a framework created by Herd and Moynihan (2018) by looking at the interactions that citizens have with the state when trying to utilize any of the public services the government provides. These burdens are not strictly an organizational idea, they were developed with public policy in mind. However, this framework fits within resource dependency theory for organizations. Resource dependency theory was developed by Pfeffer and Salancik (1978) and argues that organizations have to engage with other organizations and actors in their environment to get the resources they need. Organizations depend on these resources, and they can come in many different forms such as labor, materials, or knowledge. The control over resources that different organizations have creates a power dynamic between them. This power dynamic and the need for resources influence an organization's behavior and decision-making. Essentially, resource dependency theory is about how organizations interact with their external environment in the process of obtaining the vital resources necessary for their functioning. Administrative burdens take a micro approach, focusing on the individual and their experiences with the state. Like organizations in resource dependency theory, individuals must interact with their external environment to obtain necessary resources.

Administrative burdens can be seen in many of the interactions we have with the state and organizations every day. It is experienced in the hour-long holding period to wait for a customer service agent, or in the lengthy process to complete federal student aid funding applications. When it comes to administrative burdens, there are several main ideas. The burdens that we experience are consequential, meaning that they make a difference in our lives. Administrative burdens can impact people's ability to exercise the fundamental rights of citizenship, access benefits that can improve quality of life, and can affect the effectiveness of public programs. These burdens are also distributive, some groups will be affected more than other groups which typically aligns with the inequalities in society. Lastly, administrative burdens are constructed, they are a result of the choices that are made in the political process. There are also three mechanisms that make up administrative burdens in the organizational literature: (1) learning costs, (2) compliance costs, and (3) psychological costs (Herd & Moynihan, 2018). Each of these costs can be experienced in any combination, it is not all or nothing.

Learning costs include the time and effort that people must put in to learn or collect information about a program or service and the eligibility status of it. This is where people are unaware of a program that could be helpful to them or have trouble discovering what would make them eligible for it. Using the federal student aid funding applications as an example, we can see the learning costs where an incoming student may not be aware that FASFA exists at all to help with higher education classes. Those students who do know that FASFA exists may think they are not eligible to receive any funding and have issues determining where to find the information regarding eligibility.

The next mechanism, compliance costs, is the "provision of information and documentation to demonstrate standing; financial costs to access services; avoiding or responding to discretionary demands" (Herd & Moynihan, 2020 p. 4). This cost is fairly simple, it is the costs financial and otherwise that are required to comply with a program or service. Compliance costs can be easily seen in the process of obtaining a US visa or green card for immigration. The most obvious cost for visas and green cards is the financial cost, with the fees costing up to over $4000 (Shanks, 2022). The other compliance costs for immigration include the collection of necessary documents, time spent going to appointments, etc. (U.S. Citizenship and Immigration Services, 2020).

The last mechanism of administrative burdens is psychological costs. Psychological costs refer to the stigma that comes from interacting with an unpopular program or service, the loss of personal power or autonomy from interactions with the state, frustration dealing with the other costs, unjust or unnecessary procedures, stresses coming from uncertainty about the process and compliance (Herd & Moynihan, 2018). One example of psychological costs can be seen in filling out forms for a disability, whether that be for school or work (Christensen et al., 2019).

It can be difficult for individuals to share the specific details of their disability with administrators or the government, which may be seen as intrusive and cause them extra stress.

Now, with a better understanding of the administrative burden framework it is easier to see how it fits in the organization resource dependency theory. Just as organizations adjust their behavior and decision making based on others in their environment and the ease of access to and availability of resources, citizens adjust their behavior and decision making based on other citizens and the government based on the ease of access to and availability of public services. Administrative burdens in accessing public services create difficulties in the organization of the person obtaining the resources of the other organization, the government. This difficulty in accessing public services for citizens is similar to difficulty in accessing resources for organizations.

The experience of administrative burdens is not a universal one, some people may feel the effects much stronger than others. It is an individual experience. One of the explanations for these differences is a concept known as human capital. Human capital is also a large part of the burdens that people face as it can impact how often and how strongly burdens are experienced. Human capital is "the stock of innate abilities and characteristics that people possess and the knowledge and skills they acquire over time" (Christensen et al., 2019, p. 127). Human capital can be made up of a lot of things like an individual's education, experiences, health, knowledge, and personality traits. These different levels of human capital are part of what makes people experience administrative burdens differently (Pierce & Moulton, 2023). Human capital is the equivalent of the power dynamics between organizations in resource dependency theory. Organizations have different levels of power based on the resources they hold control of and with human capital it is a person's resources that create differences in power. For example, a person who has a lower level of education would have lower human capital and resources, meaning less power. Those who are women, disabled, racially marginalized, or low-income experience more administrative burdens, all of these things examples of human capital (Herd, 2023). To explain it in another way, say you as a senior college student are getting ready to register for your classes for the next semester. As a senior you will likely have first pick of the classes that you register for and will pick before any freshman students do. This would be because you have more human capital in that situation—a senior has already taken more classes so you would have more education and knowledge than a freshman.

Administrative burdens can have a serious impact on whether people are able to access and participate in the many processes that they encounter. I mentioned FASFA earlier and one of the administrative burdens that people may face in utilizing the federal funding. Learning costs are not the only administrative burden that can occur during the FASFA process though. There is also the issue of compliance costs as the application is long and complex (Billings et al., 2022). Those who experience these burdens with FASFA may decide that the process is not worth it and in turn acquire large amounts of student debt that they will spend decades paying off.

People may also not attend college at all because of the costs that they were using FASFA to help lighten.

When individuals are in the process of applying for some type of relief that is needed urgently, the administrative burdens may seriously inhibit their ability to obtain the assistance they need (Pierce & Moulton, 2023; Duffy & Shaefer, 2022). They may be swayed away from completing the process because of lengthy forms to complete or long wait times, leading them to stop pursuing the assistance that they truly need. As things like Medicaid and health insurance can present large administrative burdens, people can abandon the process of obtaining them as they need. Without Medicaid or health insurance though, people's physical and mental health is at risk, something especially true for older adults (Herd, 2023).

Not all negative impacts of administrative burdens are quite as direct as the ones discussed already. Bruch et al. (2010) saw an example of this in their study that examined social welfare programs. The authors there saw that when a program was designed to encourage feedback and participation of those involved then the participants had high levels of civic or political engagement. Administrative burdens do not just impact whether an individual will obtain the services or programs that they need but can impact whether or not they engage in activities outside of that as well. Addressing the unnecessary administrative burdens of programs and services is important to ensuring people can obtain those that they need and not be harmed further.

Correctional Programming

During an individual's time incarcerated they are often offered the opportunity to participate in the programs that are available at their jail or prison. The programs that residents participate in are important to their future success once they are released and help to prevent recidivism (committing another offense) and increase chances of employment (Davis et al., 2013; Perez & Leon, 2020; Vur & Nguyen, 2023). These programs can also help to ensure that residents are making productive use of their time and ensure the safety of the facility as well as give them a sense of purpose or meaning (Meyer et al., 2010; Joon Jang & Johnson, 2022).

Over 80% of correctional facilities across the United States offer some form of educational programming. Despite most facilities having these educational programs, participation rates are not quite as high—about 25%—and have been declining over time (Davis et al., 2013; Meyer et al., 2010; Barlow et al., 2022). There are many different types of educational programs that are available to residents including; GED courses, secondary education, post-secondary education, literary courses, and special education. Inside-Out programs where traditional college students take higher education courses within prisons and jails alongside residents are also offered (Perez & Leon, 2020). There are also college programs that offer just residents' courses. According to prior literature, between 35% and 42% of facilities had post-secondary programs available and only about 5% of the total incarcerated population had participated and about 11% of those that were eligible participated (Meyer et al., 2010; Brosen et al., 2019). In Florida, less than 4% of the prison population enrolled in a GED program and of that 4%, only 25% of them completed the program (Florida Department of Corrections, 2019). Educational programs can help with more than just improving residents' education. They also reduce criminal activity, improve behavior while incarcerated, improve chances of employment, help to decrease the odds of recidivism, and can help them to improve their human capital (Ellison et al., 2017; Davis et al., 2013: Duwe & Clark, 2014; Meyer et al., 2010; Brosen et al., 2019).

Employment and vocational programs are another group of correctional programs that residents can be involved in. There are many different types of employment and vocational programs available, including prison work, vocational, and work release programs. Prison work programs are those where the residents are provided the opportunity to perform a job in their facility, such as the kitchen, janitorial, or producing goods to be sold, which does not necessarily help them obtain employment once they are released (Vur & Nguyen, 2023). Vocational programs are meant to teach residents specific skills and certifications that can help them obtain employment after release such as carpentry and construction. The last type of program, work release, allows individuals to work jobs in the community and then return to their facility when they are not working (Duwe, 2015). Individuals who gain employment after their release have lower recidivism rates meaning these programs to help obtain skills for employment can help reduce recidivism (Meyer et al., 2010). Prison work programs that focus on producing goods and also have a goal of giving residents training and real work experience are known as prison industries. These are the jobs that most people think of when they consider residents working in prison including license-plate manufacturing, sewing, electronics recycling, and more (Richmond, 2014). About 30% of all state and federal adult correctional facilities have a prison industry program that employs residents (Stephan, 2008). Work release programs can also help individuals not only have lower levels of recidivism, but also better chances of finding a job and earning more money (Duwe, 2015). While work release can be incredibly helpful for individuals while they are incarcerated and after their release, one study saw that of the participants involved, 25% never finished the program (Duwe, 2015).

Aside from the increase in chances of obtaining future employment after release, employment and vocational programs can help residents and the facility in other ways as well. These programs can help them with a sense of self-worth and purpose that they may be struggling with, something that can be especially true for incarcerated women (Laub & Sampson, 2003; Richmond, 2014). For men, these programs can provide them with a sense of independence, particularly financial independence (Richmond, 2014). Similar to education, employment programs help with residents' behavior or misconduct and recidivism (Richmond, 2014; Saylor & Gaes, 1997).

Entering prison or jail while being a primary caretaker of your child is never an easy situation. There are facilities, however, that have parenting programs and classes to help those mothers and fathers separated from their children. Ninety percent of women's facilities specifically have a parenting program (Hoffman et al.,

2010). Incarcerated mothers specifically face a lot of distress due to their motherhood role being removed or reduced while they are incarcerated (Tremblay & Sutherland, 2017). While a good number of correctional facilities, specifically women's facilities, have parenting programs, they are not all the same. These programs may include parenting groups, manual based groups, visits home upon completion, homework assignments, interactions between mothers and babies, structured lessons, videos, vignettes, etc. (Tremblay & Sutherland, 2017). One of the parenting group courses is known as Parent-Child Interaction Therapy which teaches a specific type of parenting skills through role playing and in-session coaching (Scudder et al., 2014). These parenting programs can help parents to regain custody of their children once they are released and provide a method of maintaining relationships with their children (Burgess & Flynn, 2013; Eddy & Poehlmann, 2010).

In addition to the programs mentioned above, there are also many other types of correctional programming. This includes substance use treatment (Peters et al., 2017), mental health treatment (Glowa-Kollisch et al., 2014), religion or faith-based programs (Joon Jang & Johnson, 2022; Duwe et al., 2023), art and other creative programs (Jacobi, 2011; Littman & Silva, 2020), life-skills programs (Clark & Duwe, 2015), and more. These programs, like the others discussed, are implemented differently and at different rates across facilities. They all offer their own benefits though to help improve individual wellbeing and a facility.

Overall, there are many programs that are available to residents while they are incarcerated. They can take many different forms and have many benefits as well as different levels of presence and participation across facilities. These programs and classes do not come without their challenges though, as can be seen in the low participation rates across programs. These challenges or burdens are something I will discuss further in the following section.

The Burdens of Correctional Programming

We now have an overview of both administrative burdens and the programming available in correctional facilities. How do these two connect though? Where are the administrative burdens seen in correctional programming? Administrative burdens have traditionally been viewed in the process of accessing government services. They can be clearly seen in other types of programs and services though, like correctional programming. When residents attempt to engage with the programming in their facility, they may experience difficulties in doing so. Evidence of these difficulties may be inferred based on research showing that there is a higher level of interest in available programs than participation in those programs (Kaiser et al., 2020; Duwe et al., 2023). As these levels differ, it outlines the fact that barriers do exist in accessing correctional programs. These difficulties can be learning, compliance, or psychological in nature and are often a combination of the three. The section below will demonstrate examples of administrative burdens in correctional programming as they fall into the three types of costs and show the inequalities residents face in these burdens and costs.

Learning Costs

One of the ways administrative burdens can be seen in correctional programming is through the learning costs residents face. These costs, as well as the other two types, can be seen in both public and private prisons, as well as many different types of programs. Learning costs generally include the lack of knowledge of programs' existence and lack of knowledge on eligibility or participation requirements.

First, one learning cost seen in correctional programs is residents' knowledge of programs' existence. Not having knowledge about what programs and opportunities are available is the most obvious form of learning costs for residents. There have been several studies that demonstrate residents do not participate in programs because they do not know what opportunities are available (Westrheim & Manger, 2014; O'Keeffe et al., 2007; Eikeland et al., 2009; Brosens et al., 2015). This has also been seen with incarcerated women who were reentering into society who expressed they faced a lack of knowledge regarding resources available for them (Salem et al., 2023).

Learning costs may be present because the residents do not know what programs exist or they can due to a lack of information needed in order to be involved. Lack of knowledge on the eligibility or participation requirements for a program serves as an example. Residents have faced difficulty in determining if they were eligible for a program as well as difficulty in learning the process of how individuals are chosen for participation (Kaiser et al., 2020; Gustavsson, 2013). There are many nuances that go into determining if they could participate in a program and some of them were not in written policy even though they were followed. These nuances make it difficult for individuals to learn what programs they are allowed to participate in as they are denied even without a clear policy showing why. For example, in a study by Kaiser et al. (2020), residents who had a life sentence often were not allowed to participate in programs due to their sentence but there was no prison policy stating that as a disqualifier.

The requirements for initial and continued participation in a program can also be unclear to residents beyond eligibility. Even if a resident is eligible, they may still not know how to apply or register for a program (Gustavsson, 2013). Once in a program, the requirements and rules to continue participating in something like prison work can be unclear or simply not known to residents (Croux et al., 2019). This can lead them to lose their position in a program due to breaking a rule they were unaware of. Related to this, residents may reach out to the staff in their prison to obtain information on eligibility and requirements for participation. Sometimes when they seek out this information, they never receive a response from the staff they contacted, leaving them in the dark with no more knowledge than before (Brosens et al., 2015).

Lastly, as prison populations continue to grow and "warehouse" individuals, a new learning cost emerges with wait lists for programs becoming more common place. Programs may have wait lists to gain access to them as there are only so many spots in programs and a lot more people incarcerated (Brosen et al., 2019; Westrheim & Manger, 2014). Wait lists can cause all types of costs for residents, but the focus here is them as a learning cost. If programs that are available at a prison have a long wait list, they may not be discussed or advertised as much to those incarcerated as to prevent the wait list from growing. This creates a learning cost for individuals as they would no longer be gaining knowledge of every program that is available to them.

Regardless of what the circumstances are that prevent residents from gaining knowledge about programs' existence and eligibility, they all present learning costs. The burdens for residents presented in this section directly fit the definition of learning costs under the administrative burden framework as they prevent residents from being aware of programs and the eligibility for them.

Compliance Costs

Residents can face administrative burdens through compliance costs when participating in correctional programs. In this context, compliance costs most resemble those things that are traditionally seen as barriers to programming in the correctional literature. Many of the compliance costs for correctional programs arise from the specific environment of prisons, as they are unique and have their own distinct challenges. These compliance costs include things such as lockdowns, staffing, resource availability, schedules, and more.

The first compliance cost is the impact lockdowns have on participation in correctional programming. Lockdowns can occur for many different reasons such as an incident, behavior of other individuals, short staffing, or even COVID-19. Regardless of why, they are a barrier to residents' participation as they prevent residents from being able to attend their program (Lovell et al., 2023; McCarthy, 2006; Kaiser et al., 2020; Michals & Kessler, 2015). Residents are never aware of how long a lockdown may last, so it can be 1 day, or weeks of programming missed. This keeps residents from completing their programs on time which, in turn, can impact their release or parole date (Kaiser et al., 2020). These are not their own actions preventing them from being able to participate but actions of the administration at the prison making it difficult for them to do what is necessary to attend and complete a program.

Another form of compliance costs is related to the staff in a prison. Staffing shortages are increasingly common in prisons and recognized as a problem by both residents and staff (Turner et al., 2022). The shortage of staff creates a burden for residents in their access to programming, as the shortage can cause lockdowns or less movement around the prison leading to missed classes, or it can mean there is not enough staff to hold the number of programs needed for all the residents who are interested (Duwe et al., 2023; Kaiser et al., 2020). One example of this was seen in faith-based programming where the residents noted that there needed to be more access to the programs, but the lack of adequate staffing prevents that (Duwe et al., 2023).

The staff in prisons can occasionally be unsupportive of residents participating in programs or gaining an education, showing hostility or negativity towards them (Meyer et al., 2010; Vaughn-Somervell et al., 2023; Danks & Bradley, 2018; Croux et al., 2019). Sometimes the attitudes and actions of staff can become a compliance cost for residents as it prevents them from attending class (Meyer et al., 2010). Obviously, attendance is important in completing these classes and being prevented from attending class creates a compliance cost for them. They are unable to properly participate in and complete a program because of the actions of staff.

In prisons, there is an issue with schedules in programs and activities that creates a compliance cost. The first way this is seen is in the issue of overlapping schedules of different programs and activities. A program that residents are interested in or attempting to participate in may be scheduled at the same time as another program they have interest in or other activities like visits or recreational time, preventing them from being able to attend the original program of interest (Croux et al., 2019). Along the lines of schedules are transfer and release dates. This may prevent residents from participating in or completing programs when they have uncertainty about transfers and release dates (Callan & Gardner, 2005). When it comes to participating, residents may refrain from doing so because they do not know if they will be at the prison for the whole duration of the program. Unexpected transfers and release dates can come during the resident's time in a program meaning it is cut short for them and not completed.

The resources and materials needed to be successful in and complete a program present another compliance cost for residents. Many residents who were students in post-secondary education programs in several prisons indicated that they had issues with this, specifically mentioning problems obtaining tutoring and advising, finding useful materials in the library, and having access to a computer (Meyer et al., 2010). These are all things that are necessary to their education, but the setting of their education (prison) prevents them from having access to what they need. With the changes in technology and society, and pandemics, some prisons are making programs tablet based. With tablet-based programs, a new burden arises as not all residents have equal access to tablets—a necessary material (Vaughn-Somervell et al., 2023). Some residents are granted full time access and their own tablet while others only have access to a tablet for a certain amount of time. Residents not having unlimited access to tablets when needed to participate in a program can stop them from being able to do the work they need to do or keep them from attending any online meetings.

Programs may have requirements to be involved in them that create compliance costs, leading residents to act out in various ways in order to meet the requirements. For example, opioid agonist treatments may require residents to have a positive drug test to participate, leading them to search out and use illicit drugs while they are incarcerated so they can meet the requirement of testing positive when they previously did not (Komalasari et al., 2021).

Using the original administrative burden framework, time and presence (physical or online) would be the costs that are required to comply with a program in prison. The setting in prisons is different than being a citizen in outside society. Things such as lockdowns, staff, and schedules become the costs that make giving a resident's time and presence more difficult, making them the compliance costs. Access to resources and the requirements necessary to comply with a program are compliance costs that apply to both residents and citizens in society, they just look a bit different.

Psychological Costs

Psychological costs are the final cost in administrative burdens that are experienced in correctional programming. There are several things that have been discussed above as learning or compliance costs that also present psychological costs as well. Psychological costs include safety, distress experienced from lockdowns, staff, and more.

The environment itself can cause several psychological costs for residents. They may fear for their safety if they leave the confines of their cell for programs as it puts them at risk of being harmed by other residents (Croux et al., 2019). Lockdowns are another feature of the environment that can have costs for residents by causing psychological distress to individuals. They reduce the morale of residents and their interest in participating in programs because of the stress it causes and the time it would take from programs (Kaiser et al., 2020). Residents can also be worried about how the lockdowns will impact their ability to finish a program.

Some of the same things that result in compliance and learning costs can have psychological costs as well. For example, wait lists were discussed above as a learning cost but can present a psychological cost too. A long wait list can cause individuals to be stressed about their ability to get into a program or finish it in time. It can also dissuade individuals from deciding to sign up for a program, both of which create psychological costs for individuals. Another example of this are the actions of staff. In several studies it has been seen that the staff in prisons have not always been supportive of the residents gaining their education (Meyer et al., 2010; Vaughn-Somervell et al., 2023; Danks & Bradley, 2018; Croux et al., 2019). This also comes with the residents facing hostility or negativity from the staff. The actions and negativity of the staff create a psychological cost for residents as they must deal with the stigma of participation from staff. It creates additional stress for them in the process of joining and participating in programming. These psychological costs that are also learning and/or compliance costs demonstrate that administrative burdens are not mutually exclusive. One single barrier or burden such as lockdowns can cause more than one cost for residents.

The psychological costs presented here fit within the definition of psychological costs under the administrative burden framework. These costs are things that create stress for residents in their attempts to participate in correctional programming like worrying for their safety or stress surrounding lockdowns.

Inequalities and Changes in Costs

In correctional facilities, there are inequalities just as there are in society. These inequalities can be based on many things, like age (Onyeali et al., 2023), gender (Salem et al., 2023; Manger et al., 2019), education level (Manger et al., 2019), unit at the prison (Croux et al., 2019), or length of sentence (Kaiser et al., 2020; Brosens et al., 2015). Under the administrative burden framework, these inequalities are known as human capital. Programs are occasionally not available to people who have a life sentence or have a certain charge or crime on their record (Kaiser et al., 2020; Brosens et al., 2015). Individuals with a life sentence will face the burdens discussed, but because of a difference in their human capital, they experience these burdens stronger than others without a life sentence. Although the specific burdens that prevented completion are not mentioned, Pelissier (2004) saw that women were less likely than men to participate in and complete a substance use treatment program while incarcerated. This helps to demonstrate how gender is a part of human capital and impacts the burdens residents handle.

The demographic composition of prison populations can vary and often have many minorities and those at a socioeconomic disadvantage. This can create a separate issue with programming as residents may have difficulty with reading or English may not be their first language. This is another example of human capital in prison programming as those individuals would have increased difficulty learning about programs and/or participating in them compared to those without reading or language difficulties (Croux et al., 2019; Brosens et al., 2015). If available or new programs were displayed on flyers around a prison with information only in English, then those who have difficulty reading or do not speak/read English would not be able to learn about the program's existence. Their human capital puts them at a disadvantage and makes the already present burdens even more prominent. As most people in the United States speak English, most programs offered would be in English as well. This presents a problem for those who do not speak English because even if they learn about a program, they would not be able to actively engage in it and get the same benefits out of it that English speakers would.

Many of the administrative burdens discussed so far have persisted for many years. There are more recent burdens, as well however, such as COVID-19. COVID-19 was a brand new problem that correctional facilities were facing for the first time and shifted the focus from safety to health (Novisky et al., 2023). Similar to the general lockdowns for staffing or safety, there were many short- and long-term lockdowns that occurred during COVID-19 (Barlow et al., 2022; Maycock, 2022). This would again be a compliance cost for individuals as they can no longer comply with the necessary requirements of the programs, in this case that requirement is attendance and time. Programs (therapy, education, jobs, etc.) were often cut off entirely during this time or residents were given limited access to adjust for social distancing that was necessary (Zielinski et al., 2022; Maycock, 2022; Barlow et al., 2022). These changes that included lockdown and the suspension or cancelation of programs were often included in policy for prisons as well, not just practice. Once some normal activities returned to prisons, many individuals were still not allowed to participate in programs because they would not obtain the COVID-19 vaccination (Osman et al., 2023). COVID-19 not only created additional compliance costs for individuals but also psychological costs as well. Individuals now had new additional stress from the lack of programming and isolation that they faced. While COVID is not an active concern in most facilities anymore, it provides an example of temporary situations that can create new burdens.

This section identified gaps between program interest and participation as well as the burdens that prevent residents from participating or increase their difficulty in doing so. Although these costs are based upon the literature, there is still a large gap of information related to the administrative burdens residents face and how we can improve those burdens. The next section will talk about how we can fill these gaps by using administrative burdens to improve correctional programming. Another way to begin to overcome administrative burdens now would be to open the eligibility of the programs available. Some programs are only open to those with/without certain convictions or a certain amount of time left on their sentence. Ensuring that there is equal opportunity for individuals to engage in programs by eliminating these types of restriction not only in policy but in practice as well.

Improving Correctional Programming

There are many burdens that come with trying to participate in correctional programming. Herd and Moynihan (2018) have already outlined a good approach to improve programming, stating that we should not be creating new programs but we should be adjusting policy to ensure the current programs are working properly. This can be used for correctional programming as well. The problem is not directly with the programs but the ways in which they can be accessed and utilized while in prison.

Many of the studies in the current literature have looked simply at the effectiveness of a program, typically measured by how participating in that program improves a resident's behavior and recidivism. This may be a great approach for determining if a program is reaching its intended goals, but a different approach needs to be taken to determine how to improve administrative burdens. Even if a program is working effectively in achieving its' goals, effectiveness is reduced if is not accessible to those who need it. Those studies that do look at barriers to participation use different theoretical frameworks to guide their study, not administrative burdens. By treating barriers as administrative burdens, it offers practical implications for addressing them.

The research on correctional programming should not just include residents, but staff as well. While the perceptions and experiences of burdens are something that needs to be examined from the resident's perspective, staff can also provide important insight into the processes of programming. In resource dependency theory, the environment of the organization is an essential part of their access to resources and power. The staff are part of the residents' environment in prison and they impact their access to resources, making them essential to studying administrative burdens in correctional programming. The Kaiser et al. (2020) study discussed previously is a good example of the importance of staff input. The residents in the study who had life sentences were having difficulty gaining access to programs because of their sentencing but in checking with the staff and administration at the prison, it was determined that this was not a direct written policy. By combining the staff and residents' experiences and knowledge, you can gain a full picture of the burdens that exist and what exactly needs to be changed to improve access to and participation in programming. Whether this change be a new policy, a change in the wording of a current policy, or simply a change in the practices and implementation of a current policy or guideline. These are changes that would need to be made but it would be difficult to gain the information needed to change them without speaking to staff at a facility.

One of the burdens previously discussed was related to the impact socioeconomic status and language can have on involvement with programming. Future research should take an interest in those individuals who do not or cannot participate because of a lack of previous education or language barriers. Using administrative burdens, researchers can look at how large an issue these language barriers may be in prison programs. This information can then be used to help equip prison staff and administration with the tools they need to make sure that programs are not only accessible but fully beneficial to anyone who does not have a strong grasp on the English language.

Another gap in the literature that needs to be improved is the diversity of programs that are examined for administrative burdens. Many of the studies that were discussed in the chapter focused on educational programs in their different forms. There are so many other programs available in prisons that hold equal levels of importance, as education, which have been looked over. The different types of programs are representative of the different resources that an organization depends on and there is typically more than one resource for them.

Not all administrative burdens and situations in facilities are static, facilities can be ever changing. The is similar to the ever-changing environments of organizations as well with those changes impacting their access to resources and power. With these changes such as the COVID-19 example discussed, the burdens will change as well. Due to this, the knowledge about administrative burdens in programming needs to extend beyond knowing which ones exist and finding solutions to them. Attention should be given to how those working in prisons can keep updated information on the existence of burdens. An example of this would be an internal position accompanied with a system that involves periodical surveys of residents to determine the burdens they are facing over time and if those burdens have changed.

This would require a survey to be created that accurately detects administrative burdens that residents face. Outside of this suggested position, staff and program facilitators need to work together and be able to adapt quickly. This is not a new idea and is something that has been done previously. During COVID-19 due to lockdowns and social isolation, an art therapy program had to be adapted quickly to keep residents on track with the program and did so by switching to workbooks and accommodating an online format of meetings (Barlow et al., 2022). This adjustment could not have been made without staff and facilitators working together and quickly. Other examples exist as well that align more with our suggestion of using a position and survey to track burdens. A survey that could be implemented or used as a guideline is the Perceived Barriers to Prison Education Scale (PBPES) created by Manger et al. (2019). This scale looks at what prevents individuals from participating in education while they are incarcerated and how these reasons differ by demographic variables and interest. While the barriers in this survey and its analysis were split into three groups by barrier type that were from a different theoretical perspective, the groups can easily be made to align with administrative burdens. Obegi (2024) describes an effective way to implement a monitoring system for a suicide prevention program in prisons and while this is not the same as the programs discussed in this chapter, inspiration can still be drawn from the ideas and design described. From this guideline, it is gathered that the survey must include questions or measures that are not too vague, ensure there are not too many measures, ensure measures focus on the key information, and set a threshold for measures to determine when further review or action in necessary. By acknowledging the changing environment of prison and using the methods described, staff can be better accommodating and adjust to new burdens more effectively.

A system similar to this can also be used to evaluate if administrative burdens are being properly addressed beyond their acknowledgment. This would vary slightly from a system focusing on changing burdens as it would not focus on if they are new burdens but if the ones that the staff is aware of have been solved or lessened by any new actions taken by the staff to do so. Program evaluations are popular in this correctional programming literature currently to determine if programs are effective at achieving their goals, typically of lower recidivism. The administrative burden evaluation system can follow this path to determine if the action taken is in fact effective in lessening administrative burdens. As Miller et al. (2012) describe in their discussion of program evaluations, these surveys should also include qualitative data as well. This helps to give the residents a stronger voice on the burdens they are facing and allows them to give a better explanation of what they are experiencing beyond stating they are experiencing a burden.

It is important in both types of surveys outlined here and future research that the psychological costs associated with correctional programming are given attention. Residents already face higher levels of mental health and stress than the general population (Danks & Bradley, 2018; Turner et al., 2022), so it is needed to see how the burdens of programming are impacting their stress.

There are ways for those currently employed in prisons to start to address administrative burdens as well both before and after research is done. The first of these is to ensure that every program the facility has available is clearly presented in a way visible to everyone incarcerated. The two easiest ways to do this that can also be easily updated would be a bulletin board in a common area and a tablet. The tablet is most effective for those facilities that provide access to one for every incarcerated person. By presenting clear and visible information on current programs, this helps overcome one of the learning barriers that residents face. An additional way to ensure that residents are aware of programs is to employ "insiders" who are select residents chosen to share information about prison life and programs with other residents who are new to the prison (Edgar et al., 2011; Jaffe, 2012). This as a method has been suggested before and used in United Kingdom. The hiring of an individual to share information is not uncommon in organizations either. Adding a board member to a company that has new or important information can help an organization in gaining resources and power in their environment (Simmons, 2012). This would be a response that organizations use under resource dependency theory that can apply to prisons as well.

Conclusion

Programs in correctional facilities can provide residents with many benefits and cover many topics. They can gain knowledge, skills, spend time being productive for their future, remain out of trouble in the facility, reduce their recidivism, and have overall improved mood and mental health. As this chapter demonstrates though, accessing and participating in correctional programs is not always simple.

Administrative burdens, the framework from Herd and Moynihan (2018), were introduced in the beginning of this chapter and are those burdens in interactions with the state that have a negative impact on the individual. As mentioned, there are three mechanisms of administrative burdens (learning, compliance, and psychological) and although developed with public policy in mind, this framework can be situated in resource dependency theory of organizations. There is also a clear link between these burdens and programs in prisons. There is a wide range of specific administrative burdens that residents face in programs. Staff, lockdowns, stigma, access to materials, space in programs, eligibility, and more. These burdens make full use of programs more difficult for individuals by preventing learning, compliance, or causing psychological burdens. Due to these burdens interfering with participation in programs, residents can face lower mental health, higher misconduct, and higher recidivism.

These burdens discussed can have a serious impact on individuals' participation in programming and their futures after they are released. The main goal of incarceration is to rehabilitate and help individuals so they can return to the community and be successful. The programs they engage with in prison are a major way to help them succeed as they provide them with new skills and other benefits previously discussed. When these burdens stand in the way of their participation and completion of programs then they do not get the full benefits of them. Any assistance that can be provided to individuals while they are incarcerated should be taken full advantage of. Many of the burdens they encounter can be remedied, meaning it is possible to fix those things preventing them from getting benefits.

As this chapter showed, there are some things we know about the barriers and burdens in prison programming. While this is a good start, there needs to be an increase in research that focuses on these burdens and how to lessen them. The beginning of this change in research is to shift the focus from the evaluation of program effectiveness to those burdens preventing individuals from fully accessing programs. In addition to the shift in topic, there should be a shift in the methods and participants used in research. New methods need to include prison staff as well as residents in the same study, and residents with education or language barriers. The last major change to research to consider is to include a more diverse selection of types of programs as educational programs have been heavily evaluated and studied. These new directions of focus in research are supported by both the administrative burden and resource dependency literature.

Although there is much to learn still regarding administrative burdens and correctional programming, there are some things we can do to help now. The easiest fix discussed in this chapter was addressing some of the learning burdens. The suggested way to do this is to ensure that all available programs are clearly displayed on a bulletin board or tablet, to use an "insider" to distribute information, and ensuring displays are constantly updated with the changing of programs.

Immediate fixes are not the only thing needed to improve administrative burdens in programming. The field needs more research to not only empirically determine the administrative burdens that residents face but also how we can work to improve them. There are many directions that research can go using an administrative burden framework to improve instead of replace programs as Herd and Moynihan (2018) suggest. The biggest improvement is a shift in focus from the effectiveness or end goals of programs to the accessibility or lack thereof of programs. Other improvements discussed in the chapter include, including staff in study samples, examining education and language barriers in access, and look at different types of programs outside of education.

Prison programs are incredibly important and useful in the betterment and success of residents. Administrative burdens can prohibit this success and have been previously overlooked in the literature. Academics and practitioners need to acknowledge and address these burdens in the future to ensure programs and residents are both operating at their best level.

References

Barlow, C., Soape, E., Gussak, D. E., & Schubarth, A. (2022). Mitigating over-isolation: Art therapy in prisons program during COVID-19. *Journal of the American Art Therapy Association, 39*(2), 71–80.

Bell, E., Christensen, J., Herd, P., & Moynihan, D. (2022). Health in citizen-state interactions: How physical and mental health problems shape experiences of administrative burden and reduce take-up. *Public Administration Review, 83*, 385–400.

Billings, M. S., Clayton, A. B., & Worsham, R. (2022). FASFA and beyond: How advisers manage their administrative burden in the financial aid process. *Journal of Student Financial Aid, 51*(2), 1–21.

Brosen, D., Croux, F., & De Donder, L. (2019). Barriers to prisoner participation in educational courses: Insights from a remand prison in Belgium. *International Review of Education, 65*, 735–754.

Brosens, D., De Donder, L., Dury, S., & Verte, D. (2015). Barriers to participation in vocational orientation programmes among prisoners. *Journal of Prison Education and Reentry, 2*(2), 8–22.

Bruch, S. K., Ferree, M. M., & Soss, J. (2010). From policy to polity: Democracy, paternalism, and the incorporation of disadvantaged citizens. *American Sociological Review, 75*(2), 205–226.

Burgess, A., & Flynn, C. (2013). Supporting imprisoned mothers and their children: A call for evidence. *Probation Journal, 60*, 73–81.

Callan, V., & Gardner, J. (2005). *Vocational education and training provision and recidivism in Queensland correctional institutions*. National Center for Vocational Education Research.

Carson, E. A. (2022). *Prisoners in 2021 – Statistics table*. Bureau of Justice Statistics.

Carson, E. A. (2023). *Prisons report series: Preliminary data release*. Bureau of Justice Statistics.

Christensen, J., Aaroe, L., Baekgaard, M., Herd, P., & Moynihan, D. P. (2019). Human capital and administrative burden: The role of cognitive resources in citizen-state interactions. *Public Administration Review, 80*(1), 127–136.

Clark, V. A., & Duwe, G. (2015). An outcome evaluation of a prison-based life-skills program: The power of people. *International Journal of Offender Therapy and Comparative Criminology, 59*(4), 384–405.

Croux, F., Brosens, D., Vandevelde, S., & De Donder, L. (2019). Foreign national prisoners in Flanders (Belgium): Motivations and barriers to participation in prison programmes. *European Journal on Criminal Policy and Research, 25*, 171–188.

Danks, K., & Bradley, A. (2018). Negotiating barriers: Prisoner and staff perspectives on mental wellbeing in the open prison setting. *Journal of Criminal Psychology, 8*(1), 3–19.

Davis, L. M., Bozick, R., Steele, J. L., Saunders, J., & Miles, J. N. V. (2013). *Evaluating the effectiveness of correctional education: A meta-analysis of programs that provide education to incarcerated adults*. Rand Corporation.

Duffy, M., & Shaefer, H. L. (2022). In the aftermath of the storm: Administrative burden in disaster recovery. *Social Service Review, 96*(3), 507–533.

Duwe, G. (2015). An outcome evaluation of a prison work release program: Estimating its effects on recidivism, employment, and cost avoidance. *Criminal Justice Policy Review, 26*(6), 531–554.

Duwe, G., & Clark, V. (2014). The effects of prison-based educational programming on recidivism and employment. *The Prison Journal, 994*(4), 454–478.

Duwe, G., Johnson, B. R., & Hallett, M. (2023). What do correctional leaders think about faith-based programs? Results from a national survey. *The Prison Journal, 103*(6), 707–727.

Eddy, J. M., & Poehlmann, J. (2010). Multidisciplinary perspectives on research and intervention with children of incarcerated parents. In J. M. Eddy & J. Poehlmann (Eds.), *Children of incarcerated parents: A handbook for researchers and practitioners* (pp. 1–9). Urban Institute Press.

Edgar, K., Jacobson, J., & Biggar, K. (2011). *Time well spent: A practical guide to active citizenship and volunteering in prison*. Prison Reform Trust.

Eikeland, O. J., Manger, T., & Asbjørnsen, A. E. (Eds.). (2009). *Education in Nordic prisons: Prisoners' educational background, preferences and motivation*. Nordic Council of Ministers.

Ellison, M., Szifris, K., Horan, R., & Fox, C. (2017). A rapid evidence assessment of the effectiveness of prison education in reducing recidivism and increasing employment. *Probation Journal, 64*(2), 108–128.

Florida Department of Corrections. (2019). *Annual report 2018–19*.

Glowa-Kollisch, S., Lim, S., Summers, C., Cohen, L., Selling, D., & Venters, H. (2014). Beyond the bridge: Evaluating a novel mental health program in the New York City jail system. *American Journal of Public Health, 104*(11), 2212–2218.

Gustavsson, A. L. E. (2013). Serbian prisoners in Sweden. In K. Westrheim & T. Manger (Eds.), *Ethnic minority prisoners in Nordic prisons. Educational background, preferences and needs. A qualitative study of prisoners from Iraq, Poland, Russia, Serbia and Somalia* (pp. 127–156). County Governor of Hordaland.

Herd, P. (2023). Improving older adults' health by reducing administrative burden. *The Milbank Quarterly, 101*(51), 507–531.

Herd, P., & Moynihan, D. P. (2018). *Administrative burden: Policymaking by other means*. Russell Sage Foundation.

Herd, P., & Moynihan, D. (2020). Administrative burdens in health policy. *Journal of Health and Human Services Administration, 43*(1), 3–16.

Hoffman, H. C., Byrd, A. L., & Kightlinger, A. M. (2010). Prison programs and services for incarcerated parents and their underage children: Results from a national survey of correctional facilities. *The Prison Journal, 90*, 397–416.

Huynh, K. H., Hall, B., Hurst, M. A., & Bikos, L. H. (2015). Evaluations of the positive re-entry in corrections program: A positive psychology intervention with prison inmates. *International Journal of Offender Therapy and Comparative Criminology, 59*(9), 1006–1023.

Jacobi, T. (2011). Speaking out for social justice: The problems and possibilities of US Women's prison and jail writing workshops. *Critical Survey, 23*(3), 40–54.

Jaffe, M. (2012). *Peer support and seeking help in prison: A study of the Listener scheme in four prisons in England* (Doctoral dissertation). Keele University, Keele.

Joon Jang, S., & Johnson, B. R. (2022). Religion and rehabilitation as moral reform: Conceptualization and preliminary evidence. *American Journal of Criminal Justice*, 1–27. https://doi.org/10.1007/s12103-022-09707-3

Kaiser, K. A., Keena, L., Piquero, A. R., & Howley, C. (2020). Barriers to inmate program participation in a private southern US prison. *Journal of Crime and Justice, 44*(2), 165–179.

Komalasari, R., Wilson, A., & Haw, S. (2021). A social ecological model (SEM) to exploring barriers of and facilitators to the implementation of opioid agonist treatment (OAT) programmes in prisons. *International Journal of Prisoner Health, 17*(4), 477–496.

Laub, J. H., & Sampson, R. J. (2003). *Shared beginnings, divergent lives: Delinquent boys to age 70*. Harvard University Press.

Littman, D. M., & Silva, S. M. (2020). Prison arts program outcomes: A scoping review. *The Journal of Correctional Education, 71*(3), 54–82.

Lovell, B., Brown, A., Steen, M. & Esterman, A. (2023). Process evaluation of a prison parenting education program for women. *Social Sciences, (13)*(370), 1–22.

Manger, T., Eikeland, O. J., & Asbjornsen, A. (2019). Why do not more prisoners participate in adult education? An analysis of barriers to education in Norwegian prisons. *International Review of Education, 65*, 711–733.

Maycock, M. (2022). 'Covid-19 has caused a dramatic change to prison life'. Analysing the impacts of the Covid-19 pandemic on the pains of imprisonment in the Scottish Prison Estate. *The British Journal of Criminology, 62*, 218–233.

McCarthy, H. J. (2006). Educating felons: Reflections on higher education in prison. *Radical History Review, 96*, 87–94.

Meyer, S. J., Fredericks, L., Borden, C. M., & Richardson, P. L. (2010). Implementing postsecondary academic programs in state prisons: Challenges and opportunities. *The Journal of Correctional Education, 61*(2), 148–184.

Michals, I., & Kessler, S. (2015). Prison teachers and their students: A circle of satisfaction and gain. *Journal of Correctional Education, 66*(3), 47–62.

Miller, H. V., Tillyer, R., & Miller, J. M. (2012). Recognizing the need for prisoner input in correctional research: Observations from an in-prison driving while intoxicated reduction program evaluation. *The Prison Journal, 92*(2), 274–289.

Novisky, M. A., Tostlebe, J., Pyrooz, D., & Sanchez, J. A. (2023). The COVID-19 pandemic and operational challenges, impacts, and lessons learned: A multi-methods study of U.S. prison systems. *Health and Justice, 11*, 1–10.
O'Keeffe, C., Senior, P., & Monti-Holland, V. (2007). Barriers to employment, training and education in prison and beyond: A peer-led solution. In R. Sheehan, G. McIvor, & C. Trotter (Eds.), *What works with women offenders* (pp. 240–261). Willan Publishing.
Obegi, J. H. (2024). Monitoring a correctional suicide prevention program: The roles of implementation and intermediate outcomes. *Psychology, Public Policy, and Law, 30*(1), 59–65.
Onyeali, R., Howell, B. A., McInnes, K., Emerson, A., & Williams, M. E. (2023). The case for transitional services and programs for older adults reentering society: A narrative review of US departments of correction and recommendations. *International Journal of Prisoner Health, 19*(1), 4–19.
Osman, I., Williams, A., Pierson, K., Ryu, E., & Shlafer, R. J. (2023). Facilitators and barriers to COVID-19 vaccination among incarcerated people and staff in three large, state prisons: A cross-sectional study. *Health and Justice, 11*, 1–11.
Pelissier, B. (2004). Gender differences in substance use treatment entry and retention among prisoners with substance use histories. *American Journal of Public Health, 94*(8), 1418–1424.
Perez, G., & Leon, C. S. (2020). Bonds beyond bars: Impact of an inside-out prison exchange program. *The Journal of Correctional Education, 71*(3), 33–53.
Peters, R. H., Young, M. S., Rojas, E. C., & Gorey, C. M. (2017). Evidence-based treatment and supervision practices for co-occuring mental and substance use disorders in the criminal justice system. *The American Journal of Drug and Alcohol Abuse, 43*(4), 475–488.
Pfeffer, J., & Salancik, G. R. (1978). *The external control of organizations: A resource dependence perspective*. Harper & Row.
Pierce, S. C., & Moulton, S. (2023). The effects of administrative burden on program equity and performance: Evidence from a natural experiment in a foreclosure prevention program. *The Russell Safe Foundation Journal of the Social Sciences, 9*(5), 146–178.
Richmond, K. M. (2014). Why work while incarcerated? Inmate perceptions on prison industries employment. *Journal of Offender Rehabilitation, 53*(4), 231–252.
Salem, B. E., Kwon, J., Ekstrand, M. L., Hall, E., Turner, S. F., Faucette, M., & Slaughter, R. (2023). Transitioning into the community: Perceptions of barriers and facilitators experienced by formerly incarcerated, homeless women during reentry-A qualitative study. *Community Mental Health Journal, 57*, 609–621.
Saylor, W. G., & Gaes, G. C. (1997). Training inmates through industrial work participation and vocational and apprenticeship instruction. *Corrections Management Quarterly, 1*(2), 32–43.
Schubert, E. C., Duininck, M., & Shlafer, R. J. (2016). Visiting Mom: A pilot evaluation of a prison-based visiting program serving incarcerated mothers and their minor children. *Journal of Offender Rehabilitation, 55*(4), 213–234.
Scudder, A. T., McNeil, C. B., Chengappa, K., & Costello, A. H. (2014). Evaluation of an existing parenting class within a women's state correctional facility and a parenting class modeled from Parent-Child Interaction Therapy. *Child and Youth Services Review, 46*, 238–247.
Shanks, D. (2022). Entrance fees: Self-funded agencies and the economization of immigration. *University of Colorado Law Review, 93*(2), 405–458.
Simmons, C. (2012). Will you be on our board of directors? We need help: Media corporations, environmental change, and resource dependency theory. *Journalism & Mass Communication Quarterly, 89*(1), 55–72.
Stephan, J. (2008). *Census of state and federal correctional facilities, 2005*. Bureau of Justice Statistics, U.S. Department of Justice.
Tremblay, M. D., & Sutherland, J. E. (2017). The effectiveness of parenting programs for incarcerated mothers: A systematic review. *Journal of Child and Family Studies, 26*, 3247–3265.
Turner, M., King, N., Mojtahedi, D., Burr, V., Gall, V., Gibbs, G. R., Hudspith, L. F., Leadley, C. B., & Walker, T. (2022). Well-being programmes in prisons in England and Wales: A mixed-methods study. *International Journal of Prisoner Health, 18*(3), 259–274.

U.S. Citizenship and Immigration Services. (2020, July). *How to apply for a green card*. https://www.uscis.gov/green-card/how-to-apply-for-a-green-card

U.S. Prison Population vs. The World: Statistics and Insights. Background Checks.org. (2019, May 5).

Vaughn-Somervell, S., Poole, C., Gardner, R., Winters, B., Dewey, S., & Roberts, S. (2023). An evaluation of tablet-based education in two state prisons. *The Journal of Correctional Education, 74*(2), 3–25.

Vur, A. V., & Nguyen, H. (2023). Prison work and vocational programs: A systematic review and analysis of moderators of program success. *Justice Quarterly, 40*(1), 129–158.

Westrheim, K., & Manger, T. (2014). Iraqi prisoners in Norway: Educational background, participation, preferences and barriers to education. *Journal of Prison Education and Reentry, 1*(1), 6–19.

Yates, S., Carey, G., Malbon, E., & Hargrave, J. (2021). 'Faceless monster, secret society': Women's experiences navigating the administrative burden of Australia's National Disability Insurance Scheme. *Health and Social Care Community, 30*, 2308–2317.

Zielinski, M. J., Cowell, M., Bull, C. E., Veluvolu, M., Behne, M. F., Nowotny, K., & Brinkley-Rubinstein, L. (2022). Policy and public communication methods among U.S. state prisons during the first year of the COVID-19 pandemic. *Health and Justice, 10*(1), 27.

Chapter 10
Power, Discretion, and the Landscape of Contemporary Prosecution

Clayton B. Drummond and Suraiya H. Shammi

Introduction

In this chapter, we examine prosecutorial power and discretion through the lens of reforms. Specifically, we argue that increased awareness of wrongful convictions and mass incarceration, alongside related initiatives adopted by reform-minded prosecutors, have impacted the institution of prosecution, its organizations, and individuals working within this institution. Criticisms rooted in over-incarceration and systemic errors have demanded change at the institutional level, which has influenced structural and strategic shifts where contemporary prosecutors are favoring nontraditional methods. This has, in some ways, divided prosecutors in the twenty-first century. We thus explore modern prosecution practices with a two-pronged approach. First, we use institutional logics theory to examine the relationship between reforms and the landscape of contemporary prosecution. Second, we contend that the criticisms that spurred these reforms can, in part, be addressed by improving prosecutorial compliance. We explore prosecutorial compliance and accountability from the perspective of legal endogeneity theory.

C. B. Drummond (✉) · S. H. Shammi
George Mason University, Department of Criminology, Law & Society, Fairfax, VA, USA
e-mail: cdrummo@gmu.edu; sshammi@gmu.edu

D. S. Rudes, J. R. Ingram (eds.), *Using Organizational Theory to Study, Explain, and Understand Criminal Legal Organizations*,
https://doi.org/10.1007/978-3-031-66285-0_10

Power, Discretion, and the Landscape of Contemporary Prosecution

The criminal legal system is a central part of American society. It houses a "sprawling web of competing institutions," such as law enforcement, prosecutors, various boards, and political elites, who "respond to different constituencies and have different incentives" (Pfaff, 2012, p. 1240). Prosecutors, who are often referred to as the gatekeepers of criminal justice in the USA, influence a variety of processes within the legal system, and they hold tremendous power over case outcomes. As former Attorney General Robert Jackson (1940) put it, "The prosecutor has more control over life, liberty, and reputation than any other person in America" (see Robert H. Jackson Center, n.d., para. 2). Prosecutors are the system's most powerful actors, largely due to the vast discretion they exercise in the legal process. This discretion includes but is not limited to, discretion for charging decisions, pleas, litigation, and their influence on criminal sanctions.

While prosecutors have long been a pillar of criminal justice, recent criticisms have facilitated institutional, organizational, and individual shifts in the structures and strategies of contemporary prosecution. Indeed, calls for justice reform have been widespread in the twenty-first century, particularly following the "punitive turn" of the late twentieth century (Garland, 2001, p. 142). Gallup polls show that, over the past few decades, public support for punitive punishments and confidence in the legal system has declined (Brenan, 2023; Jones, 2022). Public opinion data from recent years also shows that people hold critical views toward US prosecutors (e.g., American Civil Liberties Union [ACLU], 2017a, b). Relatedly, awareness around issues like wrongful convictions and mass incarceration has increased in the twenty-first century. Prior research shows that prosecutors have—in part—contributed to heightened imprisonment rates and system errors. Prosecutor organizations across the country are changing as a result, adopting Conviction Integrity/Review Units (CIUs, CRUs) and/or prioritizing decarceration initiatives, among other reforms. Often, these prosecutors align themselves with the progressive prosecution movement. Progressive prosecutors are "committed to both public safety and reducing mass incarceration" (Young, 2020, para. 4), and many view wrongful convictions as "a key platform issue" (Webster, 2019, p. 989). Though reforms surrounding wrongful convictions and mass incarceration only illustrate a portion of the changes occurring in contemporary criminal justice, they exemplify major shifts that challenge traditional methods of prosecution.

We first provide an overview of the literature surrounding power and organizations. Then, we describe the role of prosecutors in the US legal system and their use of power and discretion before turning to our theoretical framework. From there, we explain what we refer to as the "logics of contemporary prosecution" and discuss the impact that structural and strategic changes have had on prosecutors. We then examine how concepts of legal endogeneity theory can inform accountability and compliance. We conclude with remarks surrounding the landscape of American prosecution and the legal system moving forward.

Power and Organizations

Organizational and sociological research has extensively examined power. For instance, sociologist Max Weber (1978) defined it as "the chance of a man or a number of men to realize their own will in a social action even against the resistance of others who are participating in the action" (p. 926). Weber viewed power as distributive, where one person's power increases as another's decreases (Heiskala, 2001). Additionally, Weber's concept of power requires two or more parties alongside some form of resistance (Baldus, 1975). Talcott Parsons, on the contrary, shared a different perspective. Parsons saw power as shared (i.e., collective) among multiple parties to influence third parties (Heiskala, 2001; see Parsons, 1960 on the societal distribution of power). Many prominent scholars have studied the relationship between power and society, including Marx, Foucault, and many others (see Clegg, 1998; Jessop, 2012). These definitions are examples widely used in sociological and organizational research on power.

Organizational studies provide more context on the relationship between power and individuals. Power, according to Salancik and Pfeffer (1977), is the "secret of [organizational] success," and those who have it can "bring about the outcomes they desire" (p. 3). Although power is not exclusive to organizational leaders, its distribution depends on individual and positional characteristics (Van Wart, 2003). In other words, power can be driven by individual differences in informal groups and by position in formal organizations (Scott, 2003). To this end, leaders do not solely hold power, nor is it confined to people occupying particular positions. Rather, power is broadly illustrated by one's ability to, formally or informally, "influence behavior, to change the course of events, to overcome resistance, and to get people to do things that they would not otherwise do" (Pfeffer, 1992, p. 30). Simply put, power is best defined as one's impact on organizational behaviors and outcomes.

Power is complex, particularly in the institution of prosecution. Its applications are not entirely uniform and vary depending on organizational and individual factors. Prosecutorial discretion is one of the leading uses of prosecutorial power. In the next section, we describe the structure of the US prosecution, traditional and contemporary strategies for using power and discretion, and the shifting landscape around prosecution.

Power, Discretion, and Contemporary Prosecution

Prosecutors possess a vast amount of influence over legal system outcomes, and thus, they are often cited as the gatekeepers of justice. They work in both federal and state systems. The 93 federal prosecutors who work across 94 US districts are presidentially appointed (U.S. Department of Justice, n.d.-a, b). As of 2007, more than 78,000 attorneys were employed in 2,330 state prosecutor's offices (Perry & Banks, 2011). Most state and local prosecutors are elected, though some are appointed

(Bibas, 2010; see Prosecutors and Politics Project, 2020). District attorneys lead most prosecutor organizations and oversee assistants who tend to do most of the charging and trial work (Walther, 2000). Overall, however, prosecutor organizations use various structures, strategies, and systems for labor distribution. Walther (2000), for example, described three distribution systems: horizontal (i.e., assistants are spread across procedural tasks, common in larger areas), vertical (i.e., one prosecutor assigned to an entire case, often in smaller areas), or a mixed-method approach. To this end, prosecutors are involved in all levels of the legal system, and they often get to choose how they structure their day-to-day operations.

The primary role of prosecutors is to "seek justice within the bounds of the law," aiming to solve problems rather than focusing on conviction rates (American Bar Association, 2017). Their power is virtually unmatched by any other legal official, given the authority they have over case outcomes. Prosecutors use their power to facilitate the actions of others involved in the legal process, such as enabling police investigations, engaging in plea bargains, and seeking sanctions for offenders through the judiciary (Sklansky, 2016). Prosecutors rely on discretion to carry out these duties, particularly when charging the accused or engaging in pleas.

Charging decisions are among the most influential uses of a prosecutor's discretion. Prosecutors can decide *if* they want to charge the accused and *what* crimes they will charge them with—a decision that largely cannot be overruled by other system-involved actors (Bellin, 2019). This "invisible stage" of the legal process is not legislatively nor judicially constrained in most areas, and decisions to decline prosecution are often not reviewable (Spohn et al., 2018, p. 121). Prosecutors may decline to prosecute people if success is questionable, or in favor of the defendant's culpability, alternatives, to better manage their caseload, or for no reason (Sarat & Clarke, 2008). Scholars have rigorously studied charging decisions, and there has been some debate about charging frequencies. Particularly, many have challenged the practice of overcharging, where prosecutors may stack charges against defendants to obtain guilty pleas (see Alschuler, 1968; Schoenfeld et al., 2019). Some have suggested that it is unclear, however, how overcharging—while it has been identified as prosecutorial abuse—constitutes malpractice (Gershman, 2010).

Most US criminal cases are solved by guilty pleas, and thus, prosecutors participate in them frequently.[1] According to a 2005 Bureau of Justice Statistics (BJS) report, 86% of criminal convictions included a guilty plea (Motivans, 2008). A 2022 BJS report found that around 90% of convictions were secured by guilty plea, and bench/jury trials contributed to less than 2% of dispositions (Motivans, 2024). The prevalence of pleas has led to increases in prosecutorial power over time, as they control the outcomes (e.g., sanctions, disposition) in these cases (Johnson et al., 2016). The practice of plea bargaining though widely employed, is not flawless—as evidenced by false confessions. Indeed, research shows that some defendants falsely pled guilty to crimes they did not commit (e.g., DiFava et al., 2023; Redlich et al.,

[1] Defendants have a variety of plea options—depending on the jurisdiction—including a traditional declaration of guilt, no contest (i.e., *nolo contendere*), or an *Alford* plea (a plea where one sustains their innocence) (Redlich et al., 2017; see also *North Carolina v. Alford*, 1970).

2023). At the time of this writing, false confessions have contributed to 13% of the current 3489 exonerations recognized by the National Registry of Exonerations (NRE, n.d.-a). In sum, prosecutors often use their power through discretionary actions in charging and pleas, though there are ethical considerations surrounding the evolution of these practices.

The Shifting Landscape

In recent decades, scholarly evidence has identified the pitfalls of the immense power and discretion afforded to prosecutors. The emergence of wrongful convictions and mass incarceration are among these pitfalls, both of which have facilitated widespread criticisms of prosecutors in the twenty-first century. First, prosecutors oversee much of the legal process and have inevitably been linked with the increased discovery of wrongful convictions. The rise of the innocence movement—a social movement that aims to exonerate innocent people and reform the legal system—over the last four decades has led to heightened awareness and scholarship around convictions of the innocent (see Norris, 2017a, b). At the time of this writing, 3,489 people have been exonerated in the USA since 1989 (NRE, n.d.-a). Criminal legal officials, like police and prosecutors, have undoubtedly contributed to these system errors. Misconduct is perhaps the most egregious act committed by officials in wrongful convictions, which has occurred in 60% (n = 2,091) of known exonerations (NRE, n.d.-a). The NRE (n.d.-b) stated official misconduct occurs when "Police, prosecutors, or other government officials significantly abused their authority or the judicial process in a manner that contributed to the exoneree's conviction." A report by Gross et al. (2020) identified prosecutorial misconduct in 30% of 2400 known exonerations, including acts such as withholding exculpatory evidence, witness tampering, lying in court, and permitting perjury, among others (Gross et al., 2020).[2] Other researchers have identified similar types of misconduct (e.g., Ridolfi & Possley, 2010; Scheck et al., 2000) and have linked prosecutorial misconduct—specifically, the withholding of exculpatory evidence—to false confessions (Bettens & Redlich, 2023). These scholarly findings, alongside countless others amidst the now-evident "innocence revelation," have revealed how prosecutors (and others, like police and forensic personnel, see Bonventre, 2020 & Covey, 2013) contribute to wrongful convictions (Norris, 2017b, p. 27).

Second, prior research has suggested that prosecutors helped produce mass incarceration. While mass incarceration is not solely represented by the prison population rate, the data show that the number of persons incarcerated in the USA skyrocketed throughout the late twentieth century and early aughts. The total prison population increased from 315,974 in 1980 to 1,553,570 in 2009 (Sentencing

[2] The withholding of material, exculpatory evidence is referred to as a *Brady* violation, referencing the US Supreme Court's decision in *Brady v. Maryland* (1963).

Project, n.d.). Though the prison population has decreased in recent years, more than one million people were still incarcerated as of 2020 (Sentencing Project, n.d.). There are several explanations for what caused and contributed to mass incarceration, including the rise of punitive policies (Western & Wildeman, 2009, see also Garland, 2001) and prosecutorial practices. Pfaff (2012) argued that prosecutors drove mass incarceration by increasing the frequency with which they file charges in cases of arrest. According to Davis (2016), prosecutorial power and discretion increased during the era of mass incarceration as prosecutors assumed the power of sentencing guidelines and mandatory minimum sentences. Davis (2016) wrote, "Prosecutors already exercised great discretion and power in the criminal justice system, but these sentencing policies increased that power and discretion significantly…" (p. 1070). Not to mention, many prosecutors in the era of mass incarceration favored tough-on-crime policies, facilitating the use of their discretion in a way that negatively impacted people of color (Young, 2020).

Though some, albeit not all, prosecutors have contributed to wrongful convictions and/or mass incarceration, they are positioned to remedy such injustices. Exonerees often rely on the very officials who produced their wrongful convictions to correct it (Westervelt & Cook, 2010). Additionally, prosecutors "are uniquely situated to have the greatest and most immediate impact on [mass incarceration] because of their vast discretion and power" (Davis, 2016, p. 1064). In the twenty-first century, many prosecutor organizations have adapted their structures and strategies to address these issues. One adaptation is the implementation of Conviction Integrity Units (CIUs, also referred to as Conviction Review Units [CRUs]). According to the NRE (n.d.-c), 101 CIUs currently exist in prosecutor's offices across the USA to "prevent, identify, and remedy false convictions" (para. 1) (see also Innocence Project, 2015). Another adaptation is the increase in prosecutors who favor decarceration initiatives, which stems from the progressive prosecution movement that culminated in the twenty-first century (for comparison with twentieth-century Progressive Era prosecution, see Green & Roiphe, 2020). These reform-minded prosecutors use their power and discretion to carry out equal justice, addressing issues like wrongful convictions and mass incarceration, among others (e.g., Bellin, 2020; Davis, 2019; Webster, 2019). Key leaders of the movement have been elected in California, Illinois, Philadelphia, and Washington, pushing for alternatives to traditional prosecution and/or punishment (Levenson, 2023; Young, 2020). Overall, a recent uptick in the number of prosecutors labeling themselves as "progressive"—aimed at rebranding criminal justice through critical rhetoric—has sought to challenge traditional prosecution by "promising systemic change" (Levin, 2021, p. 1423). Many of these prosecutors are "inheriting bloated prosecutorial institutions" and are thus attempting to drawback prosecution rates (Gajwani & Lesser, 2019, p. 75).

These changes in the landscape of modern prosecution are occurring at a critical time. Indeed, public opinion data shows that people are becoming increasingly critical of the legal system and its officials. From 1992 to 2020, perceptions that the legal system is "not tough enough" decreased from 83% to 41%. During this decline, views of the system being "too tough" increased from 2% to 21% (Brenan, 2023).[3] Recent polls indicate that public confidence in the criminal justice system has also declined (see Jones, 2022). Further, polling data shows that the public holds critical views of prosecutors. The ACLU's (2017a) national survey, for example, found that most people view police, prosecutors, and sentencing as contributors to inequality in the system. A poll by David Binder Research showed that voters prefer more transparency and accountability for prosecutors (ACLU, 2017b). Eighty percent of the poll's 1600 respondents support prosecutors who focus on decarceration and addressing unequal treatment in the legal system. Greenspan et al. (2022) found that, when given information about a wrongful conviction, most people favor civil liability for prosecutors engaging in misconduct. In sum, public views of the legal system have changed, and many citizens favor reforms that address injustices and accountability for US prosecutors.

Accountability, however, has proven to be difficult to achieve. Prosecutors who commit misconduct are rarely sanctioned for their wrongdoing, both generally and in their contributions to wrongful convictions (e.g., Gross et al., 2020; Ridolfi & Possley, 2010). Ridolfi and Possley (2010), for instance, found that only six prosecutors were disciplined for withholding exculpatory evidence in 707 cases. Not to mention, prosecutors are shielded from accountability. Absolute immunity is often cited as among the most problematic protections afforded to prosecutors. Absolute immunity dates to the US Supreme Court case, *Imbler v. Pachtman* (1976), which concluded that prosecutors are protected from civil liability if they are acting within the scope of their duties. This includes knowingly using false testimony but does not extend to the withholding of material evidence as established in *Brady v. Maryland* (1963) (Morrison, 1978). Prosecutors, when acting in an investigative or administrative role, can also be protected by qualified immunity (see Chemerinsky, 2008). Prosecutorial protections are quite troublesome, particularly in cases of misconduct. As Johns (2005) put it, absolute immunity "protects the dishonest prosecutor" and does not deter misconduct (p. 55).

The landscape of contemporary prosecution has been shaped by issues like wrongful convictions, mass incarceration, calls for accountability, and related reforms. Each of these areas has garnered heightened awareness in recent decades amidst societal changes in perceptions of the legal system. We find that each of these components has shaped modern prosecution practices in various ways. To reiterate, we apply organizational theory in this chapter to explore the structure and strategies of contemporary prosecution and how it deviates from traditional practices. Specifically, we examine how prosecutors have adapted to address heightened rates of incarceration and system errors through a reform-minded approach. Examples of these adaptations include but are not limited to, the implementation of CIUs/CRUs and/or initiatives undertaken by those aligned with the progressive

[3] This Gallup poll has recently shifted (i.e., 2023) toward higher responses for "not tough enough" (58%) and decreases in "too tough" (14%), but views for most of the twenty-first century are reflective of what is written. Further, current views are still less punitive than they were at the turn of the century.

prosecution movement. We also describe prosecutorial compliance with existing structures and explore future mechanisms for accountability. We next describe the two organizational theories in our framework: institutional logics and legal endogeneity.

Institutional Logics

The modern study of organizations from an institutional perspective can be traced to the late 1970s. Meyer and Rowan (1977) sought to understand how institutions shape organizational structures through "rationalized myths" and isomorphism (see p. 347). Their work, and many others, influenced a new wave of theoretical scholarship on institutions and organizations. Institutional theorists see organizations as open systems that are shaped by their environments and social norms (Scott, 2003). Institutional logics stems from this perspective.

Scholars have offered many definitions for institutional logics. Friedland and Alford (1991)—who were among the first to develop the theory—defined it as "a set of material practices and symbolic constructions—which constitutes [an institution's] organizing principles and which is available to organizations and individuals to elaborate" (p. 248). Similarly, Thornton and Ocasio (2008) defined institutional logics as "the socially constructed, historical pattern of material practices, assumptions, values, beliefs, and rules by which individuals produce and reproduce their material subsistence, organize time and space, and provide meaning to their social reality" (p. 804). These definitions suggest that environments shape logics, which in turn impact individual and organizational behaviors.

Prior research demonstrates the versatility of the institutional logics perspective. According to Thornton et al. (2012), this framework is useful for understanding how actors, both individually and at the organizational level, are impacted by the multidirectional relationship between institutions, organizations, and people within society. Logics are thus a "frame of reference" that guides decision-making, motivations, and identity for organizations and individuals (Thornton et al., 2012, p. 2). People and organizations use logics to make sense of and organize their time and space, including structures, procedures (e.g., surveying their environment and resources), culture (e.g., norms and values), and power (e.g., who holds formal/informal authority) (Haveman & Gualtieri, 2017). Individuals and organizations interact with logics through a collective identity, desire for power and status, social structures (i.e., classification and categorization), and attention (e.g., responses to economic, social, and/or institutional factors) (Thornton & Ocasio, 2008).

One's identification with logics, at the individual and organizational level, is important for understanding behaviors. Lok (2010), for instance, examined how individuals reproduce and identify with shifting logics. The study's findings showed that people reinforce and resist new logics by building on preexisting practices, embracing new logics while continuing to align with prior ones, and establishing independence. Other studies have focused on organizational—rather than individual—identities. Organizations can identify with multiple logics (e.g., Besharov & Smith, 2014; Ressler et al., 2024) or competing ones (e.g., Pache & Santos, 2013). Competing logics can spur change in organizations and thus divide adherents and resistors. These changes, according to Rao et al. (2003), can occur when activists gain power in organizations and push for new logics that deviate from traditional ones. In turn, organizations and individuals assume new identities and roles. Indeed, part of the process for creating, or perhaps even adopting, new logics includes "reconstructing rules or regulations" and "reconfiguring belief systems" (Haveman & Gualtieri, 2017, p. 19).

In summary, institutional logics is a useful theoretical framework for examining the relationship between organizations, individuals, and institutions. We are certainly not the first to study issues surrounding the legal system from a logics perspective (e.g., McPherson & Sauder, 2013; Rudes et al., 2021; Salet & Terpstra, 2022). To our knowledge, however, we are among the first to explore contemporary prosecution using the logics lens. This theoretical perspective can help scholars make sense of sweeping changes in the use of prosecutorial power and discretion, and an emerging division in the structures and strategies used by prosecutors. We proceed by describing legal endogeneity before turning to a discussion on modern prosecution.

Legal Endogeneity

In light of the previous discussion, the principles of institutional logics are helpful for examining the relationship between organizations, individuals, and the legal system. Institutional logics play a crucial role in shaping how organizations interpret and implement legal rules and regulations (Haveman & Gualtieri, 2017; Besharov & Smith, 2014), whereas legal endogeneity highlights the role of organizations in interpreting laws in ways that align with their internal logic and practices (Edelman & Talesh, 2011). Legal endogeneity theory suggests that the relationship between law and organizational behavior is reciprocal (Edelman et al., 1999). While institutional logics provides a lens for examining how organizations navigate and interpret legal requirements, the concept of legal endogeneity expands this view to consider how organizations also play a role in shaping the legal landscape. As organizations reflect their legal requirements through the lens of their specific institutional logic, they may identify and address ambiguities in existing laws. For example, they might take part in lobbying for legal changes or regulatory rule-making processes. This active engagement with the legal system can lead to changes in the law that reflect an organization's practical experiences and logic.

The notion of endogenous law is an extension of institutional theories of organizations, emphasizing the dependence on and interaction between organizations and their normative environments (DiMaggio & Powell, 1983; Edelman, 1990; Meyer et al., 1987). Professor Lauren Edelman conducted a series of studies to understand the endogenous nature of law. According to Edelman et al. (2011), "legal endogeneity theory emphasizes the extent to which organizational structures influence the content and meaning of law" (p. 890). Legal endogeneity theory argues that law and legal processes are not just external forces that impact organizations but are also shaped by organizations (Edelman et al., 1999; Gilad, 2014). Organizations respond to ambiguous laws by implementing various policies and programs that symbolize their attention to them (Edelman et al., 1992; Gualtieri, 2020).

The concept of symbolic compliance is one of the key components of this theory, where organizations adopt practices that meet legal and societal expectations without affecting substantial changes (Edelman et al., 1992; Edelman & Talesh, 2011). Symbolic compliance allows organizations to appear as if they are meeting their goals without changing their operations and maintaining public legitimacy. Organizations influence the laws they obey and how they apply them. Organizations, then, develop "symbolic responses" that formally indicate organizational compliance but do not necessarily address social problems (Gualtieri, 2020, p. 211). For example, a company might create a diversity and inclusion policy that outlines procedures for reporting discrimination but does not actually do anything to address the issue of discrimination. Symbolic responses may provide a sense of commitment to social responsibility, but they must be backed up by meaningful actions and policies to be effective.

In summary, the interplay between institutional logics and legal endogeneity provides invaluable insights into how organizations interact with the legal system. This dynamic relationship not only influences the interpretation and application of laws but also highlights the potential for organizations to shape the legal landscape in ways that reflect their internal logics. However, the challenge remains to surpass symbolic compliance and foster significant changes in prosecutorial practices and outcomes, ensuring that legal standards and societal expectations can be met meaningfully.

In the following section, we propose two emerging and, in some ways, competing logics of contemporary prosecution. Then, we apply concepts from legal endogeneity to modern practices and accountability for prosecutors moving forward.

The Logics of Contemporary Prosecution

To reiterate, the institutional logics framework is useful for making sense of the interactions between institutions, organizations, and individuals. We view contemporary prosecution as an interesting area to study in this context for several reasons. First, as mentioned earlier in the chapter, public opinion data show that critical views of the legal system and prosecutors have become prevalent in the twenty-first century. Widespread awareness of wrongful convictions and mass incarceration have further exacerbated critical perspectives of the system and prosecutors. Some prosecutors, though not all, have contributed to the proliferation of these issues and are positioned to rectify them (e.g., Davis, 2016; Westervelt & Cook, 2010). In turn, many prosecutors have adopted reforms. The implementation of CRUs/CIUs and decarceration initiatives by progressive prosecutors are examples of prevalent changes. Though the shifting landscape cannot be explained entirely by wrongful convictions, mass incarceration, or the progressive prosecution movement, we argue that prosecutors have grappled with these issues and, in some jurisdictions, have sought structural and strategic changes to address them.

We thus propose two logics that characterize twenty-first century prosecution at the organizational level, influenced by institutional shifts and led by individual prosecutors. By structural change, we mean how prosecutors have reorganized their offices to adapt to the institutional (and political) environment. By strategic change, we suggest that contemporary prosecutors have shifted their focus to uses of power and discretion that deviate from traditional forms. We first propose a logic of reformation. Prosecutors aligned with this logic often engage in progressive prosecution but nonetheless seek reform, prioritize decreases in incarceration, and aim to alleviate system errors (e.g., wrongful convictions). Collectively, those within the logic of reformation have recognized the institutional changes occurring around the legal system and are attempting to strengthen the institution (and its reputation) at the organizational and individual level. These prosecutors take on more of an activist role and, like Rao et al. (2003) suggested, deviate from traditional logics. These prosecutors thus, both individually and organizationally, have taken on different identities and roles that reconstruct traditional practices in favor of reform.

Consider the following example. Parisa Dehghani-Tafti (D–Arlington, VA), one of three Northern Virginia progressive prosecutors who won their primary elections in 2023 (and ultimately was re-elected), "embraced messages about shifting the traditional focus of district attorney offices, including directing resources to keep certain defendants out of prison" (Bland, 2023, para. 2). Dehghani-Tafti's agenda has included ending cash bail, lowering the incarcerated population, and establishing the only CRU in Virginia (Arlington, VA, n.d.-a, b). This exemplifies the logic of reformation, where a person in power aligns with initiatives that are rooted in broader critiques of an institution—in this case, the prosecution. Dehghani-Tafti is not the first, nor the only, prosecutor to engage in these practices. CIUs/CRUs have become more prevalent over the last two decades, with the first of the 101 recognized by the NRE (n.d.-c) being founded in 2002. To this end, many prosecutors have sought to address wrongful convictions through change, and likely in ways that surpass the implementation of review units. Webster (2019), in fact, found that prosecutors are adopting progressive ideas toward alleviating wrongful convictions that include a justice-oriented mindset, broadening their investigations of innocence claims and, in some instances, actively seeking independent reinvestigations. Other key figures, like Maryland Attorney General Anthony Brown, have developed partnerships aimed at tackling injustice and mass incarceration through reform (Wiggins, 2023). Brown and public defender Natasha Dartigue created a partnership called the Maryland Equitable Justice Collaborative to address discriminatory practices (Wiggins, 2023). Philadelphia prosecutor Larry Krasner has sought lower prison sentences and aims to "curb mass incarceration" (Young, 2020, para. 11; see also Palmer, 2019). Krasner's office has focused on declining particular prosecutions (e.g., marijuana possession and prostitution), increasing diversion and reentry, and seeking less harsh punishments in plea offers, among others (Philadelphia District Attorney's Office, 2018). Brown's and Krasner's efforts are examples of reformation, as they have sought change at the individual and organizational level that stems from mass incarceration.

Second, we propose a logic of endurance in contemporary prosecution. Broadly, prosecutors in this logic have *endured* the shifting landscape around contemporary criminal justice and prosecution by maintaining traditional structures and strategies. We argue that these prosecutors, in line with Lok's (2010) proposition, resist change and bolster the legitimacy of non-reformism. Prosecutors who align with the endurance logic use their power and discretion in a more traditional fashion—focusing on outcomes like incapacitation and deterrence (Green & Burke, 2012)—and are likely not as willing to prioritize change like their reformation counterparts. Traditional prosecutors often focus on processing cases and punishment and tend not to involve the community in prosecutions (Nugent et al., 2004). Further, Meldrum et al. (2021) found that traditional prosecutors prioritize convictability and that the traditional perspective is associated with higher punitive attitudes. In sum, traditional prosecutors are aligned with a logic of endurance, while those who seek to deviate from traditional norms identify with a logic of reformation. These logics illustrate variations between how prosecutors use their power and discretion.

The logics of reformation and endurance have, in some ways, divided contemporary prosecution. Broader political discourse illustrates how these logics are in conflict. On the one hand, progressive prosecutors have been scrutinized by conservative and progressive politicians in many US states (Barakat, 2023; Goodman, 2023; Herndon, 2022; Tegethoff, 2023). In 2020, Deborah Gonzalez, who ran for prosecutor as a progressive in Georgia, faced opposition from the Governor and political conservatives who sought to "redraw her two-county district in their favor" (Blakinger, 2022, para. 4). As Blakinger put it, conservative opposition to reform-minded prosecution is often rooted in concerns over public safety, viewing less punishment as a threat. Recent research shows, however, that progressive prosecution is not related to increasing crime rates (e.g., Foglesong et al., 2022, see Eisenberg & Preston, 2022). On the other hand, progressive prosecutors have countered political adversity by affirming their agendas. Dan Satterberg, a prosecutor in Seattle, supported case review by claiming, "We have to be willing to roll up our sleeves, look through the files of old cases, and really…compare them to our contemporary law and practice" (Hager, 2018, para. 18). Kings County, NY prosecutor Eric Gonzalez stated that, "I'm on the record as saying I don't think our primary responsibility should be incarceration, That should be the last option" (Witt, 2017, para. 20). Los Angeles, California prosecutor George Gascón has sought lower sentence lengths, a decision he justified by stating, "Right now, all the signs that we know about lengthy incarceration shows we're probably heading in the right direction" (Haskell, 2024, para. 8). To this end, contemporary prosecution appears to have its adherents and resistors within the institution of prosecution and across others (e.g., political institutions), which is partly demonstrated by modern political discourse.

In sum, contemporary prosecution has shifted and is, on some days, divided based on two competing logics: reformation and endurance. We explore these logics with the understanding that there are multiple assumptions. Not all progressive prosecution reforms meet their intended goals. Additionally, there are likely other prosecutors who align with the logic of reformation, which are not explicitly discussed in this chapter (e.g., cash bail abolitionists). Further, not all political progressives support reform-minded prosecution, nor do all conservatives support traditional prosecution. There is likely overlap, where conservatives favor elements of progressive prosecution and vice versa. Generally, however, discourse around these two types of prosecution proves that these are competing logics. We, too, are aware that not *all* prosecutors abuse their power or should be blamed as contributors to mass incarceration and wrongful convictions. Evidence shows, however, that *some* have cast a negative light on prosecutors and the entire legal system. Many prosecutors, on both sides of the political spectrum and across typologies of prosecution, are aware of these criticisms and have sought to engage in more equitable practices and course-correct for prior system errors. Finally, there are other models—like community prosecution—that may fall in either (or neither) of these logics (see Nugent et al., 2004). Overall, we contend that much of the discourse around contemporary prosecution illustrates an emerging divide at the institutional level. This has created at least two factions in the institution of prosecution: reformation and endurance. Though these factions have obvious political motivations, we find that the logics proposed in this chapter exemplify structural and strategies changes in the institution of American prosecution.

We now turn to a discussion on modern practices from the perspective of legal endogeneity theory.

Legal Endogeneity and Contemporary Prosecution

As prosecutorial philosophies evolved, a new approach emerged (Meldrum et al., 2021), focusing on fairness, proportionality, transparency, and a decreasing emphasis on incarceration (Sklansky, 2017). It is important to remember, however, that prosecutors will continue to hold immense power in case disposition and criminal punishments. Hence, holding them accountable for any unlawful and/or unethical practices is difficult. Legal endogeneity theory suggests that prosecutorial abuses of power stem from policies structured to protect them in the first place. Prosecutorial misconduct is rarely defined as harmful, even if one recognizes it (Johns, 2011). For example, in *Buckley v. Fitzsimmons* (1993), Stephen Buckley sought damages from the prosecutor Fitzsimmons, who had collaborated with police to fabricate evidence materials during the preliminary investigation of a rape and murder case. However, the Supreme Court's decision did not directly result in any disciplinary action or immediate personal consequences for Fitzsimmons, which clearly shows the endogenous nature of law. Not to mention, recent studies that we discussed in this chapter show that prosecutors are rarely disciplined for misconduct.

Edelman et al. (1999) developed her sociological account to explain why the Civil Rights Act of 1964, despite its progressive aspirations, failed to deliver its intended results regarding discrimination in hiring and other aspects of equal employment opportunity. It is important to note that Edelman's work focuses on statutory issues; however, this book chapter provides a theoretical argument to suggest that a similar system exists in contemporary prosecution. The legal endogeneity perspective implies that organizational processes and legal norms constantly influence each other. As prosecutors work within existing laws, their decisions and strategies shape those laws as they interact with the legal system.

Symbolic Compliance and Traditional Prosecution

The application of law in traditional prosecution tends to be more symbolic than substantive engagement with legal norms and principles. For instance, In *Brady v. Maryland* (1963), the Supreme Court ruled that prosecutors must disclose any exculpatory, material information to the defendant. Failure to comply with the ruling would be identified as *Brady* violation. However, due to the ambiguity of legal wording and lack of precision, prosecutors often choose not to disclose evidence that could be critical (Gershman, 2007). This tendency to omit crucial evidence is not an isolated issue and, in fact, can affect the entire prosecutorial process. Research shows the presence of implicit racial bias in every phase of the prosecutorial process, from charging decisions to trial strategy selection. As such, it becomes challenging for a defendant to prove a *Brady* violation since the legal standard for proving systemic discrimination is high (Davis, 2007). A 2010 analysis, based on 12 years of criminal trial cases in California, reported 707 cases with 782 instances of prosecutorial misconduct, averaging 59 cases and 65 violations per year, including 66 *Brady* violations (Ridolfi & Possley, 2010). Hence, to achieve legitimacy within the legal system, legal actors within organizations conform their formal structures to institutionalized norms where the structures symbolically represent constituent views, social norms, or legal requirements (Meyer & Rowan, 1977). In the following section, we apply concepts from legal endogeneity theory (Edelman et al., 2011) to discuss increased accountability that aligns with legal and ethical standards to reduce symbolic compliance in contemporary prosecution.

Increasing Accountability in Contemporary Prosecution

Based on the recent criticisms directed toward prosecutors, we suggest that accountability should increase to align with legal and ethical standards to reduce symbolic compliance. The three-pronged framework of legal endogeneity, which includes reference, relevance, and deference, is useful for contextualizing reform surrounding accountability for modern prosecutors (see Edelman et al., 2011). In the reference stage, organizational structures (e.g., grievance procedures or, like, employee handbooks) initially do not have an authorized legal basis but become recognized in legal contexts as judges mention them in rulings and parties reference them in legal briefs, seeing them as pertinent to legal compliance (Edelman et al., 2011). In other words, the reference stage involves acknowledging and understanding the existing legal and ethical frameworks. For prosecutors, this means being aware of laws and standard practices and understanding the broader ethical implications of their actions. For example, prosecutors acknowledge and look to establish legal norms, ethical guidelines, and court rulings as benchmarks to prove the fairness of their actions. This initial step aims to promote accountability by ensuring prosecutorial actions are justifiable according to legal standards. This process may include developing checklists or guidelines that reference specific legal and ethical standards relevant to regular uses of prosecutorial discretion, such as charging, plea deals, and dismissals of cases. Prosecutors can develop internal policies that explicitly reference these legal and ethical standards. For example, policies on case selection could reference principles of justice and equity, while policies on victim interaction could reference ethical standards for treating victims with respect and dignity.

Second, in the relevance stage, judges are more likely to find institutionalized organizational structures relevant to see if illegal discrimination has occurred. This can occur, in part, because organizations increasingly refer to their established structures to justify the fairness of their actions, and judges treat these structures as more relevant when it comes to legal liability (Edelman et al., 2011). This stage must reflect a shift from just acknowledging the existence of such structures to practical evaluation. To ensure this, prosecutorial offices need a thorough evaluation of their internal structures and processes (e.g., policies on case selection and withdrawal) to prevent discrimination. This evaluation should consider whether these structures are formalities or actively contributing to fair and equitable prosecution practices. To strengthen the evaluation process, offices need to document and demonstrate effectiveness by collecting and analyzing data on case outcomes, feedback from defense attorneys, and satisfaction surveys from the public to demonstrate the structure's impact.

In the deference stage, judges believe that an organization's established structures, such as policies or procedures, are sufficient evidence of compliance with the law (Edelman et al., 2011). To avoid this stage, prosecutor offices may conduct regular audits and independent reviews of prosecutorial actions and decisions. These audits should assess not just the existence of compliance structures but their effectiveness and the actual outcomes of their implementation. Further, prosecutor offices can use audit feedback to improve practices that align with judicial ethics. Moreover, prosecutorial offices should develop a culture of continuous improvement and learning. For example, a prosecutor's office could review their charging decisions over a one-year period to identify disparities in charging outcomes among racial or ethnic groups. Additionally, the office could develop a performance review system that focuses on prosecutors' use of evidence and their ability to effectively communicate with victims, witnesses, and defendants. Finally, prosecutors may also need to reconsider how they use evidence, witnesses, and other resources to ensure fairness and transparency.

Applying legal endogeneity theory through its stages of reference, relevance, and deference offers a strategic pathway for prosecutorial offices to reinforce accountability and navigate the complexities of legal compliance. Prosecutorial practices can achieve a deeper alignment with the principles of justice and equity by transitioning from the initial acknowledgment of legal norms and ethical guidelines to the thorough evaluation and effective implementation of organizational structures. By addressing the inherent challenges in the deference stage—through regular audits and a commitment to continuous improvement—prosecutorial offices can ensure that their practice fosters a responsive, transparent, and fundamentally just culture.

Conclusion

In this chapter, we examine the uses of prosecutorial power and discretion in the twenty-first century. Particularly, we argue that critical perspectives of the legal system and issues like wrongful convictions and mass incarceration have reshaped the structure and strategies of contemporary prosecution. Research shows that prosecutors have contributed to system errors and increasing incarceration rates (Gross et al., 2020; Pfaff, 2012), but the progressive movement has sought to address these issues (e.g., Levenson, 2023; Webster, 2019). These prosecutors align with a logic of reformation, seeking to remedy injustice in the legal system. On the contrary, prosecutors in the logic of endurance have sought to maintain traditional processes. These logics are, in some ways, in competition with one another and have led to division. Future researchers should consider expanding on these logics. For example, cash bail reform and abolition have grown increasingly popular in the last several years (see Scott-Hayward & Fradella, 2022, for more on abolishing bail). Though we do not explore bail reform in this chapter, it is plausible that it also illustrates divisions in contemporary prosecution. Additionally, scholars should continue studying the consequences of prosecutorial uses of power and discretion in both traditional and progressive avenues.

In this chapter, we suggest that contemporary prosecution can be improved by increasing accountability. Many of the mechanisms (e.g., laws and ethical standards) for achieving this goal are in place. We argue that prosecutors should take a more proactive approach, structurally and strategically, to address accountability in their organizations and to comply with the law. We have sought to address the criticisms of the legal system generally and prosecutors specifically by exploring changes in applications of power and discretion. Prosecutors are, and likely will remain, the most powerful actors in the administration of justice. To this end, more research is needed on systems of accountability for prosecutors. This includes, for example, how prosecutors can self-regulate or the impact of professional boards and commissions (e.g., the New York State Commission on Prosecutorial Conduct, see New York State, n.d.) on prosecutorial accountability. Prosecutorial structures and strategies should also be further analyzed surrounding the proliferation of wrongful convictions, mass incarceration, and other key issues plaguing contemporary legal institutions. Collectively, prosecutors are vital to the criminal legal system, and the landscape surrounding their practices in the modern era merits further analysis.

References

Alschuler, A. W. (1968). The prosecutor's role in plea bargaining. *University of Chicago Law Review, 36*(1), 50–112.
American Bar Association. (2017). Prosecution function. In *Criminal justice standards for the prosecution function*. Retrieved from https://www.americanbar.org/groups/criminal_justice/standards/ProsecutionFunctionFourthEdition/
American Civil Liberties Union. (2017a). *Smart Justice Campaign polling on American's attitudes on criminal justice*. Retrieved from https://www.aclu.org/publications/smart-justice-campaign-polling-americans-attitudes-criminal-justice
American Civil Liberties Union. (2017b). *Fact sheet: New polling of voters' opinions towards prosecutor*. Retrieved from https://www.aclu.org/documents/new-polling-voters-opinions-towards-prosecutors
Arlington, VA. (n.d.-a). *Parisa Dehghani-Tafti*. Retrieved from https://www.arlingtonva.us/Government/Departments/Courts/Commonwealth-Attorney/Meet-Parisa
Arlington, VA. (n.d.-b). *Conviction review unit*. Retrieved from https://www.arlingtonva.us/Government/Departments/Courts/Commonwealth-Attorney/Conviction-Review-Unit
Baldus, B. (1975). The study of power: Suggestions for an alternative. *The Canadian Journal of Sociology, 1*(2), 179–201.
Barakat, M. (2023). *Reform-minded prosecutors in northern Virginia face primary challenges*. Associated Press. Retrieved from https://apnews.com/article/reform-prosecutors-reelection-virginia-descano-crime-f06a4aa39902b8faa9bd0398798f5183
Bellin, J. (2019). The power of prosecutors. *New York University Law Review, 94*(2), 171–212.
Bellin, J. (2020). Expanding the reach of progressive prosecution. *The Journal of Criminal Law and Criminology, 110*(4), 707–717.
Besharov, M. L., & Smith, W. K. (2014). Multiple institutional logics in organizations: Explaining their varied nature and implications. *Academy of Management Review, 39*(3), 364–381.
Bettens, T., & Redlich, A. D. (2023). The effects of confessions on misconduct and guilty pleas in exonerations: Implications for discovery policies. *Criminology & Public Policy, 23*, 179–199.
Bibas, S. (2010). The need for prosecutorial discretion. *Temple Political & Civil Rights Law Review, 19*(2), 369–376.
Blakinger, K. (2022). *Prosecutors who want to curb mass incarceration hit a roadblock: Tough-on-crime lawmakers*. The Marshall Project. Retrieved from https://www.themarshallproject.org/2022/02/03/prosecutors-who-want-to-curb-mass-incarceration-hit-a-roadblock-tough-on-crime-lawmakers
Bland, S. (2023). Progressive prosecutors beat back primary challengers in Virginia. *NBC News*. https://www.nbcnews.com/politics/elections/progressive-prosecutors-beat-back-primary-challengers-virginia-rcna90334
Bonventre, C. L. (2020). Wrongful conviction and forensic science. *WIRES Forensic Science*. https://doi.org/10.1002/wfs2.1406
Brady v. Maryland, 373 U.S. 83. (1963).
Brenan, M. (2023). *Americans more critical of U.S. criminal justice system*. Gallup. Retrieved from https://news.gallup.com/poll/544439/americans-critical-criminal-justice-system.aspx
Buckley v. Fitzsimmons, 509 U.S. 259. (1993).

Chemerinsky, E. (2008). Absolute immunity: General principles and recent developments. *Touro Law Review, 24*(3), 473–500.
Clegg, S. (1998). Foucault, power and organizations. In A. McKinlay & K. Starkey (Eds.), *Foucault, management and organization theory: From panopticon to technologies of self* (pp. 29–48). SAGE Academic.
Covey, R. (2013). Police misconduct as cause of wrongful convictions. *Washington University Law Review, 90*(4), 1133–1190.
Davis, A. J. (2007). *Arbitrary justice: The power of the American prosecutor*. Oxford University Press.
Davis, A. J. (2016). The prosecutor's ethical duty to end mass incarceration. *Hofstra Law Review, 44*(4), 1063–1086.
Davis, A. J. (2019). Reimagining prosecution: A growing progressive movement. *UCLA Criminal Justice Law Review, 3*, 1–28.
DiFava, R. J., Bettens, T., Wilford, M. M., & Redlich, A. D. (2023). Confession evidence results in more true and false guilty pleas than eyewitness evidence. *Journal of Experimental Criminology*, 1–15. Advanced online publication.
DiMaggio, P. J., & Powell, W. W. (1983). The iron cage revisited: Institutional isomorphism and collective rationality in organizational fields. *American Sociological Review, 48*(2), 147–160.
Edelman, L. B. (1990). Legal environments and organizational governance: The expansion of due process in the American workplace. *American Journal of Sociology, 95*(6), 1401–1440.
Edelman, L. B., & Talesh, S. A. (2011). To comply or not to comply—That isn't the question: How organizations construct the meaning of compliance. In C. Parker & V. L. Nielsen (Eds.), *Explaining compliance: Business responses to regulation* (pp. 103–122). Edward Elgar Publishing.
Edelman, L. B., Abraham, S. E., & Erlanger, H. S. (1992). Professional construction of law: The inflated threat of wrongful discharge. *Law and Society Review, 26*(1), 47–83.
Edelman, L. B., Uggen, C., & Erlanger, H. S. (1999). The endogeneity of legal regulation: Grievance procedures as rational myth. *American Journal of Sociology, 105*(2), 406–454.
Edelman, L. B., Krieger, L. H., Eliason, S. R., Albiston, C. R., & Mellema, V. (2011). When organizations rule: Judicial deference to institutionalized employment structures. *American Journal of Sociology, 117*(3), 888–954.
Eisenberg, R., & Preston, A. (2022). *Progressive prosecutors are not tied to the rise in violent crime*. Center for American Progress. Retrieved from https://www.americanprogress.org/article/progressive-prosecutors-are-not-tied-to-the-rise-in-violent-crime/
Foglesong, T., Levi, R., Rosenfeld, R., Schoenfeld, H., Wood, J., Stemen, D., & Rengifo, A. (2022). *Violent crime and public prosecution: A review of recent data on homicide, robbery, and progressive prosecution in the United States*. Munk School of Global Affairs & Public Policy, University of Toronto. Retrieved from https://munkschool.utoronto.ca/research/violent-crime-and-public-prosecution
Friedland, R., & Alford, R. R. (1991). Bringing society back in: Symbols, practices, and institutional contradictions. In W. W. Powell & P. J. DiMaggio (Eds.), *The new institutionalism in organizational analysis* (pp. 232–263). University of Chicago Press.
Gajwani, S., & Lesser, M. G. (2019). The hard truths of progressive prosecution and path to realizing the movement's promise. *New York Law School Law Review, 64*(1), 69–94.
Garland, D. (2001). *The culture of control: Crime and social order in contemporary society*. Oxford University Press.
Gershman, B. L. (2007). Litigating Brady v. Maryland: Games prosecutors play. *Case Western Reserve Law Review, 57*(3), 531–566.
Gershman, B. L. (2010). Prosecutorial decision making and discretion in the charging function. *Hastings Law Journal, 62*(5), 1259–1284.
Gilad, S. (2014). Beyond endogeneity: How firms and regulators co-construct the meaning of regulation. *Law & Policy, 36*(2), 134–164.

Goodman, J. D. (2023). With an array of tactics, conservatives seek to oust progressive prosecutors. *The New York Times*. Retrieved from https://www.nytimes.com/2023/08/12/us/conservatives-progressive-district-attorneys.html?searchResultPosition=1

Green, B. A., & Burke, A. S. (2012). The community prosecutor: Questions of professional discretion. *Wake Forest Law Review, 47*(2), 285–318.

Green, B. A., & Roiphe, R. (2020). When prosecutors politick: Progressive law enforcers then and now. *Journal of Criminal Law and Criminology, 110*(4), 719–768.

Greenspan, R. L., Miller, R., & Heaton, P. (2022). Reform we can agree on: Public opinion on prosecutorial liability. *Journal of Experimental Criminology*, 1–13. https://doi.org/10.1007/s11292-022-09533-x

Gross, S. R., Possley, M. J., Roll, K. J., & Stephens, K. H. (2020). *Government misconduct and convicting the innocent: The role of prosecutors, police and other law enforcement*. National Registry of Exonerations.

Gualtieri, G. (2020). Symbolic compliance and student concerns: Legal endogeneity and Title IX at American colleges and universities. *Sociological Forum, 35*(1), 207–228.

Hager, E. (2018). *The DAs who want to set the guilty free*. The Marshall Project. Retrieved from https://www.themarshallproject.org/2018/03/20/the-das-who-want-to-set-the-guilty-free

Haskell, J. (2024). Gascón, amid reelection bid, says 'We're in a much better place today than we were four years ago'. *ABC 7 Eyewitness News*. Retrieved from https://abc7.com/george-gascon-interview-district-attorney-los-angeles-county/14471073/

Haveman, H. A., & Gualtieri, G. (2017). Institutional logics. In *Oxford research encyclopedia of business and management* (pp. 1–29). Oxford University Press. https://doi.org/10.1093/acrefore/9780190224851.013.137

Heiskala, R. (2001). Theorizing power: Weber, Parsons, Foucault and neostructuralism. *Social Science Information, 40*(2), 241–264.

Herndon, A. W. (2022). They wanted to roll back tough-on-crime policies. Then violent crime surged. *The New York Times*. Retrieved from https://www.nytimes.com/2022/02/18/us/politics/prosecutors-midterms-crime.html

Imbler v. Pachtman, 424 U.S. 409. (1976).

Innocence Project. (2015). *Conviction integrity unit best practices*. Retrieved from https://www.innocenceproject.org/wp-content/uploads/2016/09/Conviction-Integrity-Unit.pdf

Jessop, B. (2012). Marxist approaches to power. In E. Amenta, K. Nash, & A. Scott (Eds.), *The Wiley-Blackwell companion to political sociology* (pp. 3–14). John Wiley & Sons, Ltd.

Johns, M. Z. (2005). Reconsidering absolute prosecutorial immunity. *Brigham Young University Law Review, 2005*(1), 53–154.

Johns, M. Z. (2011). Unsupportable and unjustified: A critique of absolute prosecutorial immunity. *Fordham Law Review, 80*(2), 509–536.

Johnson, B. D., King, R. D., & Spohn, C. (2016). Sociolegal approaches to the study of guilty pleas and prosecution. *Annual Review of Law and Social Science, 12*, 479–495.

Jones, J. M. (2022). *Confidence in U.S. institutions down; average at new low*. Gallup. Retrieved from https://news.gallup.com/poll/394283/confidence-institutions-down-average-new-low.aspx

Levenson, L. L. (2023). Progressive prosecutors: Winning the hearts and minds of line prosecutors. *American Criminal Law Review, 60*(4), 1495–1516.

Levin, B. (2021). Imagining the progressive prosecutor. *Minnesota Law Review, 105*(3), 1415–1452.

Lok, J. (2010). Institutional logics as identity projects. *Academy of Management Journal, 53*(6), 1305–1335.

McPherson, C. M., & Sauder, M. (2013). Logics in action: Managing institutional complexity in a drug court. *Administrative Science Quarterly, 58*(2), 165–196.

Meldrum, R. C., Stemen, D., & Kutateladze, B. L. (2021). Progressive and traditional orientations to prosecution: An empirical assessment in four prosecutorial offices. *Criminal Justice and Behavior, 48*(3), 354–372.

Meyer, J. W., & Rowan, B. (1977). Institutionalized organizations: Formal structure as myth and ceremony. *American Journal of Sociology, 83*(2), 340–363.

Meyer, J., Scott, W. R., & Strang, D. (1987). Centralization, fragmentation, and school district complexity. *Administrative Science Quarterly, 32*(2), 186–201.

Morrison, L. C. (1978). Absolute immunity for prosecutors; too broad a protection: Imbler v. Pachtman. *Southwestern University Law Review, 10*(2), 305–330.

Motivans, M. (2008). *Federal justice statistics, 2005*. Bureau of Justice Statistics. Retrieved from https://bjs.ojp.gov/library/publications/federal-justice-statistics-2005

Motivans, M. (2024). *Federal justice statistics, 2022*. Bureau of Justice Statistics. Retrieved from https://bjs.ojp.gov/library/publications/federal-justice-statistics-2022

National Registry of Exonerations. (n.d.-a). *Contributing factors and type of crime*. Retrieved from https://www.law.umich.edu/special/exoneration/Pages/ExonerationsContribFactorsByCrime.aspx

National Registry of Exonerations. (n.d.-b). *Glossary*. Retrieved from https://www.law.umich.edu/special/exoneration/Pages/glossary.aspx

National Registry of Exonerations. (n.d.-c). *Conviction integrity units*. Retrieved from https://www.law.umich.edu/special/exoneration/Pages/Conviction-Integrity-Units.aspx

New York State. (n.d.). *New York State Commission on prosecutorial misconduct*. Retrieved from https://www.ny.gov/new-york-state-commission-prosecutorial-conduct

Norris, R. J. (2017a). *Exonerated: A history of the innocence movement*. New York University Press.

Norris, R. J. (2017b). Framing DNA: Social movement theory and the foundations of the innocence movement. *Journal of Contemporary Criminal Justice, 33*(1), 26–42.

North Carolina v. Alford, 400 U.S. 25. (1970).

Nugent, M. E., Fanflik, P., & Bromirski, D. (2004). *The changing nature of prosecution: Community prosecution vs. traditional prosecution approaches*. American Prosecutors Research Institute. Retrieved from https://www.ojp.gov/ncjrs/virtual-library/abstracts/changing-nature-prosecution-community-prosecution-vs-traditional

Pache, A. C., & Santos, F. (2013). Inside the hybrid organization: Selective coupling as a response to competing institutional logics. *Academy of Management Journal, 56*(4), 972–1001.

Palmer, C. (2019). Five takeaways from Philly DA Larry Krasner's 2019 budget hearing. *The Philadelphia Inquirer*. Retrieved from https://www.inquirer.com/news/larry-krasner-city-council-budget-hearing-mass-incarceration-20190424.html

Parsons, T. (1960). *Structure and process in modern societies*. Free Press.

Perry, S. W., & Banks, D. (2011). *Prosecutors in state courts, 2007 – Statistical tables*. Bureau of Justice Statistics. Retrieved from https://bjs.ojp.gov/library/publications/prosecutors-state-courts-2007-statistical-tables

Pfaff, J. F. (2012). The micro and macro causes of prison growth. *Georgia State University Law Review, 28*(4), 1239–1274.

Pfeffer, J. (1992). *Managing with power: Politics and influence in organizations*. Harvard Business Press.

Philadelphia District Attorney's Office. (2018). *Philadelphia DAO new policies*. Retrieved from https://phillyda.org/wp-content/uploads/2022/04/DAO-New-Policies-2.15.2018-UPDATED.pdf

Prosecutors and Politics Project. (2020). *National study of prosecutor elections*. University of North Carolina School of Law. Retrieved from https://law.unc.edu/wp-content/uploads/2020/01/National-Study-Prosecutor-Elections-2020.pdf

Rao, H., Monin, P., & Durand, R. (2003). Institutional change in Toque Ville: Nouvelle cuisine as an identity movement in French gastronomy. *American Journal of Sociology, 108*(4), 795–843.

Redlich, A. D., Wilford, M. M., & Bushway, S. (2017). Understanding guilty pleas through the lens of social science. *Psychology, Public Policy, and Law, 23*(4), 458–471.

Redlich, A. D., Wilford, M. M., DiPano, M., & Berger, N. (2023). Commonalities in false guilty plea cases. *Psychology, Crime & Law*. https://doi.org/10.1080/1068316X.2023.2213381

Ressler, R. W., Fulton, B. R., & Paxton, P. (2024). Activity and identity: Uncovering multiple institutional logics in the nonprofit sector. *Nonprofit and Voluntary Sector Quarterly, 53*(2), 560–575.

Ridolfi, K. M., & Possley, M. (2010). *Preventable error: A report on prosecutorial misconduct in California 1997–2009.* Northern California Innocence Project.

Robert H. Jackson Center. (n.d.). *The federal prosecutor* (originally published in 1940). Retrieved from https://www.roberthjackson.org/speech-and-writing/the-federal-prosecutor/

Rudes, D. S., Magnuson, S., Portillo, S., & Hattery, A. (2021). Sex logics: Negotiating the prison rape elimination act (PREA) against its' administrative, safety, and cultural burdens. *Punishment & Society, 23*(2), 241–259.

Salancik, G. R., & Pfeffer, J. (1977). Who gets power—And how they hold on to it: A strategic-contingency model of power. *Organizational Dynamics, 5*(3), 3–21.

Salet, R., & Terpstra, J. (2022). Conflicting institutional logics in the control of crime and disorder: The double strategy of administrative and criminal law. *Criminology & Criminal Justice.* https://doi.org/10.1177/17488958221111206

Sarat, A., & Clarke, C. (2008). Beyond discretion: Prosecution, the logic of sovereignty, and the limits of law. *Law & Social Inquiry, 33*(2), 387–416.

Scheck, B., Neufeld, P. J., & Dwyer, J. (2000). *Actual innocence: Five days to execution and other dispatches from the wrongly convicted.* Doubleday Books.

Schoenfeld, H., Durso, R. M., & Albrecht, K. (2019). Maximizing charges: Overcriminalization and prosecutorial practices during the crime decline. *Studies in Law, Politics, and Society, 77,* 145–179.

Scott, W. R. (2003). *Organizations: Rational, natural, and open systems* (5th ed.). Prentice Hall.

Scott-Hayward, C., & Fradella, H. (2022). Abolishing bail. In J. Gould & P. Metzger (Eds.), *Transforming criminal justice: An evidence-based agenda for reform* (pp. 97–123). New York University Press.

Sentencing Project. (n.d.). *Growth in mass incarceration.* Retrieved from https://www.sentencingproject.org/research/

Sklansky, D. A. (2016). The nature and function of prosecutorial power. *Journal of Criminal Law and Criminology, 106*(3), 473–520.

Sklansky, D. A. (2017). The progressive prosecutor's handbook. *UC Davis Law Review Online, 50,* 25–42.

Spohn, C., Hemmens, C., & McCann, W. S. (2018). *Courts: A text/reader* (3rd ed.). SAGE Publications.

Tegethoff, E. (2023). *Behind the right's war on prosecutors.* The Appeal. Retrieved from https://theappeal.org/conservatives-progressive-prosecutors-reform/

Thornton, P., & Ocasio, W. (2008). Institutional logics. In R. Greenwood, C. Oliver, K. Sahlin, & R. Suddaby (Eds.), *The SAGE handbook of organizational institutionalism* (pp. 99–129). SAGE Publications.

Thornton, P. H., Ocasio, W., & Lounsbury, M. (2012). *The institutional logics perspective: A new approach to culture, structure and process.* Oxford University Press.

U.S. Department of Justice. (n.d.-a). *Offices of the United States attorneys.* Retrieved from https://www.justice.gov/usao

U.S. Department of Justice. (n.d.-b). *U.S. Attorneys listing.* Retrieved from https://www.justice.gov/usao/us-attorneys-listing

Van Wart, M. (2003). A comprehensive model of organizational leadership: The leadership action cycle. *International Journal of Organization Theory & Behavior, 7*(2), 173–208.

Walther, S. (2000). The position and structure of the prosecutor's office in the United States. *European Journal of Crime, Criminal Law and Criminal Justice, 8*(3), 283–295.

Weber, M. (1978). *Economy and society: An outline of interpretive sociology.* University of California Press.

Webster, E. (2019). Postconviction innocence review in the age of progressive prosecution. *Albany Law Review, 83*(3), 989–1020.

Western, B., & Wildeman, C. (2009). Punishment, inequality, and the future of mass incarceration. *University of Kansas Law Review, 57*(4), 851–878.

Westervelt, S. D., & Cook, K. J. (2010). Framing innocents: The wrongly convicted as victims of state harm. *Crime, Law and Social Change, 53*, 259–275.

Wiggins, O. (2023). Maryland's top prosecutor, public defender to take on mass incarceration. *The Washington Post*. Retrieved from https://www.washingtonpost.com/dc-md-va/2023/10/26/maryland-incarceration-anthony-brown-natasha-dartigue/

Witt, S. (2017). *Acting DA Gonzalez makes case with smarts & experience on his side*. PoliticsNY. Retrieved from https://politicsny.com/2017/06/26/acting-da-gonzalez-makes-case-smarts-experience-side/

Young, A. (2020). *The facts on progressive prosecutors*. Center for American Progress. Retrieved from https://www.americanprogress.org/article/progressive-prosecutors-reforming-criminal-justice/

Chapter 11
Enduring Harm as a By-Product of Prosecutors' Power Over Exonerees Post-incarceration

Mary Catlin and Andrew Madrigal

Introduction

This chapter begins with an outline of legitimacy, as understood through neo-institutional theory. We then apply the concept of legitimacy to the post-incarceration relationship between prosecutors and exonerees by establishing that legitimacy is a scarce resource post-incarceration that prosecutors and exonerees cannot both obtain. Next, we highlight power as a theoretical concept within the context of organizational literature. We then argue that prosecutors are more likely to win this scarce resource because of their power over exonerees post-incarceration. Then, we combine the concepts of legitimacy and power to argue that prosecutors and exonerees are in a battle for legitimacy, a scarce resource. In the final section, we offer examples of how the power differential favoring prosecutors is evident in several concerning but growing trends post-incarceration. We end with a discussion on how an organizational framework for understanding these complex processes provides necessary leverage for policy recommendations.

Enduring Harm as a By-Product of Prosecutors' Power Over Exonerees Post-incarceration

When a wrongful conviction occurs, prosecutors have ostensibly lost some sense of legitimacy. Prosecutors are pillars of the criminal legal system, and wrongful convictions are one of the most egregious miscarriages of justice. The discrepancy

M. Catlin (✉) · A. Madrigal
George Mason University, Department of Criminology, Law & Society, Fairfax, VA, USA
e-mail: mcatlin@gmu.edu

D. S. Rudes, J. R. Ingram (eds.), *Using Organizational Theory to Study, Explain, and Understand Criminal Legal Organizations*,
https://doi.org/10.1007/978-3-031-66285-0_11

between prosecutors' pursuit of justice and the reality of wrongful convictions is compounded by the fact that most wrongful convictions involve official misconduct (Gross et al., 2020). Thus, prosecutors have a diminished claim to justice, which is the basis of their legitimacy. This loss of legitimacy should decrease their power in negotiations with exonerees.[1] Yet, prosecutors maintain power over exonerees. This power is evident in the barriers prosecutors erect for exonerees' reentering society (e.g., Shlosberg et al., 2014) and the lack of redress for prosecutors who have been implicated in wrongful convictions. For example, only 4% of prosecutors involved in a wrongful conviction have received any kind of discipline, and only one prosecutor has ever been incarcerated (Selby, 2020). Researchers have tried explaining exonerees' post-incarceration struggles through a sociological (Umamaheswar, 2023; Westervelt & Cook, 2010, 2012) and psychological (e.g., Scherr et al., 2020) lens. However, without looking at prosecutors within the context of their organizations, the imbalance in post-incarceration interactions between exonerees and prosecutors will continue to elude social scientists. Thus, to understand these dynamics, we propose using an organizational lens.

Legitimacy and Neo-institutionalist Theory

Neo-institutionalism offers a lens through which we may understand why organizations make decisions that do not improve efficiency and, in some cases, decrease it. For example, why would a petroleum company release statements about environmentally minded initiatives (e.g., BP; Van Rooij & Fine, 2018)? Meyer and Rowan (1977) suggest that BP's concern with clean energy is not a reflection of efficiency but a matter of improving their survival prospects. Organizations—who are competing for resources, jurisdiction, and social positions (Saks, 2016)—seen as legitimate are the most likely to survive in a competitive environment with limited resources (Meyer & Rowan, 1977). It is the competition for social positions, we argue, that forces exonerees to seek legitimacy. Specifically, unless exonerees' innocence is taken for granted, they are likely to be treated as other factually guilty individuals, which diminishes their ability to adjust post-exoneration. Thus, exonerees' reintegration efforts may rest on their legitimacy.

Legitimacy is gained by incorporating "rationalized myths:" when a taken for granted belief is built into society to the point of institutionalization (Meyer & Rowan, 1977). For example, it is now taken for granted that most professions should not pose a risk to workers' well-being. This rationalized myth has been incorporated into laws and is largely reflected in public opinion. Worker safety, however, was not always taken for granted (e.g., Sinclair, 1906) and integrating worker safety into

[1] It should be noted that exoneree is an official recognition that an individual has been exonerated. Throughout the piece, we will use the term exoneree for consistency and simplicity, but at times may be referring to (1) processes occurring before the point of official exoneration or (2) innocent individuals who are never exonerated.

factories arguably decreased efficiency as workers worked fewer hours. Now, however, organizations that do not heed worker safety are not only in violation of the law but risk losing workers and support from consumers, which will limit the organization's viability. Therefore, to appear legitimate, organizations will incorporate worker safety guidelines despite the possible risk to efficiency and production.

Because rationalized myths are socially constructed, they are not stable, and organizations will need to change and expand to incorporate new rationalized myths. For example, BP would not need to worry about public statements regarding clean energy 50 years ago, but they needed to expand their organization to include environmental concerns to be legitimate in today's world (Van Rooij & Fine, 2018). Similarly, legitimacy in the criminal legal system has evolved over time. Prior to the growing concerns of whether justice existed in the "justice" system, it was believed that wrongful convictions did not happen: Justice Antonin Scalia stated that the rate of wrongful convictions was so small as to be essentially nonexistent (Walsh et al., 2017), and even when one has occurred that, "Mere factual innocence is no reason not to carry out a death sentence properly reached" (*Herrera v. Collins*, 1993). Now, however, we not only recognize that wrongful convictions occur, but an "innocence movement" has begun (Norris, 2017). On the surface, therefore, it may appear that prosecutors gain legitimacy by embracing this innocence movement.

Rationalized myths are often incorporated ceremonially (Meyer & Rowan, 1977). To continue the worker safety example used earlier, to maintain an image of legitimacy, organizations will publicly demonstrate their dedication to safe working conditions through media, written procedures, policy, and displays of success (e.g., number of days since last accident signs) whether or not the reality of the organization reflects these ceremonies (see Van Rooij & Fine, 2018 and Vaughan, 1999 for examples of organizational disasters). Thus, legitimacy is not necessarily a reflection of actual behavior but perceived behaviors: Company A has signs about worker safety. Therefore, Company A cares about worker safety and is legitimate.

To maintain this perception of legitimacy, rationalized myths are often decoupled (i.e., an organizational framework describing the disparity between the actual and stated activities of an organization; DeVries & Fitzpatrick, 2006) from the daily operations of organizations. This decoupling may partially explain why inefficient adaptation of rationalized myths does not necessarily result in decreased efficiency but is necessary because ceremonies closely coupled to organizational practice are easier to evaluate. Easy evaluation leaves organizations vulnerable to clear inconsistencies between their public claims and their organizational behaviors. Thus, decoupling allows organizations to avoid evaluation, promote discretion, and overlook inconsistencies (Meyer & Rowan, 1977). For example, a survey of police chiefs suggested that chiefs were more interested in maintaining their relationships with constituents—reflecting the arbitrators of rationalized myths—than maintaining law and order. This interest resulted in a decoupling of police policies/procedures and actual policing work, resulting in "symbolic reform at the edges" (Matusiak et al., 2017). Another instance of decoupling may be occurring with wrongful convictions: prosecutors espouse the goal of justice but, in practice, often block exonerees from receiving justice.

Legitimacy as a Scarce Resource

As of February 2024, over 3400 people have been exonerated of crimes in the United States (NRE, 2024). One factor that contributes to wrongful convictions is prosecutorial misconduct, including illegal behaviors (e.g., Brady violations; *Brady v. Maryland*, 1963) and breaking professional ethics that bind prosecutors (California Innocence Project, 2021). Thus, prosecutors are either indirectly involved in wrongful convictions when they mistakenly prosecute an individual or directly involved through the actions of their office (e.g., coerced false guilty pleas). As official state actors acting in the name of justice, prosecutors' involvement in (1) not convicting the factually guilty individual and (2) wrongfully convicting an innocent individual reduces their legitimacy. In fact, Moore (2011) found that prosecutors believe that the publicity of wrongful convictions hurts their ability to convict the guilty because wrongful convictions will reduce trust (i.e., legitimacy) in prosecutors' offices.

At first glance, it may seem that prosecutors and exonerees would be on the same side post-incarceration: to restore justice by restoring exonerees to their former state. Prosecutors, however, have a variety of reasons for working against the interests of exonerees to maintain their own legitimacy. As previously mentioned, organizations often maintain legitimacy through decoupling values from practice. For prosecutors, decoupling may be observed in conviction records. On the surface, prosecutors espouse justice as their main priority (Burke, 2010; Henry, 2020), which is often displayed through conviction records (Ferguson-Gilbert, 2001). Conviction records are especially important to prosecutors in positions or jurisdictions where prosecutors are elected. As such, prosecutors are particularly motivated to maintain a strong conviction record (Ferguson-Gilbert, 2001). To maintain a strong conviction record, prosecutors often default to plea bargaining and only proceed to trial with their strongest cases. In fact, when prosecutors fear they cannot obtain a plea deal or trial conviction, they are likely not to pursue charges or drop charges that have already been filed (Wilford & Khairalla, 2019). Thus, conviction records are decoupled from the pursuit of justice to avoid a close inspection that may threaten prosecutors' legitimacy as seekers of justice.

Wrongful convictions, however, threaten prosecutors' conviction records. Thus, prosecutors are motivated to deny wrongful convictions. In fact, some prosecutors have been labeled "innocence deniers" because they repeatedly refuse to acknowledge the innocence of wrongfully convicted individuals (Bazelon, 2018). By denying wrongful convictions, prosecutors can argue they did not contribute to a miscarriage of justice and can maintain their conviction record. One way prosecutors deny wrongful convictions is to offer potential exonerees plea deals, often for perjury. Specifically, prosecutors reason that either the wrongfully convicted individual must have lied at the time of their conviction or is lying about their innocence (Raymond, 2001). Thus, the deal for pleading to perjury offers the individual a lighter sentence, which often results in time served. Individuals are tempted to accept these deals, regardless of innocence or long-term consequences, because these plea deals typically allow them to leave prison immediately (Henry, 2020). By providing these pleas, prosecutors maintain their legitimacy by maintaining their conviction record, which allows them to avoid the scrutiny that comes when wrongful convictions, and especially exonerations, occur. Thus, at this first stage, prosecutors can only maintain legitimacy if wrongfully convicted individuals lose legitimacy by accepting the mantle of a factually guilty individual.

Once a wrongfully convicted individual has been exonerated, prosecutors have lost some sense of legitimacy. Specifically, the prosecutor is implicated in a miscarriage of justice, and their conviction record has been hurt. At this point, prosecutors can mitigate the damage to their legitimacy by reducing the impact of the exoneration. To reduce the impact of the exoneration, prosecutors must cast doubt on the exonerees' innocence: the guiltier an exoneree appears, the lesser blame prosecutors share. To do otherwise (i.e., embrace the exoneration) would be to admit a mistake has been made that can be traced to the prosecutors' office either directly or indirectly. Prosecutors can reduce the impact of exonerations materially by limiting compensation for wrongful convictions, legally by limiting record expungement (Shlosberg et al., 2014), or publicly by denying innocence (Bazelon, 2018). Regardless of the mechanism, these tactics, which maintain legitimacy for prosecutors, necessarily reduce legitimacy for exonerees.

Legitimacy, therefore, is a scarce resource post-incarceration. Whether it is in the battle for the title of exoneree or in the aftermath of an exoneration, legitimacy for one party necessarily means reduced legitimacy for the other. Consider, for example, Linda Fairstein, a renowned prosecutor known for her work in sex crime cases and high conviction rates. This reputation for conviction made her an ideal candidate to prosecute the individual(s) responsible for a brutal rape in New York City's Central Park that left a female jogger fighting for her life. Under her direct supervision and prompting, her office targeted a group of five teenage boys. As a result, her office was partly—if not entirely—responsible for the wrongful conviction of the Exonerated Five. This case became the epitome of factors that lead to wrongful convictions: young, vulnerable teenage boys at the mercy of powerful criminal legal actors who were convinced the youth were guilty despite the lack of evidence. Several of the boys were threatened and beaten during their interrogations, which led to several false confessions—largely under the direction of Fairstein (Bazelon, 2018). The boys were so hated by New York City that a full-page advertisement was taken out in a local paper suggesting that New York should reinstate the death penalty specifically for these five juvenile boys (Ransom, 2019). Yet, Fairstein has not apologized for her part in the case. In fact, instead of apologizing for her actions, she has taken fault with the way she has been portrayed in the media. With the release of *When They See Us*, a docu-series on *Netflix*, Fairstein filed a civil suit against Netflix for defamation of character. Even with the state of New York paying out nearly $45 million to these exonerees (History.com Editors, 2019), Fairstein refuses to concede her legitimacy by accepting her role in this miscarriage of justice.

Whether legitimacy will be garnered by prosecutors or wrongfully convicted individuals will largely be determined by power dynamics. Specifically, in the post-incarceration relationship between prosecutors and exonerees, the party that has greater power will be the party able to win the limited resource (i.e., legitimacy).

Power and Organizational Theory

The concept of power is ubiquitous in organizational settings, often invoked to explain phenomena not easily explained by other concepts or theories (Pfeffer, 1981). For example, one might say that an individual is powerful to explain why others appear to acquiesce to this individual's demands. Or we might also say that the Democratic Party had the power to win the 2020 presidential election. Typically, power is portrayed as a negative, even evil, force that some individuals or organizations hold over others (Pfeffer, 1981). For example, researchers have proposed prosecutors can use their power to coerce defendants into plea deals which are not made knowingly, intelligently, or voluntarily (Luna, 2022). Power, however, is not inherently good or bad. In fact, power could increase the likelihood of constructive confrontation when a powerful actor shows social support to a target with little power (Hershcovis et al., 2017). For example, celebrities have been known to use their influence to pressure legal actors to consider claims of innocence from incarcerated individuals (Palmer, 2021). Unfortunately, the broader the range of observations ascribed to power, the less meaningful power, as an organizational concept, will be. To avoid this problem, organization scholars attempted redefining the scope of power (see Czarniawska-Joerges, 1988, for an overview of different conceptualizations of power). For our purposes, we conceptualized power in the same manner as Pfeffer (1981).

According to Pfeffer (1981), power is the ability of one social actor to overcome resistance in another social actor to achieve a desired outcome. Social actors may be individuals (e.g., an officer's ability to get a false confession from an innocent suspect), subunits of an organization (e.g., the biology department's ability to get the psychology department to concede workspace), or entire organizations (e.g., the FBI's ability to take credit for cases solved by local law enforcement agencies). When the social actor is an individual, power could also reflect personality and demographic variables (Anderson & Brion, 2014). Consider that of the individuals who have been wrongfully convicted and exonerated, 53% are Black, 32% are White, and 12% are Hispanic. The race/ethnicity of exonerees is important to note (1) due to the increased vulnerability to factors typically associated with wrongful convictions for minority exonerees (e.g., Black individuals are often victims of the cross-race effect [Wells & Olson, 2001]) and (2) minority exonerees are likely to lack power in interpersonal negotiations because of their diminished social capacity (Webster, 2019). It should also be noted that power requires resistance (Bellin, 2019) because (1) without resistance, social actors do not need to exercise their power, and (2) when a social actor's power is no longer resisted, power has morphed into authority (Pfeffer, 1981). In short, power may predict how differing preferences will be resolved in conflicts over the allocation of scarce resources (Pfeffer, 1981).

Resources are regularly limited in organizational settings, and therefore, power is an organizational necessity. As a basic example, time and energy are finite resources that organizational actors possess. Finite resources could cause conflict because organizational actors, even within the same organization, can hold different goals from each other. For example, prosecutor offices may want law enforcement to spend time and energy gathering more evidence for a specific case, but law enforcement may be more motivated to continue work on new cases. In this situation, and in other ubiquitous parallels, power becomes necessary for social actors as each party attempts to apply their power in order to achieve their goals with the limited resources available (Anderson & Brion, 2014). Power may be the result of hierarchical authority where one individual has power over another because they are higher in the organizational structure (e.g., a manager having power over a line worker). Perhaps related to hierarchical authority, power may also come from the ability to control desired resources. For example, a social actor who has access to an ingredient necessary for a restaurant's most popular dish has power over that restaurant. It is possible that this social actor has access to the resource because of their place in the organizational hierarchy (e.g., the ingredient vendor is more likely to approach the head chief than the line cook), but it does not have to be (e.g., perhaps the line cook's family grows the ingredient; Astley & Sachdeva, 1984).

Finally, the source of a social actor's power may be their network centrality. This concept is especially relevant for organizations that are flat as opposed to vertical. In these decentralized organizations, there will be positions that overlap between subunits. The social actors at these points of interconnection can become functionally indispensable as they are the only ones who have the knowledge inherent to the distinct organization areas they are touching. Becoming indispensable gives social actors power through network centrality (Astley & Sachdeva, 1984). For example, in an attempt to decrease sentencing disparities, judicial discretion was severely limited. Scholars have argued that discretion did not disappear from the legal system though. Instead, it simply shifted to prosecutors who have the ability to determine the charge, which limits judicial sentencing options (see Vaynman & Fondacaro, 2024). With this shift, prosecutorial power increased because prosecutors control desired resources (i.e., the charges) which defense attorneys, judges, and defendants have a vested interest in. Furthermore, this control over a mutually invested resource puts prosecutors at the center of this network, where they are unregulated as to how they leverage this power (Engen & Steen, 2000).

Of course, power (1) does not have to be exercised and (2) can also be lost. When examining the reactions of individuals who perceived they had been victims of wrongdoing, researchers note that not every victim attempted to respond with power. Several victims decided to "move on" to preserve relationships with high-status individuals, which was less likely to happen with lower-status individuals (Aquino et al., 2006). Perhaps this reflects victims' ability to recognize that maintaining the high-status relationship may be a source of power in future disagreements over scarce resources. For example, perhaps an exoneree does not "get revenge" on a prosecutor for their wrongful conviction because they know they will need the support of the prosecutor in their claims for compensation. When social actors attempt to exercise their power, they could find themselves less powerful than they believed. Because power is about the interaction between two social actors, it can vary across relationships, contexts, and time (Pfeffer, 1981). When a social actor faces environmental competition or the balance of power within the organization changes, a social actor can lose their power (Anderson & Brion, 2014). For example, a growing number of conviction integrity units are forming (NRE, 2023), and it remains unclear how these units will or will not alter the power of prosecutors in reviewing claims of innocence.

Because we are interested in the post-incarceration relationship between prosecutors and exonerees, we sought a definition of power that reflected an imbalance in social relationships (Emerson, 1962; Tost, 2015). Power is not an attribute of prosecutors because power cannot be a dispositional characteristic of any social actor (Anderson & Brion, 2014; Emerson, 1962). To understand how prosecutors maintain control over resources after a theoretical loss of power by being either directly or indirectly implicated in a wrongful conviction, we need to understand the relationship between prosecutors and exonerees after release. We apply Emerson's (1962) theoretical power formulas to better understand this relationship. Specifically, Emerson (1962) posits that social actor A has power over social actor B to the extent that social actor B is dependent on social actor A. B will be more dependent on A if B cannot obtain the resource outside of A (e.g., from C). Furthermore, B will be more dependent on A to the extent that B needs the resources to meet their goals.

Power Struggle Over Legitimacy

Applying Emerson's (1962) formula to the prosecutor–exoneree relationship, prosecutors will maintain power over exonerees to the extent that exonerees need a resource from prosecutors that cannot be granted by another organization. We suggest that the resource that exonerees need from prosecutors is legitimacy, which prosecutors, as representatives of the larger criminal legal system, can grant.

Legitimacy as Scarce, Desired Resource

Prosecutors not only play a substantial role in wrongful convictions but continue to impact exonerees post-incarceration. To the former, the majority of wrongful convictions are due to official misconduct (NRE, 2024), which can include Brady violations (Sklansky, 2018; Swisher, 2012). Brady violations are when prosecutors intentionally withhold exculpatory evidence from the defense (*Brady v Maryland*, 1963)—partially explaining why prosecutors are motivated to deny wrongful convictions. Innocent individuals, on the other hand, are highly motivated to be exonerated. Theoretically, an exoneration should provide exonerees the legitimacy of a factually innocent individual, making it easier to reintegrate into society. For example, research has found that expungement (Shlosberg et al., 2014) and compensation (Mandery et al., 2013), both markers of exoneration and legitimacy, have been linked to fewer post-release criminal charges. Thus, social actors A (prosecutors) and B (exonerees) both desire legitimacy and are in contention over this scarce resource.

Exonerees Are Dependent on Prosecutors

Matthews (2021) claims that the exacerbated suffering of exonerees is due to the significant causal role of the state and its organizations. Prosecutors are no exception as they are members of the state organization. In fact, prosecutorial misconduct was a contributing factor in approximately 30% of wrongful convictions (Gross et al., 2020). Regardless of the contributory factors, all wrongful convictions can be attributed to state harm (Stratton, 2015; Westervelt & Cook, 2010). Through the state harm framework it becomes clear that prosecutors are critical in the organizational processes which determine how exonerees can live normal lives post-incarceration. Most notably, prosecutors regulate if an exoneree's victimization by the state continues post-incarceration (Drummond & Mills, 2020; Stratton, 2015; Vick et al., 2021). Taken from Kauzlarich et al.'s (2001) theoretical foundation, groups and individuals may be identified as victims of state crime by the following six propositions:

1. Victims of state crime tend to be among the least socially powerful actors.
2. Victimizers generally fail to recognize and understand the nature, extent, and harmfulness of institutional policies. If suffering and harm are acknowledged, it is often neutralized within the context of a sense of 'entitlement.'
3. Victims of state crime are often blamed for their suffering.
4. Victims of state crime must generally rely on the victimizer, an associated institution, or civil social movements for redress.
5. Victims of state crime are easy targets for repeated victimization.
6. Illegal state policies and practices, while committed by individuals and groups of individuals, are manifestations of the attempt to achieve organizational, bureaucratic, or institutional goals. (Kauzlarich et al., 2001, p. 183–189; Stratton, 2015; Westervelt & Cook, 2010, p. 261–263).

Westervelt and Cook (2010) walk through each of these propositions and demonstrate how exonerees are victimized by the state and its prosecutors. Briefly, prosecutors hold immense power over the lives of exonerees but often fail to recognize the harm that they cause to exonerees (e.g., "innocence deniers;" Bazelon, 2018). Even if prosecutors do acknowledge any wrongdoing, they are motivated by organizational pressures to limit exonerees' legitimacy so as to maintain their own. Yet research finds that one of the main things exonerees desire post-incarceration is legitimacy in the form of an apology (Clow et al., 2011; Penzell, 2007). Whether this apology is formal or informal, just the mere acknowledgment from prosecutors can serve as a mechanism to educate other criminal legal actors on the potential for wrongful convictions, hopefully preventing future miscarriages of justice (Faison & Smalarz, 2019).

Exonerees require legitimacy to successfully reintegrate back into society. Reentry scholars posit that for formerly incarcerated individuals to feel invested and be acknowledged as contributing members of the community, they require legitimacy (Berg & Huebner, 2011). Most importantly, though, exonerees must reestablish their legitimacy as innocent individuals. For many who have been wrongfully convicted, there is an understanding that society may still view them as guilty, regardless of their exoneration status (Clow & Leach, 2015; Thompson et al., 2012). For example, Westervelt and Cook (2012) interviewed several exonerees who discussed the role of societal reaction in their reintegration efforts. In one case, prosecutors acknowledged that a grave miscarriage of justice had occurred and that the office fully endorsed Juan Melendez's innocence. When Rivera returned to Puerto Rico, he was greeted by a parade to accompany him home, which he attributed to the prosecutor's public statements. In a very different reaction, prosecutors made public announcements regarding their disbelief in Kirk Bloodsworth's innocence. Bloodsworth lost several jobs and was accosted by local residents who believed him to be a "baby killer" (Westervelt & Cook, 2012). Thus, the quest for gaining and maintaining legitimacy for exonerees lies with prosecutors.

Exonerees are clearly dependent on prosecutors, but the reverse is not true. For exonerees, the consequences of losing legitimacy can be life-altering. Prosecutors, on the other hand, are unlikely to be affected by their role in the wrongful conviction (Selby, 2020). Thus, exonerees are more dependent on prosecutors than prosecutors are on exonerees, firmly establishing prosecutors' power over exonerees. In other words, social actor B (exonerees) are dependent on social actor A (prosecutors).

Exonerees Are Unlikely to Gain Legitimacy Without Prosecutors

It is common that although released, wrongfully convicted persons are not exonerated until years later (Scherr & Normile, 2022). Though free, the lack of a legitimate title as exoneree prevents individuals from gaining compensation, expungement of their records, and obtaining housing and employment (Shlosberg et al., 2014; Sklansky, 2018). To further complicate their predicament, released but not exonerated individuals are not eligible for the support services offered to factually guilty individuals released through probation or parole (Chunias & Aufgang, 2008). For most exonerees, these battles cannot be won without support from prosecutors.

As an example of the power dynamics between prosecutors and wrongfully convicted individuals, consider the case of prosecutor Jackson and exoneree Dennis Allen. Jackson withheld vital, exculpatory evidence that Allen was innocent. As a result of the prosecutor's actions, Allen was wrongfully convicted of murder in 1999 and was released from prison in 2014. Prosecutors were able to maintain power over Allen for five years by refusing to dismiss the charges. In fact, it was not until the prosecutor declined to retry Allen that he was officially exonerated in May 2019 (Possley, 2021). This example is not just an anecdote; empirical examinations suggest that the limbo period between release and exoneration is significantly longer when official misconduct is involved (Scherr & Normile, 2022). Thus, it is not simply that wrongfully convicted individuals are motivated to gain legitimacy through exoneration but that the path to exoneration is controlled by prosecutors. When moving from wrongfully convicted to exonerated, individuals are dependent on prosecutors, giving prosecutors power over these individuals.

Yet, even after exoneration prosecutors can hinder exonerees' ability to fully reintegrate into society. This role can include restricting exonerees' ability to gain compensation, expungement of records, and other services that assist exonerees upon release (Shlosberg et al., 2014; Sklansky, 2018). In fact, Witness to Innocence (2021)—an organization exclusively dedicated to assisting death row exonerees' reintegration efforts—claims that even in states that provide compensation for exonerees, some refuse to do so. Notably, these efforts to not compensate under state statutes are largely attributed to prosecutors utilizing "arcane and arbitrary loopholes." In other words, social actor A (prosecutors) have more power over social actor B (exonerees) because social actor B cannot obtain the necessary resources (legitimacy) to reach desired outcomes from social actor C (e.g., innocence organizations blocked by prosecutors). Thus, based on Emerson's (1962) conceptualization of power, we would expect—and research supports—that prosecutors will win the post-incarceration fight for legitimacy.

Consequences of Prosecutorial Power Post-incarceration

Prosecutors can maintain their legitimacy after a wrongful conviction by either (1) denying wrongfully convicted individuals the legitimacy of the exoneree title and/or (2) limiting the perceived or real damage a wrongful conviction does to prosecutors' offices. Furthermore, wrongfully convicted individuals are highly motivated to be exonerated, and once exonerated, to gain legitimacy to be treated as factually innocent individuals. Legitimacy is desired by both prosecutors and exonerees, but the goals of these two social actors are in direct conflict with one another. Thus, legitimacy is a scarce resource to be won by the more powerful social actor. Returning to the formula for power provided by Emerson (1962), prosecutors are likely to be the more powerful social actors because exonerees need legitimacy from prosecutors and are unlikely to gain legitimacy from another source. In this section, we outline how understanding this power dynamic can explain some troubling post-incarceration trends exonerees suffer.

First, prosecutors play an important role in an exoneree's financial stability. For example, multiple states that provide compensation require an exoneree be found factually innocent or they will refuse to compensate an exoneree if they falsely plead guilty (Madrigal & Norris, 2022; Mungan & Klick, 2016). Prosecutors act as barriers to compensation when they accept false guilty pleas or do not grant a finding of factual innocence. Not only can prosecutors prevent compensation by denying exonerees the title of "factual innocence," but recent trends have indicated that prosecutors are leveraging exoneration in exchange for an agreement from exonerees that they will not even seek compensation (Webster, 2019).

In some ways, prosecutors are attempting to protect the state from further costs associated with a wrongful conviction by reducing the chance of an exoneree being compensated. This is a particular concern for states like Michigan, whose wrongful conviction costs put Detroit in a state of bankruptcy (LeBlanc, 2021). Beyond financial motivations, criminal legal actors have indicated a concern that individuals will be compensated who are not factually innocent, but merely taking advantage of legal loopholes (Reinwald, 2020). In fact, research has demonstrated that belief in exonerees' guilt reduces the likelihood that individuals will endorse financial compensation (Kukucka & Evelo, 2019) and other forms of reintegration services (Scherr et al., 2018a, b). Thus, compensation theoretically occurs only when a "real" wrongful conviction has occurred. Prosecutors can maintain their legitimacy by denying compensation, which protects their state's financial interests and implies that prosecutors were not involved in a "real" wrongful conviction.

Exonerees, however, like other formerly incarcerated individuals, have financial issues that disrupt their reintegration back into society (Norris, 2012). This can be further exacerbated when exonerees are not compensated or even assisted through state-funded reintegration services provided to individuals on parole or probation. For example, in a state like Arkansas, where incarceration rates are the fourth highest in the United States (Carson, 2022), there are reintegration policies aimed at reducing incarceration and recidivism. Yet, the state does not provide any type of compensation or assistance to exonerees. Even something as simple as the $50 in gate money that a person receives upon leaving prison in Arkansas is not available to exonerees, only factually guilty individuals.

In fact, exonerees walk out of prison with the clothing and money they went in with, as well as any funds they may have gained through employment while incarcerated (Hennessey-Fiske, 2014; Shlosberg et al., 2020). Although some states may provide compensation to exonerees, few provide adequate payment for the amount of time an exoneree may spend incarcerated, let alone the associated traumas endured during their incarceration (Madrigal & Norris, 2022). Regardless, exonerees are largely dependent on prosecutors to assist in their attempts to receive compensation. When exonerees are unable to obtain compensation, they must seek compensation through other means, which may not necessarily be legal. Specifically, exonerees who receive under $500,000 in compensation for their wrongful conviction are more likely than exonerees compensated more than $500,000 to commit criminal or deviant acts post-incarceration (Mandery et al., 2013).

Another example of post-incarceration power dynamics plays out in exonerees' post-incarceration employment. Prosecutors play a key role in exonerees being able to find employment upon release because until a person is explicitly exonerated—via dismissed charges or granting of a pardon—a person is technically a criminal, which in many cases means that the case that kept them wrongfully incarcerated for many years is still on their criminal record. As previously discussed, prosecutors are motivated to maintain their conviction records. Therefore, prosecutors are motivated to maintain exonerees' criminal convictions. Exonerees, however, need their wrongful conviction to be expunged from their records to make it easier to obtain housing, regain custody of children, and obtain employment. Again, prosecutors' power in this relationship often results in no expungement (Sholsberg et al., 2011).

Depending on the amount of time spent wrongfully incarcerated, employers may question an exoneree's gap in employment history. Additionally, if not formally exonerated, it may be difficult for an exoneree to explain their employment gap because the crime would still be on their record. In fact, expungement is more often the exception than the rule for exonerees (Madrigal & Norris, 2022; Sholsberg et al., 2011), and when exonerees' wrongful convictions are not expunged, they are more likely to offend post-incarceration (Shlosberg et al., 2014). Though just a few examples, we see how prosecutors, motivated to maintain their legitimacy, exercise their power in the contexts of guilty pleas, exoneration, financial compensation, and expungement—largely to the determinant of exonerees.

Discussion and Implications

Reentering society after being incarcerated is not an easy task for any person. A study by Haney (2003) found that due to the increase in harsh policies and deprivation of life within the United States correctional system, formerly incarcerated individuals often acquire psychological issues. Wrongful conviction scholars posit that these psychological issues are worsened because the exoneree was incarcerated for a crime they did not commit (Jackson et al., 2021). A 2003 study by the Life After Exoneration Program revealed an array of psychological issues that exonerees face, including post-traumatic stress disorder, anxiety, depression, and sleep disorders (as cited in Weigand, 2009). In fact, self-reported experiences indicate that 80% of sampled exonerees experienced a potentially traumatic event while incarcerated, and half met clinical definitions of PTSD and/or depression (Kukucka et al., 2022). Further, Brooks and Greenberg (2021) found that being wrongfully accused of any criminal offense poses immense negative psychological and psychosocial consequences to people. Even after having their innocence proven, the traumatic experience from accusation to eventual exoneration takes its toll on wrongfully convicted individuals.

Research suggests that exonerees often suffer from stigma by association. In other words, because of their time wrongfully incarcerated, individuals are associated with factually guilty individuals, which increases the stigma attached to exonerees (Clow & Leach, 2015). Thus, one way to lessen exonerees' struggles is to reduce the association between exonerees and factually guilty individuals. In other words, exonerees need to establish their legitimacy as innocent individuals. For most exonerees, the best way to establish their innocence is through the prosecutors' office. Prosecutors control when wrongfully convicted individuals are released from prison, when and how wrongfully convicted individuals are exonerated, and the extent to which exonerees have access to reintegration services like expungement and compensation. Unfortunately, prosecutors are motivated by their own concerns of legitimacy to limit the frequency and impact of exonerations. As argued throughout this chapter, because of their power in the relationship, prosecutors' desire for legitimacy is likely to win out, and exonerees are likely to suffer as a result.

To reduce this disparity, we again look at organizational theories. First, if prosecutors' motivation was changed, their incentive to reduce exonerees' legitimacy would also change. For example, if prosecutors are motivated by their conviction record, then policy could be drafted to address how conviction records are calculated. Perhaps wrongful convictions should not change prosecutors' conviction record, or guilty pleas should not count toward conviction records. Specifically, if guilty pleas do not help prosecutors, cases might be more likely to go to trial, which could reduce the number of wrongful convictions in the first place because of the higher standard of proof. Furthermore, if guilty pleas do not help prosecutors, they may not be motivated to plead out wrongfully convicted individuals to time served. Other policies could be drafted that reward prosecutors for assisting in wrongful convictions. For example, if conviction integrity units—which are mostly run by prosecutors—are rewarded with increased legitimacy for their work in uncovering wrongful convictions, then prosecutors' motivations would change. Either way, changing prosecutors' motivations could change the goal they are working toward when they engage in negotiations with wrongfully convicted individuals.

If we cannot change prosecutors' motivations for legitimacy—or how prosecutors are awarded legitimacy—then the power formula can still be readjusted by giving exonerees more power. Emerson (1962) suggests that less powerful social actors can increase their power by teaming up with other social actors. For example, when wrongfully convicted individuals work with innocence projects, they are more likely to be exonerated (Krieger, 2011), to file for compensation, and to receive compensation (Gutman & Sun, 2019). Should more innocence organizations be formed or more funds be devoted to existing innocence organizations, wrongfully convicted individuals could more easily coalesce their power with other social actors. As a result, wrongfully convicted individuals could increase the likelihood of winning legitimacy in power battles with prosecutors.

Likewise, Emerson's (1962) theory of power suggests that prosecutors' power over wrongfully convicted individuals would be greatly diminished if wrongfully convicted individuals were able to obtain their legitimacy from a source other than prosecutors. Providing exonerees with alternative paths to legitimacy provides another opening for policy. For example, perhaps exonerees could be allowed to engage in restorative justice practices (see Umamaheswar, 2023) or a ceremony that could parallel what Maruna (2011) recommends for announcing the rehabilitation of factually guilty individuals. Echoing previous calls, wrongfully convicted individuals could, at minimum, be offered the same services provided for factually guilty individuals (Chunias & Aufgang, 2008). Any of these alternatives could allow exonerees who have already been victimized by prosecutors (see victims of state harm; Westervelt & Cook, 2010) to seek legitimacy from a source outside of their abuser.

Finally, we would suggest that recognizing the power imbalance between prosecutors and exonerees post-incarceration can provide an impetus for social change. Specifically, the opportunity for social change can arise because of several conditions, three of which the prosecutor–exoneree situation meets. First, social change can arise when market mechanisms are not adequate to reduce negative externalities. Negative externalities occur when some parties (i.e., prosecutors) draw all the benefits and other parties (i.e., exonerees) are left with all the costs. Second, social change is necessary when normal incentives are not sufficient to motivate social actors to work toward the public good. As we have demonstrated in this chapter, prosecutors are currently motivated to work against public goods by denying wrongful convictions and harming exonerees. Finally, the opportunity for social change can arise when actors seeking to challenge existing arrangements (i.e., exonerees) are excluded from conventional channels of access (Rao et al., 2000). Exonerees are often excluded from conversations regarding wrongful conviction because (1) as victims of state harm, they are already less powerful (Westervelt & Cook, 2010), and (2) most exonerees are Black and brown men from traditionally marginalized communities who lack power (Anderson & Brion, 2014). Thus, wrongful convictions are ripe for a social movement (Norris, 2017; Rao et al., 2000).

In conclusion, research examining wrongful convictions from a psychological and sociological framework identified problems in the treatment of exonerees at the hands of prosecutors. These frameworks, however, have not viewed prosecutors as part of an organization. By applying organizational theories—notably the concepts of power and legitimacy—to the post-incarceration relationship between prosecutors and exonerees, we have been able to (1) argue for a pattern of exoneree struggles that are the direct result of power differentials that are used by prosecutors to win legitimacy by taking it from exonerees, and (2) to identify potential avenues that could reduce the power differential and subsequent outcomes for exonerees.

References

Anderson, C., & Brion, S. (2014). Perspectives on power in organizations. *Annual Review of Organizational Psychology and Organizational Behavior, 1*(1), 67–97.

Aquino, K., Tripp, T. M., & Bies, R. J. (2006). Getting even or moving on? Power, procedural justice, and types of offense as predictors of revenge, forgiveness, reconciliation, and avoidance in organizations. *Journal of Applied Psychology, 91*(3), 653.

Astley, W. G., & Sachdeva, P. S. (1984). Structural sources of intraorganizational power: A theoretical synthesis. *The Academy of Management Review, 9*, 104–113.

Bazelon, L. (2018). Ending innocence denying. *Hofstra Law Review, 47*, 393.

Bellin, J. (2019). The power of prosecutors. *New York University Law Review, 94*(2), 171–212.

Berg, M. T., & Huebner, B. M. (2011). Reentry and the ties that bind: An examination of social ties, employment, and recidivism. *Justice Quarterly, 28*, 382–410.

Brady v. Maryland, 373 U.S. 83, 87 (1963).

Brooks, S. K., & Greenberg, N. (2021). Psychological impact of being wrongfully accused of criminal offences: A systematic literature review. *Medicine, Science and the Law, 61*(1), 44–54.

Burke, A. S. (2010). Talking about prosecutors. *Cardozo Law Review, 31*, 2119–2138.

California Innocence Project. (2021). *Prosecutorial misconduct*. California Innocence Project. https://californiainnocenceproject.org/issues-we-face/prosecutorial-misconduct/

Carson, E. A. (2022). *Prisoners in 2021—Statistical tables*. Report for the Bureau of Justice Statistics. https://bjs.ojp.gov/library/publications/prisoners-2021-statistical-tables

Chunias, J. L., & Aufgang, Y. D. (2008). Beyond monetary compensation: The need for comprehensive services for the wrongfully convicted. *Boston College Third World Law Journal, 28*(1), 105–128.

Clow, K. A., & Leach, A. M. (2015). After innocence: Perceptions of individuals who have been wrongfully convicted. *Legal and Criminological Psychology, 20*(1), 147–164.

Clow, K. A., Blandisi, I. M., Ricciardelli, R., & Schuller, R. A. (2011). Public perception of wrongful conviction: Support for compensation and apologies. *Albany Law Review., 75*, 1415.
Czarniawska-Joerges, B. (1988). Power as an experiential concept. *Scandinavian Journal of Management, 4*, 31–44.
DeVries, D. S., & Fitzpatrick, K. R. (2006). Defining the characteristics of a lingering crisis: Lessons from the National zoo. *Public Relation Review, 32*, 160–167.
Drummond, C. B., & Mills, M. N. (2020). Addressing official misconduct: Increasing accountability in reducing wrongful convictions. *Wrongful Conviction Law Review, 1*, 270–290.
Emerson, R. M. (1962). Power-dependence relations. *American Sociological Review, 27*, 31–40.
Engen, R. L., & Steen, S. (2000). The power to punish: Discretion and sentencing reform in the war on drugs. *American Journal of Sociology, 105*(5), 1357–1395.
Faison, L., & Smalarz, L. (2019). Perceptions of exonerees: A review of psychological science. *Albany Law Review, 83*, 1021.
Ferguson-Gilbert, C. (2001). It is not whether you win or lose, it is how you play the game: Is the win-loss scorekeeping mentality doing justice for prosecutors. *California Western Law Review, 38*, 283–310.
Gross, S. R., Possley, M., Roll, K., & Stephens, K. (2020, September 1). *Government misconduct and convicting the innocent, the role of prosecutors, police and other law enforcement.* The National Registry of Exonerations
Gutman, J. S., & Sun, L. (2019). Why is Mississippi the best state in which to be exonerated: An empirical evaluation of state statutory and civil compensation for the wrongfully convicted. *Northeastern University Law Review, 11*(2), 694–789.
Haney, C. (2003). *The psychological impact of incarceration: Implications for post-prison adjustment. Prisoners once removed: The impact of incarceration and reentry on children, families, and communities* (pp. 33–66).
Hennessey-Fiske, M. (2014, December 20). Special report: Wrongfully convicted inmates fight for compensation. *The Los Angeles Times*. https://www.latimes.com/nation/la-na-exoneree-national-20141220-story.html
Henry, J. S. (2020). Smoke but no fire: Convicting the innocent of crimes that never happened. University of California Press.
Herrera v. Collins, 506 U.S. 390 (1993).
Hershcovis, M. S., Neville, L., Reich, T. C., Christie, A. M., Cortina, L. M., & Shan, J. V. (2017). Witnessing wrongdoing: The effects of observer power on incivility intervention in the workplace. *Organizational Behavior and Human Decision Processes, 142*, 45–57.
History.com Editors. (2019). The central park five. Retrieved from https://www.history.com/topics/1980s/central-park-five
Jackson, N. A., Pate, M., & Campbell, K. M. (2021). Prison and post-release experiences of innocent inmates. *Journal of Aggression, Maltreatment & Trauma, 30*, 1347–1365.
Kauzlarich, D., Matthews, R. A., & Miller, W. J. (2001). Toward a victimology of state crime. *Critical Criminology, 10*(3), 173–194.
Krieger, S. A. (2011). Why our justice system convicts innocent people, and the challenges faces by innocence projects trying to exonerate them. *New Criminal Law Review: An International and Interdisciplinary Journal, 14*, 333–402.
Kukucka, J., & Evelo, A. J. (2019). Stigma against false confessors impacts post-exoneration financial compensation. *Behavioral Sciences & the Law, 37*(4), 372–387.
Kukucka, J., Horodyski, A. M., & Dardis, C. M. (2022). The Exoneree Health and Life Experiences (ExHaLE) study: Trauma exposure and mental health among wrongly convicted individuals. *Psychology, Public Policy, and Law, 28*, 387–399.
LeBlanc, B. (2021). Michigan needs $7M to pay wrongfully convicted, avoid going into debt. The Detroit News. Retrieved from https://www.detroitnews.com/story/news/local/michigan/2021/04/25/michigan-needs-7-million-more-pay-wrongfully-convictedclaims/7356178002/
Luna, S. (2022). Defining coercion: An application in interrogation and plea negotiation contexts. *Psychology, Public Policy, and Law, 28*, 240–254.

Madrigal, A. J., & Norris, R. J. (2022). The good, the bad, and the uncertain: State harm, the aftermath of exoneration, and compensation for the wrongly convicted. *Critical Criminology, 30*, 895–913.
Mandery, E. J., Shlosberg, A., West, V., & Callaghan, B. (2013). Compensation statutes and post-exoneration offending. *Journal of Criminal Law and Criminology, 103*(2), 553–584.
Maruna, S. (2011). Reentry as a rite of passage. *Punishment & Society, 13*, 3–28.
Matthews, R. (2021). *The victimology of state crime*. Oxford Research Encyclopedia of Criminology.
Matusiak, M. C., King, W. R., & Maguire, E. R. (2017). How perceptions of the institutional environment shape organizational priorities: Findings from a survey of police chiefs. *Journal of Crime and Justice, 40*(1), 5–19.
Meyer, J. W., & Rowan, B. (1977). Institutionalized organizations: Formal structure as myth and ceremony. *American Journal of Sociology, 83*(2), 340–363.
Moore, T. (2011). Prosecutors reinvestigate questionable evidence: Dallas establishes conviction integrity unit. *Criminal Justice, 26*, 4–15.
Mungan, M. C., & Klick, J. (2016). Reducing false guilty pleas and wrongful convictions through exoneree compensation. *The Journal of Law and Economics, 59*(1), 173–189.
National Registry of Exonerations. (2023). *Conviction integrity units*. Retrieved from https://www.law.umich.edu/special/exoneration/Pages/Conviction-Integrity-Units.aspx
National Registry of Exonerations. (2024). Retrieved from https://www.law.umich.edu/special/exoneration/Pages/about.aspx
Norris, R. J. (2012). Assessing compensation statutes for the wrongly convicted. *Criminal Justice Policy Review, 23*(3), 352–374.
Norris, R. J. (2017). *Exonerated: A history of the innocence movement*. New York University Press.
Palmer, C. (2021). Charity, social justice and sporting celebrity foundations. *Celebrity Studies, 12*(4), 565–580.
Penzell, A. (2007). Apology in the context of wrongful conviction: Why the system should say it's sorry. *Cardozo Journal of Conflict Resolution, 9*, 145.
Pfeffer, J. (1981). *Power in organizations*. Pitman.
Possley, M. (2021). *Dennis Allen*. The National Registry of Exonerations. https://www.law.umich.edu/special/exoneration/Pages/casedetail.aspx?caseid=5559
Ransom, J. (2019). Trump will not apologize for calling for death penalty over central park five. The New York Times. Retrieved from https://www.nytimes.com/2019/06/18/nyregion/central-park-five-trump.html
Rao, H., Morrill, C., & Zald, M. N. (2000). Power plays: How social movements and collective action create new organizational forms. *Research in Organizational Behaviour, 22*, 239–282.
Raymond, M. (2001). The problem with innocence. *Cleveland State Law Review, 49*(3), 449–464.
Reinwald, C. H. (2020). Deal with the devil: Reevaluating plea bargains offered to the wrongfully convicted. *North Carolina Law Review Forum, 99*, 139–162.
Saks, M. (2016). A review of theories of professions, organizations and society: The case for neo-Weberianism, neo-institutionalism and eclecticism. *Journal of Professions and Organization, 1*, 1–18.
Scherr, K. C., & Normile, C. J. (2022). False confessions predict delay between release from incarceration and official exoneration. *Law and Human Behavior, 46*, 67–80.
Scherr, K. C., Normile, C. J., & Putney, H. (2018a). Perpetually stigmatized: False confessions prompt underlying mechanisms that motivate negative perceptions of exonerees. *Psychology, Public Policy, and Law, 24*(3), 341.
Scherr, K. C., Normile, C. J., & Sarmiento, M. C. (2018b). Reluctant to embrace innocence: An experimental test of persevering culpability judgments on people's willingness to support reintegration services for exonerees. *Journal of Experimental Criminology, 14*(4), 529–538.
Scherr, K. C., Redlich, A. D., & Kassin, S. M. (2020). Cumulative disadvantage: A psychological framework for understanding how innocence can lead to confession, wrongful conviction, and beyond. *Perspectives on Psychological Science, 15*(2), 353–383.

Selby, D. (2020, November 11). *Only one prosecutor has ever been jailed for misconduct leading to a wrongful conviction*. Innocence Project. https://innocenceproject.org/ken-anderson-michael-morton-prosecutorial-misconduct-jail/
Sholsberg, A., Mandery, E., & West, V. (2011). The expungement myth. *Albany Law Review, 75*, 1229–1242.
Shlosberg, A., Mandery, E. J., West, V., & Callaghan, B. (2014). Expungement and post-exoneration offending. *Journal of Criminal Law and Criminology, 104*(2), 353–388.
Shlosberg, A., Nowotny, J., Panuccio, E., & Rajah, V. (2020). "They open the door, kick you out, and say, 'go'": Reentry challenges after wrongful imprisonment. *Wrongful Conviction Law Review, 1*, 226–252.
Sinclair, U. (1906). *The jungle*. Doubleday, Page & Co.
Sklansky, D. A. (2018). The problems with prosecutors. *Annual Review of Criminology, 1*, 451–469.
Stratton, G. (2015). Wrongfully convicting the innocent: A state crime? *Critical Criminology, 23*(1), 21–37.
Swisher, K. (2012). Prosecutorial conflicts of interest in post-conviction practice. *Hofstra Law Review, 41*, 181–216.
Thompson, A. M., Molina, O. R., & Levett, L. M. (2012). After exoneration: An investigation of stigma and wrongfully convicted persons. *Albany Law Review, 75*, 1373–1413.
Tost, L. P. (2015). When, why, and how do powerholders "feel the power"? Examining the links between structural and psychological power and reviving the connection between power and responsibility. *Research in Organizational Behavior, 35*, 29–56.
Umamaheswar, J. (2023). Wrongful conviction as racialized cumulative disadvantage. *The British Journal of Criminology, 63*, 537–552. https://doi.org/10.1093/bjc/azac061
Van Rooij, B., & Fine, A. (2018). Toxic corporate culture: Assessing organizational processes of deviancy. *Administrative Sciences, 8*(3), 23.
Vaughan, D. (1999). The dark side of organizations: Mistake, misconduct, and disaster. *Annual Review of Sociology, 25*(1), 271–305.
Vaynman, A. D., & Fondacaro, M. R. (2024). Prosecutorial discretion, justice, and compassion: Reestablishing balance in our legal system. *Stetson Law Review, 52*. 31–53.
Vick, K., Cook, K. J., & Rogers, M. (2021). Lethal leverage: False confessions, false pleas, and wrongful homicide convictions in death-eligible cases. *Contemporary Justice Review, 24*(1), 24–42.
Walsh, K., Hussemann, J., Flynn, A., Yahner, J., & Golian, L. (2017). *Estimating the prevalence of wrongful convictions*. US Department of Justice, National Criminal Justice Reference Service, document, 25115.
Webster, E. (2019). A postconviction mentality: Prosecutorial assistance in exoneration cases. *Justice Quarterly, 36*, 323–349. https://doi.org/10.1080/07418825.2017.1399212
Weigand, H. (2009). Rebuilding life: The wrongfully convicted and exonerated. *Boston University Public Interest Law Journal, 18*(2), 427–438.
Wells, G. L., & Olson, E. A. (2001). The other-race effect in eyewitness identification: What do we do about it? *Psychology, Public Policy, and Law, 7*(1), 230.
Westervelt, S. D., & Cook, K. J. (2010). Framing innocents: The wrongly convicted as victims of state harm. *Crime, Law and Social Change, 53*(3), 259–275.
Westervelt, S., & Cook, K. J. (2012). *Life after death row: Exonerees' search for community and identity*. Rutgers University Press.
Wilford, M. M., & Khairalla, A. (2019). Innocence and plea bargaining. In *A system of pleas: Social sciences contributions to the real legal system* (pp. 132–150). Oxford University Press.
Witness to Innocence. (2021). *Justice after exoneration*. Witness to Innocence. https://www.witnesstoinnocence.org/justice-after-exoneration

Chapter 12
Misconduct Routinization in Criminal Legal Organizations: An Explosive Cluster of Feedback Loops

Lakia Faison

Introduction

The proposed model of official misconduct routinization essentially argues that specific stimuli (internal or external to criminal legal organizations) cause organizational leaders to make decisions that induce increasingly dramatic and frequent misconduct-conducive cognitions and behaviors in their subordinates. These cognitions and behaviors eventually permeate the entire organization, and the acts of misconduct become routine. The consequences of misconduct routinization include damage to the people who should benefit from the organization as well as the organization itself. Efforts should be made to disrupt these processes because they are damaging to the people who should benefit from criminal legal organizations as well as the legitimacy of the organizations themselves, and a loss of legitimacy for any organization could be detrimental or even fatal. To facilitate such efforts, I present an empirically supported method of disrupting misconduct routinization.

The criminal legal system is a network of distinct, but interrelated, organizations: police, courts, and corrections (Sullivan, 1977). Each organization is intended to manage people suspected, accused, and convicted of crime. And, as per the United States' founding ideals, their methods of management should be fair, impartial, and constitutional, thereby ensuring the guilty are convicted, the innocent remain free, and there is justice for all. However, we know the criminal legal system fails to consistently meet those standards. Indeed, consider the evidence: there are over 3000 cases of known wrongful convictions (National Registry of Exonerations [NRE], 2024) that represent only the "tip of the iceberg," (Gross et al., 2005, p. 8) and although investigated far less extensively, there is burgeoning evidence of

L. Faison (✉)
George Mason University, Department of Criminology, Law & Society, Fairfax, VA, USA
e-mail: lfaison@gmu.edu

D. S. Rudes, J. R. Ingram (eds.), *Using Organizational Theory to Study, Explain, and Understand Criminal Legal Organizations*,
https://doi.org/10.1007/978-3-031-66285-0_12

wrongful acquittals (Gould et al., 2022). These miscarriages of justice cause severe and enduring harm to the wrongfully convicted and society as a whole.

Criminal Legal Misconduct

Innocence scholars and advocates have found official misconduct to be a leading culprit of justice miscarriage (Gould et al., 2022; NRE, 2024), contributing to approximately 60% of all known wrongful convictions (NRE, 2024). Official misconduct is a broad term that encompasses any behavior committed by legal officials (e.g., police, lawyers, and forensic analysts) that "produces unreliable, misleading, or false evidence of guilt, or that conceals, distorts, or undercuts true evidence of innocence" (Gross et al., 2020; p. iii). A report on official misconduct in wrongful convictions found the most common forms to be witness tampering (e.g., coercion), interrogation misconduct (e.g., physical abuse), evidence fabrication or concealment, and trial misbehavior (e.g., perjury; Gross et al., 2020), each of which expressly undermines the criminal legal systems management standards. That is, they are unfair, partial, and unconstitutional. Thus, we must ask, why does official misconduct occur?

The authors of the aforementioned report argued that "the most powerful explanation...is structural" (Gross et al., 2020, p. 133). Or, in other words, official misconduct occurs because it is embedded in the routine practices of criminal legal organizations. Official misconduct is an organizational issue. Thus, the purpose of this chapter is to explain the routinization of official misconduct by describing and applying an organizational concept that is sorely underutilized in criminal legal scholarship: organizational feedback loops. More specifically, I describe much of the existing literature on organizational feedback loops, propose a model of feedback loops that may explain the process of official misconduct routinization within criminal legal organizations, and demonstrate the applicability of the model by applying it to the routinization of official misconduct within police organizations—particularly police misconduct induced by the war on drugs.

Basic Organizational Feedback Loops

The proposed model of official misconduct routinization is based on the following principle: Any routinized organizational behavior is a product of feedback loops. That is, something influences one person's behavior, which influences another person's behavior, which then influences the first person's behavior, and so on. Although social scientists have long recognized this fact (e.g., Weber, 1947), it has seldom been applied in social science—particularly in the study of criminal legal organizations. Feedback loops are most often discussed in the context of biological, ecological, and cybernetic systems (or organizations). Biologists, ecologists, and mathematicians recognize two forms of feedback loops: negative and positive.

Negative feedback loops are a series of looping responses to an *initiating event* (i.e., a stimulus or disturbance to an organization's typical manner of operation); the first response triggers a separate response that inhibits the first (Bolton, 2002). In this way, these loops are self-stabilizing. They help organizations restore and maintain their pre-initiating event manner of operation (Katz & Kahn, 1978; Marinescu, 2016). Take, for example, blood glucose regulation (see Asarian et al., 2012). When we eat a meal, our blood glucose levels spike and could potentially damage our bodies (i.e., our bodily systems or organizations). To prevent that damage, our bodies release insulin to break down the glucose. As long as our blood glucose levels are higher than normal, our bodies produce insulin to reduce the amount of glucose in our blood. Eventually, our glucose levels normalize, and we stop producing insulin. In this example, the initiating event is the meal, the initial response is the spike in glucose, and the inhibiting or stabilizing response is the production of insulin.

Positive feedback loops, on the other hand, are a series of inherently destabilizing, self-perpetuating, and self-exaggerating loops (Haraoubia, 2018; Marinescu, 2016). These loops are triggered by an initiating event. The initial response to that event triggers a separate response, which induces more of the initial response, which, in turn, triggers more of the second response, and so on (Bolton, 2002). Positive feedback loops can completely destroy an organization if they are not stopped (Meadows, 1999), as is the case with a serious stab wound. If someone is stabbed, they lose blood. The more blood they lose, the more their blood pressure will decrease. The more their blood pressure decreases, the less blood is circulated to their heart. Those responses can loop until there is no longer enough blood for the heart to function and, consequently, the person dies.

Although the concepts of positive and negative feedback loops are usually applied to biological, ecological, and cybernetic organizations, they can also be applied to social organizations, such as those within the criminal legal system. The only substantial difference in the basic conceptualization of feedback loops in nonsocial and social organizations is the requisite of a physical, tangible, or otherwise observable initiating event or *reference point*—as they are dubbed by social scientists. In social organizations, the reference point can be characterized by a multitude of things, separately or in tandem: an observable event, a *desired normative standard* (i.e., a desired state of organizational operation or society; Masuch, 1985), or the *factual state of the organization* (i.e., what the organization is or is not at any given time; Masuch, 1985). Other differences in the social and nonsocial conceptualizations of feedback loops are merely terminological.

In social sciences, a negative feedback loop is referred to as *deviation-counteracting* when its reference point is a desired normative standard and *self-correcting* when its reference point is the factual state of the organization (Masuch, 1985). Both loops may result in a *virtuous cycle* or series of looping responses that help an organization achieve a desired normative standard or factual state (e.g., Zahra, 2008). Positive feedback loops are called *deviation-amplifying* when related to normative standards and *self-reinforcing* when related to the factual state of the system (Masuch, 1985). Both loops are harmful to the organizations in which they occur; however, deviation-amplifying loops are considered to be the most harmful (Masuch, 1985). Given the particularly detrimental nature of positive feedback loops, they are often dubbed *vicious cycles/circles*. Every type of feedback loop can occur at any given moment and either simultaneously or independently; consequently, there are infinite combinations of feedback loops.

Social scientists tend to agree that all possible combinations of feedback loops can be categorized as either explosive or monitored clusters (Masuch, 1985): *Explosive clusters* consist of two or more positive feedback loops, at least one of which is a vicious cycle. An equally suitable name is killer clusters because they can destroy any organization in which they occur. *Monitored clusters*, on the other hand, consist of one or more vicious cycles and at least one negative feedback, or inhibiting response. These clusters do not result in the death of an organization. Instead, they produce stagnation, or the creation of organizational stability after a period of growth. Throughout this chapter, I argue that the routinization of official misconduct is essentially the result of an explosive cluster with an embedded monitored cluster.

Identifying a Reference Point

The first step in analyzing organizational feedback loops, and the first part of the official misconduct routinization model, is the identification of a reference point. In the context of criminal legal organizations, it is important to identify reference points in relation to specific organizations rather than the entire system because the reference point for the latter does not change: The criminal legal system's desired normative standard is efficient and consistent procurement of justice for all, and the factual state of the criminal legal system is always suboptimal. The reference points of the criminal legal system's suborganizations, on the other hand, do change over time. Take, for example, the police: They consistently want to prevent crime and apprehend individuals suspected of criminal activity, but the manner and rate at which they believe those ends should be met changes. In other words, their desired normative standard changes. Their success rates, or their factual state, also change over time. The desired normative standards of the police and their perceptions of the state of their organization can also be changed by specific observable events.

A clear example of a reference point that involves a change in the desired normative standard, factual state, and an observable event is President Nixon's morally evocative declaration of war on drugs, in which he stated:

> America's public enemy number one, in the United States, is drug abuse. In order to fight and defeat this enemy, it is necessary to wage a new all-out offensive… It is essential to the American people to be alerted of this danger—to recognize that it is a danger that will not pass [without action] (Richard Nixon Foundation, 2016).

Shortly thereafter, the Reagan administration encouraged police to fight in the war on drugs by flushing them with cash. Or, more specifically, they created the Byrne program to supply willing police organizations with large grants in exchange for the prioritization of drug law enforcement (Nedelkoff, 2002) and amending the Comprehensive Drug Abuse Prevention and Control Act, allowing them to retain up to 80% of the value of assets seized during drug arrests (see Alexander, 2020). Thus, police were both morally and financially incentivized to fight in the war on drugs with guns blazing.

The declaration and incentivization of the war on drugs altered the desired normative standard of policing (see Alexander, 2020): drug law enforcement needed to be a top priority, and, accordingly, they needed to make more drug-related arrests and seizures. In an effort to move toward their desired normative standard and factual state, many police leaders instated drug-related arrest and asset seizure quotas (e.g., Blumenson & Nilsen, 1998), although, for legal reasons, quotas are often masked as productivity goals (Johnson & Hoopes, 2019). Regardless, the instatement of arrest and asset seizure quotas triggered a vicious cycle.

Vicious Cycles Within Organizations

Although all vicious cycles are deviation-amplifying positive feedback loops and thus are inherently damaging to the organizations within which they occur, social scientists tend to describe them as either downward spirals (e.g., Den Nieuwenboer & Kaptein, 2008; Hambrick & D'Aveni, 1988; Merton & Merton, 1968) or expanding loops (e.g., Masuch, 1985).

Downward Spirals

Downward spirals refer to self-deleterious vicious cycles in which each response reduces the magnitude of another response—effectively evoking an image of a large loop that gets smaller and smaller with each revolution. The magnitude of the vicious cycle will continue to reduce until it reaches a *critical threshold*, or a point of no return. At this point, one of two things may occur (Masuch, 1985): An organization can recognize that they are in a downward spiral and begin allocating resources toward cycle disruption, or the organization may fail to recognize that they are in a downward spiral, pass the critical threshold, and die.

Downward Spiral of Legitimation

One type of downward spiral that is particularly relevant to criminal legal organizations—but especially the police—is that of *legitimation*, or the means by which organizations seek to obtain, maintain, and increase their *legitimacy*. An organization is legitimate so far as its purpose and means are considered unquestionably necessary, appropriate, and socially normative by people within and outside the organization (Dowling & Pfeffer, 1975; Perrow, 1970; Pfeffer, 1980; Suchman, 1995). Systems seek legitimacy so that they can exercise *authority* or legitimate power (Pfeffer, 1980). Without legitimacy, and thereby authority, organizations struggle to fulfill their purpose (e.g., Walters & Bolger, 2019)—this is especially the case for organizations whose legitimacy is predicated on a moral mission or high levels of trust (Ashforth & Gibbs, 1990), such as the police. Therefore, organizations have a vested interest in legitimation. Importantly, however, "clumsy, nervous, or overzealous" efforts can trigger, what I call, a *downward spiral of legitimation* (Ashforth & Gibbs, 1990, p. 191).

In downward spirals of legitimation, organizational leaders implement policies that damage the organization's legitimacy; in turn, leaders implement even more damaging policies, and so on. This behavior-response loop can theoretically revolve until the organization has lost all legitimacy and is no longer able to operate or fulfill its purpose.

Downward Spiral of Legitimation: War on Drugs

The responses to the war on drugs by leaders of police organizations may have triggered a downward spiral of legitimation. They were morally and monetarily incentivized to implement and enforce arrest and asset seizure quotas. To meet those quotas, officers began committing acts of misconduct (e.g., planting false evidence) and, more often than not, their targets were Black people (Gross et al., 2020). The racial disparities in police misconduct are likely caused by the racist, yet pervasive, *bad is Black* heuristic, in which people assume immoral acts are committed by Black and/or dark-skinned people (Alter et al., 2016). Racially discriminatory misconduct has likely contributed to the loss of legitimacy among the general population, but especially people of color. Indeed, people have lost trust in the police (Jones, 2015) and are hesitant to report crime to the police (Carr et al., 2007; Desmond et al., 2016), among other things.

Police legitimacy seems to be approaching a critical threshold, as indicated by the fact that defunding and abolishing the police have become hot-button topics (see Kesslen, 2020). Although, defunding and abolishment are unlikely to occur anytime soon. Police have an abundance of resources at their disposal (e.g., external governmental funding and support), which they can use to stave off organizational death—despite hemorrhaging legitimacy. However, death cannot be avoided forever. For the police to survive as they are, they must disrupt this downward spiral of legitimation. To do so, police leaders must first understand the process by which problematic means of legitimation are routinized (i.e., expanding loops), and then they must learn how to prevent and disrupt these processes.

Expanding Loops

Expanding loops refer to self-exaggerating vicious cycles in which each response increases the magnitude of another response (Masuch, 1985)—effectively evoking an image of a small loop that gets larger and larger with each revolution. In order for the magnitude of the loops to grow, resources must be fed into the loop from sources external to the organization; growth, however, is finite due to the fact that resources in social organizations are limited (Mazur, 1978). Once resources have been depleted, the expanding loop has passed a critical threshold; thus, they become stagnant. There are many forms of expanding loops that are detrimental to organizations, the most well known of which has been dubbed the vicious circle of bureaucracy (Masuch, 1985).

Vicious Circle of Bureaucracy

The *vicious circle of bureaucracy*, as coined by Merton and Merton (1968), refers to the following pattern of intraorganizational behaviors: An organizational leader wants to change their organization in ways conducive to the purpose of the organization. To do so, the organizational leader makes rules, places people under more supervision, or takes other bureaucratic measures (i.e., increasing *formalization*). The people within the organization respond negatively to the increased formalization, and those negative reactions result in behaviors that are harmful to the organization.

Although Merton and Merton do not make this distinction, it is important to note that harm can be immediate and obvious, or it could be delayed and discrete. In the first condition, organizational leaders respond to negative reactions by increasing formalization even more—hoping to stifle those negative reactions and produce their desired results (Merton & Merton, 1968). In the second condition, the reactions may initially seem to produce results that benefit the organization and help it to fulfill its purpose but are actually covertly damaging the organization; in other words, the reactions result in *superficial benefits*. Consequently, organizational leaders may increase formalization in hopes of increasing the magnitude of superficial benefit.

When organizational leaders increase formalization in ways that produce negative reactions among the people within the organization, the organization is damaged. With each revolution of the vicious circle of bureaucracy, the negative reactions are more thoroughly embedded into the organization. Recall that resources for loop expansion are limited (Mazur, 1978), so eventually, further formalization is no longer possible. At this point, the vicious circle of bureaucracy stops expanding, the negative reactions get *walled in* (Gouldner, 1954), and the organization is *blocked* (Crozier & Friedberg, 2017), thereby forcing a state of stagnation. In other words, the final degree of formalization and its corresponding negative reactions are normalized or routinized.

Vicious Circle of Bureaucracy: War on Drugs

The war on drugs produced a clear example of a vicious circle of bureaucracy. In an effort to fight the war on drugs, police leaders increased formalization by instating drug-related quotas. Officers responded negatively by committing acts of misconduct to meet those quotas (e.g., Marzulli, 2011). To the leaders of police organizations, the quotas seemed to produce beneficial results: From the mid-1980s to 1997, the number of people incarcerated for nonviolent drug offenses increased from 50,000 to over 400,000 (Drug Policy Alliance, 2021). What they failed to recognize was that implementing drug-related quotas would ultimately damage their legitimacy. Thus, police leaders kept increasing formalization and, consequently, exaggerated the frequency of police misconduct. Eventually, the leaders could not increase formalization any further, so police misconduct was walled in, and the organization was blocked. In this way, police misconduct induced by the war on drugs became routinized. The mechanism by which officers come to commit and routinize police misconduct can be best understood as a monitored cluster of vicious cycles of corruption.

Vicious Cycles of Corruption

Although police (and other official) misconduct is often defined as behavior committed by criminal legal personnel that distorts evidence used to reach verdicts (e.g., Gross et al., 2020), a broader definition may also be appropriate. Official misconduct may be redefined as *corruption*, or the "abuse of entrusted power for private gain" (Pozsgai-Alvarez, 2020, p. 435). To elaborate, abuse is the prioritization of personal goals over the official goals of the organization; entrusted power is essentially Pfeffer's (1980) concept of authority, and private gain refers to self or in-group interest (Pozsgai-Alvarez, 2020). A specific form of corruption that is particularly relevant to criminal legal organizations, but especially police organizations, is *noble cause corruption* or acts committed by people who believe they are justified by their ends (Delattre, 2011; Klockars, 1980; Van Halderen & Kolthoff, 2017).

Corruption, noble or otherwise, proliferates organizational practices and becomes a part of the routines of everyone within the organization via vicious cycles of corruption. Den Nieuwenboer and Kaptein (2008) delineate three vicious cycles that can result in routinized corruption: the vicious cycle of pressure, the vicious cycle of opportunity, and the vicious cycle of divergent norms. In describing their proposed cycles, I make two notable modifications: (1) I categorize these cycles as expanding loops, whereas Den Nieuwenboer and Kaptein categorize them as downward spirals. (2) I propose that these cycles are sequential—one cycle triggers another cycle, and so on. Once a cycle has been triggered, it expands until it reaches a state of stagnation. In this way, these cycles of corruption constitute a monitored cluster of vicious cycles.

The routinization of corruption among non-leaders begins with the *vicious cycle of pressure*, or the process by which increasing pressure to meet and exceed performance expectations leads to an increase in corruption. In this cycle, organizational leaders place pressure on people within an organization to meet a certain standard of behavior. They may do so by making wages, desirable work hours, or other privileges contingent on meeting certain goals or quality of performance; Den Nieuwenboer and Kaptein (2008), however, emphasize the importance of *status*, or the "relative rank that an individual holds with attendant rights, duties, and lifestyle, in a social hierarchy based upon honor or prestige" (Britannica, 2019). Indeed, Den Nieuwenboer and Kaptein purport that people within organizations are chiefly concerned with maintaining and improving their status within organizations. When people consider their status to be contingent upon their ability to meet performance standards, and corruption makes it easier for people to meet those standards, they are likely to commit corrupt acts. As status increases, the pressure to meet performance standards also increases. With each iteration of the cycle, the likelihood of corruption increases. Den Nieuwenboer and Kaptein argue that people who achieve status via corruption are quickly blocked into this cycle: They must continue committing corrupt acts to maintain their status. In short, the vicious cycle of pressure entails reciprocal increases in perceived pressure of performance-contingent status and the likelihood of committing corruption. It should be noted, however, that people are unlikely to overtly justify corrupt behavior with status-related goals when they are committing or facilitating a corrupt act. It is only when (and if) they are chastised for the corrupt behavior that they will cite performance-contingent status as an excuse (e.g., Marzulli, 2011). At the time of the offense, however, they are more likely to rationalize corruption in ways that complement their sense of self (Ashforth & Anand, 2003; De Klerk, 2017).

The *vicious cycle of divergent norms* refers to the mechanism by which people develop increasingly problematic rationalizations which perpetuate the routinization of corrupt acts. This cycle is largely dependent on the tendency for groups of people to establish *positive distinctiveness* or to ascribe favorable qualities to the people within their group that differentiate them from people outside of their group (Tajfel & Turner, 1978). The effect of firmly established positive distinctiveness is twofold: (1) people within the group feel superior to those outside of the group; (2) people within the group foster a strong and positive social identity.

Because positive distinctiveness is essentially a feeling of superiority, it is an object of competition between groups. When competing for positive distinctiveness, people within each group grow closer to one another and become isolated from people outside of their groups (Cloward & Ohlin, 1969; Staw et al., 1981). Moreover, the social norms within an organization evolve to allow for increasingly corrupt behavior against their competitors. People within the group either dismiss the corrupt nature of their behaviors or fail to notice it because they rationalized the behavior in such a way that it seems legitimate and beneficial to the people in the group. People also tend to over-rationalize their corrupt behaviors, thereby paving the way for more egregious acts of corruption (Zyglidopoulos et al., 2009).

In short, the vicious cycle of divergent norms involves increasingly dramatic rationalizations of increasingly problematic positive-distinctiveness-seeking behaviors in ways that make corruption seem legitimate and beneficial to an organization. After the vicious cycle of divergent norms has had many iterations, the rationalization of corrupt behaviors will have perforated the vast majority of the organization; at which point, most people within an organization will not report corrupt behaviors to organizational leaders, who could then punish the corrupt actors. Therefore, the vicious cycle of divergent norms creates more opportunities for corrupt acts to occur.

The *vicious cycle of opportunity* is embodied in the following statement: Organizational leaders indirectly reward people for corrupt acts when they fail to punish people for those acts. The more instances of corruption that organizational leaders fail to punish, the more likely people within the organization will commit corrupt acts. The magnitude of failure (and thereby reward) and the likelihood that people will commit corrupt acts increases with each revolution of the cycle until leaders no longer attempt to punish the act, and the act is incorporated into the common practices of the organization.

Vicious Cycles of Corruption: War on Drugs

These vicious cycles of corruption have been observed in police organizations during the war on drugs. Indeed, as previously discussed, the war on drugs triggered a vicious circle of bureaucracy in which police leaders implemented and enforced quotas and other formalization measures. The ever-increasing formalization triggered negative reactions throughout law enforcement organizations. Those negative reactions are best described in terms of vicious cycles of corruption. First, the implementation of quotas induced perceptions of performance-contingent status: Police officers felt that if they did not meet those quotas, they would lose their status within the organization. To prevent that from happening, they resorted to corruption. After they began committing corrupt acts to maintain and improve their status, they had to keep doing so (see Marzulli, 2011). However, that was not the primary rationalization of their behavior prior to and during the misconduct. Instead, they probably employed more self-favoring forms of rationalization.

Recall that the declaration of the war on drugs incited a change in the desired normative standard of policing: Police were in charge of protecting the general population from the dangers of drugs and drug-associated people. Thus, the war on drugs strengthened the positive distinctiveness of police organizations by firmly positioning police as protectors and people associated with drugs as villains. Also, historically, Black people have been stereotyped as being criminals, drug dealers, and drug abusers (Bennett & Plaut, 2017; Nunn, 2002). As such, the villains here were primarily Black people. This is why corruption related to the war on drugs disproportionately impacts Black people (Drug Policy Alliance, 2016).

The tendency for the police to target their legitimate and corrupt forms of policing on Black people resulted in conflict between the groups, thereby encouraging the police to close ranks, disengage from extra-organizational social norms, and exaggerate their antidrug (and discriminatory) rationalizations of corrupt acts. Over time, the rationalization of corrupt behaviors saturated policing procedures, and most police became unwilling to report corrupt behaviors to organizational leaders or became ignorant of the fact that they should have done so. This limited the opportunities for police leaders to punish acts of corruption.

When police leaders failed to identify and punish officers who used corrupt means to meet quotas, they indirectly rewarded the officers for their corruption by rewarding them for meeting quotas. The failure of the police leaders to identify and punish corrupt officers led officers to believe they could get away with committing corrupt acts, thereby paving the way for future corruption. Moreover, officers who join the organization after a corrupt act is being routinized may be unsure of its legitimacy. If directly encouraged by their peers to commit an act or indirectly encouraged to do so by observing the success of corrupt officers, the new officers will be more likely to commit the same corrupt act. In this way, corrupt acts become normalized and incorporated into the routine activities of officers.

Summarizing the Feedback Model of Official Misconduct Routinization

I have described a complex series of interwoven positive feedback loops, or vicious cycles, that result in the routinization of corrupt acts or official misconduct. The model, depicted in Fig. 12.1, is as follows: A reference point of some sort triggers a downward spiral of legitimation, in which organizational leaders seek to maintain and improve the legitimacy of their organization in ways that ultimately damage their legitimacy. Their methods of seeking legitimacy are damaging when they are the product of a vicious circle of bureaucracy, in which organizational leaders increase formalization in ways that both induce negative reactions (e.g., corruption) from the people subject to that formalization and produce superficial benefits for the organization.

The negative reactions from officers are cultivated and routinized via the three vicious cycles of corruption: First, the formalization measures foster perceptions of performance-contingent status, which leads to more corruption. Second, people begin to rationalize their corruption in increasingly exaggerated and self-favoring

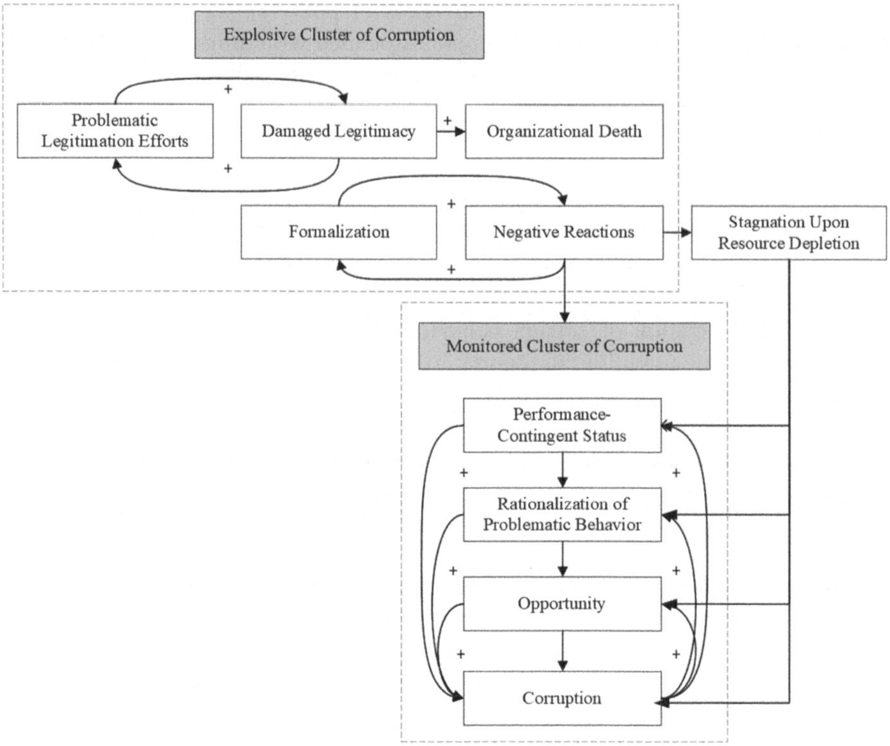

Fig. 12.1 Feedback model of official misconduct routinization in organizations. (*Note*. Resource depletion acts as negative feedback on the monitored cluster)

ways, which pave the way for more intense and/or frequent corruption. This occurs until most people within the organization believe the corruption is legitimate. Consequently, people stop reporting one another for corrupt acts. This leads to the third and final vicious cycle; organizational leaders become increasingly unable to identify and punish corrupt actors, and eventually, they stop trying. This results in an environment where corruption can occur with impunity and reward. At this point, the corrupt act is normalized and incorporated into the routine practices of the people within the organization.

Why Do People Within Organizations Perpetuate Vicious Cycles?

The proposed model of official misconduct routinization is essentially an explosive cluster composed of a downward spiral with an embedded monitored cluster of vicious cycles. To prevent the explosive cluster from exploding, people within the organization need to disrupt the current vicious cycles and disavow negative reactions that are currently blocked into the organization. If the downward spiral is not stopped, the organization will eventually die—or lose the ability to operate and achieve its ends because it lacks legitimacy. Organizational death is never sought after, so why do people within organizations perpetuate the explosive cluster of misconduct routinization? Masuch (1985) posits that the answer lies in the self-sealing nature of vicious cycles and the limitations of human cognition.

Vicious cycles are self-sealing because they are too complicated for people within them to perceive, especially in organizations with hierarchical power structures like criminal legal organizations (Berti & Simpson, 2021; Rosenblatt, 2012). Moreover, human cognition is typically limited to singular causal chains (see Greene, 2013); therefore, it is extremely difficult for a person to recognize the fact that they are trapped in a cluster of vicious interconnected loops—let alone disrupt the vicious cycles that they themselves perpetuate.

Disrupting Vicious Cycles

Although it is very difficult for people trapped in vicious cycles to recognize that they are, in fact, trapped and, therefore, disrupt the vicious cycles—it is not impossible. Indeed, recent research suggests that vicious cycles can be broken. Pradis and colleagues (2021) conducted action research at a European subsidiary of a multinational energy company that was caught in a vicious cycle. Through that research, they identified a three-phase method of disrupting vicious cycles and replacing them with virtuous cycles. In the first phase, people trapped in a vicious cycle must first become frustrated with at least one side effect of the vicious cycle. Once frustration sets in, a neutral agent within the organization who is external to the vicious cycle should then inform the frustrated people of the dysfunctional beliefs and patterns of behaviors that constitute the vicious cycle. In the second phase, the neutral agent should suggest and facilitate new positive beliefs and behaviors that can break the vicious cycle and thereby alleviate the frustration of the people trapped in the vicious cycle. Moreover, people within the vicious cycle must be willing to test and adopt those new beliefs and behaviors. In the third phase, the neutral agents and the people trapped in the vicious cycle should work to normalize the new positive behaviors, thereby instating a virtuous cycle: the more people working to normalize something, the more people will think it is normal, and so on.

Future research should aim to determine if the model delineated by Pradis and colleagues (2021) could effectively disrupt vicious cycles in criminal legal organizations and replace them with virtuous cycles. For example, this model could easily be applied to police organizations. First, police officers would need to become frustrated with at least one side effect of a vicious cycle in which they are trapped. Neutral agents within individual police organizations (e.g., crime analysts) should determine if the police officers within the organization are frustrated with the side effects of their vicious cycles. If the officers are frustrated, the neutral agents should work with the police officers to identify, implement, and normalize new positive behaviors to replace behaviors that perpetuate vicious cycles—thereby instating a virtuous cycle. Unfortunately, as it stands, Pradis and colleagues (2021) could only work at the micro level. Neutral agents must be close enough to the people within the organization to implement Pradis and colleagues' methods but be external to the vicious cycles. Such agents only exist within individual police organizations.

Scholars should aim to delineate a method of disrupting vicious cycles at the macro level, or across all the individual organizations that constitute a single criminal legal organization (e.g., the NYP-PD is an individual organization within the larger police organization). Most forms of police misconduct and misconduct committed in other criminal legal organizations pervade all individual organizations. In other words, criminal legal misconduct is systematic.

Future Directions and Limitations

In addition to identifying a method of disrupting vicious cycles at a macro level, researchers should aim to do several other things. For one, qualitative (and, if possible, quantitative) empirical research should be conducted to determine the validity of the proposed model of misconduct routinization. Optimally, future research would involve case studies on criminal legal organizations in which researchers identify upcoming initiating events and observe the subsequent routinization of misconduct. Of course, research of this kind would be extremely difficult to conduct because of the secretive nature of most criminal legal organizations; however, difficulty alone is insufficient cause to abandon a line of research.

Researchers should also aim to refine my proposed model of official misconduct routinization. There is at least one area in which my model can be expanded, and that is in acknowledging the feedback loops that exist between multiple organizations that perpetuate the vicious cycles within each organization. Within the criminal legal system, the most notable intraorganizational network of feedback loops exists between police and prosecutors.

Scholars have observed that prosecutors seem to enable police misconduct because doing so creates more opportunity for prosecutors to win cases (see Trivedi & Van Cleve, 2020). The tendency for prosecutors to enable police misconduct is the result of misconduct routinization within their organization; there may also be complicated web feedback loops between the cycles that perpetuate prosecutorial misconduct and those that perpetuate police misconduct. To describe such a web, however, is far too complicated for this chapter—or any single chapter, for that matter. It is truly a novel worthy topic that requires an evaluation of the entire history of the American legal system to identify the initiating event which triggered the web of feedback loops. Such an investigation could provide insight into what we should expect from the police-prosecutor relationship: If the police-prosecutor relationship is characterized primarily by a downward spiral or explosive cluster, we should expect their dynamic to kill them—or their legitimacy. If the police-prosecutor relationship is characterized primarily by an expanding loop or a monitored cluster, we can determine if we have reached, or are approaching a point, of stagnation.

Before pursuing any of the aforementioned future directions, scholars should aim to refine several concepts that are frequently employed in discussions of feedback loops in social sciences. First and foremost, what is a reference point? As it stands, reference points can be an observable event, a desired normative standard, or the factual state of the organization (Masuch, 1985). So perhaps a better question would be, what is *not* a reference point? Currently, a reference point could be anything; therefore, there is no systematic or standardized method of identifying the starting point of any network of feedback loops. Without a clear and refined definition of reference points, how do we determine what is and is not a valid starting point? Furthermore, how do we determine what a critical threshold is prior to crossing it? Recall that critical thresholds are essentially the point at which organizations can recognize that they are approaching organizational death and change their behaviors to avoid dying, or they can fail to notice that they are approaching organizational death and dying. Potentially, a systematic—or even mathematic—method of identifying that threshold should be created so that organizations can have a tool for identifying their critical thresholds and avoiding them altogether.

Conclusion

Although much has been discussed in this chapter, the main takeaway is as follows: The routinization of official misconduct, particularly police misconduct, is the product of an explosive cluster of feedback loops. Therefore, organizations caught in this network of feedback loops will eventually deplete their resources (i.e., legitimacy) and die. To avoid organizational death, organizations should make efforts to disrupt their vicious cycles and replace them with virtuous cycles. Doing so would ultimately allow them to achieve their goals. Thus, in the case of criminal legal organizations, we may one day achieve justice for all.

References

Alexander, M. (2020). *The new Jim Crow mass incarceration in the age of colorblindness*. New Press.

Alter, A. L., Stern, C., Granot, Y., & Balcetis, E. (2016). The "bad is black" effect: Why people believe evildoers have darker skin than do-gooders. *Personality and Social Psychology Bulletin, 42*(12), 1653–1665. https://doi.org/10.1177/0146167216669123

Asarian, L., Gloy, V., & Geary, N. (2012). Homeostasis. In *Encyclopedia of human behavior* (2nd ed.). Elsevier. https://doi.org/10.1016/B978-0-12-375000-6.00191-9

Ashforth, B. E., & Anand, V. (2003). The normalization of corruption in organizations. *Research in Organizational Behavior, 25*, 1–52. https://doi.org/10.1016/S0191-3085(03)25001-2

Ashforth, B. E., & Gibbs, B. W. (1990). The double-edge of organizational legitimation. *Organization Science, 1*(2), 177–194. https://doi.org/10.1287/orsc.1.2.177

Bennett, M. W., & Plaut, V. C. (2017). Looking criminal and the presumption of dangerousness: Afrocentric facial features, skin tone, and criminal justice. *University of California Davis Law Review, 51*, 745–803.

Berti, M., & Simpson, A. V. (2021). The dark side of organizational paradoxes: The dynamics of disempowerment. *Academy of Management Review, 46*(2), 252–274. https://doi.org/10.5465/amr.2017.0208

Blumenson, E., & Nilsen, E. (1998). Policing for profit: The drug war's hidden economic agenda. *The University of Chicago Law Review, 65*(1), 35–114. https://www.jstor.org/stable/1600184

Bolton, W. (2002). *Control systems*. Newness.

Britannica, T. Editors of Encyclopaedia. (2019, September 13). *Social status*. Encyclopedia Britannica. https://www.britannica.com/topic/social-status

Carr, P. J., Napolitano, L., & Keating, J. (2007). We never call the cops and here is why: A qualitative examination of legal cynicism in three Philadelphia neighborhoods. *Criminology, 45*(2), 445–480. https://doi.org/10.1111/j.1745-9125.2007.00084.x

Cloward, R. A., & Ohlin, L. E. (1969). The evolution of delinquent subcultures. In *Delinquency, crime, and social process*. Harper & Row.

Crozier, M., & Friedberg, E. (2017). *The bureaucratic phenomenon*. Routledge.

De Klerk, J. J. (2017). "The devil made me do it!" An inquiry into the unconscious "devils within" of rationalized corruption. *Journal of Management Inquiry, 26*(3), 254–269. https://doi.org/10.1177/1056492617692101

Delattre, E. J. (2011). *Character and cops: Ethics in policing* (6th ed.). AEI Press.

Den Nieuwenboer, N. A., & Kaptein, M. (2008). Spiraling down into corruption: A dynamic analysis of the social identity processes that cause corruption in organizations to grow. *Journal of Business Ethics, 83*(2), 133–146. https://doi.org/10.1007/s10551-007-9617-8

Desmond, M., Papachristos, A. V., & Kirk, D. S. (2016). Police violence and citizen crime reporting in the black community. *American Sociological Review, 81*(5), 857–876. https://doi.org/10.1177/0003122416663494

Dowling, J., & Pfeffer, J. (1975). Organizational legitimacy: Social values and organizational behavior. *Pacific Sociological Review, 18*(1), 122–136. https://doi.org/10.2307/1388226

Drug Policy Alliance. (2016). *Race and the drug war*. Drugpolicy.org. Retrieved on November 07, 2021, from https://drugpolicy.org/issues/race-and-drug-war

Drug Policy Alliance. (2021). *A brief history of the drug war*. Drugpolicy.org. Retrieved on October 31, 2021, from https://drugpolicy.org/issues/brief-history-drug-war

Gould, J. B., Smiegocki, V. M., & Leo, R. A. (2022). Theorizing failed prosecutions. *The Journal of Criminal Law and Criminology, 112*(2), 329–367. https://www.jstor.org/stable/10.2307/48656974

Gouldner, A. W. (1954). *Patterns of industrial bureaucracy*. Free Press.

Greene, J. (2013). *Moral tribes*. The Penguin Press.

Gross, S. R., Jacoby, K., Matheson, D. J., & Montgomery, N. (2005). Exonerations in the United States 1989 through 2003. *Journal of Criminology Law & Criminology, 95*(2), 523–560.

Gross, S. R., Possley, M., Roll, K., & Stephens, K. (2020). *Government misconduct and convicting the innocent, the role of prosecutors, police and other law enforcement: The role of prosecutors, police and other law enforcement*. The National Registry of Exonerations. https://doi.org/10.2139/ssrn.3698845

Hambrick, D. C., & D'Aveni, R. A. (1988). Large corporate failures as downward spirals. *Administrative Science Quarterly, 33*(1), 1–23. https://doi.org/10.2307/2392853

Haraoubia, B. (2018). *Nonlinear electronics 1: Nonlinear dipoles, harmonic oscillators and switching circuits*. Elsevier.

Johnson, C., & Hoopes, J. (2019). The war on drugs and the case for rehabilitation. *Brigham Young University Prelaw Review, 33*(17), 17–10. https://scholarsarchive.byu.edu/byuplr/vol33/iss1/17

Jones, J. (2015). In U.S., confidence in police lowest in 22 years. Gallup. Retrieved on November 07, 2021 from https://news.gallup.com/poll/183704/confidence-police-lowest-years.aspx
Katz, D., & Kahn, R. L. (1978). *The social psychology of organizations*. Wiley.
Kesslen, B. (2020). *Calls to reform, defund, dismantle and abolish the police, explained.* NBC News. Retrieved on November 07, 2021, from https://www.nbcnews.com/news/us-news/calls-reform-defund-dismantle-abolish-police-explained-n1227676
Klockars, C. B. (1980). The Dirty Harry problem. *Annals of the American Academy of Political and Social Science, 452*(1), 33–47. https://doi.org/10.1177/000271628045200104
Marinescu, D. C. (2016). *Complex systems and clouds: A self-organization and self-management perspective*. Morgan Kaufmann.
Marzulli, J. (2011, October 13). *We fabricated drug charges against innocent people to meet quotas, former detective testifies*. NYDailynews.com. Retrieved on November 07, 2021, from https://www.nydailynews.com/news/crime/fabricated-drug-charges-innocent-people-meet-arrest-quotas-detective-testifies-article-1.963021
Masuch, M. (1985). Vicious circles in organizations. *Administrative Science Quarterly, 30*(1), 14–33.
Mazur, M. (1978). Cybernetic theorems on feedback in social processes. In *Sociocybernetics*. Springer.
Meadows, D. H. (1999). *Leverage points: Places to intervene in a system*. Sustainability Institute.
Merton, R. K., & Merton, R. C. (1968). *Social theory and social structure*. Simon and Schuster.
National Registry of Exonerations. (2024). *Interactive map*. Retrieved on October 30, 2021, from http://www.law.umich.edu/special/exoneration/Pages/Exonerations-in-the-United-States-Map.aspx
Nedelkoff, R. (2002). *Edward Byrne memorial state and local law enforcement assistance program*. Bureau of Justice Assistance. https://www.ojp.gov/pdffiles1/bja/195907.pdf
Nunn, K. B. (2002). Race, crime, and the pool of surplus criminality: Or why the war on drugs was a war on blacks. *Journal of Gender, Race, & Justice, 6*, 381–445.
Perrow, C. B. (1970). *Organizational analysis: A sociological view*. Brooks/Cole.
Pfeffer, J. (1980). *Power in organizations*. Pitman.
Pozsgai-Alvarez, J. (2020). The abuse of entrusted power for private gain: Meaning, nature and theoretical evolution. *Crime, Law and Social Change, 74*, 433–455. https://doi.org/10.1007/s10611-020-09903-4
Pradies, C., Tunarosa, A., Lewis, M. W., & Courtois, J. (2021). From vicious to virtuous paradox dynamics: The social-symbolic work of supporting actors. *Organization Studies, 42*(8), 1241–1263. https://doi.org/10.1177/0170840620907200
Richard Nixon Foundation. (2016, April 29). *President Nixon declares drug abuse "public enemy number one"* [Video]. Available from https://www.youtube.com/watch?v=y8TGLLQlD9M&t=254s
Rosenblatt, V. (2012). Hierarchies, power inequalities, and organizational corruption. *Journal of Business Ethics, 111*(2), 237–251. https://doi.org/10.1007/s10551-012-1204-y
Staw, B. M., Sandelands, L. E., & Dutton, J. E. (1981). Threat rigidity effects in organizational behavior: A multilevel analysis. *Administrative Science Quarterly, 26*, 501–524.
Suchman, M. C. (1995). Managing legitimacy: Strategic and institutional approaches. *Academy of Management Review, 20*(3), 571–610. https://doi.org/10.5465/amr.1995.9508080331
Sullivan, J. (1977). *Introduction to police science* (3rd ed.). McGraw-Hill.
Tajfel, H., & Turner, J. (1978). The social identity theory of intergroup behavior. In *The social identity theory of intergroup behavior*. Brooks-Cole.
Trivedi, S., & Van Cleve, N. G. (2020). To serve and protect each other: How police-prosecutor codependence enables police misconduct. *Boston University Law Review, 100*, 895–993.
Van Halderen, R. C., & Kolthoff, E. (2017). Noble cause corruption revisited: Toward a structured research approach. *Public Integrity, 19*(3), 274–293. https://doi.org/10.1080/10999922.2016.1230689

Walters, G. D., & Bolger, P. C. (2019). Procedural justice perceptions, legitimacy beliefs, and compliance with the law: A meta-analysis. *Journal of Experimental Criminology, 15*(3), 341–372. https://doi.org/10.1007/s11292-018-9338-2

Weber, M. (1947). *The theory of social and economic organizations*. Free Press.

Zahra, S. A. (2008). The virtuous cycle of discovery and creation of entrepreneurial opportunities. *Strategic Entrepreneurship Journal, 2*(3), 243–257. https://doi.org/10.1002/sej.47

Zyglidopoulos, S. C., Fleming, P. J., & Rothenberg, S. (2009). Rationalization, overcompensation and the escalation of corruption in organizations. *Journal of Business Ethics, 84*(1), 65–73. https://doi.org/10.1007/s10551-008-9685-4

Chapter 13
Boycotting the Uniform Crime Report: Organizational Theory Analysis of the Causes and Consequences of Cooperative Failures by Police for Federal Crime Reporting

Thomas K. Hargrove

Introduction

The rate at which local and state police and sheriff's departments fully and accurately report crime data to the Federal Bureau of Investigation's 94-year-old Uniform Crime Report has been deteriorating in recent years. Police underreporting of homicides, for example, has worsened significantly over time so that nearly one in four murders went unreported to the federal government in 2020, the lowest reporting rate on record. This decline occurred during the run-up to the federal mandate that police must upgrade their reporting systems by 2021 to the more complex National Incident-Based Reporting System (NIBRS). This chapter examines in detail the extent to which interagency cooperation can be explained and predicted by organizational theory and explores, statistically, the nature of these cooperative failures. A regression analysis of reporting rates among 3,131 counties found homicide underreporting was most likely to occur in rural areas, counties with high poverty rates, politically conservative areas, counties with relatively high homicide rates, urban counties that do not contain FBI field offices, and in states that generally have poor crime reporting traditions. The implications of these findings to interagency cooperation and police organizational theory are discussed.

T. K. Hargrove (✉)
George Mason University, Department of Criminology, Law & Society, Fairfax, VA, USA

D. S. Rudes, J. R. Ingram (eds.), *Using Organizational Theory to Study, Explain, and Understand Criminal Legal Organizations*,
https://doi.org/10.1007/978-3-031-66285-0_13

Organizational Theory, the UCR, and NIBRS

Interagency cooperation between local police and sheriff's departments to report crime data to the Federal Bureau of Investigation has deteriorated rapidly in recent years to the point that nearly one in every four homicides was not reported to the federal government in 2020. This was the worst undercount on record for the 94-year-old Uniform Crime Report (UCR), the nation's official accounting for major crime. This deterioration in data reporting occurred during the FBI's preparations to mandate a new, much more robust data standard called the National Incident-Based Reporting System or NIBRS. The NIBRS standard would provide case-level details for most criminal investigations conducted by local police departments, granting unprecedented insight (critics might say oversight) into local law enforcement operations.

Why did intergovernmental cooperation for data reporting to the federal government collapse within hundreds of local law enforcement agencies? Given the UCR's successful collaborative history, the reluctance to participate in the broader NIBRS program might seem mysterious. However, growing scholarship into organizational theory suggests such refusals were not only possible but even inevitable.

Organizational theory provides insight into the FBI's cooperative collapse through an understanding of what interagency cooperation requires. The resource dependency theory (RDT) warns that cooperation becomes problematic if resources are not controlled and shared. Network theory and interorganizational collaborative capacity (ICC) theory give insight into the challenges of interagency communication, especially over significant geographic distances. Organizational theory also signals that cooperation will be threatened if the collaboration is attempted across differing organizational cultures and, especially, when such cooperation threatens "reputational uniqueness" for participants.

The issues raised by organizational theory will be validated in this study through an empirical review focusing on the nature of law enforcement agencies that are not reporting complete data to the FBI. This analysis found that these cooperative failures were influenced by politics, poverty, population size, homicide rates, state traditions of participation in federal data reporting, and agency proximity to FBI field offices. These findings are commensurate with widely acknowledged and increasing strains in interorganizational cooperation between federal authorities and local and state police (Mosher et al., 2011; Maltz, 1999; Geller & Morris, 1992). These strains have long been recognized by scholars but were exacerbated in recent years during community stresses from the COVID pandemic, local anti-police tensions, and—probably most importantly—by the insistence of federal authorities that local police must update their reporting standards to the much more complex and intrusive NIBRS format.

The quantitative elements of this study are based upon an analysis of homicide reporting rates by comparing data from the UCR and its Supplemental Homicide Report (SHR), both voluntary reporting systems, against the mandatory reports that coroners and medical examiners must make in reporting homicides to the Centers for Disease Control and Prevention's National Vital Statistics System (NVSS). Unlike voluntary reporting to the FBI, medical authorities and individuals are, in most states, required under criminal penalty to report suspicious deaths to the federal government (Anderson, 2021; Regoeczi et al., 2014).

This study will make detailed comparisons of homicide reporting rates to the CDC and FBI by region, state, victim race, victim sex, victim age, and method of killing. To determine the broad patterns in the types of local agencies that underreport homicide data, a regression analysis of reporting rates among 3,131 counties will focus on rural areas, counties with high poverty rates, politically conservative areas, counties with high homicide rates, counties with greater exposure to FBI personnel, and in states with generally poor crime reporting traditions. These findings will be addressed later in this chapter.

At the outset, it is important to see how the reporting participation rate has changed over recent years. In previous decades, scholars have estimated homicide underreporting rates averaged about 9%, meaning reporting rates were about 91% complete (Rokaw et al., 1990). But a much different picture emerges with more recent comparisons of the numbers of homicides reported to the FBI against the numbers reported by medical authorities to the CDC.

Why local police agencies began abandoning crime data reporting to the FBI years before NIBRS became mandatory has not been addressed by federal authorities and is the focus of this study.

Previous Scholarship: History of a Much-Doubted Crime Report

Congress created the UCR in September 1930 when it approved the language currently codified in 28 U.S. Code § 534 to empower the US attorney general to "acquire, collect, classify, and preserve" information for major crimes committed in the nation. Federal lawmakers took the action at the urging of the International Association of Chiefs of Police (IACP). The police chiefs recognized that local crime statistics had become a mishmash of conflicting legal definitions and reporting rules that made comparisons between police jurisdictions virtually impossible (Tibbitts, 1932; Barnett-Ryan, 2007; Mosher et al., 2011). The IACP also hoped the data would "help reduce media pressure on local jurisdictions and police chiefs from sensational or sporadic increases in crime" (Congressional Research Service, 2008).

However, the police chiefs did not ask—and Congress did not require—that UCR reporting be mandatory, complete, or even accurate. The earliest federal publication of the nation's official crime statistics faced immediate academic denigration. University of Chicago academic Clark Tibbitts noted that the 1931 federal UCR annual report was widely criticized by his colleagues because the data clearly were incomplete and implied a degree of accuracy that did not exist (Tibbitts, 1932).

Minnesota academic George B. Vold questioned whether increases in major crime occurrences reported by the St. Paul Police Department were real or the result of better counting practices compared to previous years (Vold, 1935; Mosher et al., 2011). Others, like Ronald H. Bettie in his 1941 review of the sources of crime statistics, conjectured that crime numbers would wax or wane according to the exigencies of the reporting departments to give the appearance of good administration (Beattie, 1941; Mosher et al., 2011).

A growing body of scholars, with the venerable sociologist Donald T. Campbell leading, warned of a generally perverting influence when statistics become both official and important. "The more any quantitative social indicator is used for social decision-making, the more subject it will be to corruption pressures and the more apt it will be to distort and corrupt the social processes it is intended to monitor," Campbell wrote (Campbell, 1979, p. 85; Johnston & Carley, 1981). Even A.E. Leonard, an accountant by training and one of the first chiefs of the FBI's Statistical Section, admitted to the social pressures local police executives face when making crime summaries publicly available. He urged local police to report completely and accurately, even when the data do not indicate an attractive picture of crime (Leonard, 1954).

Since the fundamental concerns with the Uniform Crime Report were over its incompleteness and worries that it was manipulated by parochial and political pressures within police departments, an alternative and overlapping data source judged to be more complete than the UCR could be a valuable tool in spotlighting exactly where crime reporting to the FBI is deficient. Scholars soon realized there is an even older reporting system whose accuracy and completeness are mandated by law (Barnett-Ryan, 2007; Loftin et al., 2008; Loftin et al., 2017). The National Vital Statistics System (NVSS) is maintained by the National Center for Health Statistics at the Centers for Disease Control and Prevention (CDC). It gathers and disseminates data obtained from death certificates. In most jurisdictions in the United States, it is unlawful to transport and dispose of human remains without a death certificate. Failure to report a human death can—and often does—result in criminal prosecution.

The Centers for Disease Control and its federal predecessors confronted death reporting challenges similar to the crime reporting hurdles faced by the FBI. But unlike the crime reporting system, medical authorities aggressively labored to standardize and improve death reporting for more than a century. The US health system developed and refined a nationally standardized death certificate. The Department of Health and Human Services approved the current standard in 2003 which has been ratified by all 50 states and the District of Columbia (Ventura, 2018, p. 50). Also, the federal–state partnership for vital records evolved in 2010 under the optimistic title of the "Getting from Good to Great Partnership" with a goal of developing "a reengineered, responsive, and nimble vital statistics system" that included robust use of electronic record exchange (Ventura, 2018, p. 23).

In recent decades, the homicide counts provided by the NVSS consistently outperformed the still often erratic reporting rates found in the UCR and SHR, prompting crime scholars to look to medical examiners for a more complete (although not without error) accounting of homicide. A comparison for the period 1976 to 1982 found that the vital records system routinely had a greater number of homicides than the UCR, with an annual average difference of 1,791 homicides. That meant the vital records system was reporting 9% more homicides than were police (Rokaw et al., 1990). The study also found that Black victims were more likely to be reported in both systems than were white victims, although the lowest reporting was for victims of "other" races. These "other" race victim data had high variability due, the authors concluded, to the relatively low frequencies being compared. One of the most recent FBI/NVSS comparisons covered the period 1981 to 2011 and also concluded that the vital records were significantly more reliable, although they did not cite exact statistical differences. The study was led by Wendy Regoeczi with Bureau of Justice Statistics and CDC scholars. They concluded that the NVSS consistently showed a higher number and rate of homicides compared to FBI data, likely due to the "voluntary versus mandatory nature of the data collection." They estimated that the NVSS covers 99% of the birth and death events in the United States (Regoeczi et al., 2014).

Methodology Used in This Study

As with previous studies (Vold, 1952; Rokaw et al., 1990; Regoeczi et al., 2014), the number of homicide cases reported by police to the FBI was compared to the count of cases of "fatal assault (homicide)" reported by medical examiners to the CDC's National Vital Statistics System during the 10-year period of 2010 to 2019. For the purposes of this study, only the actual number of homicides reported by police is used rather than the national homicide estimates released by the FBI's Criminal Justice Information Services (CJIS) division in Clarksburg, West Virginia. CJIS seeks to account for at least some of the missing data and will rely entirely on estimates starting in 2021, when the National Incident-Based Reporting System became mandatory. The percentage of unreported homicides was calculated for a variety of geographies and victim demographics using the formula: (CDC – FBI)/CDC then multiplied by 100.

The percentage of missing homicides was calculated for 3,131 counties and was used as the dependent variable for regression analysis. The independent variables included the county's 5-year population average provided by the U.S. Census Bureau's American Community Survey, the county's 5-year average poverty rate also from the ACS, the homicide rate per 100,000 population calculated using the CDC homicide count, the county's vote percentage the Republican presidential candidate received in 2016, and whether the county has an FBI Field Office. Dummy variables were also created to evaluate the effect of region and state in informing the model's ability to predict the homicide reporting performance by local police and sheriff's departments within each county.

The reporting rates based on victim demographics were made using an augmented version of the UCR's Supplemental Homicide Report provided by the nonprofit Murder Accountability Project. This group seeks to supplement missing SHR data through negotiation or Freedom of Information Act lawsuits. It has obtained more than 33,000 records of unreported homicides from Alabama, Florida, Illinois, and the District of Columbia.

A Previously Unrecognized Cause of Inaccurate Crime Reporting

Although crime scholars for 94 years have questioned the accuracy of the nation's official accounting of crime, few, if any, have suggested a major source of reporting error could be interagency disputes or deliberate noncooperation between local police and the FBI. Yet growing scholarship into organizational structure suggests such competitions and cooperative challenges and failures were inevitable (Bardach, 1998; McChrystal et al., 2015). Recent comparisons between the total homicide cases reported by police to the FBI and the murders reported by medical examiners to the CDC's National Vital Statistics System show a steadily declining reporting rate by police. By 2020, local police and sheriff's departments failed to report one in every four murders to the official federal accounting of major crime. This represents a significant decline from 1980s and 1990s estimates when the UCR was thought to be about 91% complete (Rokaw et al., 1990).

Although the technical challenges of upgrading to the more complex NIBRS standard have been cited as the cause of rapidly diminishing crime reporting by local police to the federal government, this study's analysis of the kinds of local law enforcement agencies that already had ceased federal crime reporting prior to the implementation of the NIBRS mandate suggests other factors rooted in organizational theory are deeply involved. The transition to NIBRS has forced local police to reassess their level of commitment to the reporting program, especially considering the costs involved. The Bureau of Justice Statistics in 2017 requested estimates from private records management vendors and concluded the top two vendors would upgrade a local mid-sized police department's records system to NIBRS compliance at an initial cost of \$367,000 to \$377,000 with annual maintenance costs of \$48,000 to \$53,500 for every year thereafter (Smith, 2017). This 2017 estimate puts a cash value to the price local police must pay to continue to participate in the completely voluntary federal crime reporting program.

It is hardly surprising that hundreds of police departments opted out of the UCR program during the run-up to the more expensive NIBRS program. Under the original UCR program, police departments were asked to report summary information on the number of occurrences and clearances (cases resulting in the arrest of offenders) for nearly 30 major crime types and to provide case-level information such as victim age, race, gender, and ethnicity and other details only for homicides. For most police departments, their annual UCR report could easily fit into a manila envelope. But under NIBRS, police are asked to provide a much larger depth of reporting for thousands of crimes in their jurisdiction, an unprecedented exchange of information with the federal government (Strom & Smith, 2017; Rantala & Edwards, 2020).

The transition to NIBRS, with its significant financial costs and expectations for disclosure of internal operations to the federal government, has essentially rewritten the original 94-year-old contract for reporting crime. Recent studies into NIBRS participation have found considerable cultural, practical, and technical barriers to participation and cooperation from local police. Some police agencies report they are concerned the transition to incident-based reporting "will give the appearance that an agency's crime rate has increased" because NIBRS does not impose the hierarchy rule (that crime only be counted once under old UCR procedures) and that NIBRS "also captures data on a wide range of criminal offenses" (Strom & Smith, 2017, p. 1035; James & Council, 2008; Watson, 2000).

Traditional Organizational and Cooperative Theory

German sociologist, historian, and political economist Max Weber was among the first to systematically study the nature and structure of the rapidly developing business and governmental institutions that we today call bureaucracies. Weber concluded that the internal records of such systems are the holiest of holy grails. Weber wrote:

> The management of the modern office is based upon written documents which are preserved in their original and draught form. There is, therefore, a staff of subaltern officials and scribes of all sorts. [These files along with a body of public officials and associated apparatus, make up a bureau] (Weber, 1946, p. 196–198).

The extent to which any bureaucratic organization will openly and freely exchange details about the contents of "the files" is a matter of considerable organizational theory and study (Lutzker, 1982).

Organizational cooperative theorists generally recognize that "one of the primary tasks" any organization faces is developing and maintaining its relationships with other organizations, sometimes termed the dyadic environment. Broadly, organizations would be expected to adopt "the least constraining" of any interorganizational associations "sufficient to maintain autonomy and ensure access to critical resources" (Scott & Davis, 2007, p. 242–244). This focus on access to resources developed into the formal resource dependence theory (RDT), which demonstrates how the external resources of an organization influence the practices and behavior of the organization (Pfeffer & Salancik, 1978). Procurement of external resources is an important principle of both the strategic and tactical management of any organization and the give-and-take of such relationships can easily result in "power imbalances" (Scott & Davis, 2007, p. 243). Put most simply, agency collaboration is much more likely with another agency that controls resources.

Even the mere act of communication between cooperating agencies can be problematic. Public policy scholar Eugene Bardach used network theory to describe the capacities that facilitate efficient communications and information exchange between government agencies for particular purposes, such as delivering services to citizens and seeking out partners with complementary resources. He noted, as the old joke goes, collaboration between government agencies is an unnatural act committed by nonconsenting adults. Bardach suggested that current public opinion favoring more results-oriented government makes collaboration more natural, but still far from easy (Bardach, 1998).

A more recent analysis of state and local government interagency cooperation found that such efforts might seem a beneficial way for state governments to capitalize on local knowledge, but the "benefits to local government are less clear" (Mullins & Daley, 2009, p. 757). Local agency personnel may often have goals that diverge from their state counterparts and make significant constraints on their resources, forcing them to consider the opportunity costs of collaboration. Interorganizational collaborative capacity theory (ICC) suggests efforts to sustain interagency systems in pursuit of collective outcomes can become more problematic with the perceived distance between governmental levels. Getting distant agencies to "cohere and create functionality" becomes a greater challenge (Comiskey, 2020, p. 112; Bardach, 1998). Successful collaboration requires iterative cycles of discovery and determination to develop trust, but all too often, "organizational cultures and rivalries, regulations, and inadequate training could impede interagency collaboration" (Comiskey, 2020, p. 113).

Police agencies operating at different levels of government will generally have different organizational cultures not ideally suited to developing effective countermeasures against crime and the related problems each agency targets (Geller & Morris, 1992). As shall be seen in this study, the lines of authority, resource control, communication, and cooperative benefits have become complicated between local law enforcement agencies and the federal government in general—and the FBI in particular.

Warning Signs from Europe: When Police Agencies Do and Don't Cooperate

Recent European scholarship has provided important insight into the sources of cooperation or noncooperation between police agencies. The studies have contrasted Europol, officially called the "European Union Agency for Law Enforcement Cooperation" headquartered at the Hague, and Frontex, officially the "European Border and Coast Guard Agency," also an agency of the European Union headquartered in Warsaw, Poland. At issue was why Europol suffered extensive turf-protective tendencies and a general lack of cooperation to share information about criminal activity while Frontex experienced much smoother cooperation and extensive information sharing about criminal activity at European border crossings.

The conclusion of one scholar was that at Europol, "cooperation depletes important reputational resources of national authorities, threatening their 'reputational uniqueness' and triggering turf-protective tendencies" (Busuioc, 2016, p. 41). Open sharing of information about criminal activities in each European nation threatened the reputation of the nation itself and its criminal legal agencies. The reputation an agency cultivates is "the primary source of its power, which can allow it to enlist public support, build its autonomy, protect it from external attacks, and ultimately help ensure its survival. Organizations, therefore, expend a great deal of time and effort cultivating this valuable political asset" (Busuioc, 2016, p. 41).

In contrast, Frontex experienced vertical and horizontal cooperation efforts to bring important gains to national authorities' abilities to discharge their tasks successfully and, thus their reputation-building efforts. Information sharing between nations was crucial to maintaining secure borders. Such complete and open exchange about criminal activities was perceived to enhance the reputations both of reporting and data-receiving nations (Busuioc, 2016, p. 41).

However, the cooperative failures within Interpol became endemic at the outset of the organization's creation. National police authorities were "reluctant to share information" with the international agency (Groenleer, 2009, p. 296). The failure became politically embarrassing. "I cannot influence the member states to insert more data. I appeal, I remind them all the time, and now they are getting very tired," concluded one Europol director. "The system is by far not filled as it should be" (Busuioc, 2013, p. 147). Qualitative interviews concerning what one European police official termed the "information dehydration" of crime reporting to Interpol proved enlightening. There is a tendency of local police to proclaim, "It's my data." One respondent said local police "are afraid that by cooperating someone will steal the case" and that "I want to have all the credit from this one" (Busuioc, 2016, p. 48).

Meanwhile, in America, Discontentment with the FBI

Law enforcement agencies in the United States are no more immune from turf wars, reluctance to share detailed case information and reputational concerns than are their European cousins. One of the central tensions for this problem is what scholars have termed the "lack of a rational basis" for the delineation of federal and nonfederal jurisdictions that inhibits strategic planning for efficient, effective, and coherent anticrime efforts (Geller & Morris, 1992, p. 231). The "federated" structure of national, state, and local government means that most law enforcement in America is a mishmash of overlapping jurisdictional authority. This naturally resulted in a "chaotic state of affairs" throughout police jurisdictions and in the development of "different organizational cultures" at various levels of government that challenge the development of effective countermeasures for crime (Geller & Morris, 1992, p. 232).

Much of the intergovernmental tensions for law enforcement have focused on the degree of information sharing between local police and the FBI, the nation's largest and best-funded law enforcement agency. "Local police have complained for many years about being patronized, alienated, upstaged, or simply ignored by FBI agents" (MaGuire & King, 2011, p. 322). The observation extends back decades. According to many "practitioners and observers," there is a historic pattern in which federal agencies, especially the FBI, were "principally information takers but not information providers" when working with local law enforcement (Geller & Morris, 1992, p. 266) (Also see Morgan, 1983; Lupsha, 1991). Even when interagency law enforcement partnerships did work well, local and state agencies working with the FBI often "felt that information was a one-way street" (Weiss & Davis, 2002, p. 80).

Unlike the era of the 1930s when the Uniform Crime Report was created and when the Federal Bureau of Investigation was a new and little-known agency, the modern FBI is widely understood and suffers a deeply checkered history of cooperative information sharing with state and local police. It is against this relational backdrop that the bureau asked police departments to dramatically expand the level of federal oversight into crime investigation at the local level. The much more complex level of reporting requires most police departments to adapt to expensive, technologically challenging records management systems that will be especially burdensome to small and mid-sized police agencies (Strom & Smith, 2017; Smith, 2017; Addington, 2004).

Organization theory suggests such changing technical requirements and expanded information sharing conditions can, and probably will, cause stress to the strength of association bonds between local, state, and federal agencies. Practical police studies have confirmed the theory. Manning (1996) reported that technological changes frequently "destabilize the power balance between organizational segments by altering communication patterns, role relationships, the division of labor, established formats for organizational communication, and taken for granted routines" (Manning, p. 54). Sometimes, the reactions within police agencies can be severe. Chan (2001) found that forced, from-on-high technology changes "alter the balance of power between workers and supervisors and between sworn officers and civilians. When officers feel that their autonomy is threatened by internal surveillance or external interference, they are likely to resort to resistance or sabotage where possible" (Chan, 2001, p. 146).

Local Police Objections to NIBRS Reporting

To understand the nature and depth of local and state resistance to expanded, incident-based crime reporting to the federal government, the FBI and Bureau of Justice Statistics conducted a series of focus groups with local law enforcement officials from 64 agencies attending regional discussions held in five cities in 1996 (Roberts, 1997). The concerns about NIBRS that local police expressed at those meetings reinforced the cooperative failures predicted by organizational theory.

Since cooperative theory predicts that agency collaboration is much more likely with another agency that controls—or at least partially provides—resources (Pfeffer & Salancik, 1978; Scott & Davis, 2007), it's hardly surprising the number one objection to NIBRS raised by local police was the financial and labor costs of voluntarily providing dramatically expanded crime data to the federal government. "There is a general and widespread perception that implementing NIBRS is very costly for local law enforcement," the authors of the focus group study concluded (Roberts, 1997, p. 9). Local police complained they would require larger data entry staff, will need to significantly modify their records management systems, and will need to increase staff training, even down to street-level officers, to accommodate the "substantive increases" in case data acquisition and processing (Roberts, 1997, p. 10).

Studies of the European police reporting failures to Europol concluded that data-sharing cooperation would threaten the "reputational uniqueness" of each nation and, therefore, triggered a "turf-protective tendency" (Busuioc, 2016, p. 41). Likewise in the United States, local police reported they feared a "potential public relations disaster for local law enforcement agencies and government officials" if they participated in NIBRS reporting (Roberts, 1997, p. 10). This complaint demonstrated a cunning understanding of the statistical effect of the changes in crime reporting that the NIBRS standard presents. Under the old UCR Summary Report, a crime was counted only one time according to a hierarchy rule with homicide at the apex. Thus, an incident in which a victim was robbed, sexually assaulted, and killed would only be counted as a single homicide. Local officials expressed a widespread belief that crime will appear to increase in their jurisdictions if for no other reason than that NIBRS allows the reporting of multiple offenses within a single incident (Roberts, 1997).

Just as importantly, the federal study into local resistance to NIBRS found widespread proof of the "different organizational cultures" found in federal versus non-federal police (Geller & Morris, 1992; Mullins & Daley, 2009; Comiskey, 2020; Bardach, 1998). There was widespread doubt of the benefits to local governments if they commit resources to NIBRS. Each of the regional focus groups concluded there was "no clear operational value" at the state and local levels. NIBRS only has value in "macrolevel analyses" at the national level, they concluded (Roberts, 1997, p. 10). Even law enforcement officials sympathetic to NIBRS warned that the national reporting systems "can make your department look like it is failing." Retired Colorado Police Chief Joel F. Shults cautioned his colleagues with the old wisdom that a man can drown in a river that is 6 inches deep—on average (Shults, 2019).

It is against this backdrop of intergovernmental mistrust, conflicting organizational cultures, fears of reputational damage, and local agency resource concerns that participation in the 94-year-old Uniform Crime Report dropped to just 76% of homicides in 2020, the worst reporting rate on record up to that time. The plunge in intergovernmental cooperation occurred even before the NIBRS standard became mandatory in 2021.

Major Statistical Findings of Interagency Noncooperation

The performance of police in reporting homicides to the FBI eroded significantly during the past decade. Using a previous estimate (Rokaw et al., 1990) that an average of 1,791 homicides went unreported each year by police during the period 1976 to 1982, the UCR beat this numerical performance level only twice in the last decade, in 2010 and 2011, when 1,682 and 1,687 homicides, respectively, went unreported (See Table 13.1). However, if missing homicides are evaluated as a percentage of all murders, then the UCR has failed consistently to match Rokaw's 9% undercount estimate. The deterioration in homicide reporting grew steadily from 2010, when 10% of homicides were not reported by police, until 2020, when 24% of murders went unreported.

Why has police performance in homicide accounting eroded so significantly in recent years? Since the finding that nearly one in four murders went unreported by police in 2020 has not been previously published, scholars have yet to evaluate the causes. However, there can be little doubt that police departments faced significant challenges in recent years. The workforce disruptions caused by the COVID-19 pandemic, the widespread and sometimes-violent protests over the police killing of George Floyd in Minneapolis, and the politically potent challenges from the Black Lives Matter movement could not have helped the always-challenging process of accurately tabulating data to the FBI. Also, it should be said that the approaching transition in crime reporting standards may have added to police accounting woes. There may have been confusion as to when this new standard was to be applied, probably contributing to the 2019 UCR's historically low reporting rate. Of course, datasets can still be useful analytic tools even if they suffer a significant undercount, especially if the error rate is evenly distributed throughout the sample.

Table 13.1 Homicide Reports to CDC and FBI from 2010 to 2020

Year	CDC	FBI	Missing	Percent missing	National population	CDC rate
2010	16,259	14,577	1682	10.3	308,745,538	5.3
2011	16,238	14,551	1687	10.4	311,591,917	5.2
2012	16,688	14,822	1866	11.2	313,914,040	5.3
2013	16,121	14,103	2018	12.5	316,128,839	5.1
2014	15,872	13,923	1949	12.3	318,857,056	5.0
2015	17,793	15,594	2199	12.4	321,418,820	5.5
2016	19,362	16,891	2471	12.8	323,127,513	6.0
2017	19,510	17,004	2506	12.8	325,719,178	6.0
2018	18,830	15,877	2953	15.7	327,167,434	5.8
2019	19,141	15,449	3692	19.3	328,239,523	5.8
2020	26,031	19,719	6312	24.2	331,449,281	7.8

Note: The FBI undercounts reached historic highs in 2021 when NIBRS reporting became mandatory. More than 43% of the nation's homicides were not reported that year. This study, however, focuses on the growing undercount when police agencies still had the option of reporting Data under the UCR standard

Unfortunately, the UCR's undercount was disproportionately distributed according to every dimension measured in this study. The generalizability of crime data is threatened by very large geographic disparities. Among states, Mississippi had the worst undercount since most of its homicides (50.4%) were not reported to the FBI during the last decade.

Homicide undercount disparities were also found to be significant by region. The undercount for homicides reported by police in Northeastern states was only 6%, compared to the 17% undercount by police in Southern states. Using the Census Bureau's expanded 8-category region system, police in New England states had the lowest undercount at 5%, while police in Southeastern states had the worst at 18%. Police in Mid-Atlantic and Far Western states had undercounts nearly as low as New England states.

Homicide reporting also varied enormously by county population size, suggesting available economic and staffing resources influenced cooperation with crime reporting (See Table 13.2). Rural counties had homicide undercount rates five times larger than in urban counties.

Significant undercount disparities were also found according to victim demographics obtained from the augmented Supplemental Homicide Report, which has a lower undercount of 8% because of augmentation. The undercount for male victims was 9%, while female victims were undercounted by a rate of 5%. Larger undercounts were found among homicides of infants and the elderly than among victims in other age groups. As was first described by Rokaw in 1990, homicides of African Americans were more likely to be counted than Caucasian killings. However, this study found a much larger undercount for American Indian and Alaskan Native murders and for Asian and Pacific Islander homicides. Nearly half (48%) of Indian homicides went unreported during the last decade, while 23% of Asian and Pacific Islander homicides were not counted. Homicides in which the offender used firearms were more likely to be undercounted than homicides by all other means. This pattern is partially explained by the fact that male murders are more likely to be undercounted than female murders and that men are more likely than women to be victims of firearms.

To study homicide undercounting at the local level, the NVSS and FBI data were compared among 3,131 US counties for simple Ordinary Least Squares regression analysis. The dependent variable was the percentage of homicides reported to NVSS

Table 13.2 Homicide Reporting by County Population from 2010 to 2019

County population	CDC	SRS	Missing	Percent	CDC rate per 100,000
Less than 25,000	8999	5618	3381	37.6	4.8
25,000 to 50,000	9843	7346	2497	25.4	4.4
50,000 to 100,000	11,908	9381	2527	21.2	4.3
100,000 to 500,000	46,579	39,789	6790	14.6	4.9
500,000 to 1 million	41,903	38,230	3673	8.8	6.3
More than 1 million	56,582	52,427	4155	7.3	6.3
Total	175,814	152,791	23,023	13.1	5.5

that were not reported to the FBI. To test whether homicide undercounting was more likely among police departments with scarce resources, independent variables included county population, county poverty rate, and county homicide rate per 100,000 using the NVSS count. To test political factors in reporting homicide, the model included the percentage of votes going to the 2016 Republican presidential candidate in the general election and whether the FBI had a field office in the county. These political elements were used because the Republican Party promotes limited government and might be less disposed than Democrats to insist on crime reporting to the federal government.

Whether the county was one of 54 counties with FBI field offices was deemed "political" because more common interaction between police and federal agents may improve attitudes toward crime reporting to the central government.

The five-independent-variable model performed well in the analysis of variance (ANOVA) score for predicting the percentage of homicide undercounts: $F(5, 3{,}126) = 61.57$, $p = < 0.001$. Four of the variables scored as significant under the $p < 0.05$ assumption. They were the dummy variable for the presence of an FBI Field Office ($\beta = -25.192$, p < .001), the homicide rate per 100,000 population ($\beta = 1.788$, $p < .001$), the percentage of the 2016 general election vote going to the Republicans ($\beta = .297$, $p < .001$), and the percentage of county population living below the poverty rate ($\beta = .271$, $p = .016$). Simply put, the presence of an FBI Field Office was found to reduce the county's expected homicide undercount by 25%. Meanwhile, every unit increase in the homicide rate was associated with about a 1.8% increase in homicide underreporting. This makes sense since the homicide rate can reflect small counties, which tend to have much lower homicide rates, or can also reflect whether police manpower resources are challenged by high homicide rates regardless of population size. Every percent increase in the countywide Republican vote or a percent increase in the poverty rate was associated with a 0.297% or 0.271% increase (respectively) in the rate of homicide underreporting.

The R^2 score for the model was modest (.09), meaning it accounted for 9% of the variance in homicide undercounting. However, this analysis found that knowing the state in which a county resides significantly improves the model's performance. This is because most states have reporting traditions or are guided by expectations from a statewide UCR program administrator. When dummy variables were added to the model for each state using Mississippi as the reference group since it has the worst performance rate, the R^2 score improved to (.183), accounting for 18% of the variance in homicide undercounting.

Discussion of Data Findings and Their Implications

Statistical results of this study underscore much of organizational theory's predictions for interagency data reporting. It is hardly surprising that local police agencies geographically proximate to FBI field offices had significantly improved data reporting rates, even when compared to major urban areas without Bureau field offices. Law enforcement personnel in agencies proximate to FBI facilities would have increased contact with federal personnel and would be more likely to share manpower in cooperative investigations.

However, much more problematic for future FBI data acquisition is the much-reduced data-reporting cooperation rates among resource-challenged law enforcement agencies from rural areas and areas with high poverty rates. The financial cost of the acquisition of new record-management technology, especially if perceived to be solely for the purpose of cooperating with a voluntary federal reporting program, would be a major impediment to future data reporting. This pattern underscores organizational theory's focus on formal resource dependence theory (RDT), which demonstrates how access to external resources of an organization affects the practices and behavior of the organization (Pfeffer & Salancik, 1978; Scott & Davis, 2007).

Perhaps even more alarming for future data-cooperation efforts by local police is the finding that data reporting was significantly lower in counties with large Republican voting patterns and from Southern and Midwestern states, the traditional geographic centers of GOP political strength. There is relatively little scholarship about the effect of partisan politics on interagency law enforcement cooperation, but the late political scientist James Q. Wilson found that "local political culture" was a "major determinant of variation in policing styles" in his study of police organization more than 50 years ago (Wilson, 1968).

Organizational Implications

The significant decline in cooperative crime data reporting by local police to the FBI occurred even before the new and much more complex National Incident-Based Reporting System became mandatory starting for crimes committed in 2021 and thereafter. That reporting participation by local police tumbled well before NIBRS became obligatory was predictable under current organizational theory. Yet the FBI, in its preparations to make NIBRS the mandatory standard for crime data reporting, showed an astonishingly deaf ear to understanding the organization theory challenges it faced.

The effect of widely differing "organizational cultures" between local and federal police deeply impacted compliance with a new national data standard and was fully documented by scholars well in advance (Geller & Morris, 1992; Mullins & Daley, 2009; Comiskey, 2020; Bardach, 1998). For decades, local police officers have complained that they frequently were alienated, upstaged, and ignored by FBI agents who rarely shared important case information (MaGuire & King, 2011, p. 322). This tension did not exist when the Uniform Crime Report began in 1930, and the FBI was a new and little-known agency.

Cooperative theory predicts that agency collaboration is much more likely with another agency that controls—or at least partially provides—resources (Pfeffer & Salancik, 1978). Many years before NIBRS became mandatory, there was a "general and widespread perception" that NIBRS would be costly for local law enforcement (Roberts, 1997, p. 9). This expenditure quickly became the leading objection to participation with federal authorities, perhaps becoming a widely accepted excuse not to cooperate with federal authorities.

The Bureau failed to understand the very serious threat to "reputational uniqueness" that NIBRS posed for local police by eliminating the old hierarchy rule so that each crime incident would be counted according to all statutory violations involved. Local police warned they faced a "public relations disaster" if the official crime counts in their communities seemed to double, triple, or even quadruple because of the new standards.

Even law enforcement officials sympathetic to NIBRS warned that the national reporting systems "can make your department look like it is failing" (Shults, 2019). Little attempt was made to amend the program after local police warned they found "no clear operational value" to them in upgrading to the massively more complex national reporting standard.

References

Addington, L. A. (2004). The effect of NIBRS reporting on item missing data in murder cases. *Homicide Studies, 8*(3), 193–213.

Anderson, R. (2021). *The Record Increase in Homicide During 2020, National Center for Health Statistics, recorded interview with the Chief of NCHS Mortality Statistics Branch*. https://www.cdc.gov/nchs/pressroom/podcasts/2021/20211008/20211008.htm. Accessed 30 Nov 2021.

Bardach, E. (1998). *Getting agencies to work together: The practice and theory of managerial craftsmanship*. Brookings Institute Press.

Barnett-Ryan, C. (2007). Introduction to the UCR reporting program. In J. P. Lynch & L. A. Addington (Eds.), *Understanding crime statistics: Revisiting the divergence of the NCVS and the UCR* (pp. 55–89). Cambridge University Press.

Beattie, R. (1941). The sources of criminal statistics. *American Academy of Political and Social Science, 217*, 19–28.

Busuioc, E. M. (2013). *European agencies: Law and practices of accountability*. Oxford University Press.

Busuioc, E. M. (2016). Friend or foe? Inter-agency cooperation, organizational reputation, and turf. *Public Administration, 94-1*, 40–56.

Campbell, D. T. (1979). Assessing the impact of planned social change. *Evaluation and Program Planning, 2*, 67–90.

Chan, J. B. L. (2001). The technological game: How information technology is transforming police practice. *Criminal Justice, 1*(2), 139–159.

Comiskey, J. (2020). Interagency collaboration (chapter 6). In J. D. Ramsay, K. Cozine, & J. Comiskey (Eds.), *Theoretical foundations of homeland security: Strategies, operations, and structures*. Routledge.

Congressional Research Service, Domestic Social Policy Division. (2008). *How crime in the United States is measured*. CRS Order Code RL34309.

Geller, W. A., & Morris, N. (1992). Relations between federal and local police. *Crime and Justice: A Review of Research, 15*. https://doi.org/10.1086/449196

Groenleer, M. (2009). *The autonomy of European Union agencies: A comparative study of institutional development*. Eburon.

James, N., & Council, L. R. (2008). *How crime in the United States is measured.* Congressional Research Service.

Johnston, D. F., & Carley, M. J. (1981). Social measurement and social indicators. *Annals of the American Academy of Political and Social Science., 453*, 237–253.

Leonard, A. E. (1954). Crime reporting as a police management tool. *The Annals of the American Academy of Political and Social Science, 291*, 127–134.

Loftin, C., McDowall, D., & Fetzer, M. D. (2008). A comparison of SHR and vital statistics homicide estimates for U.S., cities. *Journal of Contemporary Criminal Justice, 24*(1), 4–17.

Loftin, C., McDowall, D., & Xie, M. (2017). Underreporting of homicides by police in the United States, 1976–2013. *Homicide Studies, 21*. https://doi.org/10.1177/1088767917693358

Lupsha, P. (1991). Organized crime. In W. A. Geller (Ed.), *Local government police management*. International City Management Association.

Lutzker, M. A. (1982). Max Weber and the analysis of modern bureaucratic organization: Notes toward a theory of appraisal. *The American Archivist, 45*(2), 119–130.

MaGuire, E. R., & King, W. R. (2011). Federal-Local Coordination for homeland security, chapter 14. In *Criminologists on terrorism and homeland security* (pp. 322–356). Cambridge University Press.

Maltz, M. D. (1999, September). *Bridging gaps in police crime data*, NCJ 176365. U.S. Department of Justice, Office of Justice Programs, Bureau of Justice Statistics.

Manning, P. K. (1996). Information technology in the police context: The "sailor" phone. *Information Systems Research, 7*(1), 52–62.

McChrystal, S., Collins, T., Silverman, D., & Fussell, C. (2015). *Team of teams: New rules of engagement for a complex world.* Penguin Random House.

Morgan, R. E. (1983). Federal Bureau of Investigation: History. In S. H. Kadish (Ed.), *Encyclopedia of crime and justice*. Free Press.

Mosher, C. J., Miethe, T. D., & Hart, T. C. (2011). *The mismeasure of crime*. Sage Publications.

Mullins, M., & Daley, D. M. (2009). Working with the state: Exploring interagency collaboration within a federalist system. *Journal of Public Administration Research and Theory, 20*(4), 757–778.

Pfeffer, J., & Salancik, G. R. (1978). *The external control of organizations: A resource dependence perspective*. Harper & Row.

Rantala, R. R., & Edwards, T. J. (2020). *Effects of NIBRS on crime statistics*. Bureau of Justice Statistics Special Report, U.S. Department of Justice, Office of Justice Programs. Released in July as NCJ 178890.

Regoeczi, W. C., Banks, D., Planty, M., Langton, L., & Warner, M. (2014). *The nation's two measures of homicide*. Bureau of Justice Statistics.

Roberts, D. J. (1997). *Implementing the National Incident-Based Reporting System: A project status report.* A joint publication by Bureau of Justice Statistics and the Federal Bureau of Investigation. NCJ-165581.

Rokaw, W. M., Mercy, J. A., & Smith, J. C. (1990). Comparing death certificate data with FBI crime reporting statistics on U.S. homicides. *Public Health Reports, 105*(5), 447–455.

Scott, W. R., & Davis, G. F. (2007). *Organizations and organizing: Rational, natural and open system perspectives*. Routledge.

Shults, J. F. (2019). *How UCR stats can make your department look like it is failing, online article published by Lexipol.* https://www.police1.com/chiefs-sheriffs/articles/how-ucr-stats-can-make-your-department-look-like-it-is-failing-vXDHcGXV9G5H9Odi/. Accessed 2 Dec 2021.

Smith, E. L. (2017). *Estimating costs for transitioning to the national incident-based reporting system.* Bureau of Justice Statistics, a Power Point presentation released online at: https://bjs.ojp.gov/sites/g/files/xyckuh236/files/media/document/local_agency_-_estimating_cost_for_transitioning_to_nibrs_01232017.pdf. Accessed 20 Oct 2021.

Strom, K. J., & Smith, E. L. (2017). The future of crime data. *Criminology and Public Policy, 16*(4), 1027–1048.

Tibbitts, C. (1932). Crime. *American Journal of Sociology, 37*, 963–969.

Ventura, S. J. (2018). *The U.S. National Vital Statistics System: Transitioning into the 21st century, 1990–2017*. U.S. Department of Health and Human Services. Hyattsville, Maryland. DHHS Publication No. (PHS) 2018–1338.
Vold, G. B. (1935). The amount and nature of crime. *American Journal of Sociology, 40*, 796–803.
Vold, G. B. (1952). Murder and the penalty of death. *The Annals of the American Academy of Political and Social Science, 284*, 1–7.
Watson, W. M. (2000). Working with the local media: When NIBRS is the news. *Criminal Justice Information Services, 4*, 11–12.
Weber, M. (1946). *Max Weber's essays in sociology*. Oxford Publishing.
Weiss, J., & Davis, M. (2002). Information partnering and the FBI. *Law and Order, 50*, 1.
Wilson, J. Q. (1968). *Varieties of police behavior: The management of law and order in eight communities*. Harvard University Press.

Chapter 14
Beyond Just a Few "Bad Apples": Organizational Understandings of Police Misconduct as Deviant Subcultures

Allison G. Kondrat

Introduction

Law enforcement officers are responsible for the difficult task of enforcing the laws of the land and protecting the peace in their community. While protecting and serving, police are responsible for the lives and liberty of the individuals under their authority and, therefore, undertake a tremendous duty. Opportunity (positive and negative) develops alongside the significant power and authority of the position. Of particular concern, these opportunities open the door for the creation and sustainment of deviance among officers and organizations. Deviance in the workplace is not unique to police organizations. However, the extent of authority and its impact on the lives of civilians exacerbates the seriousness of police deviant subcultures.

This chapter provides a broad definition of deviance and lists common types of deviance among law enforcement officers. Specifically, this chapter examines police misconduct. Aligning with prior literature's examination of police misconduct as a form of deviance, individual characteristics conducive to police misconduct are discussed. While individual characteristics offer some insight into the motivations of officers who commit misconduct, they fail to address how policing, as an organization, creates opportunities for deviant subcultures of misconduct to fester. Using a recent example of extreme misconduct, the importance of organizational and individual characteristics in permitting and/or cultivating deviance subcultures of misconduct is emphasized. Finally, this chapter also discusses some integrated interventions, that previous literature offers.

A. G. Kondrat (✉)
Sam Houston State University, Department of Crimial Justice and Criminology, Huntsville, TX, USA
e-mail: agk017@shsu.edu

D. S. Rudes, J. R. Ingram (eds.), *Using Organizational Theory to Study, Explain, and Understand Criminal Legal Organizations*,
https://doi.org/10.1007/978-3-031-66285-0_14

Deviance and the Individual

Broadly, deviance is thought of as any voluntary behavior, attributes, and/or conditions that violate norms (formal or informal) and/or appear to be, and are held by others, as negative (Cohen, 1966; Heckert & Heckert, 2002; Katz, 1972; Merton, 1966). Deviance acts as an umbrella term for a vast number of situations with differing levels of seriousness. Context becomes increasingly important for determining deviance, as norms act as determinants of deviance (Merton, 1966). Further, while something may be considered deviant, it is not necessarily harmful or impactful to others (e.g., dying one's hair a bright color). However, deviance is more often associated with more negative, extreme violations of norms.

Types of Deviance

Under the umbrella of deviance, existing literature on policing discusses three prominent typologies: corruption, crime, and misconduct. Police corruption occurs when an officer's action/inaction contradicts their duty and/or achieves some sort of unapproved reward (e.g., money or gifts) by an external, corrupting force/person(s) (Porter & Warrender, 2009; Punch, 2000). Often, researchers view police crime as an extension of corruption, where police officers break other laws, such as sexual assault or using illicit substances (Porter & Warrender, 2009; Punch, 2000). The final typology, police misconduct, is at the heart of this chapter's discussion; police misconduct occurs when there is a violation of rules, policies, and/or procedures of police organizations (e.g., use of force or sleeping while on duty). Oftentimes, agencies address and sanction misconduct internally. Again, while deviance and misconduct also occur outside of police officers/organizations, the responsibilities and authority that police officers receive can exacerbate the seriousness of these occurrences (Porter & Warrender, 2009). To be able to handle the intense demands of their profession, officers receive a significant amount of discretion in their decision-making (see Bronitt & Stenning, 2011; Goldstein, 1963). However, sizable discretion (that typically lacks supervision/oversight) can open more opportunities and ability to perpetrate misconduct. Some previous literature explains this use of discretion and power (to commit deviance) as actions of just a "few bad apples."

"Bad Apples"

Existing literature largely focuses on police deviance as an individual phenomenon. Oftentimes, police misconduct is labeled as a problem of "a few bad apples" (see Alpert & MacDonald, 2001; Berkow, 1996; Walker et al., 2000). In this understanding of misconduct, deviance is isolated, individualistic actions/behaviors, and is rejected as aberrant and damaging to the perception of police (see Armacost, 2004). Under this framework, a few bad apples will not spoil the bunch, so the "isolated" actions of a small number of officers responsible for perpetrating police misconduct bring (seemingly) untoward national attention to even the "good apples" (Alpert & MacDonald, 2001; Armacost, 2004; Berkow, 1996; Jain et al., 2022; Walker et al., 2000). In theory, when you remove bad apples, you also remove deviance (Alpert & MacDonald, 2001; Armacost, 2004; Berkow, 1996; Jain et al., 2022; Simpson & Kirk, 2023; Walker et al., 2000). Prior literature also regards officer characteristics as an integral aspect of the "bad apples" argument.

Officer Characteristics Prior literature offers insights concerning the characteristics of officers who have favorable attitudes toward misconduct and officers who commit misconduct. Generally, male officers are more likely to engage in misconduct than their female peers (see Boateng et al., 2023; Brandl et al., 2001; Harris, 2010, 2014; Hickman et al., 2000; Kane & White, 2009; Kish-Gephart et al., 2010; Lersch & Mieczkowski, 1996). Both age and job experience increase the likelihood of engaging in misconduct, whereas younger, less experienced are more likely to engage in misconduct; this is probably due to the challenges of inexperience and limited supervision during this stage of their careers (Kane & White, 2009; Meredith, 1984; McElvain & Kposowa, 2004). However, younger officers with less experience are also likely to interact with the public (as they typically have line/patrol assignments), yet they are concerning more likely to perceive citizen interactions as threatening and use/escalate force (Harris, 2014; McElvain & Kposowa, 2004).

Personality characteristics are also possible predictors of misconduct among police. Traits such as cognitive moral development, idealistic moral philosophies, and high job satisfaction have negative associations with police misconduct (Kish-Gephart et al., 2010). In contrast, officers with relativistic moral philosophies, higher Machiavellianism (i.e., amorality that favors ruthless tactics to achieve personal goals), and/or who perceive their locus of control to be external share stronger associations with misconduct (Kish-Gephart et al., 2010).

While existing literature regularly considers police deviance as the problematic actions of "a few bad apples," some scholars challenge the ascription of police deviance beyond merely individual-level problems. To begin to understand the subculture(s) of policing in organizations, the definitions of organizations and organizational deviance must be clarified, as does the difference between subculture(s) and culture.

Organizations and Organizational Deviance

The word "organization" describes a plethora of phenomena across time, context, and spaces. Organizations may be formal or informal, weak or powerful, and encompass a small or large group of people/ideas (Bittner, 1965). In this application, therefore, organizations will describe the workplaces in which police operate.

Organizational Deviance

Marasi et al. (2018) define workplace deviance as the "voluntary, norm-violating behavior that threatens the well-being of an organization and/or its members" (p. 8). While deviance may be extremely harmful, it does not always have a devastating impact on organizations and their functioning (see Lawrence & Robinson, 2007; Mertens et al., 2016; Vadera et al., 2013); people tend to hold some degree of deviant tendencies and likely perpetrate some (low-level) form of deviance in their workplace (Bennett & Robinson, 2003). While (generally) this may be harmful to the effectiveness of the organization, deviant subcultures exist in a variety of different forms and severities (Bennett et al., 2008; Mertens et al., 2016; Robinson & Bennett, 1995). Early examinations of workplace deviance focus more on the act(s) (e.g., stealing office supplies), but organizational deviance demands more comprehensive examinations of *both* situational (e.g., individual beliefs, actions, and circumstances) and organizational (e.g., culture, hiring, and managerial practices) factors (see Bennett & Robinson, 2003; Berry et al., 2007; James & Jones, 1976).

While workplace deviance may be voluntary and benefit the self-interests of the individual, scholars also critically examine the role (and culpability) of organizations themselves. Organizational structure, then, is thought to possibly contribute to the development and pervasiveness of deviant subcultures (see Bennett, 1998; Bennett & Robinson, 2003; Berry et al., 2007; James & Jones, 1976; Lawrence & Robinson, 2007; Marasi et al., 2018; Pugh, et al., 1968). Particularly, organizations that are increasingly reliant on hierarchical authority structures (i.e., top-down chain of command) and individual participation in decision-making (i.e., discretion) (especially among low-level workers) experience higher rates of deviance within the workplace (Marasi et al., 2018).

Seemingly, this (structural) definition of organizations is ripe for deviance, such as in modern policing, where line and patrol officers often face the least amount of supervision while having an immense amount of discretion. Further, these organizations rely on informal social regulations/norms rather than the direct input/supervision of managers, something apparent in the daily operations of police organizations (Bennett, 1998; Bennett & Robinson, 2003; Berry et al., 2007; James & Jones, 1976; Lawrence & Robinson, 2007; Litzky et al., 2006; Marasi et al., 2018; Načinović Braje et al., 2020). Larger organizations, with fewer hours of in-service training, also have some in the literature as organizational traits influencing the prominence of deviance (Bonanno, 2015; Eitle et al., 2014; Groeneveld, 2005) Despite this, discussions of organizational approaches to deviance should not exclude the role of management. Generally, poor/abusive management relates to employee/subordinate misconduct (see Mitchell & Ambrose, 2007; Tepper et al., 2008). More specific to policing, officers who perceive fair treatment by their supervisor(s) (i.e., organizational justice) are less likely to engage in misconduct and are more likely to treat members of the public fairly and hold deeper commitments to their organization's goals (Wolfe et al., 2018).

The Role of Organizational Culture Organizational culture (i.e., the values and norms, individuals share, as to why an organization operates and behaves the way it does) is the antecedent to subcultures in the organization (Hofstede, 1998; Sackmann, 1992; Schneider et al., 2017). Subcultures may develop independently or align with the broader organizational culture(s) (Lok & Crawford, 1999). Development of subcultures may be a result of an unstable/ambiguous organizational culture or as an outcome of smaller interactions' norms and beliefs (Lok & Crawford, 1999).

Occupational characteristics of policing, like exposure to danger and the legitimization of authority to coerce behavior (e.g., through the use of force), create an organizational culture unique to police (Paoline, 2003). The insular nature of police socialization significantly contributes to the creation and maintenance of the culture of policing (Kleinig, 2001; Paoline, 2003; Westmarland, 2008); officers have to rely on other officers for social support or (physical) backup and respond to (sometimes) dangerous calls for service (Westmarland, 2008). Therefore, an extreme "us-versus-them" mentality develops among police officers, where there is (generally) a distrust for non-officers (Paoline, 2003; Westmarland, 2008). Simultaneously, a deep-rooted (sometimes blind) loyalty to the other members of their occupation develops. These prominent aspects of policing culture are often called the "thin blue line" and the "blue wall of silence."

The Thin Blue Line and the Blue Wall of Silence First coined by a Dallas prosecutor's closing arguments in 1977, the thin blue line broadly represents the role that police have in maintaining social order: "The thin blue line separating civil order from violent anarchy" (Ristroph, 2018). This sense of ever-present danger posed by civilians also serves as reinforcement for group solidarity and loyalty (Paoline, 2003; Ristroph, 2018; Westmarland, 2008). This extreme loyalty to fellow officers and the institution of policing leads officers to be extremely reluctant (or flat-out refuse) to raise issues concerning the organization or fellow officers' misconduct. By refusing to "snitch" on fellow officers, even when the action/behavior is objectively wrong, police officers adhere to the standards of the blue wall of silence (Kleinig, 2001; Skolnick, 2002).

Chin and Wells (1998) define the blue wall of silence as "an unwritten code in many departments which prohibits disclosing perjury or other misconduct by fellow officers, or even testifying truthfully if the facts would implicate the conduct of a fellow officer" (p. 237). They call this cultural norm a "wall," as it is so deeply ingrained in the organization's culture that it's almost entirely impenetrable. Furthermore, for attorneys, judges, internal investigators, media, or other critical viewers of the organization, successfully getting an officer to violate this norm (regardless of the circumstance) is rare (Heck, 1992). Officers who choose to act as whistleblowers to police deviance face extreme ostracism by their peers and serious, sometimes dangerous repercussions (Heck, 1992).

Therefore, a culture of permissiveness concerning subcultures of deviance in policing organizations is established. As previously mentioned, the structure of policing organizations creates opportunities in which subcultures of deviance can thrive: hierarchical chains-of-command where entry/low-level workers are responsible for a plethora of the (largely without supervision) decision-making throughout their daily tasks. Due to the peculiarities of policing as an organization, an insular, severe boundary is set between the police ("us") versus non-police ("them"). While this comradery is important to the social bonds between members of the organization, the norms surrounding the related phenomenon of the blue wall of silence manifest into (at best) a culture of passivity toward subcultures of deviance in police organizations.

These cultural phenomena also link directly to officer misconduct. Armacost (2004) describes this phenomenon where "the same organizational culture that produces extraordinary heroism also facilitates shocking misconduct, sometimes by the very same actors" (p. 44). Wolfe and Piquero (2011) found that officers who have ties to peers who accepted/engaged in minor police misconduct are more likely to hold code-of-silence attitudes. However, officers with stronger senses of organizational justice (i.e., perception of fairness among an organization/managers in distributive and procedural justice matters) are likely to have weaker adoptions of code-of-silence attitudes. Consistent peer supervision is also woven into introductory-level policing positions, like field training officers. Some literature supports this phenomenon of learning misconduct, where field training officers (and the experience(s) they foster) correlate to later allegations of misconduct (Bonanno, 2015; Getty, 2012). Officers who think that their peers embrace code-of-silence attitudes are more likely to hold noble-cause attitudes (i.e., misconduct is acceptable when achieving/pursuing a noble cause), but those who believe that management acts fairly have less favorable attitudes toward noble-cause misconduct (Bonanno, 2015; Wolfe & Piquero, 2011).

More than Just a Workgroup The role of police workgroups/"crews" has recently gained increased scholarly attention. Inherently, these groups are social and voluntary: while officers may be in the same department, on the same shift, or even working on the same assignment, they may not be in the same crew (Barker, 1977; Haarr, 1997; Jain et al., 2022; Lundman, 1979). In a recent study of misconduct among Chicago police workgroups, in 2022, researchers found that despite less than 4% of all Chicago police officers being in workgroups/crews, these crews/crew members represent a disproportionate number of officers receiving misconduct complaints (Jain et al., 2022). Unfortunately, the vast majority of these complaints surround the arrest/mistreatment of people of color, especially Black Americans (Jain et al., 2022). These findings should be disturbing, especially when considering the gross underreporting of police misconduct (Dunn & Caceres, 2010; GBD 2019 Police Violence US Subnational Collaborators, 2021; Gingerich & Oliveros, 2018; Jain et al., 2022; Murphy, 2016; Rozema & Schanzenbach, 2019). Furthermore, even if reports of misconduct are made, cultural norms like the "blue wall of silence" may ensure that these reports are handled discreetly (if at all). While the actions of individuals may drive initial misconduct, organizations (particularly its leaders) have an important role in identifying and stopping misconduct (Hofstede, 1998; Jain et al.,

2022; Sackmann, 1992; Schneider et al., 2017; Zhao & Papachristos, 2020). As a better understanding of the complex nature of deviant subcultures of misconduct among police officers emerges, a recent case serves as an (extreme) example of the importance of both individual and organizational considerations.

Case Study: The Mississippi "Goon Squad"

In Rankin County, Mississippi, in 2023, years of terror by six Rankin County police officers have been uncovered in a Mississippi courtroom. Hunter Elward, Daniel Opdyke (both patrol Deputies in the Rankin County Sheriff's Office (RCSO)), Christian Dedmon (Narcotics Investigator with the RCSO), Joshua Hartfield (Narcotics Investigator with the Richland Police Department in Rankin County), Brett McAlpin (Chief Investigator with the RCSO), and Jeffrey Middleton (Lieutenant with the RCSO) gleefully call themselves (publicly) the "goon squad" due to their willingness to use excessive force and not report it (*USA v. McAlpin.*, 2023). In their guilty plea to federal civil rights violations, the sordid details of terror are finally available to the world.

Case Facts

After a complaint made by a neighbor about a group of Black men staying at a nearby home (citing undisclosed suspicious behavior) with a white female homeowner, McAlpin spoke with Dedmon to take care of the complaint (USA v. McAlpin et al., 2023). Dedmon then contacts the shift of officers, who call themselves the goon squad, and their leader, RSCO Lieutenant Middleton. In a group chat with other members of the goon squad, Dedmon asks if anyone is available for a "mission" and warns others that there is a possibility of cameras on the property (i.e., they should not kick in the door). Then, Dedmon messages that "If we don't see cameras go" (i.e., execute a warrantless search and entry of the property) and that there should be "no bad mugshots" (i.e., excessive force should be used only in places not visible in a mugshot).

After determining that there were no security cameras on the house, the officers took turns trying to kick the back door open, and when it eventually opened, they entered the home (with no warrant or exigent circumstances that would supplement a warrant). Upon entering the home, they saw two Black men, whom they immediately barked orders at and handcuffed. The men immediately comply and while in handcuffs, the men are tased multiple times and kicked in the abdomen. Dedmon demands that the men tell him (and the other officers) where the drugs are, to which the men deny the presence of any drugs. Dedmon then fires his service weapon into the house, asking again about drugs. After again denying the presence of any drugs, the officers drag the men to another part of the house, where they repeatedly call them racial slurs and tase them (again) repeatedly. After officers search the home, they find a sex toy in the bedroom of the homeowner and began to sexually assault the two men with it, threatening to rape them, and begin to undress one of the men, only stopping when the officer saw that the man had defecated himself.

Changing strategies, the officers begin to force the men to involuntarily ingest a multitude of different drinks, threw eggs at the men, force them to shower (to remove evidence of the assault), and continue their assault. They each took turns tasing the men to determine who had the most powerful taser. The officers stole property from the home (including a military dress uniform). Finally, before loading the men into the police vehicles, Dedmon shot his service weapon into the yard. Following suit, Elward removes a bullet from his service weapon, forces the firearm into one of the man's mouth, and fires (but did not discharge a bullet). With the same man, Elward forces the firearm into the man's mouth and shoots the man, shattering his jaw, damaging his tongue, and creating an exit wound in his neck; the man did not receive medical attention but survived after undergoing intensive medical treatment (including the surgical removal of his tongue) (Corpuz, 2023).

Creating a Cover Story

The six police officers decide that they will tell investigators that one of the men consented to a search of his person outside of the house. In their lies, the officers decided that they would claim that there were two bags of methamphetamine in the man's pocket and, when discovered, he fled into the house, leading to a foot chase. They decide to justify the shots fired by claiming that one of the men was willing to do a controlled drug buy over the phone but instead was trying to shoot the officer (a firearm belonging to the Lieutenant, but not registered to him, was offered, but a BB gun used during part of the assault was ultimately used). They dispose of the spent taser cartridges, the clothes of victims, and shell casings and internally submit methamphetamine (previously turned over by a confidential informant) as the baggies of meth.

A History of Misconduct

According to subsequent investigative reports, two of the members of the goon squad have also been in four other (known) violent encounters with Black men since 2019 (Goldberg, 2023a). Tragically, these incidences resulted in the deaths of two men and left one man with permanent wounds after one of the deputies pulled his service weapon's trigger (Goldberg, 2023a). A Chancery Judge had to order the RCSOs to turn over the documents related to these violent encounters to enter them into the public record, as the department repeatedly refused to do so after multiple inquiries (Goldberg, 2023a).

Implications

While an extreme example of police misconduct, the actions of the goon squad serve as important case study in understanding the multidimensionality of police deviant subcultures of misconduct. Members of leadership actively participating, failing to intervene, and encouraging fellow good squad members to remain silent suggest a horrifying integration of misconduct (and racism) into the RCSO.

This failure is additionally noxious when considering that other members of the organization, and its leadership, seem unwilling to consider the possibility of such misconduct. At the highest level, RCSO Sheriff Bryan Bailey's refusal to investigate the incident and simply trusting the officers' word, despite the severity of the allegations should be concerning (see Goldberg, 2023b). Interestingly, Sheriff Bailey is refusing to resign his position after the findings of the Department of Justice Investigations are now public, despite demands from members of the public.

Further, the previously mentioned incidences (made public record only after court orders) uncover a pattern of misconduct that has not been checked. These incidences have been well documented in the RCSO since at least 2004 (Howey et al., 2023). Despite the Rankin County Sheriff sharing his shock and belief that "never in my life did I think it would happen in this department," investigations reveal a "pattern of violence that was neither confined to a small group of deputies nor hidden from department leaders" (Howey et al., 2023). Over 50 people have reported witnessing or experiencing torture from officers of this department, taser logs present a damning picture of practice, and 20 deputies in the department were active members in one or more of these incidences (including an undersheriff and current police chief elsewhere in Mississippi) (Howey et al., 2023). Further, multiple civil suits have been raised (two settled out of court), and over a dozen individuals have bravely confronted Sheriff Bailey and other commanding officers about the system of misconduct.

Therefore, it is unreasonable to believe that these events are isolated (e.g., goon squad members having established code words and strategies for executing these "missions"). The individual officers' depravity cannot be ascribed (immediately) to the organization, but clearly the systems of detecting and punishing misconduct are so absent (or without enforcement) that the misconduct was able to escalate to this degree, seemingly with no prior intervention(s). Additionally, one must consider the racial overtones in these horrific cases. All officers of the goon squad are white men. The known victims of the goon squad are Black men, that faced physical, sexual, psychological, and racial abuse by these officers.

Generally, this tragic story provides an (extreme) example of organizational culture operationalized to protect the "thin blue line" by maintaining the "blue wall of silence." Unfortunately, this incident mirrors a pattern of horrendous misconduct that officers were witness to (even if not an active participant) and subsequently ignored by management. As investigative reports note, almost every incident involving misconduct stems from small/petty drug charges (Howey et al., 2023). As this county has a tumultuous history with substance use, likely a mission to protect the fragile balance "between civil order and violent anarchy" motivates officers to use extreme, expeditious means perceived to be necessary (Ristroph, 2018).

In maintaining this thin blue line, officers, and management are choosing to turn a blind eye, or actively participate, in (tragic) misconduct. Instead of transparent reporting, noting the shortcomings and faults of the department that can be changed, the Department continued to hide information (including undeniable evidence of misconduct) like the taser logs. Moreover, leadership and management continue to feign ignorance of these deviant "workgroup" patterns, even after a decade's worth of concerning misconduct (Howey et al., 2023). Individuals witnessing these atrocious acts of misconduct and failing to oppose their fellow officers/their actions are now in high-ranking positions (including other locations). With the duty to protect *all* members of their community, the ease with which these officers engaged in racial abuse (including calling the men racial slurs and telling the victims that they needed to remain on "their" side of town) also speaks to a vast culture of permissiveness in the organization.

Conclusion

Certainly, misconduct can, and often does, occur individually. However, integrated, organizational examinations may be more appropriate for explaining police misconduct. Inherently, deviant subcultures are dependent on the socializations and norms of an organization. Therefore, accounting for the socialization of neutralization strategies, attitudes/behaviors encouraging deviance, and self-protection tactics (especially when confronting misconduct) is integral (see Kane, 2002; Micucci & Gomme, 2005; Punch, 2000).

Another possible avenue of addressing misconduct is in addressing compassion fatigue. Originally conceptualized and applied in the field of medicine, compassion fatigue is a form of occupational burnout where one's prolonged exposure to traumatic, stressful, or intense scenarios causes frontline workers to develop physical and psychological exhaustion from the demands of their job (Andersen & Papazoglou, 2015; Figley, 2002; Grant et al., 2019; Joinson, 1992; Potter et al., 2010). As a result of experiencing compassion fatigue, cynicism, decreases in empathy, hostility, and dichotomous world views (consistent with that of the thin blue line) heightens and can possibly lead to misconduct (Anshel, 2000; Grant et al., 2019; Hendy et al., 2019). Hendy et al. (2019) suggest that workplace deviance can actually be the result of maladaptive coping to workplace stressors, something easily linked to compassion fatigue, which law enforcement officers experience.

However, to truly address police misconduct as a subculture of deviance, researchers and practitioners must look beyond the mere individual. While a more palatable explanation, literature shows that removing a deviant individual from an organization, including policing, does not remove underlying deviance (see Greve et al., 2010; Sierra-Arévalo & Papachristos, 2021; Zhao & Papachristos, 2020). Mixed findings seem common among studies concerning officer misconduct: some studies find support for misconduct not being a "contagious" phenomenon among routine interactions with their police peers who commit misconduct (see Simpson & Kirk, 2023), yet other studies like Ouellet et al. (2019) show that officer characteristics and social networks influence misconduct rates (i.e., use of force incidences). Whether Schrödinger's cat is in a blue box or a murky barrel of apples, an organization's culture garners consideration and increased scholarly attention. As Gottschalk et al. (2012) highlight, "the distinction of bad apples and systems failure is simplistic and that overlaps are likely to occur such that systems failures can allow or encourage bad apples to thrive" (p. 25).

In continuing to examine the impacts of organizational culture on police misconduct, there must be greater efforts to monitor, address, and sanction misconduct at the organizational level. Fostering and maintaining a climate that uplifts and addresses the well-being of multiple stakeholders is shown to have fewer incidences of misconduct; for police organizations, this can take shape in the form of consistent and proper enforcement of codes of conduct (Bonanno, 2015; Kish-Gephart et al., 2010). Another possible avenue is extending early warning systems (that flag officers at a high risk for misconduct) to include strategies for accountability, rather than focusing solely on the individual act(ions) (Chalfin & Kaplan, 2021). As Sierra-Arévalo and Papachristos (2021) and Simpson and Kirk (2023) note, addressing individual police misconduct is incredibly important and can have meaningful impacts on deviance. Therefore, researchers and practitioners need to integrate approaches that monitor and address misconduct at the individual *and* organizational levels.

As Sierra-Arévalo and Papachristos (2021) argue, longitudinal data (e.g., a five-year time period) on officer behavior can be a part of an extended warning system. This extended monitoring system may be a successful means of integrating both individual and "spillover" (social) effects on the organization (Sierra-Arévalo & Papachristos, 2021). In incapacitating and removing individual, deviant officers, agencies can address the immediacy of the problem and hold space for comprehensive initiation and maintenance of appropriate cultural changes (Sierra-Arévalo & Papachristos, 2021; Simpson & Kirk, 2023). In conjunction with extended early warning systems, Maskály et al. (2020) have introduced a promising assessment tool for police integrity, something that can assess officers' integrity (in an agency) effectively in cross-sectional and longitudinal data.

Another important aspect of changing organizational culture is recruitment: specifically, Kane and White (2009) found that a more diverse police force that has higher levels of educational attainment and professional training is significantly less likely to be separated from the policing profession due to misconduct. Organizations should also be mindful of the importance of flexibility and tailoring recommendations to one's agency: interventions at large agencies (e.g., the New York Police Department) will likely not translate to small agencies (and vice versa).

Acknowledging that there are limits to what police organizations can do to curb misconduct, these recommendations can begin to address the permissiveness and plausible deniability that persists in policing organizations. Protections like qualified immunity create opportunities to shield excessive and unconstitutional force from civil liability (Armacost, 2004; Rozema & Schanzebach, 2019). Additionally, no (official) tracking of this misconduct is available to the public, leaving community members subject to opaque lines of communication and accountability. In the wake of Tamir Rice, Elijah McClain, Tyre Nichols, Atatiana Jefferson, and so many more, the impacts of police misconduct can be fatal and unjust (Murphy, 2016; Potter, 2013; Rozema & Schanzenbach, 2019). Similarly, misconduct can leave lifelong, haunting psychological and physical scars, like the victims of the goon squad. Therefore, the need for police organizations to address and quash deviant subcultures of misconduct is immediate and imperative.

References

Alpert, G. P., & MacDonald, J. M. (2001). Police use of force: An analysis of organizational characteristics. *Justice Quarterly, 18*(2), 393–409.

Andersen, J. P., & Papazoglou, K. (2015). Compassion fatigue and compassion satisfaction among police officers: An understudied topic. *International Journal of Emergency Mental Health and Human Resilience, 17*(3), 661–663.

Anshel, M. H. (2000). A conceptual model and implications for coping with stressful events in police work. *Criminal Justice and Behavior, 27*(3), 375–400.

Armacost, B. E. (2004). Organizational culture and police misconduct. *George Washington Law Review, 72*(3), 453–546.

Barker, T. (1977). Peer group support for police occupational deviance. *Criminology, 15*(3), 353–366.

Bennett, R. J. (1998). Perceived powerlessness as a cause of employee deviance. In R. W. Griffin, A. O'Leary-Kelly, & J. M. Collins (Eds.), *Dysfunctional behavior in organizations: Violent and deviant behavior* (pp. 221–239). Elsevier Science/JAI Press.

Bennett, R. J., & Robinson, S. L. (2003). The past, present, and future of workplace deviance research. In *Organizational behavior: The state of the science* (2nd ed., pp. 247–281). Lawrence Erlbaum Associates Publishers.

Bennett, R. J., Robinson, S. L., Tepper, B. J., Henle, C. A., Lambert, L. S., Giacalone, R. A., & Duffy, M. K. (2008). Organization deviance scale: Abusive supervision and subordinates' organization deviance. *Journal of Applied Psychology, 93*(4), 721–732.

Berkow, M. (1996). Weeding out problem officers. *Police Chief, 63*, 21–29.

Berry, C. M., Ones, D. S., & Sackett, P. R. (2007). Interpersonal deviance, organizational deviance, and their common correlates: A review and meta-analysis. *Journal of Applied Psychology, 92*(2), 410–424.

Bittner, E. (1965). The concept of organization. *Social Research, 32*(3), 239–255.

Boateng, F. D., Pryce, D. K., & Hsieh, M. L. (2023). The criminal police officer: Understanding factors that predict police crime in the United States. *Crime & Delinquency, 69*(9), 1700–1735.

Bonanno, E. R. (2015). *An evidential review of police misconduct: Officer versus organization.* University of Western Ontario Undergraduate Awards, 9. https://ir.lib.uwo.ca/ungradawards_2015/9?utm_source=ir.lib.uwo.ca%2Fungradawards_2015%2F9&utm_medium=PDF&utm_campaign=PDFCoverPages

Brandl, S. G., Stroshine, M. S., & Frank, J. (2001). Who are the complaint-prone officers?: An examination of the relationship between police officers' attributes, arrest activity, assignment, and citizens' complaints about excessive force. *Journal of Criminal Justice, 29*(6), 521–529.

Bronitt, S., & Stenning, P. (2011). Understanding discretion in modern policing. *Criminal Law Journal, 35*(6), 319–332.

Chalfin, A., & Kaplan, J. (2021). How many complaints against police officers can be abated by incapacitating a few "bad apples?". *Criminology & Public Policy, 20*(2), 351–370.
Chin, G. J., & Wells, S. C. (1998). The blue wall of silence as evidence of bias and motive to lie: A new approach to police perjury. *University of Pittsburgh Law Review, 59*(2), 233–300.
Cohen, A. K. (1966). *Deviance and control*. The Free Press.
Corpuz, M. (2023, February 16). Rankin County deputies beat, tortured two Black men, leaving one in the hospital for weeks, lawyers allege. *Mississippi Today.* http://mississippitoday.org/2023/02/15/mississippi-deputies-jenkins-parker/
Dunn, A., & Caceres, P. J. (2010). Constructing a better estimate of police misconduct. *Policy Matters Journal, 7*(2), 10–16.
Eitle, D., D'Alessio, S. J., & Stolzenberg, L. (2014). The effect of organizational and environmental factors on police misconduct. *Police Quarterly, 17*(2), 103–126.
GBD 2019 Police Violence US Subnational Collaborators (2021). Fatal police violence by race and state in the USA, 1980–2019: A network meta-regression. *The Lancet, 398*(10307), 1239–1255.
Figley, C. R. (2002). *Treating compassion fatigue*. Brunner-Routledge.
Getty, R. M. (2012). *Does the apple fall far from the tree?: Police field training officers, their trainees and allegations of misconduct* (Publication no. 3507626) [Doctoral dissertation, University of Texas at Dallas]. ProQuest Dissertations Publishing.
Gingerich, D. W., & Oliveros, V. (2018). Police violence and the underreporting of crime. *Economics and Politics, 30*(1), 78–105.
Goldberg, M. (2023a, March 27). Deputies accused of shoving guns in mouths of 2 Black men. *AP News.* https://apnews.com/article/mississippi-deputies-black-violent-arrests-61acf712b13fc3c77dce76e508fa94c1
Goldberg, M. (2023b, August 6). Racist abuse by Mississippi officers reveals a culture of misconduct, residents say. *AP News.* https://www.usnews.com/news/us/articles/2023-08-06/racist-abuse-by-mississippi-officers-reveals-a-culture-of-misconduct-residents-say
Goldstein, H. (1963). Police discretion: The ideal versus the real. *Public Administration Review, 23*(3), 140–148.
Gottschalk, P., Dean, G., & Glomseth, R. (2012). Police misconduct and crime: Bad apples or systems failure? *Journal of Money Laundering Control, 15*(1), 6–24.
Grant, H. B., Lavery, C. F., & Decarlo, J. (2019). An exploratory study of police officers: Low compassion satisfaction and compassion fatigue. *Frontiers in Psychology, 9*, 2793.
Greve, H. R., Palmer, D., & Pozner, J. E. (2010). Organizations gone wild: The causes, processes, and consequences of organizational misconduct. *The Academy of Management Annals, 4*(1), 53–107.
Groeneveld, R. F. (2005). *Arrest discretion of police officers: The impact of varying organizational structures*. LFB Scholarly Publishing.
Haarr, R. N. (1997). They're making bad name for the department exploring the link between organizational commitment and police occupational deviance in police patrol bureau. *Policing: An International Journal of Police Strategies & Management, 20*(4), 786–812.
Harris, C. J. (2010). Problem officers? Analyzing problem behavior patterns from a large cohort. *Journal of Criminal Justice, 38*(2), 216–225.
Harris, C. J. (2014). The onset of police misconduct. *Policing: An International Journal of Police Strategies & Management, 37*(2), 285–304.
Heck, W. P. (1992). Police who snitch: Deviant actors in a secret society. *Deviant Behavior, 13*(3), 253–270.
Heckert, A., & Heckert, D. M. (2002). A new typology of deviance: Integrating normative and reactivist definitions of deviance. *Deviant Behavior, 23*(5), 449–479.
Hendy, H. M., Can, S. H., & Black, P. (2019). Workplace deviance as a possible "maladaptive coping" behavior displayed in association with workplace stressors. *Deviant Behavior, 40*(7), 791–798.

Hickman, M. J., Piquero, A. R., & Greene, J. R. (2000). Discretion and gender disproportionality in police disciplinary systems. *Policing: An International Journal of Police Strategies & Management, 23*(1), 105–116.

Hofstede, G. (1998). Identifying organizational subcultures: An empirical approach. *Journal of Management Studies, 35*(1), 1–12.

Howey, B., Rosenfield, N., & Today, M. (2023, November 30). How a 'goon squad' of deputies got away with years of brutality. *3 WLBT*. https://www.wlbt.com/2023/11/30/how-goon-squad-deputies-got-away-with-years-brutality/

Jain, A., Sinclair, R., & Papachristos, A. V. (2022). Identifying misconduct-committing officer crews in the Chicago police department. *PLoS One, 17*(5), e0267217.

James, L. R., & Jones, A. P. (1976). Organizational structure: A review of structural dimensions and their conceptual relationships with individual attitudes and behavior. *Organizational Behavior and Human Performance, 16*(1), 74–113.

Joinson, C. (1992). Coping with compassion fatigue. *Nursing, 22*, 116–120.

Kane, R. J. (2002). The social ecology of police misconduct. *Criminology, 40*(4), 867–896.

Kane, R. J., & White, M. D. (2009). Bad cops. *Criminology & Public Policy, 8*(4), 737–769.

Katz, J. (1972). Deviance, charisma, and rule-defined behavior. *Social Problems, 20*(2), 186–202.

Kish-Gephart, J. J., Harrison, D. A., & Treviño, L. K. (2010). Bad apples, bad cases, and bad barrels: Meta-analytic evidence about sources of unethical decisions at work. *Journal of Applied Psychology, 95*(1), 1–31.

Kleinig, J. (2001). The blue wall of silence: An ethical analysis. *International Journal of Applied Philosophy, 15*(1), 1–23.

Lawrence, T. B., & Robinson, S. L. (2007). Ain't misbehavin: Workplace deviance as organizational resistance. *Journal of Management, 33*(3), 378–394.

Lersch, K. M., & Mieczkowski, T. (1996). Who are the problem-prone officers? An analysis of citizen complaints. *American Journal of Police, 15*(3), 23–44.

Litzky, B. E., Eddleston, K. A., & Kidder, D. L. (2006). The good, the bad, and the misguided: How managers inadvertently encourage deviant behaviors. *Academy of Management Perspectives, 20*(1), 91–103.

Lok, P., & Crawford, J. (1999). The relationship between commitment and organizational culture, subculture, leadership style and job satisfaction in organizational change and development. *Leadership & Organization Development Journal, 20*(7), 365–374.

Lundman, R. J. (1979). Police misconduct as organizational deviance. *Law & Policy Quarterly, 1*(1), 81–100.

Marasi, S., Bennett, R. J., & Budden, H. (2018). The structure of an organization: Does it influence workplace deviance and its' dimensions? And to what extent? *Journal of Managerial Issues, 30*(1), 8–27.

Maskály, J., Kutnjak Ivković, S., Haberfeld, M., Donner, C., Chen, T., & Meyers, M. (2020). Assessing the validity of police integrity scale in a comparative context. *Policing and Society, 30*(6), 618–638.

McElvain, J. P., & Kposowa, A. J. (2004). Police officer characteristics and internal affairs investigations for use of force allegations. *Journal of Criminal Justice, 32*(3), 265–279.

Meredith, N. (1984). Attacking the roots of police violence. *Psychology Today*, *18*(5), 20–26.

Mertens, W., Recker, J., Kohlborn, T., & Kummer, T.-F. (2016). A framework for the study of positive deviance in organizations. *Deviant Behavior, 37*(11), 1288–1307.

Merton, R. K. (1966). Social problems and sociological theory. In R. K. Merton & R. Nisbet (Eds.), *Contemporary social problems* (pp. 775–827). Harcourt Brace.

Micucci, A. J., & Gomme, I. M. (2005). American police and subcultural support for the use of excessive force. *Journal of Criminal Justice, 33*(5), 487–500.

Mitchell, M., & Ambrose, M. (2007). Abusive supervision and workplace deviance and the moderating effects of negative reciprocity beliefs. *The Journal of Applied Psychology*, *92*, 1159–1168.

Murphy, T. R. (2016). When numbers lie: The under-reporting of police justifiable homicides. *Berkeley Journal of Criminal Law, 21*(1), 42–94.

Načinović Braje, I., Aleksić, A., & Rašić Jelavić, S. (2020). Blame it on individual or organization environment: What predicts workplace deviance more? *Social Sciences, 9*(6), 99.

Ouellet, M., Hashimi, S., Gravel, J., & Papachristos, A. V. (2019). Network exposure and excessive use of force: Investigating the social transmission of police misconduct. *Criminology & Public Policy, 18*(3), 675–704.

Paoline, E. A. (2003). Taking stock: Toward a richer understanding of police culture. *Journal of Criminal Justice, 31*(3), 199–214.

Porter, L. E., & Warrender, C. (2009). A multivariate model of police deviance: Examining the nature of corruption, crime and misconduct. *Policing and Society, 19*(1), 79–99.

Potter, G. (2013). The history of policing in the United States. *Eastern Kentucky University School of Justice Studies, 1*, 1–16.

Potter, P., Deshields, T., Divanbeigi, J., Berger, J., Cipriano, D., Norris, L., & Olsen, S. (2010). Compassion fatigue and burnout: Prevalence among oncology nurses. *Clinical Journal of Oncology Nursing, 14*, E56–E62.

Prenzler, T. (2009). *Police corruption: Preventing misconduct and maintaining integrity*. CRC Press.

Pugh, D. S., Hickson, D. J., Hinings, C. R., & Turner, C. (1968). Dimensions of organization structure. *Administrative Science Quarterly, 13*, 65–105.

Punch, M. (2000). Police corruption and its prevention. *European Journal on Criminal Policy and Research, 8*(3), 301–324.

Ristroph, A. (2018). The thin blue line from crime to punishment. *The Journal of Criminal Law and Criminology, 108*(2), 305–334.

Robinson, S. L., & Bennett, R. J. (1995). A typology of deviant workplace behaviors: A multidimensional scaling study. *Academy of Management Journal, 38*(2), 555–572.

Rozema, K., & Schanzenbach, M. (2019). Good cop, bad cop: Using civilian allegations to predict police misconduct. *American Economic Journal: Economic Policy, 11*(2), 225–268.

Sackmann, S. A. (1992). Culture and subcultures: An analysis of organizational knowledge. *Administrative Science Quarterly, 37*(1), 140–161.

Schneider, B., González-Romá, V., Ostroff, C., & West, M. A. (2017). Organizational climate and culture: Reflections on the history of the constructs in the *Journal of Applied Psychology*. *Journal of Applied Psychology, 102*(3), 468–482.

Sierra-Arévalo, M., & Papachristos, A. (2021). Bad apples and incredible certitude. *Criminology & Public Policy, 20*(2), 371–381.

Simpson, C. R., & Kirk, D. S. (2023). Is police misconduct contagious? Non-trivial null findings from Dallas, Texas. *Journal of Quantitative Criminology, 39*(2), 425–463.

Skolnick, J. (2002). Corruption and the blue code of silence. *Police Practice and Research, 3*(1), 7–19.

Tepper, B. J., Henle, C. A., Lambert, L. S., Giacalone, R. A., & Duffy, M. K. (2008). Abusive supervision and subordinates' organization deviance. *Journal of Applied Psychology, 93*(4), 721–732.

USA v. McAlpin, Dedmon, Middleton, Elward, Opdyke, No. 3:23-cr-00062-TSL-LGI (S. D. Miss. N. D. July 31, 2023).

Vadera, A. K., Pratt, M. G., & Mishra, P. (2013). Constructive deviance in organizations: Integrating and moving forward. *Journal of Management, 39*(5), 1221–1276.

Walker, S., Alpert, G. P., & Kenney, D. J. (2000). Early warning systems for police: Concept, history, and issues. *Police Quarterly, 3*(2), 132–152.

Westmarland, L. (2008). Police cultures. In T. Newburn (Ed.), *Handbook of Policing* (2nd ed., pp. 253–280). Willan Publishing.

Wolfe, S. E., & Piquero, A. R. (2011). Organizational justice and police misconduct. *Criminal Justice and Behavior, 38*(4), 332–353.

Wolfe, S. E., Rojek, J., Manjarrez, V. M., & Rojek, A. (2018). Why does organizational justice matter? Uncertainty management among law enforcement officers. *Journal of Criminal Justice, 54*, 20–29.

Zhao, L., & Papachristos, A. V. (2020). Network position and police who shoot. *The Annals of the American Academy of Political and Social Science, 687*(1), 89–112.

Chapter 15
Leadership in Law Enforcement

Tyler Houser

Introduction

Executive officers have several different leadership styles, strategies, and behaviors to choose from when navigating the rigors of a law enforcement organization. Depending on the style or strategy used, leaders may significantly impact a range of subordinate and organizational outcomes. For instance, leaders might affect their subordinates' productivity, organizational commitment, mental health, and overall job performance (among several other phenomena) (Schaveling et al., 2017; Andreescu & Vito, 2010; Dick, 2011). Additionally, leaders might shift the culture of a police agency, which, in turn, may significantly affect how police officers operate within that organization (Darroch & Mazerolle, 2012; Santos & Santos, 2020).

Although outdated and almost always ineffective, many police leaders use an authoritative leadership strategy (Jermier & Berkes, 1979). The typical paramilitary design of law enforcement organizations creates a hierarchical structure that suits a leader who leads top-down. However, several disadvantages are commonly associated with authoritative leadership relating to organizational, subordinate, and cultural outcomes. Instead of utilizing an authoritative approach, law enforcement supervisors should look elsewhere to properly lead their subordinates and attain organizational goals. This chapter focuses on three other styles available to police leaders: transformational, transactional, and participative.

Although the transformational, participative, and transactional styles often produce more desirable results than authoritative leadership, a combination of the three styles produces the most optimal outcomes. Law enforcement is an ever-changing field that presents leaders with varying challenges daily (Hoggett et al., 2019; Engel

T. Houser (✉)
George Mason University, Department of Criminology, Law & Society, Fairfax, VA, USA
e-mail: thouser@gmu.edu

D. S. Rudes, J. R. Ingram (eds.), *Using Organizational Theory to Study, Explain, and Understand Criminal Legal Organizations*,
https://doi.org/10.1007/978-3-031-66285-0_15

et al., 2020; Easton, 2018). Leaders will seldomly resolve those challenges utilizing one strategy (at least successfully). Given specific circumstances, leaders must have the ability to intertwine or adopt different leadership styles and specific traits and behaviors to receive the most output from their personnel.

Thus, this chapter presents evidence (using the existing literature) and argues that executives must combine leadership strategies and styles to proficiently meet the organizational demands of a police agency.

This chapter presents a general overview of the four leadership styles commonly found in law enforcement: authoritative, transformational, participative, and transactional. This chapter then reviews literature detailing how each style, a combination of the styles, and specific traits and behaviors affect subordinate, organizational, and cultural outcomes. Finally, this chapter endorses a transformational leadership style with applications of participative and transactional strategies. Ultimately, the approach provides researchers and practitioners a framework to effectively lead in law enforcement.

Overview of Prominent Leadership Styles

Authoritative Leadership

As noted in Jermier and Berkes (1979), the organizational construct of law enforcement agencies is related to Weber's (1947) rational-legal authority. Organizations create rational-legal authority through the implementation of strict rules and procedures meant to obtain organization-wide obedience. The obedience provides the organization with its legitimacy, and subordinates rarely challenge that authority. Individuals within a rational-legal authority organization internalize the rules because they are considered law within the agency. Relating to law enforcement, the chain of command creates an ordered structure for subordinates to follow. If subordinates disobey an order from a superior, they are subjected to punishments or sanctions, creating obedience throughout the chain of command (United Nations, 2011).

If law enforcement agencies attempt to obtain legitimacy through strict obedience, authoritative leaders will provide the organization with the most efficient course of action. The authoritative leader expects (and receives) complete obedience and strict adherence to commands from their subordinates (Schuh & Zhang, 2013). Complete obedience and strict adherence to commands do not allow subordinates to question any decisions or provide input that could positively affect organizational processes and outputs. Subordinates have relatively little autonomy or power, and authoritative leaders possess all the power and control in the organization. In theory, the strict obedience allows police organizations to efficiently respond to emergencies. If organizations create democratic environments (where participation is encouraged), efficiency might be lost. Nonetheless, this chapter illustrates the negative impacts of leaders keeping subordinates at "arm's length" and running their organization in ways that are akin to a dictatorship.

Although not all authoritative leaders are cold or insensitive, many display traits that negatively impact their subordinates and an organization's overall vision. For instance, an authoritative style of leading often instills a sense of distrust and causes a range of psychological issues in subordinates (Chan et al., 2013). By consolidating all the organizational power and not involving subordinates in decision-making, leaders signal to their followers that they are not trusted to influence the organization's processes or goals. The lack of trust may damage the self-esteem and confidence of subordinates, potentially jeopardizing their job performance and the overall effectiveness of an organization.

Transformational Leadership

Instead of solely using subordinates as a means to achieve end goals (like the authoritative approach), humanistic management requires leaders to put their personnel ahead of organizational outcomes, consider their needs and wishes, and, above all, treat them with dignity and respect (Melé, 2016). Leaders can exhibit a more humanistic approach in law enforcement through applications of transformational leadership. Transformational leadership strategies focus on "motivating followers to transcend their own personal goals for the greater good of the organization" (Murphy & Drodge, 2004, p. 2).

Murphy and Drodge (2004) detail that police managers should utilize the "Four I's" to properly display transformational leadership: individualized consideration, idealized influence, inspirational motivation, and intellectual stimulation. Individualized consideration posits that leaders should authentically care for the well-being of their subordinates. Transformational leaders must recognize individual achievements, take time to develop officers, and obtain the necessary resources for each person to carry out their job function (Murphy, 2008; Pearson-Goff & Herrington, 2013). Individualized consideration also helps leaders build interpersonal relationships with their subordinates (Yammarino & Dubinsky, 1994), which is lacking in authoritative environments.

Many transformational leaders use charisma to build idealized influence (Hinkin & Tracey, 1999). According to Weber, charismatic leaders are uniquely equipped to bring about change in an organization because of their "superhuman" and "supernatural" powers to influence their subordinates (Weber, 1947, p. 358). Concepts associated with charisma include emotional expressiveness, self-confidence, self-determination, and separation from internal conflict (Hall & Grant, 2018). By possessing those traits, leaders create a strong moral conviction, causing their subordinates to righteously admire them (and their vision). The idealized influence also allows leaders to build trust, respect, and a perception of fairness with their personnel (Murphy & Drodge, 2004; Can et al., 2017; Yammarino & Dubinsky, 1994).

Most importantly, transformational leaders create a collective vision through inspirational motivation (Murphy & Drodge, 2004; Aarons, 2006; Andreescu & Vito, 2010; Pearson-Goff & Herrington, 2013). The collective vision is the primary driving force for change in an organization. The collective vision includes the overarching goals of the organization and how the organization will achieve those goals. Transformational leaders utilize inspirational motivation by uniting subordinates around a collective vision and demonstrating to subordinates how they fit into and may impact the vision (Murphy & Drodge, 2004). Between emotional bonds, interpersonal relationships, trust, and respect, a transformational leader can easily utilize inspirational motivation for subordinates to buy into the collective vision.

Finally, transformational leaders intellectually stimulate their subordinates, causing them to critically, strategically, and creatively think about how to solve problems that may impact the collective vision of the organization (Murphy & Drodge, 2004; Aarons, 2006; Andreescu & Vito, 2010; Pearson-Goff & Herrington, 2013). The increased intellectual stimulation should yield a more effective problem-solving approach for law enforcement organizations (as all personnel are involved rather than only the leader).

Participative Leadership

Participative leaders are opposites of authoritative leaders. A participative leader creates an environment where employees of all ranks can innovatively and creatively think to better the organization (Steinheider & Wuestewald, 2008). Essentially, participative leadership strategies provide power to subordinates to help create and amend an organization's overall vision (Hassan et al., 2018). Leaders who empower their subordinates listen to their input, allow them to be involved in critical decisions that affect the organization, and allow subordinates to make decisions independently without asking for permission (McGregor, 1957). The participative environment creates free-flowing communication up and down the chain of command, allowing for both management and employees of lower ranks to voice questions, frustrations, and concerns (Shaed, 2018). The increased responsibility stemming from participative environments also provides subordinates with a sense of importance and trust. By allowing subordinates to influence key organizational decisions, they will feel valued by the organization.

A participative work environment also increases the overall productivity of an organization (Shaed, 2018; Hassan et al., 2018; Steinheider & Wuestewald, 2008). Instead of all key ideas, decisions, and actions stemming from one level of the organization, a participative environment allows all employees to think and act, increasing the overall organizational output. Similar to the adage, *two hands are better than one;* leaders can increase the organizational output by delegating and increasing the number of employees working on key tasks. Additionally, Murphy and Drodge (2004) note that intellectual stimulation requires a participative environment. Thus, if a leader does not allow subordinates to provide input for critical organizational processes, challenges, or decisions, subordinates will be far less likely to think innovatively on their own. However, if subordinates can influence policy, they will be far more likely to innovate as they have the power to make a substantial impact on the organization. Ultimately, the newly obtained power given to subordinates will provide them with a sense of purpose and allow them to feel valued by their leaders, creating a variety of positive outcomes.

Transactional Leadership

Compared to the transformational leadership style, a transactional leader is more task-oriented and practical in nature (Aarons, 2006). Where a transformational leader focuses on connecting with and inspiring their subordinates, a transactional leader's primary emphasis is placed on personnel completing tasks efficiently. Thus, the transactional leadership strategy is centered around a give-and-take relationship between the supervisor and their subordinate (Aarons, 2006; Andreescu & Vito, 2010). The supervisor will provide the employee with positive reinforcements and rewards if they complete their job functions appropriately and efficiently. For the subordinate to produce satisfactory work, the transactional leader will create a structure that clearly defines the roles and standards of procedures for personnel (Aarons, 2006; Andreescu & Vito, 2010; Hassan et al., 2018). The clearly defined guidelines provide subordinates with information on expectations and how to earn positive benefits.

However, like the authoritative leader, a transactional leader will be quicker to utilize negative reinforcement, criticism, and negative feedback when performance suffers (Aarons, 2006; Andreescu & Vito, 2010; Hassan et al., 2018). Because a transactional leader's priority is task completion, they will be less likely to coach or discipline subordinates in a positive manner. Thus, it is less likely that a transactional leader will build the emotional bonds that transformational leaders rely on to carry out an organization's goals. Nevertheless, through appropriate uses of rewards and reinforcements, leaders can improve organizational output using transactional leadership strategies.

Leadership and Impacts on Subordinates

Authoritative Leadership

As previously mentioned, many leaders in law enforcement still employ an authoritative strategy when leading their subordinates. However, there are several disadvantages associated with consolidating power at the top of the chain of command. For instance, Jermier and Berkes (1979) and Bruns and Shuman (1988) utilized surveys of 158 and 365 police officers to understand how leaders affect subordinates. The authors found that authoritative leaders who have poor interpersonal skills are highly directive and only offer routine tasks to their subordinates were more likely to have officers with lower job satisfaction and organizational commitment levels. Those with higher levels of organizational commitment are more likely to perform their job functions more effectively than those with lower levels of organizational commitment (Kehoe & Wright, 2013). Additionally, it is essential that police officers are satisfied with their job. Prior research illustrates that those with higher job satisfaction levels in complex jobs (e.g., policing) are more likely to have a higher performance rating than those with lower satisfaction levels (Judge et al., 2001). Thus, authoritative leaders often cause poor work performance due to their subordinates' lack of commitment to and satisfaction with the organization.

Authoritative leaders also create environments that allow ethical issues to grow. Zheng et al. (2021) surveyed 522 police personnel to determine how authoritative leaders affect their confidence to question unethical issues in their organization. The results indicate that subordinates who work for an authoritative leader are less likely to feel comfortable speaking out against unethical practices. Authoritative leaders are less likely to allow input in decision-making, creating uncertainty for subordinates. Thus, if police officers feel they cannot speak up, they most likely will not speak up when agencies act unethically, compounding issues.

Furthermore, authoritative leadership styles adversely affect the emotional well-being of subordinates. For instance, in testing how authoritative practices affect subordinates outside of law enforcement, Chan et al. (2013) surveyed 1372 employees and their leaders at a manufacturing firm in China. The results illustrated that subordinates are more likely to feel disrespected, devalued, and demoralized when working for an authoritative leader. Similarly, Karakitapoglu-Aygün et al. (2020) surveyed 409 subordinates and 72 leaders of varying organizations in Turkey to determine the negative effects of an authoritative leadership style. The results indicated that authoritative leadership strategies cause adverse effects on subordinates' psychological health and willingness to innovatively perform. Additionally, subordinates under an authoritative leader are more likely to have the following negative emotions: fear, anger, distrust, and anxiety.

Research also suggests that authoritative leaders may resort to cruel practices to force subordinates to follow their commands. Karakitapoglu-Aygün and Gumusluoglu (2013) interviewed 31 subordinates and leaders from various organizations in Turkey. Their results illustrate that authoritative leaders will often utilize aggression, threats, and coercion to make their subordinates obey rules and commands. The participants noted that they displayed strong work ethics because of their leaders' aggression, threats, and other possible negative consequences and not because their leaders inspired them. Similarly, Einarsen et al. (2007) show that authoritative leaders often achieve their goals at the cost of their subordinates, utilizing humiliation, manipulation, and other negative concepts to force their subordinates to work harder.

Participative Leadership

As previously mentioned, the opposite of an authoritative leader is a manager who creates a participative environment. Several advantages stem from the power given to subordinates to influence organizational processes and goals. For example, Steinheider and Wuestewald (2008) examined how a shared leadership initiative impacted various subordinate outcomes at a police agency through pre- and post-survey data (over 18 months). The agency created a leadership team consisting of 12 individuals that represented the labor union, management, and most agency ranks. The team's main goal was to create an inclusive environment where all employees had a voice and were involved in the organization's critical decisions. The results indicated that police officers felt their work conditions dramatically improved, their organizational commitment increased, and they held higher perceptions of their executive officers after the study period.

The leadership team also yielded other positive outcomes. Organizational processes and policies were more predictable and transparent, turnover was lower, and morale was improved (Steinheider & Wuestewald, 2008). Additionally, police officers felt more empowered to participate in agency decisions because management took their input seriously. The officers' productivity also improved as they were more motivated to be proactive in discretionary time. Officers were more likely to engage in community-oriented policing, make more arrests, issue more citations, and conduct more field interviews. The authors also noted that citizen satisfaction levels with police services improved, indicating that officers were more efficiently and appropriately carrying out their job functions.

In addition to the findings relating to authoritative leadership, Jermier and Berkes (1979) and Bruns and Shuman (1988) found positive effects stemming from participative environments in their policing studies. Both studies found that officers favor a participative leader compared to an authoritative leader. Jermier and Berkes (1979) found that participative leaders had subordinates with higher organizational commitment and job satisfaction levels. Bruns and Shuman (1988) found that productivity significantly increased under a participative leader. Thus, allowing subordinates to contribute to critical decisions increases organizational commitment, providing employees with a stake in their agency.

Transformational Leadership

Like participative environments, the existing literature suggests that transformational leadership styles also produce positive outcomes and should be prioritized over authoritative practices. Dobby et al. (2004) surveyed 1066 England and Wales police officers to determine how leadership affects their organizational commitment, mental health, and job satisfaction. The results demonstrated that transformational leaders were more likely to have subordinates with better psychological health, and non-transformational leaders led to poorer psychological health in subordinates. Leaders who displayed transformational traits also predicted higher levels of job satisfaction and organizational commitment in their subordinates. Finally, motivation to exceed job expectations improved under transformational leaders.

Similarly, Adebayo (2005) surveyed 184 police officers in Nigeria and found that transformational leadership was positively associated with subordinates' motivation to exceed job requirements. Additionally, Morreale (2002) and Sarver (2008) surveyed 177 patrol officers in New England and 161 police chiefs in Texas. Like the previous studies, their results also indicated that transformational leaders were more successful in improving the work motivation of subordinates and inspiring them to "go the extra mile."

Transactional Leadership

In addition to participative and transformational leadership styles, research also suggests that transactional leadership strategies can be effective. In testing how leadership affects the productivity of patrol officers, Johnson (2006) surveyed 320 patrol officers and 79 patrol supervisors to determine how specific behaviors can motivate officers to issue more citations and enforce more DUIs. The productivity of police officers seemed to hinge on appropriate uses of transactional leadership. The availability of positive rewards predicted more citations and DUI enforcement. Thus, if leaders appropriately reward task accomplishments, they can expect greater productivity from their officers.

Additionally, important to transactional leadership, the study revealed that leaders must clearly communicate their expectations to patrol officers regarding traffic enforcement (Johnson, 2006). Patrol officers need to understand that traffic enforcement is a priority and why it is a priority for them to be more motivated to carry out the required tasks. By communicating expectations and explaining why traffic enforcement is essential, leaders were able to define the roles of their police officers clearly. Similarly, MacDonald (1986) interviewed and surveyed Canadian police officers. Like Johnson (2006), the findings demonstrated the importance of setting clear roles for subordinates, communicating expectations, and explaining why various job functions are essential.

Brewer et al. (1994) utilized observations of 20 police sergeants. The results indicated that as sergeants spent more time monitoring the performance of their subordinates, the overall performance of their unit increased. Although the sergeants were not micromanaging their subordinates, they monitored their officers to ensure that they carried out their job functions efficiently and appropriately to produce desirable results. Interestingly, following the successful completion of job tasks, police sergeants who utilized neutral feedback or rewards/consequences predicted higher performance. Thus, significant positive rewards were not required to use transactional leadership effectively. Simple messages of encouragement and direct or indirect feedback were enough to motivate officers.

Finally, Johnson (2015) utilized survey data from 292 police officers who had been out of the academy for one year in Phoenix, Arizona. The results demonstrated that patrol work is not "black and white," creating difficulties for officers to understand if they are successfully carrying out their job functions. Again, using transactional strategies, leaders can inform subordinates on the expectations of their performance by explicitly stating the rules and policies, providing immediate feedback, and offering informal rewards after carrying out tasks efficiently and appropriately (Johnson, 2008). Thus, for new patrol officers, transactional leadership might prove vital.

Combining Leadership Styles and Strategies

Leaders within the field of law enforcement confront a range of challenges on a daily basis. Although the three non-authoritative leadership styles produce positive results, they may not always be successful in varying situations. Thus, this chapter argues for a combination of styles to fully equip leaders with the proper skills needed to lead in law enforcement in the twenty-first century.

Although the previous sections primarily concentrated on one leadership strategy, Schaveling et al. (2017) demonstrate that leaders must possess multiple styles to be successful. In a survey of 134 participants, the authors examined how charismatic, empowering, and transactional leadership traits improve the performance of police units. The results indicate that combining the three leadership styles significantly and positively affects how units perform; however, the strategies do not necessarily succeed independently. The authors argue that police leadership does not operate in a "one size fits all" vacuum, indicating that leaders must employ different strategies in different circumstances to receive the most out of their subordinates.

Like Schaveling et al. (2017), Andreescu and Vito (2010) examined multiple leadership strategies and whether police officers were more likely to prefer a transformational, transactional, or laissez-faire leadership style through a survey of 126 police managers. The results illustrated that most participants favored leaders who utilized a transformational leadership style compared to a transactional or laissez-faire style. However, the participants admitted that leaders must be able to maintain order within the organization and set clear rules and roles for subordinates. Thus, despite preferring transformational leadership styles, the participants revealed other strategies are also important to effectively lead a law enforcement organization (i.e., transactional).

In a survey of 670 law enforcement personnel at a county police force in the UK, Dick (2011) examined which factors were most likely to increase police officers' organizational commitment. Dick (2011) found that successful leaders allow subordinates to participate in critical decisions, create supportive environments that focus on learning rather than punishment (i.e., positive coaching), and demonstrate clear and consistent communication about one's job performance and role. Thus, the author found that all three strategies are critical to effective leadership.

Furthermore, in studying a combination of the three leadership strategies, Hassan et al. (2018) examined how empowering leadership can influence an organization's overall performance through a survey of hundreds of law enforcement personnel in Ohio. The authors described empowering leadership as listening to input from subordinates, allowing subordinates to make decisions, and allowing subordinates to carry out tasks without asking for permission (similar to participative leadership). Their empowering leadership approach also contains transactional and transformational leadership properties, including coaching subordinates, rewarding good work, and providing necessary information and tools to carry out job functions. The results illustrated that empowering leadership improved the overall job performance of police officers and the overall performance of police units.

Similarly, Can et al. (2017) surveyed 152 law enforcement personnel to understand the impact that varying leadership styles have on the psychological well-being of police officers. Can et al. (2017) created a leadership scale, which included 20 items that measure the following three concepts: clear and consistent communication, fairness and honesty, and training and cooperation. Psychological well-being was measured through self-esteem, perceived police social support, and romantic partner conflict. Can et al. (2017) found that their leadership scale was able to explain the variance in the three measures of psychological well-being. Leaders must be fair and honest to create a trusting relationship with subordinates. Leaders must utilize clear and consistent communication to allow subordinates to understand job functions. Finally, leaders must allow subordinates to influence the vision of the organization through participative management. Thus, all three leadership strategies were apparent in increasing the mental health of police officers.

Other Traits and Behaviors of Effective Leaders

Although the three presented leadership styles provide law enforcement supervisors with ample flexibility in leading their personnel, supervisors must understand how other traits and behaviors also influence subordinate performance. For instance, Pearson-Goff and Herrington (2013) analyzed 66 studies to understand the traits and activities of effective police leaders. The results illustrated that leaders must be effective communicators, honest, and show integrity to build interpersonal relationships with personnel. Leaders should model appropriate behavior for their subordinates to ensure the agency acts in an ethical manner. Leaders must also establish legitimacy, or they will have difficulties in making their personnel respect their authority. Additionally, effective leaders tend to be problem-oriented as they can critically, creatively, and strategically think to accomplish goals and improve agency outcomes.

The review also presented results for different leadership traits and behaviors for police supervisors at all levels (frontline, middle managers, and executive managers) (Pearson-Goff & Herrington, 2013). Executive officers should focus on transformational and participative leadership strategies to create a vision for the organization and allow all subordinates to provide input on how to achieve that vision. Middle managers must possess the ability to provide administrative and logistical support for the organization. Finally, frontline supervisors should focus on leading by example, supervising and training subordinates, and evaluating the performance of their subordinates. Similarly, Hawkins and Dulewicz (2007) also found that leadership strategies should differ depending on the rank and job responsibilities of police personnel.

Schafer (2010) and Garner (2018) surveyed police chiefs and leaders to understand which traits and behaviors are critical to lead in law enforcement. Like Pearson-Goff and Herrington (2013), both studies found that police chiefs should possess integrity and honesty to build trust with their subordinates and model proper behavior on- and off-duty. Garner's (2018) results also demonstrate that supervisors should possess humility, patience, accountability, and maturity to lead effectively. Furthermore, similar to transformational leadership, both Schafer (2010) and Garner (2018) found that leaders must put the agency's goals ahead of their own and create a vision to help accomplish those goals. The studies also revealed that leaders should have an open-door policy, be open to advice, criticism, and new ideas from subordinates, and allow subordinates to aid in decision-making (like participative management).

Another emergent theme in Schafer (2010) and Garner's (2018) studies was the concept of micromanagement. Similar to authoritative leadership, micromanagers overly control and supervise their subordinates to ensure tasks are completed to their liking (Serrat, 2017). Micromanaged subordinates do not have the freedom to carry out tasks independently, and their leader requires permission for all tasks to be completed. Like authoritative leadership, micromanagement slows down the organizational output and creates attitudes of distrust and disrespect in subordinates. Leaders should avoid micromanaging to allow personnel to accomplish routine tasks without asking for permission and to help speed up the organizational output of the agency (while also increasing job satisfaction in employees).

Additionally, Schafer (2010) and Garner (2018) found that supervisors must refrain from playing politics when making decisions. Leaders must base all decisions on what is best for the agency and not on personal relationships or how agency outsiders view them. The authors also noted that supervisors must possess sufficient communication skills to ensure requirements are fully understood by all personnel, to clearly explain their decisions, and to build interpersonal relationships with their officers. Finally, the participants noted that leaders who have a poor work ethic often struggle to instill a stronger work ethic in their personnel. Thus, leaders must lead by example.

Engel (2000) derived data from the Project on Policing Neighborhoods to examine how specific leadership behaviors affect subordinate outcomes. The four specific leadership tactics of interest were traditional, innovative, supportive, and active. Engel (2000) found that the active leadership style was most likely to influence subordinate behavior. Active supervisors spend more time in the field with their subordinates than other leader types and set an example for the work and roles of their subordinates. The findings also suggest that transformational leaders might struggle to change their subordinates' behavior if they are not active. Thus, transformational leaders may have to model their vision in the field to be effective.

Interestingly, Engel (2000) found that having an active supervisor could be considered a double-edged sword. The results demonstrated that active supervisors were more likely to have patrol officers utilize force. The author theorized that active supervisors might create environments where aggressive tactics are permitted. However, the findings also highlighted that subordinates with active supervisors are more likely to engage in police-initiated activities (e.g., problem-oriented policing and community-oriented policing) rather than just responding to calls. Thus, officers under an active supervisor will be more likely to find themselves in circumstances where they must use force. Future research should further examine the role active leaders have on subordinates' policing activities and their use of force.

Finally, prior research has also explored qualities and steps that can make a leader more effective. Krimmel and Lindenmuth (2001) surveyed 205 municipal managers to understand how education, training, and the promotional process affect the likelihood that one is an effective leader in law enforcement. The results demonstrated that supervisors are more likely to be more effective if they are college-educated, have participated in leadership education and training, and were promoted from within the organization. Taken together, just as leaders need to rely on varying leadership styles to be effective, they must also possess various other traits and behaviors to successfully lead within a law enforcement organization. Table 15.1 provides a brief overview of the successful leadership strategies and traits/behaviors discussed.

Leadership and Culture

A law enforcement organization's culture is dependent on those in power within the agency. Several studies have shown that police culture can significantly influence how officers perform their job tasks and behave while on duty (both positively and negatively) (e.g., Terrill et al., 2003; Paoline & Terrill, 2005; Paoline, 2003; Worden, 1995). Although much literature has examined police culture, less often do scholars assess the influence leadership has on an organization's culture. The available evidence suggests that leadership is important in creating, maintaining, and changing the culture of a law enforcement organization. Thus, positive or negative police culture often stops and ends with those in management positions.

For instance, to make large-scale changes to the culture of law enforcement organizations, Santos and Santos (2020) stress the importance of executive officers. For widespread shifts to be implemented, executive officers must be fully engaged and committed to creating an environment where culture change can thrive. If leaders stray from their vision in their actions or words, it will become exponentially more difficult for cultural changes to survive. Santos and Santos (2020) also demonstrate that culture change will meet resistance at each level of a police organization. Thus, the executive leader should continually stress the importance of adopting the

Table 15.1 Overview of leadership styles and successful traits/behaviors

Style and traits/behaviors	Description
Authoritative leadership	Expects strict obedience, little power given to subordinates, and many authoritative leaders display negative traits
Transformational leadership	Individualized consideration, idealized influence, inspirational motivation, and intellectual stimulation
Participative leadership	Free-flowing communication up and down the chain of command, all contribute to decision-making, and subordinate empowerment
Transactional leadership	Task-oriented, rewards are contingent on job accomplishment, and provides a structure for subordinates to understand and carry out duties
Successful traits	Humility, accountability, integrity, patience, honesty, selflessness, strong communication skills, and college-educated
Successful behaviors	Active modeling, refraining from playing politics, avoiding micromanagement, strong work ethic, problem-oriented, creating a supportive environment, properly providing feedback, monitoring performance (but not micromanaging), attending leadership education/training programs, and being promoted from within the organization

changes (through their collective vision) and explain why change must occur at all rank levels. In addition to the continual championing of their organizational vision, leaders must also hold personnel accountable if they do not change with the vision and culture. By having a collective vision and holding the entire organization accountable, leaders will be equipped to make seismic culture changes in law enforcement organizations.

The available empirical evidence also demonstrates the importance of leadership in affecting police culture. Aston et al. (2019) examined how police leadership affected cultural change surrounding the use of stop and frisk in Scotland. The results demonstrated that police officers are less likely to view cultural shifts (reducing the use of stop and frisk) in a fair and just way if management strictly enforces the changes and provides no explanations for the changes. Leaders must create open dialogue and clear communication to allow personnel to express their views and opinions. By creating open communication up and down the chain of command, officers will be more likely to believe that their superiors take their input seriously and authentically care for their opinions/concerns. The open dialogue will also allow subordinates to fully understand why culture change is necessary and how the organization plans to amend policies. Thus, until subordinates feel that culture shifts are fair and just and believe their supervisors respect and appreciate their input, leaders will face difficulties instituting cultural change organization-wide.

Relatedly, Darroch and Mazerolle (2012) utilized surveys of 286 New Zealand police officers (in addition to 30 interviews) to determine which factors are more likely to influence a police agency into changing its culture and adopting intelligence-led policing (rather than continuing reactive policing). The results demonstrated that the agencies most likely to adopt intelligence-led policing strategies were more likely to employ transformational leaders, allow for a participative environment, and successfully utilize specific transactional leadership behaviors.

Similar to Darroch and Mazerolle (2012), Koper et al. (2014) conducted interviews, focus groups, surveys, and field observations at four large police agencies to understand the difficulties of new technological implementation. The findings demonstrate that culture significantly influences the implementation of new technologies. For example, if an agency's culture focuses on traditional policing (i.e., reactive policing), a new crime analysis technology is unlikely to make a significant, positive impact on the agency. However, if a leader creates a vision of proactive policing, it is more likely that subordinates will be motivated and inspired to adopt new technologies. Additionally, the authors found that many of the new technologies directly (and almost solely) affect patrol officers (i.e., license plate readers, record management systems, and body cameras). However, patrol officers often lack a voice in how the technologies are designed, used, and adopted. A participative leadership environment would allow affected personnel to test new technologies, provide input and feedback, and provide suggestions for the best applications of the new technologies (McGregor, 1957; Steinheider & Wuestewald, 2008; Hassan et al., 2018).

Finally, Eterno et al. (2021) assessed how leadership affected cultural change surrounding CompStat in New York City. The authors surveyed 1962 retired police officers (of all ranks) of the New York City Police Department (NYPD) to examine CompStat's effects on policing. When the NYPD first implemented CompStat, leadership was able to significantly and positively affect the agency's policing. Leaders (at the time) fully bought into using the technology to improve how the agency operated. The leaders created a vision of more efficient and appropriate policing, and CompStat was the means to accomplish those goals. However, when those leaders left the agency, new management solely focused on meeting numerical goals and not improving the overall effectiveness of their officers, leading to adverse impacts on subordinates. Additionally, not only did the culture change negatively affect lower-level officers, but it also led to adverse outcomes for the public (through over-policing). Thus, just as leadership can influence an organization's personnel, it can also affect an agency's culture depending on the strategies utilized at the top of the chain of command.

The Successful Police Leader

Despite the ill effects of authoritative leadership, many police executives still wield the strategy in their organization (Jermier & Berkes, 1979; Bruns & Shuman, 1988). Instead, police leaders should utilize a more humanistic approach, focusing on transformational leadership with applications of participative and transactional strategies. Although transformational, participative, and transactional leadership strategies were successful on their own, the literature suggests that a combination of the styles produces the most optimal results. Because policing is an ever-changing field that presents new challenges daily, managers must be flexible in their leadership habits. By applying transformational, participative, and transactional styles correctly (among the other-mentioned traits and behaviors), leaders can navigate the many issues they face in law enforcement.

Based on the literature, leaders should begin with a transformational leadership style. Transformational leadership will create a collective vision for an organization's goals (Murphy & Drodge, 2004). The transformational style also provides leaders with the means to motivate subordinates to buy into the collective vision. The leader will utilize charisma, individualized consideration, and idealized influence to build interpersonal bonds with their subordinates. The interpersonal bonds afford the leader capital with their personnel, making the buy-in process easier. The transformational approach will also raise the motivation levels of their subordinates, allowing for more production toward achieving the collective vision (Dobby et al., 2004; Adebayo, 2005; Morreale, 2002; Sarver, 2008).

Once subordinates buy into the collective vision, leaders should then utilize a participative approach. A participative environment enables subordinates to critique or supplement the collective vision (Steinheider & Wuestewald, 2008). By utilizing a participative style, leaders will receive input from all organizational personnel to ensure the collective vision is feasible, practical, and successful. Additionally, the participative environment provides leaders with alternative perspectives that they might have neglected, leading to a more complete vision (Schafer, 2010; Garner, 2018).

After creating the collective vision and allowing subordinates to influence it, leaders should then utilize transactional leadership to hold their personnel accountable and further motivate them to succeed. However, leaders should not become too reliant on transactional leadership. The literature suggests that subordinates' organizational commitment and job satisfaction levels can suffer when leaders become obsessed with performance-management strategies (Eterno et al., 2021). Thus, leaders should utilize transactional leadership narrowly to keep personnel motivated (e.g., Johnson's (2006) research relating to traffic enforcement).

In addition to combining transformational, participative, and transactional strategies, leaders must also realize that other traits, behaviors, and tools will impact their likelihood of success. For instance, leaders could adopt an active leadership strategy to properly model the correct behavior for their officers (Engel, 2000). By displaying an active leadership style, leaders provide subordinates with a framework to carry out their job functions and meet the collective vision. Additionally, many of the traits and behaviors listed in the literature (e.g., honesty, integrity, work ethic, communication skills) provide leaders with opportunities to further build relationships with their subordinates and motivate them to carry out the collective vision (Schafer, 2010; Garner, 2018; Pearson-Goff & Herrington, 2013).

It is also important to note that not all individuals possess innate abilities to lead in law enforcement. Agencies can better prepare their personnel for leadership roles by requiring them to complete college credits or training prior to starting a management position (Krimmel & Lindenmuth, 2001). College education provides individuals with opportunities to enhance their communication skills, foster professional development, and increase exposure to varying perspectives. Leadership programs like the Federal Bureau of Investigation's National Academy provide law enforcement officers with education and real-world training to hone successful leadership strategies relevant to policing (Federal Bureau of Investigation, n.d.). Agencies might also find success by promoting from within their organization. Promoting from within creates more trust, respect, and interpersonal relationships between supervisors and subordinates, leading to fewer challenges in implementing organizational changes (Krimmel & Lindenmuth, 2001). Any of those steps will help leaders engage in transformational, participative, and transactional leadership.

Despite possessing the abilities mentioned in this chapter, many leaders often fail to create real change within an organization. As mentioned in Santos and Santos (2020), cultural change will be met with resistance at each level of the chain of command. Leaders must regularly create environments where the new culture can take root and sustain, and the existing culture can filter out of the organization's processes. Thus, leaders must continually champion their collective vision, promote participative working environments, and reward good work completed by subordinates. If leaders stray from their new initiatives, it will become increasingly more difficult to influence the trajectory of the organization and will allow for negative processes to resurface.

Future Research

Many have offered new research and policy directions to improve policing in the twenty-first century. Ranging from defunding the police to mandating body-worn cameras, researchers, practitioners, and advocates have continued to develop strategies to curb corrupt behavior and improve accountability. However, few have offered directions that start from within the organizational structure of police agencies. Although technological advances and accountability efforts to improve policing are valuable, researchers, practitioners, and advocates must not neglect specific organizational features that influence law enforcement capabilities.

This chapter illustrates that leaders who increase organizational commitment and work satisfaction in subordinates are predictive of higher citizen satisfaction levels (Steinheider & Wuestewald, 2008). The existing literature also demonstrates that leaders are instrumental in changing police culture, including reducing fatal force incidents (Wu, 2020). Is that not a priority of many defund the police movements? Thus, instead of attempting to "reinvent the wheel," future research and practitioners should shift their focus toward improving the organizational component of leadership in law enforcement agencies.

Future research should also explore how leaders of varying demographics influence organizational outcomes. For instance, Wu (2020) utilized the Washington Post Fatal Force database and examined how a police chief's race is associated with fatal police shootings. The findings demonstrate that agencies that employ Black police chiefs are less likely to utilize deadly force than agencies that employ White police chiefs. Although Wu (2020) cannot explain why fatal killings are less likely under Black police chiefs, the author argues that Black chiefs might create a different culture for their agency. For example, Black police chiefs might emphasize de-escalation, take brutality cases more seriously, or create a stricter adherence to policies and procedures than White police chiefs.

Relatedly, Huber and Gunderson (2023) examined the impact gender has on leadership outcomes. The authors found that female police chiefs are more likely to be perceived as effective in addressing gender-related crime (e.g., domestic violence), corruption and police brutality, and increasing community partnerships. The study also revealed that communities are more likely to provide more support to female police chiefs versus male police chiefs. Given the distinctions between Black and White and male and female leaders in law enforcement, future research should explore why leaders of different demographics might be more (or less) effective. A further understanding of the demographic effects would yield insight into how all leaders can improve their skills and abilities.

Future research should also explore how law enforcement agencies can better prepare their leaders to step into the role. Although Krimmel and Lindenmuth (2001) illustrated the effects of college education, prior training, and promoting from within, future research needs to further explore how individuals can become better leaders. By further understanding how to improve leadership capabilities, law enforcement agencies across the country (and the world) can implement policies and programs to improve their executive, middle, and frontline leaders.

Conclusion

The existing literature demonstrates the importance of leadership in law enforcement. Leaders can influence a range of subordinate and organizational outcomes, including organizational commitment, job satisfaction, and police culture. However, the literature revealed that leadership styles differ in their effectiveness. Police leaders should distance themselves from authoritative practices and focus more on humanistic strategies, primarily found in transformational leadership, while including aspects of participative and transactional styles.

Although the three styles can be effective, leaders must not solely rely on one strategy to successfully navigate their way through the perils of law enforcement. Just because one strategy worked in one circumstance, it does not mean that it will succeed in all other situations. Thus, a combination of strategies provides leaders with the greatest likelihood of success in varying environments. Ultimately, by focusing on appropriate uses of transformational, participative, and transactional leadership, leaders can produce positive subordinate outcomes, cultural shifts, and an overall more effective law enforcement organization.

References

Aarons, G. A. (2006). Transformational and transactional leadership: Association with attitudes toward evidence-based practice. *Psychiatric Services, 57*(8), 1162–1129. https://doi.org/10.1176/appi.ps.57.8.1162

Adebayo, D. (2005). Perceived workplace fairness, transformational leadership and motivations in the Nigeria police: Implications for change. *International Journal of Police Science and Management, 7*(2), 110–122.

Andreescu, V., & Vito, G. F. (2010). An exploratory study on ideal leadership behavior: The opinions of American police managers. *International Journal of Police Science & Management, 12*(4), 567–583. https://doi.org/10.1350/ijps.2010.12.4.207

Aston, E., Murray, K., & O'Neill, M. (2019). Achieving cultural change through organizational justice: The case of stop and search in Scotland. *Criminology & Criminal Justice, 21*(1), 40–56. https://doi.org/10.1177/1748895819839751

Brewer, N., Wilson, C., & Beck, K. (1994). Supervisory behavior and team performance amongst police patrol sergeants. *Journal of Occupational and Organizational Psychology, 67*(1), 69–78. https://doi.org/10.1111/j.2044-8325.1994.tb00550.x

Bruns, G. H., & Shuman, I. G. (1988). Police managers' perception of organizational leadership styles. *Public Personnel Management, 17*(2), 145–157. https://doi.org/10.1177/009102608801700205

Can, S. H., Hendy, H. M., & Can, M. B. E. (2017). A pilot study to develop the police transformational leadership scale (PTLS) and examine its associations with psychosocial well-being of officers. *Journal of Police and Criminal Psychology, 32*(2), 105–113. https://doi.org/10.1007/s11896-016-9204-y

Chan, C. S. H., Huang, X., Snape, E., & Lam, C. K. (2013). The Janus face of paternalistic leaders: Authoritarianism, benevolence, subordinates' organizational-based self-esteem, and performance. *Journal of Organizational Behavior, 34*(1), 108–128. https://doi.org/10.1002/job.1797

Darroch, S., & Mazerolle, L. (2012). Intelligence-led policing: A comparative analysis of organizational factors influencing innovation uptake. *Police Quarterly, 16*(1), 3–37. https://doi.org/10.1177/1098611112467411

Dick, G. P. M. (2011). The influence of managerial and job variables on organizational commitment in the police. *Public Administration, 89*(2), 557–576. https://doi.org/10.1111/j.1467-9299.2010.01874.x

Dobby, J., Anscombe, J., & Tuffin, R. (2004). *Police Leadership: Expectations and Impact (20/04)*. Home Office Research, Development & Statistics Directorate. https://citeseerx.ist.psu.edu/viewdoc/download?doi=10.1.1.610.4853&rep=rep1&type=pdf

Easton, M. (2018). Managing innovation in policing. In G. Bruinsma & D. Weisburd (Eds.), *Encyclopedia of criminology and criminal justice*. https://link.springer.com/referenceworkentry/10.1007/978-1-4614-5690-2_388

Einarsen, S., Aasland, M. S., & Skogstad, A. (2007). Destructive leadership behavior: A definition and conceptual model. *The Leadership Quarterly, 18*(3), 207–216. https://doi.org/10.1016/j.leaqua.2007.03.002

Engel, R. S. (2000). The effects of supervisory styles on patrol officer behavior. *Police Quarterly, 3*(3), 262–293. https://doi.org/10.1177/1098611100003003003

Engel, R. S., McManus, H. D., & Isaza, G. T. (2020). Moving beyond "best practice": experiences in police reform and a call for evidence to reduce officer-involved shootings. *The Annals of the American Academy of Political and Social Science, 687*(1), 146–165. https://doi.org/10.1177/0002716219889328

Eterno, J. A., Silverman, E. B., & Berlin, M. M. (2021). Police leadership of tomorrow: Comprehensive compstat performance management moving from stagnation to innovation. *Police Practice & Research, 22*(1), 886–902. https://doi.org/10.1080/15614263.2020.1725273

Federal Bureau of Investigation. (n.d.). *National Academy.* Retrieved December 2, 2021, from https://www.fbi.gov/services/training-academy/national-academy

Garner, R. (2018). Leadership as a police chief: Advice from those who've been there. *Applied Psychology in Criminal Justice, 14*(2), 171–182.

Hall, R., & Grant, D. (2018). Charismatic leadership. In M. Augier & D. J. Teece (Eds.), *The Palgrave encyclopedia of strategic management*. https://doi.org/10.1057/978-1-137-00772-8_735

Hassan, S., Park, J., & Raadschelders, J. C. N. (2018). Taking a closer look at the empowerment-performance relationship: Evidence from the law enforcement organizations. *Public Administration Review, 79*(3), 427–438. https://doi.org/10.1111/puar.12978

Hawkins, J., & Dulewicz, V. (2007). The relationship between performance as a leader and emotional intelligence, intellectual and managerial competences. *Journal of General Management, 33*(2), 57–78. https://doi.org/10.1177/030630700703300205

Hinkin, T. R., & Tracey, B. J. (1999). The relevance of charisma for transformational leadership in stable organizations. *Journal of Organizational Change Management, 12*(2), 105–119. https://doi.org/10.1108/09534819910263659

Hoggett, J., Redford, P., Toher, D., & White, P. (2019). Challenges for police leadership: Identity, experience, legitimacy and direct entry. *Journal of Police and Criminal Psychology, 34*(2), 145–155. https://doi.org/10.1007/s11896-018-9264-2

Huber, L., & Gunderson, A. (2023). Putting a fresh face forward: Does the gender of a police chief affect public perceptions? *Political Research Quarterly, 76*(3), 1418–1432. https://doi.org/10.1177/10659129221142598

Jermier, J. M., & Berkes, L. J. (1979). Leader behavior in a police command bureaucracy: A closer look at quasi-military model. *Administrative Science Quarterly, 24*(1), 1–23. https://doi.org/10.2307/2989873

Johnson, R. R. (2006). Management influences on officer traffic enforcement productivity. *International Journal of Police Science & Management, 8*(3), 205–217. https://doi.org/10.1350/ijps.2006.8.3.205

Johnson, R. (2008). Effectively communicating performance expectations to subordinates: Patrol officer perceptions. *Law Enforcement Executive Forum, 8*, 103–112.

Johnson, R. R. (2015). Police organizational commitment: The influence of supervisor feedback and support. *Crime & Delinquency, 61*(9), 1155–1180. https://doi.org/10.1177/0011128712466887

Judge, T. A., Thoresen, C. J., Bono, J. E., & Patton, G. K. (2001). The job satisfaction-job performance relationship: A qualitative and quantitative review. *Psychological Bulletin, 127*(3), 376–407. https://doi.org/10.1037/0033-2909.127.3.376

Karakitapoglu-Aygün, Z., & Gumusluoglu, L. (2013). The bright and dark sides of leadership: Transformational vs. non-transformational leadership in a non-Western context. *Leadership, 9*(1), 107–133. https://doi.org/10.1177/1742715012455131

Karakitapoglu-Aygün, Z., Gumusluoglu, L., & Scandura, T. A. (2020). How do different faces of paternalistic leaders facilitate or impair task and innovative performance? Opening the black box. *Journal of Leadership & Organizational Studies, 27*(2), 138–152. https://doi.org/10.1177/1548051819833380

Kehoe, R. R., & Wright, P. M. (2013). The impact of high-performance human resource practices on employees' attitudes and behaviors. *Journal of Management, 39*(2), 366–291. https://doi.org/10.1177/0149206310365901

Koper, C. S., Lum, C., & Willis, J. J. (2014). Optimizing the use of technology in policing: Results and implications from a multi-site study of the social, organizational, and behavioral aspects of implementing police technologies. *Policing, 8*(2), 212–221. https://doi.org/10.1093/police/pau015

Krimmel, J. T., & Lindenmuth, P. (2001). Police chief performance and leadership styles. *Police Quarterly, 4*(4), 469–482. https://doi.org/10.1177/109861101129197950

MacDonald, V. N. (1986). *Study of leadership and supervision in policing*. Canadian Police College.

McGregor, D. M. (1957). The human side of enterprise. *Management Review, 46*, 22–28.

Melé, D. (2016). Understanding humanistic management. *Humanistic Management Journal, 1*(1), 33–55. https://doi.org/10/1007/s41463-016-0011-5

Morreale, S. (2002). *Analysis of perceived leader behaviors in law enforcement agencies* (Dissertation Abstracts International).
Murphy, S. A. (2008). The role of emotions and transformational leadership on police culture: An autoethnographic account. *International Journal of Police Science & Management, 10*(2), 165–178. https://doi.org/10.1350/ijps.2008.10.2.72
Murphy, S. A., & Drodge, E. N. (2004). The four I's of police leadership: A case study heuristic. *International Journal of Police Science & Management, 6*(1), 1–15. https://doi.org/10.1350/ijps.6.1.1.34461
Paoline, E. A. (2003). Taking stock: Toward a richer understanding of police culture. *Journal of Criminal Justice, 31*(3), 199–214. https://doi.org/10.1016/S0047-2352(03)00002-3
Paoline, E. A., & Terrill, W. (2005). The impact of police culture on traffic stop searches: An analysis of attitudes and behavior. *Policing: An International Journal of Police Strategies and Management, 28*(3), 455–472. https://doi.org/10.1108/13639510510614555
Pearson-Goff, M., & Herrington, V. (2013). Police leadership: A systematic review of the literature. *Policing: A Journal of Policy & Practice, 8*(1), 14–26. https://doi.org/10.1093/police/pat027
Santos, R., & Santos, R. (2020). *Stratified policing: An organizational model for proactive crime reduction and accountability*. Rowman & Littlefield.
Sarver, M. (2008). *Leadership and effectiveness: An examination of the leadership styles of Texas police chiefs and the correlates of the most effective leaders* (Doctoral Dissertation, Sam Houston University). WorldCat.
Schafer, J. A. (2010). The ineffective policy leader: Acts of commission and omission. *Journal of Criminal Justice, 38*(4), 737–746. https://doi.org/10.1016/j.jcrimjus.2010.04.048
Schaveling, J., Blaauw, S., & Montfort, K. V. (2017). Predictors of group performance in a police criminal investigation department: The role of gender homogeneity, leadership and team characteristics. *Journal of Police and Criminal Psychology, 32*(4), 358–368. https://doi.org/10.1007/s11896-017-9227-z
Schuh, S. C., & Zhang, X. (2013). For the good or the bad? Interactive effects of transformational leadership with moral and authoritarian leadership behaviors. *Journal of Business Ethics, 116*(3), 629–640. https://doi.org/10.1007/s10551-012-1486-0
Serrat, O. (2017). *Knowledge Solutions: Tools, methods, and approaches to drive organizational performance*. Springer.
Shaed, M. M. (2018). Participative management theory and feminist leadership styles. *Malaysian Journal of Society and Space, 14*(4), 332–345. https://doi.org/10.17576/geo-2018-1404-27
Steinheider, B., & Wuestewald, T. (2008). From the bottom-up: Sharing leadership in a police agency. *Police Practice and Research, 9*(2), 145–163. https://doi.org/10.1080/15614260802081303
Terrill, W., Paoline, E. A., & Manning, P. K. (2003). Police culture and coercion. *Criminology, 41*(4), 1003–1034. https://doi.org/10.1111/j.1745-9125.2003.tb01012.x
United Nations. (2011). *Handbook on police accountability, oversight, and integrity.* https://www.unodc.org/pdf/criminal_justice/Handbook_on_police_Accountability_Oversight_and_Integrity.pdf
Weber, M. (1947). *The theory of social and economic organizations*. Free Press.
Worden, R. E. (1995). Police officers' belief systems: A framework for analysis. *American Journal of Police, 14*(1), 49–81. https://doi.org/10.1108/07358549510152979
Wu, S. (2020). Leadership matters: Police chief race and fatal shootings by police officers. *Social Science Quarterly, 102*(1), 407–419. https://doi.org/10.1111/ssqu.12900
Yammarino, F. J., & Dubinsky, A. J. (1994). Transformational leadership theory: Using levels of analysis to determine boundary conditions. *Personnel Psychology, 47*(4), 787–811. https://doi.org/10.1111/j.1744-6570.1994.tb01576.x
Zheng, Y., Graham, L., Farh, J., & Huang, X. (2021). The impact of authoritarian leadership on ethical voice: A moderated mediation model of felt uncertainty and leader benevolence. *Journal of Business Ethics, 170*(1), 133–146. https://doi.org/10.1007/s10551-019-04261-1

Chapter 16
Conclusion and Future Directions

Danielle S. Rudes and Jason R. Ingram

Organizations are complex, interconnected, and dynamic entities comprised of formal rules, policies, and protocols. Organizations also employ, serve, house, and/or host *people*. If you thought organizations were complex, people are even more multifaceted. The people, whether organizations like it or not, do not always follow the formal rules, policies, and protocols. Sometimes, this is because they simply do not want to or do not agree with them, but other times, it may be because they do not know what those rules and policies are or they do not understand them. Both aspects—the formal and the informal—components of organizations are critical, yet difficult to assess and comprehend. This creates a challenge for individuals working within or receiving services from organizations and for scholars and researchers who are trying to understand how these systems and organizations operate. It is also incredibly difficult for anyone to think about how to change and/or improve organizations, as the first step in implementing change is often assessing the current form and processes to decide what to change and how best to do so.

The US criminal legal system is a vast network of organizations that are themselves organized into branches with specialties and roles that fit the different ways criminal legal organizations work and the various people they serve/supervise. In broad terms, the criminal legal system is home to law enforcement/police, law and courts, institutional and community corrections, and juvenile justice. All of the agencies, departments, and units within these branches are interconnected with various other systems, agencies, and departments.

Researchers, students, and scholars working within criminology and criminal justice disciplines—as well as individuals within other disciplines such as health/

D. S. Rudes (✉) · J. R. Ingram
Sam Houston State University, Department of Criminal Justice and Criminology, Huntsville, TX, USA
e-mail: drudes@shsu.edu

D. S. Rudes, J. R. Ingram (eds.), *Using Organizational Theory to Study, Explain, and Understand Criminal Legal Organizations*,
https://doi.org/10.1007/978-3-031-66285-0_16

medicine, sociology, political science, law and society, and social work—often study various components or people within the criminal legal system. Some of this research is robust and critically important, and yet without fully understanding the organizations of study and the context within which they operate, the analyses often lack additional depth, depth that may be hugely helpful for knowledge expansion and policy/practice reform. Think about doctors, for example. When a person wants to become a doctor, regardless of their specialty, they attend medical school. Through years of reading, practicing, and training, all doctors have a basic command of the human body. That is, they have a holistic approach to medicine first, and then they specialize in a particular area. Unfortunately, criminology and criminal justice scholars/students do not often get holistic training in organizations prior to choosing a specialty area such as courts, policing, or corrections. For many people, this may mean that they understand the intricacies of their area of focus but do not know much about that area in a broader sense, nor do they understand the intra- and inter-organizational features, components, and/or relationships (formally and informally) within that area. We can—in fact—we must do better! Together, we can help expand organizational theory into criminal justice and criminology programs and into our broader thinking about criminal legal organizations. Only then will we be aptly equipped to engage with understanding and perhaps reforming the organizations that make up this hugely complex system.

Learning Organizational Theory

With very few ways to formally learn about organizational theory in courses, classes, or trainings, many people are left on their own to figure things out. While we cannot solve this for everyone, we hope to provide a starting guide for interested learners, particularly students and researchers. In this section of the book, we offer some assistance in this organizational theory learning quest.

Perhaps the most important part of learning organizational theories and the related concepts and ideas is that in many cases, particularly when considering criminal legal organizations, it will be difficult to find research articles or theoretical arguments where the researchers are studying criminal legal organizations. This largely stems from the lack of attention to organizational theory in undergraduate and graduate criminology and criminal justice programs (as discussed in the introduction to this volume). While some students and scholars learn organizational theory in public administration, sociology, political science, and some business programs, the people most likely to work in and study criminal legal organizations are overwhelmingly under-trained in organizational theory. This is challenging, but it also creates tremendous opportunity. Sure, not all organizations operate the same way; the cultures and climates vary, and their goals, roles, and processes are unique in many ways. However, studying different organizational environments sometimes provides valuable insights in unexpected ways if the reader/learner creates a bridge between the concepts presented in noncriminal legal settings and uses them to understand criminal legal settings.

One example emerges when trying to understand culture. In a book written by labor relations scholar, Gideon Kunda (1992), he researches organizational culture with a technology firm. To do this, he considers how managers *create* culture (what he calls engineering culture) and how employees working under these supervisors internalize that created culture. For Kunda, culture is established through normative control. Normative control is "The attempt to elicit and direct the required efforts of members by controlling the underlying experiences, thoughts, and feelings that guide their actions" (p. 11). Additionally, Kunda finds workers are driven by "internal commitment, strong identification with company goals, intrinsic satisfaction from work" (p. 11). Kunda's analysis considered workers in a tech firm and his subsequent analysis examined how managers create culture and then how workers come to embody that culture—all of this benefiting the organization. One of the editors of this volume, Rudes (2012), used Kunda's (and others) work as a springboard for understanding how a parole agency in one US state navigated a change in policy mandated by the state's governor. During Rudes' ethnographic fieldwork in parole offices, she noticed a series of mixed messages and misunderstandings about the governor's mandate and began to examine how both the agency and its staff, as well as the associated union, understood and accepted or resisted the change. While at differing levels of analysis (Kunda at the mezzo/organizational level and Rudes at the micro/street level), Kunda's analysis of culture in a tech firm gave Rudes purchase over what was happening in parole during this state-wide change. For Rudes, the parole unit and union managers were framing the mandate differently based on the way they were embodying the engineered culture of their organization and their role within it.

The point here is that criminal justice- and criminology-focused scholars may have to do some additional work—called *bridging*—to fully learn and engage with organizational scholarship and theory in their research within criminal legal organizations. This involves considering the theories and concepts presented within contexts that are not criminal legal organizations. However, instead of discarding these as irrelevant, bridging involves reading materials for their framework and deeper meaning and, at least in part, ignoring the organizational context within which they are presented. There are several examples of bridging, like the Kunda–Rudes example mentioned earlier. The good news is that doing this affords learners and researchers a whole new literature to help explain their findings within criminal legal organizations while it also expands knowledge and makes important contributions to the field.

Teaching Organizational Theory

To teach organizational theory to yourself or within a criminal justice or criminology program will take a bit of work, but the rewards are endless. In this section of the book, editors Rudes and Ingram present their syllabi, some assignments to help organizational theory students learn, and some of the "why" behind their pedagogical choices for an organizational theory course in a criminal justice or criminology program.

A great book to assign or read is Richard W. Scott's *Organizations and Institutions* (2005). This book—although dense—is a wonderful handbook for individuals learning organizational theory and concepts for the first time. Scott's early framing within the book begins chronologically, with *Rational Systems*—the first way we thought about organizations as somewhat rigid and formal (ala Weber). The book next turns to *Natural Systems*—when scholars and researchers began to understand that in addition to the formal/rational organizational components, *people* also worked in these organizations and they were not quite rational, and their behaviors/actions were, many times, informal—yet still a part of the organization. And finally, to *Open Systems*—a framework that begins to understand organizations as both rational and natural but with connections to other organizations and people outside of them (interconnected). As Scott walks readers through this trilogy of frameworks, learners begin to recognize the trajectory of thinking about organizations and how/why it matters that we see criminal legal organizations as open systems today.

After that introduction and field structure overview, the remaining weeks of a course (or independent learning) might move into key challenges that organizations face, including some of the topics included in this volume. These could include decision-making, power/politics, technology/structure, culture/climate, conflict/resistance, social inequality, ethics/deviance, leadership/authority, and change. While there is certainly a litany of other topics that might be considered, this list highlights some of the most relevant for criminal legal organizations and provides an excellent starting place for learners/students.

An important caveat to keep in mind that reading about organizations via organizational theory is not easy. For many new learners, it is a bit like learning a new language. There are some concepts in organizational work that students have heard before and yet their meaning in organizational writing is different and more robust than the colloquial way they likely understand them now. These include terms like group think, irrationality, sensemaking, and even culture. There are also some ideas and concepts that seem like they might better belong in a science textbook. These include loose coupling, isomorphism, equifinality, and endogeneity. To help learners with these terms, ideas, and concepts, it may be important to spend some time in the learning process working through the definitions and applying them directly to a criminal legal example in courts, corrections, or policing. New criminal justice and criminology learners may need a bit of handholding when trying to grasp these concepts and they make a lot more sense in the context of the organizations they already know—criminal legal organizations. If you are prepping an undergraduate or graduate (MA or PhD) course on organizational theory, consider lecturing a bit more than you might usually do…particularly in graduate seminars. The articles and book chapters on the sample syllabi are challenging, and students often struggle with the content. It is absolutely alright to provide a bit more structured lecturing in a course like this. Help students understand what they are reading, and they will begin making connections and bridging all on their own as the course continues.

Think of the syllabi presented here as a learning guide. Each week contains suggested multidisciplinary readings on an organizational theory, concept, or idea and, when possible, each week also provides readings where a scholar or researcher applied organizational theory to a criminal legal organization or topic. Finding criminology articles that use organizational theory (and use it well) was exceptionally difficult ~15 years ago, but with each year, a few more scholars make this task a bit easier. For each weekly topic, there is also a set of guiding questions. Students/learners can use these questions if they feel overwhelmed with the depth and complexity of the readings. The questions are like signposts, helping readers understand why the chosen articles are part of this topic and what the students should be getting out of them.

In addition to the vocabulary exercises suggested above, it is also a good idea to go beyond just reading the articles/chapters on each topic. Instead, try to find ways of using them in your own work, either as an organizational employee or a criminal justice or criminology scholar, researcher, or student. Both Drs. Rudes and Ingram do this on their syllabus by engaging students in their graduate courses to pick a topic within criminology that interests them and write a paper or a chapter about it iteratively throughout the course. The students choose a topic, prepare a brief (short notes) of 12 articles and then outline their argument. Next, they draft an expansive literature review that comes together a bit like an anthology or annual review. It makes an argument, but it does so by presenting what we know about a topic already in conjunction with what we do not yet know. The students engaging with this assignment present their draft for comments and then make revisions. This process, of course, helps students with their writing and argumentation, but it also digs deeply into the organizational theories and concepts they are using and helps them really understand them.

Other ideas to help learners/students include making them a vocabulary or concept list and playing a round of jeopardy-like questions and answers using that list. The more they know and more confident, they will feel using the materials to understand, assess, evaluate, and/or examine the criminal legal organizations they are most interested in. Also, in addition to the guiding questions, students learn a lot via analytic memoing on a posed question either in class or as homework. We provide a sample vocabulary list and some analytic questions in the appendix of this book. Dr. Rudes even provided students in her class with a sample dataset one semester from a probation study she was conducting. The sample data contained ten de-identified interview transcripts from interviews with probation officers about their views on reforms and changes occurring within their units. The students were given a brief qualitative methods training so they could complete some fairly basic analysis of the interviews. Their assignment involved using their analysis from the ten interviews and writing a mini-empirical paper using an organizational theory, concept, and/or idea to frame and explain what they "found." Through practicing the application of organizational theories and concepts using real data, the students learned a lot about bridging and how organizational theory helps explain criminal legal data in new and innovative ways.

Over many years, Dr. Rudes' doctoral students have published the papers they wrote for her doctoral seminar in organizational theory. Below is a list of published works not found in this volume but available in other books and journals. In addition to the chapters in this book, these works may be particularly useful for students/learners who are new to organizational theory—as the authors of these pieces were new to it too. They represent students all trying to make sense of organizational theories, concepts, and ideas and to use them to explain something found within a criminal legal organization or within the broader criminal legal system. We also provide two graduate-level syllabi (from Rudes and Ingram) in Appendix A. These syllabi provide a host of additional readings for anyone wanting to learn more about organizational theories, ideas, and concepts.

Previously Published Student Work Using Organizational Theory to Explain Criminal Legal Settings

Appleton, C. J. & Rudes, D. S. (2022). Organizational factors affecting EBP implementation in community supervision. *Oxford Research Encyclopedia of Criminology and Criminal Justice*.

Azam, M., Sim, C., & Rudes, D. S. (2022). The influence of organizational structures on police decision-making on stop, question, and frisk. In the *Research Handbook on the Sociology of Organizations* with Edgar Elgar Publishing, LTD.

Davis, L., Houston, P. J., & Rudes, D. S. (2021). Probation officers, discretion, and participatory management. *Oxford Research Encyclopedia of Criminology and Criminal Justice*.

Ingel, S.N., Richards-Karamarkovich, A., Bietsch, S., & Rudes, D. S. (2020). Privacy violations and procedural justice in United States prisons and jails. *Sociology Compass,* 15(2). https://doi.org/10.1111/soc4.12847

Mackey, B. & Rudes, D. S. Discretion in the U.S. parole system. (2021). *Oxford Research Encyclopedia of Criminology and Criminal Justice*..

McPherson, M. & Rudes, D. S. (2022). Carceral goals: The role of correctional officers in organizational goal attainment. In the *Research Handbook on the Sociology of Organizations* with Edgar Elgar Publishing, LTD.

Peterson, K. & Rudes, D. S. (2022). Crime control, community relations, and barriers to community-based reform in policing. *Oxford Research Encyclopedia of Criminology and Criminal Justice*.

Prince, H., Kuen, K., & Rudes, D. S. (2022). Police self-legitimacy shaped by organizational factors leads to racially biased decision making. *Oxford Research Encyclopedia of Criminology and Criminal Justice*.
Rudes, D. S. & Viglione, J. (2013). Correctional workers in the change process. Invited entry for the Encyclopedia of Criminology and Criminal Justice (Editors-in-Chief Gerben Bruinsma and David Weisburd). Springer.
Zastrow, T. & Rudes, D. S. (2022). Civilian oversight of police in the U.S. *Oxford Research Encyclopedia of Criminology and Criminal Justice*.

Concluding Thoughts

We thank you for taking the time to read this book and think about the theories, concepts, and ideas presented here. However, this is only the first step in your journey toward learning more. Also, get ready because, in many ways, you will be a bit of a pioneer for a while without much existing published research that uses organizational frameworks to study or understand criminal legal organizations. You will have to do a lot of *bridging* (taking concepts/ideas that use organizational theories to study other types of organizations or organizational actors outside of the criminal legal system and applying those to your own work). This work is worth it, though, and you know it. Dig in, expand your thinking, and see how much more is possible.

Index

D. S. Rudes, J. R. Ingram (eds.), *Using Organizational Theory to Study, Explain, and Understand Criminal Legal Organizations*,
https://doi.org/10.1007/978-3-031-66285-0

The manufacturer's authorised representative in the EU is Springer
Nature Customer Service Centre GmbH, Europaplatz 3, 69115 Heidelberg,
Germany. If you have any concerns regarding our products, please
contact ProductSafety@springernature.com

Printed and bound by CPI Group (UK) Ltd, Croydon, CR0 4YY
01/10/2026
02225909-0007